# Gold, Gals, Guns, Guts

# Gold,

A History of Deadwood, Lead, and Spearfish, 1874-1976

# Gals,

Bob Lee, Editor
Stan Lindstrom & Wynn Lindstrom, Assistant Editors

# Guns,

With a New Introduction by Bob Lee

# Guts

South Dakota State Historical Society Press
Pierre, South Dakota

This publication is funded in part by the Deadwood Publications Fund provided by the City of Deadwood and the Deadwood Historic Preservation Commission.

Library of Congress Cataloging-in-Publication Data
Gold, gals, guns, guts : a history of Deadwood, Lead, and Spearfish, 1874-1976 / Bob Lee, editor ; Stan and Wynn Lindstrom, assistant editors ; with a new introduction by Bob Lee.
p. cm.
Originally published: Deadwood, S.D. : Deadwood-Lead 76 Centennial, 1976.
Includes bibliographical references and index.
ISBN 0-9715171-8-5 (pbk.)
1. Deadwood (S.D.)—History. 2. Frontier and pioneer life—South Dakota—Deadwood. 3. Lead (S.D.)—History. 4. Frontier and pioneer life—South Dakota—Lead. 5. Spearfish (S.D.)—History. 6. Frontier and pioneer life—South Dakota—Spearfish. I. Lee, Bob, 1920–
II. Lindstrom, Stan. III. Lindstrom, Wynn.
F659.D2G64 2004
978.3'91—dc22
2004045223

Printed in the United States of America

9 8 7 6 5 4 3 2

Gold, Gals, Guns, Guts *is dedicated to Nell Perrigoue, who not only devoted her life to publicizing the golden past of "Deadwood Country," but also envisioned and worked for an even brighter future for her beloved Black Hills.*

# Acknowledgements

This 100-year history, the first ever to be published about Lawrence County, has been achieved through the efforts of the Deadwood-Lead '76 Centennial and the South Dakota Bicentennial Commission. It has been written with the hope that it will prove to be as valuable a legacy for generations to come as were the personal recollections, the early-day newspapers and authors in the compiling of this century of authentic material.

Compilation of the researched information was under the direction of the Deadwood-Lead '76 Centennial Historic Research Committee, which included S. Cushman Clark, chairman; Sue Firestone, Helen Clark, Elizabeth Ludeman, Reed Richards, Esther Richards, Lyle Elward, Irma Klock, Don Clowser, Kenneth Lee, Will Severns, Mary Jo Grinager, Edna Grieb, Mary F. Fredrickson, Dorothy Delicate, Pat McGibney and Carl Lindstrom Jr.

Untiring cooperation was given by Marjorie Pontius, Deadwood Carnegie Library, and Marion Bedsaul and her staff at Lead's Homestake Library. Of great value were the Deadwood Library files of the early-day issues of the *Pioneer*, the *Black Hills Times* and the *Pioneer-Times*, as was the Lead Library's microfilm of the *Daily Call* newspapers of that city.

Posthumous recognition is extended to the Rev. Eugene Szalay whose assistance in the writing of this history was interrupted by his unexpected death. However, his extensive collection of research, made available by the E. Y. Berry Library, Black Hills State College, Spearfish, proved invaluable in compiling the information on Spearfish.

Acknowledgement should also go to previous researchers under the direction of Camille Yuill, former Historic Research chairman, who contributed to an extensive file of information on the area. They include: Mary Lou Teller, Patricia Mechling, Margaret Severns, Eleanor Smith, Mari Caron, Thelma Jaynes, Roselyn Ridley, Hermina Hemminger, Ethylle Quillian, Kathryn Hight, Marie Lawler, Clinton Richards, Kenneth Lewis, Harry Daniels, George Hunter, Henry Frawley family, Linda Miller, Phyrne Ulrich, Alberta Mattson, Arthur Davis, Karen Rossow, Loretta Blanchard, and Jeff Moye.

Barry Cepak assisted in writing the text.

# Contents

# Introduction to the New Edition

Over a quarter of a century has passed since this book was published to commemorate the first hundred years of Lawrence County's turbulent history. As one of the three original Black Hills counties created by the Dakota Territorial Legislature in 1875, Lawrence County was not formally organized until after the region was opened for legal non-Indian settlement in 1877. By that time, thousands of gold seekers were trespassing in the portion of the Black Hills that lay within the confines of the Great Sioux Reservation established years earlier. Lawrence County and its communities have experienced tremendous change, much of it highly controversial, since that troubled time. *Gold, Gals, Guns, Guts*, originally published by the Deadwood-Lead Centennial Committee in 1976, chronicles the exciting early events that shaped the county's unique character. This introduction offers a synopsis of the major changes that have taken place since 1976.

Controversy is as much a part of Lawrence County's heritage as James Butler ("Wild Bill") Hickok and Martha ("Calamity Jane") Canary. These two colorful frontier personalities, among many other figures of like repute, made brief appearances in Lawrence County. Their enduring legends in the historical life of the county seat at Deadwood continue to enrich the community's character and coffers to this day. In reviewing the significant events that have taken place in Deadwood and Lawrence County since 1976, it is apparent that the past twenty-eight years have produced some pretty exciting and controversial times, too.

For instance, take prostitution. Although outlawed when Dakota Territory was separated into South Dakota and North Dakota in 1889, prostitution had been a locally tolerated, if not totally accepted, part of the Deadwood scene despite the protestations of the clergy and other moral guardians. Every once in a while, in a valiant but usually vain effort to uphold the law, a reform-minded states attorney would attempt to close down the "upstairs" brothels known to exist in a number of buildings in the 600 block of Deadwood's Lower Main Street. Such misguided reformers usually were not reelected.

On the morning of 21 May 1980, however, state and federal officials (with short notice to local law enforcement agencies) raided, padlocked, and permanently closed the city's three remaining brothels. A newspaper survey taken in Deadwood the following month showed that 42 percent of those polled opposed the closings, 35 percent favored them, and 23 percent were undecided. The South Dakota Committee on the Humanities subsequently sponsored a panel discussion in Deadwood on the social, religious, and historical aspects of the world's oldest profession. Most of the locals sided with the lone madam who showed up to defend the practice and turned unsympathetic ears to the beleaguered states attorney who staunchly pointed out that prostitution was illegal. Nonetheless, the infamous brothels of Deadwood remain closed to this day, and the services of prostitutes are no longer available there—or so they say.

Whether the closing of the brothels had anything to do with what followed is debatable, but Deadwood was in dire economic straits by the mid-1980s. Once the "metropolis of the Black Hills" with a population exceeding that of the territorial capital, Deadwood found it could no longer thrive year-round on its historical legacy. It did well enough during the summer months when tourists thronged there to visit its numerous historic sites, such as the saloon where Wild Bill had been murdered in 1876 and Mount Moriah Cemetery where Calamity Jane is buried alongside Wild Bill, and to attend the reenactment of the trial of Jack McCall for the killing of Wild Bill. The chamber of commerce had taken over the abandoned Broken Boot Mine and opened it to tourists as a reminder of the community's robust mining past.

In the off-season when the tourists were gone, businesses had a hard time keeping their doors open, and more than a few of them closed or left town. Some Deadwood residents survived by working in area mines, most notably the durable Homestake at nearby Lead, but their numbers dropped drastically as the number of operating gold mines in the region gradually diminished because of falling prices and rising costs. Deadwood's population, only a bit over two thousand in the 1980 census, continued its downward plunge throughout the following decade.

Consequently, the citizens of Deadwood—a determined lot—decided they had to do something to save their community. An aggressive "Deadwood You Bet" committee, composed of energetic community leaders, was formed to lobby vigorously for legalized gambling in Deadwood. Gambling, like prostitution, had been part and parcel of Deadwood's lusty historical past (Wild Bill had been fatally shot while playing poker) and was seen as the salvation of the dying town. Gaining approval was a Herculean undertaking, as gambling was prohibited in the state constitution and would require the support of a majority of the state's voters as well as their elected representatives in the state legislature. Miraculously, both tasks were accomplished despite the controversy the proposal generated among those morally opposed to gambling of any kind for any purpose.

Members of the Deadwood You Bet committee and other Deadwood citizens made frequent trips to Pierre to lobby the legislature for a statewide vote on the issue. Their efforts paid off as lawmakers placed a constitutional amendment to permit limited gambling solely in Deadwood on the ballot in 1988. Sixty-four percent of those voting approved it. Deadwood voters gave the proposal an even greater majority (75 percent) in a special election the following year. The measure placed a five-dollar limit on bets and restricted the gambling to slot machines, poker, and blackjack. State voters approved another constitutional amendment in 2000 to raise the bet limit to one hundred dollars.

Federal legislation authorized gaming on American Indian reservations in states that otherwise permit it, even on a limited basis. Consequently, there are now nine casinos in South Dakota operated by Indian tribes under compacts with the state. These enterprises have brought varying amounts of revenue to the reservations, where poverty rates are higher than elsewhere in the state. There has been about as much controversy about the merits of this activity among American Indians as among other citizens of the state, but Deadwood remains the only place in the state where non-Indian-operated gambling is legal.

Gambling was widespread, but unlawful, in Deadwood in the 1930s until law-enforcement officials conducted a crackdown that (at least publicly) ended the activity there. Legalized gambling began in November 1989 and brought about spectacular changes in the formerly depressed community—again not without controversy. Property values leapt upward as speculators and entrepreneurs competed for building space for casinos. Longstanding retail businesses that could not afford to pay the rising taxes on their higher-valued buildings either sold out to the casino operators or moved out of the community. Housing for casino employees also became scarce and expensive, forcing many to commute daily from neighboring communities. By 2004, Deadwood offered gaming activities in thirty casinos of various sizes and inducements, including stage shows, dancing, and dining, as well as in gift shops and grocery stores. Gaming also brought a boom in hotel and motel construction and expansion to accommodate the ever-increasing number of visitors who now converge on Deadwood year-round.

The revenue produced by gaming in Deadwood and the changes it has wrought in the community, economically and aesthetically, have been astonishing. Moreover, legalized gambling has provided increased revenue to governmental agencies on the state, county, and local levels that far exceeds earlier expectations. Deadwood collects a yearly license fee of two thousand dollars for every card table and slot machine in the casinos. There is also an 8 percent tax on the adjusted gross revenue. Forty percent of the tax collected is used by the state for tourism promotion, 10 percent is paid to Lawrence County, and 50 percent goes to the South Dakota Commission on Gaming. The latter agency regulates the industry out of offices in Pierre and Deadwood with sixteen employees who are mostly investigators, auditors, accountants, or inspectors. The commission deducts its expenses and one hundred thousand dollars for the State Historical Preservation Loan and Grant Fund, which makes grants for preservation projects anywhere in the state. The remaining money goes to Deadwood for its own historical preservation fund and for marketing.

Since 1995, any time Deadwood's annual share of the gaming revenue reaches $6.8 million, the remaining proceeds are distributed under a different formula: 70 percent goes to the state's general fund, 10 percent is awarded to Deadwood, 10 percent is distributed to the other Lawrence County municipalities, and the remaining 10 percent is sent to the school districts of the county. However, the recipient school districts lose state aid equal to the amount they receive in gaming taxes and fees. This proviso has generated considerable controversy among school administrators, who point out that their schools gain nothing by the exchange.

Deadwood gaming reached a milestone in November 2003 when it completed its fourteenth year. By that time, more than $7.2 billion had been wagered and gross revenues had exceeded $664.5 million. The 8-percent gaming tax had produced more than $51.5 million, the state's tourism program had benefited by more than $20.6 million, and Lawrence County had received in excess of $5.1 million. The State Gaming Commission's 50-percent share amounted to over $25.7 million. August has consistently been the leading revenue-producing month, principally due to the Sturgis Motorcycle Rally, which draws thousands of bikers to the Black Hills. Deadwood's assessed valuation of all its real property totaled $28.6 million in 1989 when gaming was launched. It soared to $111.6 million by 2003, reflecting the explosion in casino, hotel, motel, and home-construction activity.

The gaming industry undeniably has transformed Deadwood from a dying community to a thriving "Little Las Vegas" that complements its historical heritage, although there are still South Dakotans who oppose the change on moral grounds. It is also undeniable that there have been benefits in the transformation, particularly in the many local, county, and state historical preservation projects financed by gaming revenue. The muddy streets that plagued the oxen wagon trains that first brought supplies into the budding Deadwood mining settlement during its pioneer era have been replaced by brick streets paid for with gaming revenue. The old-fashioned open-air trolleys (enclosed during the winter months) that carry visitors from their hotels and motels to the casinos and to local historical attractions are a plus, too. So is the transformation of the historic Adams Museum from a cobweb-lined antique collection operated by an untrained curator to a vital, well-organized community asset offering a host of intriguing programs directed by a well-funded professional staff.

Many area residents are especially pleased that most of the casinos have restaurants offering fine food at cut-rate prices as an inducement to visit gaming tables and slot machines. Senior citizens, who constitute a major segment of the gaming patrons, are particularly attracted to the casinos that offer them free meals on specific days. The old bromide "There is no free lunch" fails to hold true in Deadwood today. Not all gaming revenue retained by the city goes to historical-preservation projects, although a major portion of it does. Some of it is also spent in hiring highly skilled professional marketing specialists, whose mission is to devise innovative ways of attracting visitors to town throughout the year. So far, they have been remarkably successful, hosting a Chinese New Year celebration, a Mardi Gras, street concerts, and numerous other special entertainment events.

All has not been wine and roses in Lawrence County during recent decades, however. At the end of 2001, the venerable Homestake Mining Company at Lead permanently closed down after 125 years of almost continuous operation. Its employees suspected what was coming when the company laid off half of its 850-person workforce in 1989 because of falling gold prices and increasing costs. The company abandoned further exploration efforts and concentrated on recovering the gold in its known reserves. Unfortunately, most of it was low-grade ore and cost an average of $198 an ounce to retrieve and process the metal at a time when gold was barely topping $200 an ounce on the world market. The company had experienced negative cash flows since December 1999. Two other northern Black Hills gold producers had already shut down: the Golden Reward near Terry Peak in 1996 and Brohm's Gilt Edge near Galena in 1999. The three closings dropped Lawrence County's mining-property tax base from $106 million to about $25 million within six years, the brunt of the loss coming from Homestake's demise. Wharf Resources, whose open-pit mine near Lead produced slightly over one hundred four thousand ounces of gold in 2001, is the only large-scale mining operation remaining in the Black Hills.

Two weeks before its official closing, the Homestake Mining Company merged with Barrick Gold Corporation, a Canadian firm founded in 1983 with mining properties in South America and Australia. The merger made Barrick the second-largest gold producer in the world. By the time it closed down, the Homestake mine had produced some forty million ounces of gold since George Hearst bought the Lead property from Moses and Fred Manuel on 9 April 1876. Its production during those 125 years amounted to about 10 percent of all the gold produced in the United States, making the mine the largest single gold producer in the nation. The company's shafts had extended to the seven-thousand-foot level when operations ceased, and in 2003 the pumps that kept water from flooding the mine were turned off. The Homestake workforce was down to 249 employees at the time of the closing, compared to 1,200 workers at the peak of its hirings in 1940. Only a fraction of the remaining personnel will be needed during the eight years the company estimates it will take to dismantle the mine's superstructure and accomplish the required reclamation work at a cost of about eighteen million dollars.

Meanwhile, Barrick has offered to turn the Homestake mine over to the state of South Dakota to create a $281-million underground astrophysics laboratory to be operated by the National Science Foundation (NSF). Governor M. Michael Rounds favors the proposal and has asked the state legislature to accept the offer since the facility is projected to provide upwards of twenty-three hundred jobs for highly-paid, skilled workers. Congress has appropriated $10 million in start-up funds for the project after the state and federal governments resolve some thorny problems concerning future environmental liability. Underground scientific research has been conducted in the Lead mine as a separate and independent undertaking for quite some time. Raymond Davis, Jr., a chemist, won the Nobel Prize in physics for his experiments there during the 1960s relating to elusive particles of nuclear reactions known as neutrinos. The state legislature passed the laboratory proposal in 2004 but is still awaiting a decision by the National Science Foundation on whether the Homestake mine is the best place for its underground scientific research projects.

Governor Rounds sees the NSF laboratory project as offering exciting opportunities for the state and for revitalizing the depressed economy of Lead. Like so many other projects in the history of Lawrence County, this one has aroused considerable controversy. Most debate centers around questions of benefits versus costs, state and federal responsibilities, and public and scientific support. These questions will likely have to be resolved before the proposed project can become reality.

The mine closings have been a serious blow to the economy of Lead, in particular, and to other northern Black Hills communities that provided workers. The Homestake mine, especially, was historically a pillar of stability, prospering even during the Great Depression of the 1930s. It provided jobs that were scarce elsewhere, and its taxes over the years greatly enriched the city, county, school district, and state treasuries. Even so, the loss of taxable income from the mine closings has been more than offset by the spectacular growth in Lawrence County in recent years, largely because of legalized gambling in Deadwood. The county's director of equalization reports that the assessed valuation of taxable property in the entire county jumped from $432.3 million to $973.5 million during the fourteen years since gaming was authorized in Deadwood. It is expected soon to top $1 billion for the first time in the county's history. The director attributes part of the change to the reappraisal of property to bring it more in line with its higher market value. She adds, however, that most of the increase comes from the boom in construction, particularly in casinos, hotels, and motels in Deadwood, and in new residences throughout the county.

Lawrence County, especially Deadwood, has also benefited from highway improvements made since the county celebrated its centennial in 1976. Portions of the three major highways that funnel traffic into the historic city have been reconstructed and vastly improved at a total cost exceeding $36.9 million in federal and state funds. In 1993-1994, a 5.7-mile stretch of United States Highway 85 from the Interstate 90 interchange east of Spearfish to Deadwood was rebuilt at a cost of $10.9 million. Then, in 2000-2001, $5.5 million was spent on widening 6.4 miles of the scenic Boulder Canyon road (United States Highway 14-A) between Sturgis and Deadwood. More recently, 6.4 miles of United States Highway 385 over Strawberry Hill south of Deadwood and Lead was reconstructed in 2002-2003 to eliminate some steep, hilly curves at a cost of $20.5 million. These projects, while generally welcomed by residents of the northern Black Hills, also generated controversy. Some residents feared the wider and faster roads would encroach on the scenic beauty of the surrounding countryside, but, in most cases, that did not happen.

A forest fire in Grizzly Gulch south of Deadwood and Lead in 2002 forced the evacuation of most of both cities, burned an estimated ten to twelve thousand acres, and destroyed a few dwellings on the edge of Deadwood. The cities had not been evacuated since 1959, when a fire that began near Gayville caused considerable property damage and cost over $1.6 million to control. Neither fire was as disastrous as the 1879 fire that wiped out most of Deadwood's original business district.

There have, indeed, been extensive changes in Lawrence County since this book was first published. The people fortunate enough to live there, like their pioneer predecessors, are a hardy lot acclimated to, if not unanimously accepting of, change. They are survivors, as were those who lived there before them. The pioneers would be proud of the way residents have preserved and promoted their historical heritage. Conversely, the present-day inhabitants appreciate the legacy left by the early settlers. They are also pleased that their new-found prosperity permits the reprinting of the centennial chronicle of those early-day accomplishments. Enjoy!

Bob Lee
Boulder Canyon
January 2004

# foreword

# Enter At Your Own Risk

**A cryptic message carved on a slab of stone was found at the base of Lookout Mountain near Spearfish in 1877. It told of the Ezra Kind Party hunted down and killed by the Indians in 1833. No trace of any of the seven miners, their ponies loaded with gold, have ever been found. The Thoen Stone is viewed by thousands each year at the Adams Museum in Deadwood.**

**(Fassbender Photo)**

An island in a sea of grass. That's how early white visitors to the Black Hills viewed this incongruous mountain range within the vast expanse of the Great Plains. Others considered them "an oasis in a dreary desert." They were — and are — a bit of both. An island because they jut skyward from the undulating surface of the grassy plains that surround them. An oasis because of their isolation, sparkling streams, forested slopes and park-like meadows rising mirage-like from the stark prairielands enveloping them.

The Black Hills, an oblong area of about 4,500 square miles along the west-central border of present-day South Dakota and eastern Wyoming, were formed about 40 million years ago. They were born in a massive eruption of the earth's bowels. The violent upheaval created a mountain range from the rocky bed of an inland sea that covered the area eons ago. The Cheyenne River grips the range between its north and south branches as it courses eastward. While apart from them, the Black Hills are generally considered to be the eastern ramparts of the taller Rocky Mountains.

In truth, however, the Hills are actually mountains too. They were the "Black Mountains" to the early Indians of the vicinity, probably because of their dark appearance when viewed from a distance. It was the white man, coming much later, who reduced them to hills. The corruption may have resulted from comparing them with the loftier Rocky Mountains to the west. The whites were intimately acquainted with the towering snow-capped Rockies long before they located the lonely Black Hills. But there's no higher point than 7,240-foot Harney Peak, in the granitic center of the Black Hills, eastward from the majestic Rockies to the Atlantic Ocean.

There is archaeological evidence of human inhabitation of the fringes of the Black Hills in pre-historic times. One site near Bear Butte a few miles east of their outer rim dates back about 4,000 years.

The closest fur trading post to the Black Hills was established at the forks of the Cheyenne River in Meade County. It was first heard of in 1832 with F. A. Chardon as fur trader. He and William Laidlaw had been there in 1831 and they were followed later by Joseph Jouet, Joseph Picotte, F. Laboue, Leon Corena and Andrew Drips. It was a branch of Fort Tecumseh and Fort Pierre, trading posts of John Jacob Astor's American Fur Co. There may have been a post at Oglala in eastern Pennington County but little is known about it.

Deadwood Pioneer-Times

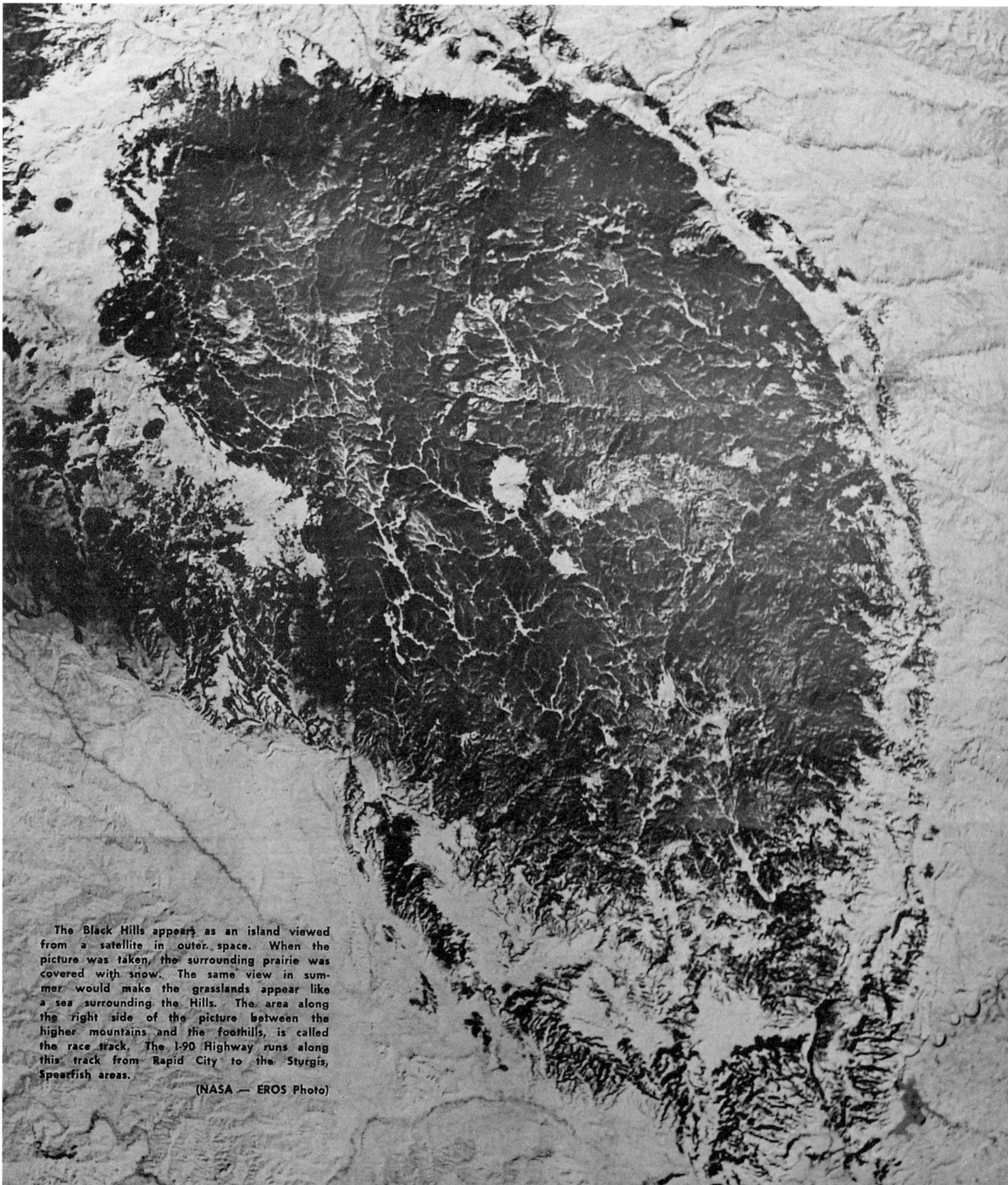

The Black Hills appears as an island viewed from a satellite in outer space. When the picture was taken, the surrounding prairie was covered with snow. The same view in summer would make the grasslands appear like a sea surrounding the Hills. The area along the right side of the picture between the higher mountains and the foothills, is called the race track. The I-90 Highway runs along this track from Rapid City to the Sturgis, Spearfish areas.

(NASA — EROS Photo)

The first white men known to have pierced this long-hidden mountain range were the Verendrye brothers, noted French-Canadian explorers, who came to the region in 1742 while searching for a mysterious "Sea of the West." Guided by Mandan Indians from the Missouri River area to the east, the Verendryes found sub-bands of the Crow, Cheyenne and Kiowa tribes scattered about the "Black Mountains."

Here, too, they found the "Mountain of the Horse Indians." The exact mountain and tribe so described have not been positively identified. The mountain could have been any one of a number of prominent peaks in the region. The tribe might have been a band of the fearsome Teton Dakotahs then mounted and spreading westward from the Missouri River. The Tetons, a loose confederation of distinct tribes, comprising "Seven Council Fires" when congregated, composed the western branch of the powerful Sioux Nation. An ancient winter count, a hide painting recording significant tribal events and outstanding individual exploits, places the Tetons in the Black Hills vicinity as early as 1775-76. This most war-like arm of the Sioux gained possession of the region by conquest over the tribes that had preceded them there.

**An artist depicts the Verendrye brothers who buried a lead tablet to claim the region for France in 1743. It was buried near what is Fort Pierre, South Dakota today.**

More than half a century passed after the Verendrye visit before white men again ventured to the Black Hills. There are sketchy reports of whites reaching or passing near them in the first half of the 19th century. Wilson Price Hunt is said to have led a party of Astorians to Oregon by way of the Black Hills in 1811. That intrepid adventurer, Jedediah Smith, was reportedly mauled by a grizzly bear while passing through the southern portion of the Black Hills in 1823. By the 1830's fur trappers were passing along the Cheyenne waterways from the Missouri to the Yellowstone. An American Fur Company outpost at the mouth of Rapid Creek, on the eastern fringe of the Hills, is known to have blown up in 1832. A candle falling into a keg of powder caused the explosion and killed the white trader.

It was more than a full century after the Verendryes that the first evidence was uncovered of white men in the Black Hills as gold prospectors. The evidence, long questioned, is circumstantial at best. Valid or not, the incident is now firmly rooted in Black Hills legend. In 1887, at the base of Lookout Mountain near present-day Spearfish, in what is now Lawrence County, a small sandstone slab was found that told a cryptic tale. Crudely carved on one side of it was this message:

"Came to these Hills in 1833 Seven of us All ded (dead) but me Ezra Kind Killed by Ind. beyond the high hill Got our gold June 1834."

The same side listed the names of the seven. With the exception of an "Indian Crow," they apparently were all white men. On the reverse side was carved this poignant information:

Sometime last summer an old revolver of Colt's manufacture was found in one of the placer mines at the rear of the TIMES office, at a depth of about sixteen feet, which at the times excited much curiosity. Numerous conjectures and much speculation as to how and when it got there were indulged in. The most plausible theory was that it had been the property of some miner who lost it years ago while working in this gulch.

The revolver, which is now in our possession, is numbered 11293, and from inquiries made of Mr. W. E. Webster of the Colt Manufacturing company, we learn from a letter recently received from him that this identical revolver was manufactured in the year 1853.

This instance and others are proof conclusive that the existence of gold in the Black Hills is not of recent discovery and that at least twenty-five years ago mining was carried on here. The theory that the revolver was lost by a hunter and not a miner is not tenable, as it was found on bed-rock in what may have been at that time a drain ditch; whereas, had it been lost by a hunter it would have been lying nearer the surface.

B H Daily Times
June 8, 1877

"S. D. Porter has discovered upon a tributory to Spruce Gulch, an old drift, 12 or 15 feet deep, which judging from a blazed tree standing at the mouth of the drift, and whose age can be clearly determined by its circles, was made in 1865. A blazed trail leads up from Spruce Gulch and was probably made in the same year, adding one more to the many indications that the Hills were visited by adventurous miners years ago."

B H Daily Times
Nov. 10, 1877

"Got all the gold we could carry our ponys all got by the Indians I have lost my gun and nothing to eat and Indians hunting me."

The author of these frantic lines apparently was later "got" by the Indian pursuers too. Who were these unfortunate adventurers and where did they originate? Frank Thomson, the late Spearfish author and historian, spent most of his 93-year lifetime trying to find out. Through prodigious research, he succeeded in tracing most of them. Like many others, before and since, these tragic victims had "gone West" from the eastern settlements and "were never heard from again."

The members of the ill-fated Kind Party may have been the first gold-seekers to invade the mysterious Black Hills. But they were far from the last. Nor were they the last to suffer the consequences of lust for gold in the jealously-guarded Indian country. Oddly, despite their idyllic environment, the Indians did not live in the Black Hills for prolonged periods. The Sioux, who lorded over the region when the white man began coveting it, were a nomadic people. They roamed the Great Plains in constant search for the immense buffalo herds that sustained them in so many ways. But the Black Hills were sacred to them and they made frequent pilgrimages there. Perhaps they reminded the Sioux of their former woodland culture in the forested lands of Minnesota and Wisconsin where they had lived prior to migrating west of the Missouri River.

In any event, game was plentiful in the Black Hills and the Indians cherished them as their "Meat Pack." In addition, the level, wooded bottom lands cradled by tree-clad bluffs or ridges made ideal winter camping grounds. Here, too, the Sioux sought refuge from the forces of the white man's civilization crowding in on them. In 1873, the Army proposed a fort there.

A treaty with the Sioux consummated at Fort Laramie in 1868 called for the abandonment of military posts in the Indian country rather than the establishment of any new posts there. Red Cloud of the fierce Oglala Sioux, who had led the costly raids against the Bozeman Trail forts, had vowed his people would not stop the fighting until this humiliating condition was met. He won his point along with an agreement that all roads leading through the Indian country to the Montana gold fields would be closed.

Further, the treaty set aside all of the vast country west of the Missouri River in Dakota, including the coveted Black Hills, for the "absolute and undisturbed use and occupation of the Sioux Nation." It also committed the government to preventing white encroachment on the region, with troops if necessary. The historic treaty effectively slammed the door on white expansion into the Indian country, and dashed the hopes of the people of Dakota for settlement of the Black Hills — for a few years anyway.

"The United States hereby agree and stipulates that the country north of the North Platte River and east of the summits of the Big Horn Mountains shall be held and considered to be unceded Indian territory, and also stipulates and agrees that no white person or persons shall be permitted to settle upon or occupy any portion of the same; or without the consent of the Indians, first had and obtained, to pass through the same; and it is further agreed by the United States, that within ninety days after the conclusion of peace with all the bands of the Sioux Nation, the military posts now established in the territory in this article named shall be abandoned, and that the road leading to them and by them to the settlements in the Territory of Montana shall be closed."

Article XVI
Laramie Treaty of 1868

# chapter I

# Custer Opened The Gate

**Gen. George A Custer started Black Hills history, at least as far as the white man was concerned, when his expedition to the area in 1874 opened the gate to the Indian's sacred hunting ground. All that transpired before Custer arrived was called "B.C." and all after Custer was referred to as "A.C."**

No other single event contributed more to eventual Indian loss of the region than the now famous Custer Expedition to the Black Hills in the summer of 1874. There had been earlier explorations of the mysterious Sioux sanctuary and there would be a later one of significance. But it was the Custer Expedition that triggered the explosion of white colonization of the coveted Indian country. Lt. Col. George A. Custer and his Seventh Cavalry spent almost 60 days reconnoitering the Black Hills and the Indian country around it. The expedition was described as the best equipped on the Northern Plains up to that time. In addition to the soldiers, the command included scientists, practical miners, a corps of newspapermen and, happily for history, a photographer. All told, the expedition familiarized about 1,000 men — and one woman, a colored cook hired by the teamsters — with the Black Hills. The presence of the civilians, of course, strained the terms of the Laramie Treaty. The newspapermen, at least, were not in the employ of the government. They clearly were not covered in the category of whites permitted in the region. The entourage also included 110 wagons, mules to pull them, horses to carry the command and a beef herd to feed it.

Ostensibly, the purpose of the expedition was to thoroughly explore the interior of the Black Hills and to locate a suitable site for a future military post. It embarked from Fort Abraham Lincoln near present-day Bismarck, N.D., on July 2, 1874. It returned there on August 30 after covering 1,205 miles on the round trip. The expedition entered the primeval Black Hills from the west on July 24 when it marched down Castle Creek into a picturesque floral valley. Its entry occurred in the southwestern portion of what later became Lawrence County. Enroute home, the command camped for two days at Bear Butte in what was later to become another sector of Lawrence County. Between the dates of its penetration of the Black Hills and its departure from them the expedition had unlocked many secrets of the enchanting Sioux haven.

"In pursuance of instructions from the headquarters of the Military Division of the Missouri, an expedition will be organized at Fort Abraham Lincoln, Dakota Territory, for the purpose of reconnoitering the route from that post to Bear Butte, in the Black Hills, and exploring the country south, southeast, and southwest of that point . . . The expedition will start from Fort Abraham Lincoln as soon after the 20th of July as practicable; Lieutenant Colonel Custer will proceed by such route as he may find to be most desirable to Bear Butte, or some point on or near the Belle Fourche, and thence will push his explorations in such direction or directions as in his judgment will enable him to obtain the most information in regard to the character of the country, and the possible routes of communication through it . . . "

Excerpt from Brigadier General Alfred Terry, Commanding, Military Department of Dakota, orders for the Black Hills Expedition of 1874.

Mrs. Annie D. Tallent, born April 12, 1827, near York, Livingston County, New York, was 46 years old when she became the first white woman to enter the Black Hills in the winter of 1874 with her husband, nine-year-old son, and 25 other men of the Gordon Party. She died at the home of her son in Sturgis on February 13, 1901.

Overshadowing all other findings of the expedition was its momentous discovery of gold in French Creek in the Southern Hills. Custer was exuberant in reporting the presence of the precious metal long suspected to exist in the region, stating it could be found "from the grass roots." His official dispatches were replete with poetic references to the pristine beauty of the region. But it was the gold discovery that caught the public eye. Custer himself was so elated about the historic gold discovery that he failed to even mention a possible site for a future military post in his verbose dispatches. It is doubtful that he even looked for one.

News of Custer's sensational gold find electrified the nation and brought renewed demands for opening of the Black Hills to white settlement. The government agreed to negotiate with the Sioux for sale or lease of the gold fields. But some whites were too impatient to await the outcome of the negotiations. Custer had opened the gate and thousands were determined to burst through it. They took off for the new-found El Dorado despite government prohibitions against it. Most of them were quickly intercepted by Army patrols and turned back. But there was one notable exception.

On December 23, 1874, some four months after the Custer Expedition had left the Hills, the first party of white prospectors to illegally invade them reached French Creek. The interlopers, known as the Gordon Party for its leader, included 26 men, one woman and her nine-year-old son. The lone woman was Mrs. Annie Tallent immortalized ever since as the first "white" woman in the Black Hills. The emphasis is on the "white" because Sarah Campbell, the colored cook with the Custer expedition, had preceded her.

The Gordon Party built a stockade near where Custer's men had made their gold strike and they lived within it while prospecting the area that winter. The Army, true to its commitment to protect the sanctity of the Indian country, located the unlawful encampment in April of 1875 and expelled the intruders. But countless other civilian expeditions stampeded to the region from all directions.

Army troops at the Gordon Stockade on French Creek where the first illegal prospectors in the Black Hills after the Custer Expedition of 1874 spent the winter. There were six cabins within the stockade for the 26 men, one woman and nine-year-old boy in the Gordon Party.

(S. D. State Historical Society)

Army troops, principally from Fort Laramie in Wyoming and Fort Robinson in Nebraska, were repeatedly ordered to the Black Hills to eject the illegal prospectors. It soon became a hopeless task, however, as the heavily-forested gulches afforded the elusive miners numerous hiding places.

It was at this point that the government decided to send still another expedition to the Black Hills for additional information on them. It wasn't that Custer's remarkable findings weren't believed. But his inspection of the interior had been necessarily hurried, considering the difficulty of movement within it, and the extent of the gold fields was not definitely known. It was important, the Secretary of the Interior wrote in the spring of 1875, to determine whether the precious metal existed there in large quantities. "To settle this question," he explained, "the Department has decided, under the advice of the President, to send a competent geologist to explore the region . . . " Moreover, it was essential to know whether the Black Hills were worth a war with the Sioux. The prospect of war became very real when the Sioux refused to sell or lease their beloved stronghold, and they strongly protested the unlawful invasions of it.

Walter P. Jenney, who later became Geologist in Charge, Division of Zinc, U. S. Geological Surveys, was a co-leader of the Jenney-Newton Expedition to the Black Hills in 1875. The other co-leader, a faculty member of the Columbia School of Mines, New York City, returned to the Black Hills for further information and died in Deadwood of typhoid fever on August 5, 1877.
(S. D. State Historical Society)

Nevertheless, a scientific expedition was sent to the Black Hills in May of 1875. It consisted of 16 civilian specialists in technical fields, headed by two prominent geologists, Walter F. Jenney and Henry Newton, and a military escort of about 600 troopers from Fort Laramie commanded by Lt. Col. Richard I. Dodge. Unknowingly at first, unlike the previous two expeditions with women, it also included a lone woman. She was the ubiquitous frontier character Calamity Jane who, dressed in men's clothing, avoided detection until the expedition had almost reached its destination. She was ordered back to Fort Laramie, but somehow managed to frequently reappear as the command advanced. Whether she actually reached the Black Hills with the expedition has never been definitely established. Nevertheless, she was to leave a lasting imprint on the history and legends of the region "A.C." It is possible that she was the third woman, the second of her race, to enter the forbidden Hills.

The Jenney-Newton Expedition arrived in the Black Hills on May 25 and returned to Fort Laramie on October 23. It thoroughly scoured every aspect of the region's resources during its almost five months in the Hills. Topographical surveys were conducted in all sections of them and reports were written on the geological, botanical, water courses, soil fertility, timber stands and climatic conditions of the region. The expedition also named all the prominent peaks in the surveyed area, mostly for outstanding military leaders like Warren, Terry, Crook, Harney and Custer. The campsites were generally named for these officers too and for members of the expedition. The party, although not given the press coverage of the more exciting Custer Expedition, gathered more information on the Black Hills than had ever before been collected on them.

"That most curious of the many curious features of the Black Hills, the 'outer rampart,' must, at some time in earth's history, have been a reef around the island now called the Black Hills. The Red Valley was a reservoir in which were collected the waters which flowed from the 'Hills.' These cut their way through the barrier, not necessarily on the natural prolongation of any stream, but wherever they found the easiest outlet . ."
Excerpt from report of Lieutenant Colonel Richard I. Dodge, Military Commander, Jenney-Newton Expedition to the Black Hills, 1875.

" . . . Every step towards the heart of these 'sacred fastnesses' is beset with innumerable difficulties. These overcome, the venturous explorer is amply repaid for all his hardships and privations. Almost any moderately good country would seem a 'Paradise' after passing the 'Purgatory' of such approaches to it; but, allowing for the full extravagance of pleasure which the traveler must feel under such circumstances, after mature judgment derived from several months of actual sojourn, and the cool comparison which a return to civilization enables me to make, I but express my fair and candid opinion when I pronounce the Black Hills, in many respects, the finest country I have ever seen . . . "

Lieutenant Colonel Richard I. Dodge
Military Commander, Jenney-Newton
Expedition to the Black Hills, 1875.

In addition to confirming Custer's reports of gold in the Hills "in paying quantities," the Jenney-Newton Expedition also made a less welcome discovery. It reported the presence of between 1,000 and 1,500 illegal prospectors in the Hills. Again troops were dispatched to remove the intruders. But they experienced only limited success. Gen. George Crook and his troopers escorted about 600 miners out of the region in August of 1875. But many others eluded capture and fanned out throughout the mountainous terrain.

Strangely, these early prospectors had few encounters with the resentful Sioux. Most of the Sioux were apparently hunting out on the plains for much of that eventful year. But, as winter approached, the growing number of white interlopers heading for the Hills became too conspicuous to remain undetected. Travel in the vicinity became extremely hazardous as the Sioux began picking off the unprotected invaders. The Sioux had cause for swearing vengeance on "Yellow Hair," as Custer was known to them, for exposing their revered Black Hills to the greed of the white man. They were to achieve their revenge on Custer and his Seventh Cavalry on the bluffs of the Little Big Horn in 1876.

Col. Dodge, in his report of the Jenney-Newton Expedition, included advice on a possible site for a future military post that Custer had neglected to do. Dodge wrote that there were many good sites for a post in the region. But the best one, in his opinion, would be on "Spear-fish" Creek in the Northern Hills. This was in the vicinity of the Raynolds Expedition campsite of July 12, 1859. Col. Dodge recommended the establishment of a military reserve 10 miles wide from east to west and 20 miles long from north to south on that constantly running stream. It would, he explained, be a strategic location in relation to the Indian trails to their favorite hunting grounds in the Powder River country. These trails converged on the Belle Fourche River, as the north branch of the Cheyenne River was then known, northwest of the Hills.

**Lt. Col. Richard I. Dodge, escorting the Jenney-Newton Scientific Expedition to the Black Hills, recommended the best site for a fort in the region was "Spear-fish" creek (left center). White tents of the expedition's encampment are seen in the right center.**
**(S. D. State Historical Society)**

"A military post established within a reasonable distance of the trail," Col. Dodge reported, "will be in the direct line of north and south, east and west travel of these bands of Sioux. Answering to these strategic conditions, nature has provided on the large creek known as Spear-fish, the most admirable spot for a military post to be found in the Hills. The creek is large enough for all necessary water power, has a fall of quite one hundred feet to the mile, the water is pure and delicious, the country very fertile. Beautiful hay bottoms line the creek; fine building stone is on every hill, and the canon (canyon) of Spear-fish affords easy access to the very heart of the best pine and spruce forests in the Black Hills."

Dodge also urged prompt action in establishing the military reserve before the best lands could be taken up by the hordes of white settlers streaming into the promising valley. But his pleadings went unheeded until it was too late.

Before any action could be taken on Dodge's recommendations, the vital issue of Sioux title to the Black Hills had to be resolved. Efforts to obtain peaceable cession of the Hills through negotiation ended unsuccessfully in September. The Sioux simply would not give up their esteemed "Paha Sapa" as they called the Black Hills. President Grant, in apparent disgust, authorized the withdrawal of troops from the Sioux reserve. The government continued to issue public proclamations against further encroachments in the region. But it also halted all attempts to expell the adventurous parties that ignored the proclamations. Those reckless enough to risk the wrath of the watchful Sioux on the roads to the gold fields were free to do so, and there were many who were. It was estimated that about 4,000 whites were unlawfully occupying the Black Hills by the end of 1875.

At first, the Black Hills mining boom was concentrated in the Southern Hills where the initial gold discoveries had taken place. It shifted to the Central Hills as the frenzied prospectors spread out from the discovery site. Every report of fresh strikes, fancied or factual, sent the eager miners scurrying in new directions. Word quickly spread in the fall of 1875 that a major strike had occurred on a long-neglected stream in the Northern Hills which a small band of prospectors had reached in August. The stream was known as Whitewood Creek. It was only about 10 miles long from its headwaters to where it emerged onto the plains near the northeastern tip of the Hills. Although located in one of the most inaccesible sectors of the Hills, the stream could be identified by the mass of dead wood lining its upper banks. The fallen timber proved to be more of a guidepost than an obstacle to the excited miners rushing northward.

It had taken less than six months after the eviction of the Gordon Party, first of the white civilian trespassers, for the center of the gold boom to settle in the Northern Hills. It was here, among the dead wood of Whitewood Creek, that the destiny of the Black Hills was ultimately settled. For underfoot was the "Mother Lode."

"Far out of the ordinary lines of plains travel, surrounded by all sides by the arid wastes of the 'Bad Lands,' by bands of hostiles and treacherous savages, the 'Black Hills' loomed up in silent majesty, mysterious, unknown. More than 200 miles east of north of the 'Laramie Range,' in the midst of a desert of dreary alkaline plains, rises a magnificent mass of mountains, covering a country almost as large as the State of Vermont, and closely embraced within the two principal branches of the Cheyenne River. To this country all the tribes of the great Dakota or Sioux Nation give the name 'Pah-sappa,' which liberally interpreted, is 'black hill,' Pa-hill, sappa, black.' . . . . "

Excerpt from report of
Lieutenant Colonel Richard I. Dodge,
Military Commander, Jenney-Newton
Expedition to the Black Hills, 1875.

**This battered marker located about three miles south of Bear Butte designates the location of the Black Hills Expedition campsite of August 15, 1874.**

**(Bob Lee Photo)**

**This picture was probably the first one taken of Deadwood in 1876. It was snapped by a Henry Garlick who designated his tent store on the left by making a dot on it on his original print. His son, Harry Garlick of Denver, who visited Deadwood many years later, sent the Adams Museum a copy of the print. (Adams Museum)**

# chapter II

# Seven Started It All

The Bryant Party first discovered gold at the mouth to Spruce Gulch in 1875. Where these primitive cabins stood in 1876, the Deadwood Amusement Park and rodeo grounds now stand. The Days of '76 rodeos, intermingled with early-day pageantry, now commemorate the gold discovery in Deadwood Gulch at this site.

(Centennial Collection)

Precipitating the stampede of gold seekers into the Northern Hills were the sensational discoveries there by the small party of prospectors who were the first to penetrate that rugged region. The party included James B. Pearson, Frank Bryant, Richard Lowe, Thomas Moon, James Pierman, Samuel Blodgett, and George Hauser. It had assembled in the vicinity of Fort Pierre and reached Whitewood Creek in early August of 1875. Pearson, a resident of Yankton, was the most experienced miner of the lot, having prospected in Australia and British Columbia as well as in the gold fields of California, Idaho and Montana. The party built a cabin, the first structure in that sector of the Hills, at the mouth of Spruce Gulch near the banks of Whitewood Creek. Pearson told about the wealth of the region in a statement published in the Yankton Daily Press and Dakotan. By the time the statement was published, the richness of the region was no secret to the horde of prospectors already in the Hills. The party of seven that had made the initial exciting strikes was soon crowded on all sides by other mining hopefuls. But the statement gave the outside world a glimpse into the cause of all the excitement.

"The Whitewood rich gold producing region," Pearson disclosed, "embraces an area that will average eight miles in width by twenty in length, its largest area extending north and south. It embraces a number of streams and gulches known as Deadwood, Bob Tail, Gold Run, Two Bit, Split Tail, Cape Horn and others, and has been divided by the miners into four districts called Cape Horn District, Whitewood District, Lost District, which includes Deadwood; and Gold Run."

Moreover, Pearson informed the Press and Dakotan that the Deadwood area was yielding $10,000 a day and he optimistically estimated it would average a daily yield of $100,000 a day when fully

**One of the big placer mining claims on Whitewood Creek in 1876 was at the upper end of Sherman Street in Deadwood.**
**(Centennial Collection)**

It is estimated between three and four million dollars worth of placer gold was taken from the streams that converged in Deadwood during 1876 and 1877. Most of the records of the fabulous claims were destroyed in the great Deadwood fire of 1879. Following are the records available of owners and value of gold placer mined: No. 1 below Discovery, Ed Murphy, $50,000; No. 2 below Discovery, $150,000 in four months with $250,000 in all; No. 4 and 5 below Discovery, $75,000; No. 6 below Discovery, $70,000; No. 8 below Discovery, McLeer, $40,000; No. 13 below Discovery — lived up to its name; No. 17 and 18 below Discovery, Smith and Oaks, sold to Wybell and Andres, $40,000 and $50,000 respectively; No. 22 below Discovery, J. J. Williams, $40,000; No. 1 and 2 above Discovery, Wheeler Brothers, $65,000 each; No. 5 above Discovery, $40,000; No. 6 above Discovery, $70,000. Many of the other claims were the richest.

Fred Borsch
Galena Pioneer

opened. "It lays over Alder Gulch, Montana, the richest placer mines ever before discovered," Pearson added, "because Alder Gulch was spotted while the Deadwood is regular and the streak wider, and is the richest and most extensive placer gold field that has ever been struck."

Bryant and two others staked out "Discovery Claim" at the mouth of Spruce Gulch on November 8. Pearson had joined up with a party of eight others he found prospecting in the Central Hills. He urged them to approach Deadwood Gulch from upstream, and they staked out their "Discovery Claim" on November 9 near the mouth of Blacktail Gulch, two miles above the center of present-day Deadwood.

Because of the tangle of dead wood and beaver dams below the Discovery Claim, the party all staked their claims above Discovery, and these turned out to be a real bonanza. Claim No. 2 below Discovery, for example, produced about $140,000 in gold in an early four-month period.

By the first of 1876 over 50 miners were working Deadwood Gulch. The rich two mile area was divided by early January into 300-foot claims all taken up. Bobtail and Blacktail Gulches which feed into Deadwood Gulch near Discovery were being successfully worked, as was Gold Run, coming down from what was soon to be Lead City, into Whitewood Gulch, a mile above Deadwood. Whitewood Creek below Gold Run and below the confluence with Deadwood Creek returned good gold values, but nothing as rich as the two miles up past Blacktail.

The other gold placers of consequence in Lawrence County were in the Tinton area, about 20 miles northwest of Deadwood. Activity commenced here at the same time as Deadwood. The hot spot became known as Nigger Hill because it was worked very successfully by a group of colored miners. They left early with their gold, avoiding loss in saloons and gambling joints. Iron, Potato, Beaver and Bear Creeks draining from Nigger Hill were thoroughly prospected and worked. They were about played out in 1878. This area was easily accessible from foothills to the north and from Spearfish and could easily have been the source of the gold made famous by the Thoen Stone.

Even before all the placer claims had been staked, experienced prospectors began looking for the Mother Lode, the origin of the placer gold that had washed down into the creeks. Two sources were found: conglomerates high up the hillsides in the Central City area, and hard-rock lodes in the general area from Central City through Terraville to Lead.

The conglomerates are actually solidified debris from the disintegration and erosion of hard-rock ore above the Central City-

Terraville vicinity millions of years ago. They are considered to be "fossil placers." Their erosion in Blacktail and other nearby gulches is thought to be largely responsible for the unusually rich placers found in Deadwood Gulch just below Blacktail.

These conglomerates were mined and milled extensively starting in September 1876, but the more accessible deposits were mined out by 1881.

The hard-rock gold deposits have a longer history. Prospectors searching for the Mother Lode found gold in quartz-type ore not far from the conglomerates in Terraville and Central City, and then especially over the ridge in Lead City. Several stamp mills occupied the best available sites in the narrow gulch, and almost all houses had to be built on narrow ridges or steep hillsides. The general area of the early hard-rock ore can be traced today by following the Open Cut from the highway in Central City, south through Terraville, and right up to Main Street in present-day Lead. This is the outcropping of the world-famous Homestake mine ore body that today extends deeply underground southeast to a mine depth of 8,000 feet.

Pearson is credited with locating the Giant quartz claim on January 7, 1876 in what is now the "Open Cut" in Lead. He didn't know how close he was to "bonanza." He was right on top of the Homestake! It was winter and he failed to dig out any ore.

It was left to Moses Manuel to find and prove the Homestake. He and his brother Fred were experienced miners, fresh in the Hills from diggings in Montana and points west. The Manuels located claims February 21, 1876, on Bobtail Gulch, the mouth of which is opposite Blacktail Gulch and the site of the "Discovery" claim of November 9, 1875. Bobtail leads steeply up into present-day Terraville, just over the ridge from Lead. Gold Run Creek is short, running down a mile from the Open Cut area to its juncture with Whitewood Creek, a mile up from Deadwood.

Thomas Carey had discovered placer gold in Gold Run Creek in February. It must have been obvious to the Manuels that gold-bearing ore should exist on or near the ridge between Terraville and Lead. They had found some rich float quartz in March, presumably in Gold Run. The Manuels looked for the lode but the snow was too deep. Moses persisted alone, and after a week's search, when the snow began thawing, his search ended! He had found some rich quartz in the bottom of a draw cleared by a small stream from the melting snow. The Homestake claim was located the next day, April 9, 1876. The surface ore proved very rich, and an arrasta — a crude method of crushing ore — was built down Gold Run on Whitewood Creek. Panning, sluicing, or using quick-silver would recover the gold released by pulverizing the rock in this manner.

**Fred and Mose Manuel were experienced miners who saw beyond the rich placer deposits in Deadwood Gulch to the "Mother Lode." They knew that somewhere up on the mountain was the source of all the gold in the lower creeks. Mose found the Homestake bonanza on April 9, 1876. In June, 1877 the Manuels sold the Homestake to George Hearst, father of William Randolph Hearst. Millions have been taken out of the Homestake Mine during the century completed in 1976.**
**(Centennial Collection)**

Lead City

"This pleasant little mining town which is located about four miles directly south of Deadwood is prospering finely. Rich quartz leads have been struck which are yielding abundantly by the aid of quartz mills now in operation. Many new buildings are in the process of erection and they are of a class second to none in Hills. The camp is settling up fast and many new comers to the Hills are taking up their residence at the place."

B H Daily Times
June 19, 1877

The Manuels' Homestake claim was later found to be squarely on top of Pearson's Giant claim staked on January 7, as was their Old Abe claim, staked alongside of and east of the Homestake. Others were hard at work locating and working quartz claims in the vicinity. The Giant and nearby Gold Run claims were lost to their locators because they failed to stay for the spring thaw and perform the drudgery of hard rock mining.

Several small stamp mills were operating in Lead City by the summer of 1877 on ore from the Homestake, Old Abe, Golden Star, and others. "Lead," (pronounced Leed) in mining lingo, means a lode or vein of ore. The Manuels had worked hard during the first year proving the worth of their claims. In June, 1877, the Homestake was sold to George Hearst for $70,000 and thus began the celebrated Homestake Mining Co. The story of Homestake's growth and eventual acquisition of the Central City, Terraville, and Lead mining areas is a complex one. It is a story of shrewd consolidations and the importance of proper capitalization.

The really intensive and profitable gold mining operations were concentrated in the few square miles of the Deadwood-Lead vicinity. However, extensive prospecting for the hard-rock lodes went on in the 1876-1878 years. Thousands of prospectors had deserted Custer for Deadwood in the summer of '76. Those not finding any prospects in the Deadwood vicinity fanned out through the Northern Hills.

**It is believed that this early-day picture is one of the first of Golden Gate. It is identified by the name of Rainwater on the sign above Cash Store on the left. News reports name a Rainwater as a pioneer of the mining town who specialized in selling whiskey.**

**(Courtesy of George Fassbender)**

**James Conzette's cabin at Galena was built by him in 1877 and was sturdy enough to be used as a fort. Conzette helped lay out the city of Deadwood with only the use of a length of rope.**

**(Centennial Collection)**

. . . We only wish the laboring class of the East and all parts of the Union had equal chances with us, and would once more advise the seeker after fortune to wend his steps this way, where the cry of hard times is little heard, and where the thrifty and industrious man can see some chances for a fair return for his work.

B H Pioneer
Jan. 13, 1877

Many mines developed in these early years, especially those within about six miles of the Homestake.

The largest of these was the Bald Mountain Mining Co., a consolidation of many smaller mines in the Bald Mountain area. The first discovery was made near Trojan in 1877 at the beginning of Deadwood Creek, four miles up the gulch from Deadwood. It resulted in the formation of the Portland Mining Co. in 1880. Two other consolidated mines in the Ruby Basin area, about three miles south of Bald Mountain, the Mogul and the Golden Reward, also became major gold producers.

Two other mining areas were discovered and developed by prospectors panning for gold on their way north to Deadwood. The first was in March, 1876, at present-day Galena, named for the galena (lead) ore discovered when panning in Bear Butte Creek, six miles southeast of Deadwood. The ore was very rich in silver, with some gold. It required smelting to extract the silver, hence only the highest grades could be mined and soon three smelters were operating. Further search disclosed rich silver ore deposits and a local boom was on. Ten months later, Galena boasted about 75 structures for housing and the usual businesses common to mining camps. About 400 men were at work on various mining ventures.

The other area was at present-day Roubaix, first known as Perry, on Elk Creek, seven miles south of Deadwood. The first lode discoveries were made in 1878. These were later consolidated in a mine known as the Uncle Sam, later named the Clover Leaf. It produced well, on and off, until 1937. Excessive water had finally made it unprofitable.

"One hundred passengers leave Deadwood today. They could not see any gold on the sidewalks."

B H Daily Times
April 27, 1877

"The largest gold hunting party yet in these Hills are now enroute for this city, by way of Kearney. They number about 200 souls. They have all the conveniences of overland travel, and are a sort of portable city. They have a minister and divine service is held in the open air."

B H Daily Times
May 15, 1877

"Yesterday was pay day with most of our mining and milling companies. The boys were all happy and flying high. Ye gay and festive faro dealer stole a smile of happiness as he raked in ye golden chips and quarters of ye boys."

B H Daily Times
Feb. 6, 1879

**The first saloon to be erected in Central City, located between Deadwood and Lead, was the "Shoofly."**

**(Centennial Collection)**

Elizabethtown, one of the earliest sections of Deadwood in 1876, was named for Elizabeth Card, the first white woman in this section of the Black Hills.

Black Hills of Dakota
Deadwood Board of Trade, 1881

The new town of Cleveland is located on Whitewood about one mile from Deadwood.

B H Pioneer
April 7, 1877

Other mining camps had their early beginnings in the 1876-1880 period but didn't really amount to much until the 80's and 90's. Terry was about two and a half miles southwest of Lead and situated about halfway down the east slope of Terry Peak in the Ruby Basin District. Maitland was on a back road gulch connecting with Spearfish, four miles northwest of Lead. Carbonate, another silver area, was six miles northwest of Lead and three miles west of Maitland, in the high country. Flatiron served the Wasp gold mine, on Whitewood Creek two miles directly south of Lead.

These were the very earliest found and at least partially developed by the first rush of prospectors to the Northern Hills.

The first mining camp in the Northern Hills was Gayville, located November 1875 on Deadwood Creek just below the junction with Blacktail Gulch. It was here that the Gay brothers and other members of the Lardner party located placer claims on November 9, 1875. Gayville was often in the news and was the site of one of the first murders in the area, the killing of a miner named Jack Hinch July 9, 1876. Located immediately upstream the following spring were South Bend, Central City, Golden Gate and Anchor which were at the foot of Poorman Gulch, leading to the upper end of Lead. These were all shortly merged into Central City, subsequently on one of the two main highways between Deadwood and Lead. Central City was formally organized in January, 1877, being named after the city by the same name in Colorado.

There were at least 15 stamp mills operating in the area by 1878, averaging about 20 stamps each. These operated on both gold quartz ores from the south side of the gulch and up Bobtail Gulch, and on the conglomerate ores from Hidden Treasure and Blacktail gulches, running north. The famous DeSmet mine and mill was located on the south side of the hill in the Golden Gate part of Central City, and was the northern anchor of the Homestake ledge. The present Open Cut runs from DeSmet southerly to Lead's Main and Mill streets, a mile in length.

By the spring of 1877, Central City's population was estimated at 3,000, and it had the usual stores, hotels, saloons, and two newspapers. The first established public school in the Black Hills is said to have opened in the fall of 1877. In the Deadwood area, the first camp to be located was Elizabethtown. It was started in the early spring of 1876 about a half-mile below the center of present-day Deadwood, which was located next. Fountain City and Montana City came next, down Whitewood Creek below Elizabethtown and in the vicinity of the November 8, 1875, "Discovery Claim." South Deadwood was laid out next, up Whitewood Creek and a half-mile from Deadwood proper. It provided badly-needed space for businesses and homes on level ground.

J. B. Pearson, the first man to discover gold in Deadwood Gulch, sat on Brown Rocks, high above this same view but minus the buildings. He tried to decide whether to start panning gold in the gulch to his left or the one twisting up on the right. He chose the one to the right and discovered the richest placer mining area the world has ever known.
(Centennial Collection)

**Sluice boxes honeycombed Deadwood Gulch in 1876 after the first miners discovered that more loose gold in nuggets and dust, than in any other mining area in the world, had been washed down into the creek beds after millions of years of erosion.**
**(Centennial Collection)**

The original Deadwood was laid out April 26, 1876, below the junction of Deadwood and Whitewood creeks, with the well-known White Rocks high above on the steep hill to the east. As in Central City and Lead, there was room for one main street and it ran the length of the gulch toward Central City. A branch, Sherman Street, followed alongside Whitewood Creek up through South Deadwood, where a road went to Lead by way of Pluma. Lots were 25 by 100 feet where possible. Placer mining was going on at the same time, generally between the buildings going up and down the creek. Occasionally, tunneling was resorted to under the buildings to get to the gold dust trapped at bedrock.

A small log cabin was the first structure erected in Deadwood itself, completed April 30, on the location of the later telephone building. Small sawmills were being set up, and the first frame building was completed in June adjoining the log cabin. It housed a well-equipped grocery store. Structures for other businesses followed rapidly. Within four months both sides of Main Street for half a mile were filled solidly with a varied lot of log and frame structures, some two stories. Lee, Gold and Wall streets, the main cross streets, ended up about half their platted widths due to the intense demand for business locations. The population is said to have grown in this period to 7,000.

Washington and adjoining Lead City were organized, following the discovery of gold-bearing ore at the head of the north fork of Gold Run Creek in the spring of 1876. It is not certain which was located first, but certainly the first to be platted was Lead City, later simply Lead. This was completed on July 11, 1876, when an organizational meeting was held and rules were set for the sale of lots. The hub of the city was the junction of Main and Mill streets, the south end of the Open Cut of today. Washington was platted a few weeks later, just a short quarter mile from Main and Mill. Ultimately, Washington became a part of Lead, their few businesses moving to locations in the Main and Mill area. Mill Street was the main business street for years, until it was swallowed up by the gradual extension of the Open Cut.

James Lawler, a great friend of Seth Bullock, was born in Dublin, Ireland. He arrived in Deadwood on March 8, 1876, a member of the second Bryant Party Expedition into the Black Hills. The party tried to enter Deadwood at the mouth of Spruce Gulch but hostile Indians forced them to enter on the Deadwood side of Speagle Gap where the wagons had to be lowered by ropes. Lawler was wounded in the cheek by an Indian arrow, a mark he carried the rest of his life. He owned a claim at Golden Gate between Central City and Lead and had an interest in the MC97 claim located where the Sunnyside Motel, Grace Lutheran Church and Penny's Motel are located on upper Main Street in Deadwood. Two of Lawler's daughters, Marie Lawler and Dorothy Curnow were still living in Deadwood at the printing of this book. A son Bramble lives in Omaha, Nebraska.

Lead had the terrain for side streets and homes could be built with little difficulty, especially on the south slopes. In the first few years, 11 small stamp mills were built to process ore from the close-by mines. By the fall of 1878, Lead boasted a post office, hotels, hospital, churches, a bank, besides the usual saloons and business places. Population was estimated at 1,500. Terraville, in upper Bobtail Gulch, got going in 1877. It was the center of intense mining and milling activity, situated as it was between the rich DeSmet mine in Central City and the still richer mines in Lead. Several stamp mills occupied the best available sites in the narrow gulch, and almost all houses had to be built on narrow ridges or steep hillsides. Portland, later renamed Trojan, was founded in 1877 near the head of Deadwood Creek in the Bald Mountain area.

Even Pearson, among the first prospectors to look down upon the quiet, serene, deep emptiness of Deadwood Gulch in August of 1875, probably did not realize what a wild, pent-up mass of humanity his party had unleashed upon the rugged scene with their historic gold finds.

It was like turning over a hidden ant hill with his shovel. Like ants, the gulches, ravines and mountainsides were suddenly swarming in every direction with men in their mad, half-crazed search for yellow glitter. Gold taken from the Hills in 1876 was estimated at $1,500,000 and the toiling mass of men who retrieved it was somewhere between 7,000 and 8,000. There was no way to accurately count the human invasion with a constant stream of hopefuls coming and the disappointed ones returning home. But the majority crowded into Deadwood Gulch.

It is estimated they came a hundred a day; beds were rented by the hour and food could not come in fast enough to feed the mob. There was not even enough gold or shovels to shovel it for all who came even though it was the richest strike of all. As usual, as in every stampede, the number of people was far greater than the amount of gold, bountiful as it was in the Black Hills. If the gold taken out in that first year had been equally divided among those who came, it was estimated it would have been a paltry $200 per person. From all walks of life, they came in groups, some on foot, horseback, burros in caravans of covered wagons and heavy wagon trains.

The placer gold rush reached its climax in the spring of 1877. The Engineering and Mining Journal continually warned the poor, without mining skills, to stay away from the Hills as there were not enough mines or jobs to go around. By May 1877 the booming population in the Black Hills was roughly estimated at 15,250 with Deadwood and Whitewood topping the list at 5,500; Gayville (Central City) 3,000; Crook City, 400; Centennial City, 100; Rapid City, 250; Bear Butte Gulch, 500; Central Hills, 2,500; and a floating population of 3,000.

By 1880, the last of the nation's big gold rushes was over. Placer mining had "petered out." Hard rock mining was the thing. Gold production (mostly placer), at $1,500,000, in 1876, had climbed to $3,305,843 (hard rock) by 1880. It was reported that from 1874 to 1880 more than 30,000 persons had passed through the Hills, and that of all the boom towns, Deadwood (which included Elizabethtown, Gayville and South Bend) was the largest and wildest. It reputedly had "the prettiest women, the bravest men, the laziest dogs, the meekest hackmen, the homeliest newspaper reporters and the toniest bartenders in the world."

It is estimated that about $2,000,000 worth of gold dust was taken out of these Hills in the last year, surrounded as were the miners with danger and difficulty.

B H Daily Times
May 18, 1877

Throughout the 1879 papers, there were numerous items showing that residents were getting "Leadville fever" and with the exodus of many braver souls, the news carried reports showing that living conditions were better in Deadwood and warning the miners to investigate before leaving the Black Hills. To the headline carried in the local papers, 'Mortuary Report Fearful', the Leadville paper retaliated with the statement: "We have never urged people to come here."

**Deadwood was growing so fast between 1876 and 1880 that space was at a premium as supplies brought in by freighters piled up on the porches of stores on Main Street. The Big Horn Store, later changed to Goldberg Grocery, is still operating at the same location 100 years later.**
**(S. D. 500 Years of Progress)**

## The Deadwood Country

We do not believe this or any other country affords such another example of rapid development as what is now known as "The Deadwood Country." Three months ago it was occupied by only a few hardy miners—scarce fifty in number — who had placed their lives in peril, both from Indians and starvation, living on "meat straight," without even salt, for months, and undergoing nearly every privation known to man in search of the precious metal. Now Deadwood, Whitewood, and their tributaries, are peopled by more than seven thousand of as hardy, energetic and intelligent men as there are in the country; men who have left home, wife and children, and endured hardships and incurred dangers that those in the States little dream of, in search of a better country — more money. They have found it, and today, go where you will, the sound of the pick, shovel, rocker and sledge greets your ear, and sluice-boxes, ditches and dams are on every hand.

Six weeks ago the site of Deadwood City was a heavy forest of pine timber; now it extends nearly a mile along Deadwood and Whitewood, and contains nearly two thousand of the most energetic, driving people on the continent. Every branch of business is represented, and many of them are overdone. Houses are going up on every hand — immense trains are constantly arriving loaded with goods of all kinds, business is rushing, and bargains are driven here that would put Wall Street to blush. In addition to Deadwood, Montana City, Centennial and Spearfish have sprung into existence, and each and all are growing rapidly.

Let the Government but protect this people and give them mail facilities, and within two years the Black Hills will contain more than 200,000 of prosperous and happy souls. We know that the country is wonderfully rich in its mines of gold, silver, and other minerals, in its vast forests of pine and in its grazing and agricultural resources.

The Black Hills are a success — complete, entire, in spite of rival mining districts, "croakers," "tender-feet" and barbarous Indians. Let those who have found the fight and won the battle work together patiently, earnestly, unitedly. We have full faith that the government will soon come to our assistance — extend a helping hand, and throw around us its strong arm of protection and welcome us as no longer outlaws. May God in His providence speed the day.

**Black Hills Pioneer**
**June 24, 1876**

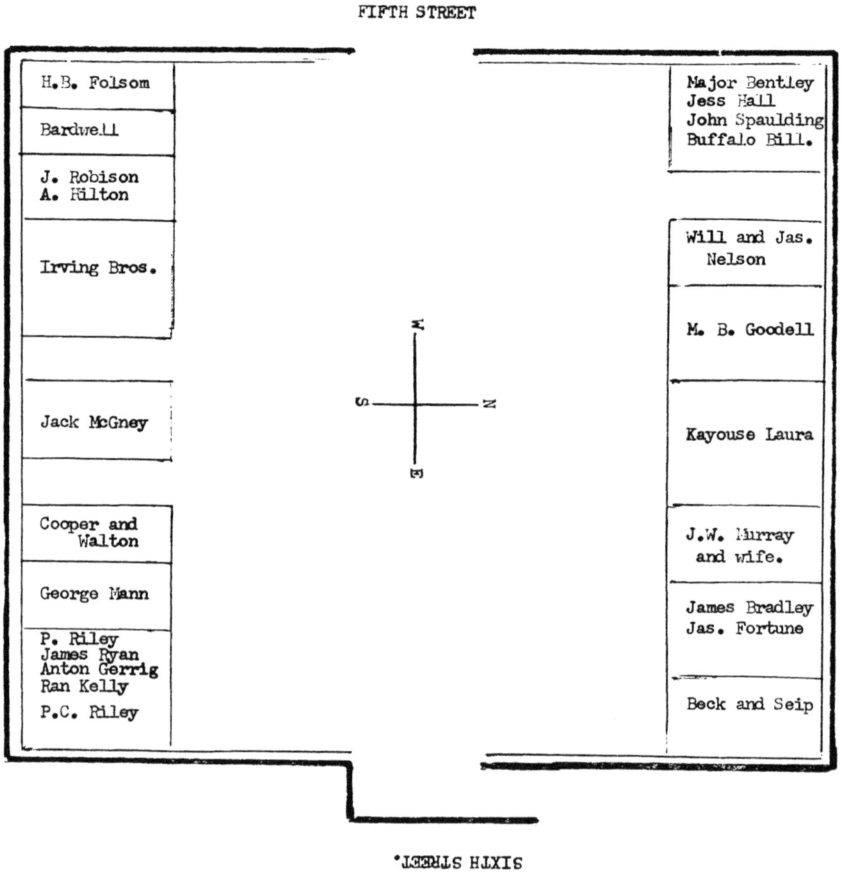

**Spearfish was a typical western town before the big fire of 1886. It looked like a scene from "Gunsmoke" with its wide, dirt streets and false-front buildings. The street is believed to be Hudson with the Overland House facing on Main Street. Several blocks were destroyed in the 1886 fire including part of the buildings shown in the photo.**
**(Black Hills State College Photo)**

# chapter III

# Grass, Grains Vie With Gold

**Crook City was located between Deadwood and Whitewood. It was once selected as the site for the seat of Lawrence County but Deadwood was finally the logical choice. The promising community suffered a quick death when the railroad selected Whitewood as a focal point. Crook City residents then moved to Whitewood.**

**(Centennial Collection)**

Among the many groups which converged on Deadwood in the Gold Rush Days was the Montana Party. Whereas others came from Bismarck and the north, Fort Pierre and the east, Sidney and Cheyenne to the south, this group came overland from Montana and the west. Thus it can be rightly said that the early gold-seekers came to Deadwood from all points of the compass.

Montana had had its own Gold Rush Days in the Bannock and Virginia City areas in 1862. Now the gold strike of 1876 at Deadwood in Dakota Territory loudly called some of these hardy frontiersmen back eastward. They could have taken a boat downstream on the Missouri and avoided the hazards of crossing Indian lands. This is what Seth Bullock, Sol Star and John Manning did later in August. But a large group of Montanans had become interested in Dakota gold and they organized the largest party to seek entry into the Black Hills at one time.

Organization of the party started as early as February of 1876 at Helena and within a month 200 members were gathered together at a rendezvous point on the Yellowstone River. Bill Langston was appointed as their leader and his assistant was Joseph Cook. With 100 pack mules and a long train of supply wagons the party started on March 20 to retrace the Bozeman Trail. All were expert frontiersmen but not all were miners. Many were cattlemen and tradesmen, whose skills would be in great demand in the full mining operations. They passed the place where Fort Phil Kearney had stood and where the Fetterman massacre had taken place. Before reaching the Platte River, they broke away from the Bozeman Trail. They left the Powder River Valley and crossed directly across the hunting grounds of the Indians, always alert to possible attack.

They crossed the Belle Fourche River and were in sight of the looming land-mass known as the Bear Lodge Mountains, reaching the

The head of an Indian killed near Crook City was brought into town and after being viewed by a number of citizens, it was turned over to Dr. Schultz, who upon removing the brain, found it to weigh 44 ounces. When we remember that Webster's brain weighed just 54 ounces we can rest assured that the Indian killed was one of no mean intellect. He was a young brave about 26 years of age.

B H Pioneer
Aug. 5, 1876

Headlines:
Unfriendly Neighbors
They Make Dash Through the Streets
Of Spearfish and Try Their
Needleguns on Its Citizens
Crook City Receives Call —
Stock Stolen by Red Devils
Indians All Around Us —
And Only One Good One —

Under the headline, the long story goes into elaborate detail about Indian attacks on Spearfish, the Valley, Crook City and Centennial and accounts of horse and cattle stealing.

B H Pioneer
**Aug. 5, 1876**

The raid of the Indians on Spearfish City last Sunday morning occasioned not a little excitement. Notwithstanding the suddenness of the attack the citizens were soon aware of the situation and a volley from their guns put the red devils to flight. So endeth the raid of the red in Spearfish City July 30, '76.

B H Pioneer
**Aug. 22, 1876**

James Irion, the young man who was killed by Indians in False Bottom on Saturday last, was employed by Boughton and Berry on account of his courage and skill as an Indian fighter and for the purpose of watching the movements of the red devils who infest the locality . . . Irion had ridden to the brow of the hill to look around with field glasses. He met a deadly fire that broke both his legs. One bullet struck his cartridge belt over his shoulder and exploded several of the cartridges. The concussion from the exploding shells brought immediate death.

B H Pioneer
**Oct. 23, 1876**

southern section in the early part of May. It was here they lost one of their party to the Indians. Their large numbers and constant vigilance had proved effective in protecting themselves. In the area just south of Devil's Tower, one of the party, George Miller, went ahead scouting for a good route through the canyons. His body was found later and his name was given to the creek, a reward which remains as a memorial to this day. An eye-witness was Mary Wilson McFarland, later of Sturgis, who made the trip as a chiid of eight. She recalled that when the party reached Deadwood Gulch, some of the wagons were lowered on ropes down the steep canyon walls into the mining camp.

Another noteworthy event involving Indians took place after the party had cleared the Bear Lodge Mountains and was in the Red Canyon area east of Sundance. The event is now called the Rifle Pit incident and was described by Mrs. Stella Howe, later of Spearfish, who with her husband, George, homesteaded there for many years. When the party reached a dry lake near the present Roubideaux Ranch it split, the pack train going into the lower canyon and the wagon train remaining on the high divide. An alarm of near-by Indians was sounded and the wagon train was placed into a defensive circle. Twelve rifle pits were dug around the encirclement in preparation for the attack. It never materialized and the party went onward the next day unmolested to join the pack train near present-day Beulah. Some of these pits are still visible on the Paul Smith Ranch. The pack train itself made a notable discovery when it reached Sand Creek. The travelers found a cabin by the stream with a sign above the door, "American Fur Company." Its year of origin was unknown, but it had undoubtedly sheltered some of the first trappers in that isolated region.

Continuing on eastward, the party crossed the fertile Spearfish and Centennial Valleys. Arriving in Deadwood, not all of them joined the mining enterprises. J. E. Cook and Mike Burton returned to the Polo Creek area in the Centennial Prairie and established the "Montana Herd," building a stockade for horses and supplying feed and custody for them. Others of the party, R. H. Evans, G. H. Jones, James Ryan, G. W. Reid, F. R. Cooper, G. W. Rosenbaum, Hiram Ross, and J. A. Walton established homestead claims along Spearfish Creek. They became involved with the agricultural resources of the area and helped to build Spearfish into a thriving community. They also helped furnish the miners deeper in the Hills with their fresh food supplies and gave the Hills advanced warning of Indians lurking about the foothills.

The first white men to settle in the area now known as Spearfish after those adventurers described by the Thoen Stone were members of the Centennial Party. This expedition of 14 men was organized in Iowa to explore the gold fields of the Black Hills. The Centennial

Party, named in honor of the nation's 1876 Centennial, left Ames, Iowa, in March 1876 and in July only six men had reached the Spearfish Valley. John Johnston, the leader of the group, was one of the first settlers in the valley, and also held the distinction of establishing, in connection with Captain C. V. Gardner, the first newspaper published in Spearfish. Others claim that James Butcher was the first actual settler on the northern frontier, having located and built a cabin, prior to the location of the townsite, on ground afterward occupied by J. C. Ryan's store. It was also claimed that Colorado Jack had pre-empted the townsite but was soon driven off by the Indians, abandoning his claim.

Other groups were formed to develop the Spearfish Valley. Townsite speculators believed that the land in the fertile valley could be worth more than any gold found. Land speculation rather than prospecting became important. The Smith, Gay, and Montana parties began the Spearfish Townsite Company in late May 1876 and a site along Spearfish Creek was selected and surveyed.

Accordingly, on May 29, 1876, Spearfish was laid out on the beautiful banks of the stream from which it later derived its name. The site was surveyed and platted by H. S. Burke with the aid of the traditional pocket compass. The original stockholders of the townsite company were Alfred Gay, A. J. Arnold, J. E. Smith, T. K. Bradley, William Gay, W. L. Kuykendall, E. B. Farnum, H. B. Young, Thomas Jefferson, R. H. Evans, J. H. Biglers, C. L. Craig, J. Fitzimmons, J. McHenry, J. R. Frost, H. S. Burke, D. G. Tallent, A. F. Wood, T. G. Murphy, J. J. Crawford, E. F. Slater, C. F. Thomas, C. C. Spades, J. J. Bump, J. Laham, M. Gearney, William Plaudney, S. D. Peters, P. O. Mill, M. B. Goodsell and R. Holt, 32 in all. J. E. Smith was chosen president of the company.

Early in September, the Spearfish Townsite Company decided that with the increased Indian hostilities and with the coming of winter, protection was needed by the settlers of the valley and town. The building of an enclosure was begun. A precedence had already been set for them at Rapid City and by the Gordon Party at Custer. A few log cabins had already been built close to the center of the townsite. In this area, where present-day Hudson Street joins Fifth and Sixth Streets, four cabins were built on four respective corners that enclosed a plat of ground described as north tier on lots in Block 42 and the south tier of lots in Block 29. Logs were set vertically in the ground between the cabins enclosing the area and completing the stockade. Helping in the work were John Bronson, Ran Kelly, and G. Hauser. John Johnston, one of the leaders of the Centennial Party, described the stockade as follows:

> "John Ward's cabin was built on the northeast corner, where Court and Bell's building now stands; P. C. Riley's on the southeast corner, where Gammon's livery stable

On Wednesday morning last, as Mr. William Smith was out looking after his herd in the neighborhood of Spearfish, he noticed a number of Indians coming toward him. He at once gave the alarm and a number of mounted men rode out in pursuit of the Indians, who had by that time run off a large herd of horses. The pursuing party followed the redskins for about 40 miles to the Belle Fourche, and succeeded in recapturing the horses excepting 20. The Indians were better mounted than the pursuers, consequently got away; but they did not have time to gather up their war tepee, which fell into the hands of the whites, together with their moccasins, medicine pipe and dried meat. Of the stock missing, eight horses belonged to Ryan and Reilly, seven to Tomling and Dawson and five to different individuals living in Spearfish.

**B H Pioneer**
**Dec. 23, 1876**

The news reached us yesterday afternoon that 200 head of stock had been run off by the Indians from the herder who had them in charge at Centennial. One hundred head belong to Mr. M. V. Boughton of this city; 30 head to the proprietors of the Buffalo Corral; 6 head to Mr. John A. Smith and the remainder to parties here. Mr. Boughton, who had just arrived on the stage from the East organized a party of 20 men to go in pursuit. At press time no report available as to their success. Mr. Boughton also telegraphed the news to Gen. Sheridan but as yet no answer has been received. It is no longer a matter of doubt, the Indians are upon us and prompt action is the only thing that will save us from further loss of life and destruction of property.

**B H Pioneer**
**Feb. 17, 1877**

A surveying party under J. D. McIntyre, while out on a survey last week, found a deserted Indian camp on Bear Butte Creek about 13 miles from the Custer road. From appearances they decided there were 200 Indian, 50 lodges, 300 to 500 ponies. Believed to be Indians who upon Feb. 21, stampeded the cattle and murdered two men.

**B H Times**
**April 9, 1877**

"While we do not wish unnecessarily to alarm our people, yet again we will warn those who may be about the foothills, and on the adjoining prairies to be vigilant as undoubtedly Indians are raiding for the purpose of plunder and murder. Report comes to us through channels which we deem reliable, that a ranchman was killed by them the fore part of the week in Spearfish Valley, and another, Mr. McNocton, was chased by them. Mr. McN. says they were genuine Indians as he saw them, and had abandoned his hay ranch in consequence of their presence. Let our stage companies and freighters take note.

B H Times
June 8, 1877

"After a remarkable lull in Indian affairs, the red devils put in an appearance near Crook City yesterday, to the number of forty, and succeeded in running off every head of stock, thirty in all, along the Whitewood Valley, the principle losers being Messrs. Fletcher Stewart, Shannon and Flood. Stewart and a hand pursued the depredators a long distance, pouring in hot lead upon them until they abandoned his stock.

B H Times
Nov. 22, 1877

At Spearfish there is indication of further trouble, that will in all probability have to be settled in court. It appears that the townsite of Spearfish claims more land than is allowed for a townsite by the statutes. Knowing this fact, a party came and located adjacent to, and partially intersecting this townsite, a ranch. A few days ago a sub-committee appointed and empowered by the general committee of the townspeople, notified these so-called jumpers, to vacate the premises forthwith or await the consequences. The jumpers, in pursuance of the demand, came to this city and instituted proceedings against the town of Spearfish, in Justice Gooding's court this morning.

B H Daily Times
May 2, 1877

now is, the two 100 feet apart; John Spalding's on the northwest corner where Nutt's store is, and Henry Folsom's on the northwest corner, now vacant, same distance apart, the space enclosed being 140 x 100 feet."

John C. Ryan, who arrived after Johnston in the spring of 1877 from St. Joseph, Mo., with goods for a store, also gave a diagram of the stockade in an article published in the Queen City Mail for February 6, 1895, and added these observations:

> "Outside of this stockade there were several other houses, or more properly, cabins and in spite of the danger from Indian depredations, others were in the process of erection. There were but two entrances to the stockade, and the entire population could be called in at short notice, if deemed necessary for purposes of protection or defense."

Johnston reported that this protection was sought by all the ranchmen and settlers for the winter by their moving into the stockade. W. B. Lown told his son in later years that the farmers down Spearfish Valley came to the stockade for safety every evening.

By July 1877 about 150 settlers resided in Spearfish and a large number of farmers and ranchers lived nearby. The Indians, still bold after the Battle of the Little Big Horn, were a constant threat. The United States survey party under Rollin Reeves was ambushed by Indians near the Dakota Territory-Wyoming border and sought refuge in the Spearfish Stockade. During that year a tragic event occurred. David Abernathy and a deputy sheriff were in pursuit of thieves when they were ambushed by Indians and killed near Spearfish. The Sioux lost title to the Black Hills by the Agreement of August 15, 1876, and later settlers could legally claim the land they had taken. Soon after Indian attacks diminished and the stockade was no longer needed.

In the late 1870's, the town was a small group of log cabins and wood frame buildings. The first store was open for business in 1877 and a United States Post Office was established the same year. The Spearfish school district was organized and pupils attended school in a log cabin.

The early days of Spearfish were as wild as the pioneer days of Deadwood and Lead. Gun and fist fights were common. Rowdy cowboys on occasion would walk up a street shooting at sidewalks and doorknobs. Law and order eventually prevailed.

The white man came to the Black Hills not only for gold but also for land. Farmers and ranchers followed the prospectors seeking riches produced by the land. The stampede of miners and prospectors of the gold rush era became a ready market for the grain, meat, and dairy products of the local agriculture industry. Numerous herds of cattle were brought by ranchers to the Hills and with the ranchers came the cowboys. The cowboys were mostly adventurous young men looking for excitement. The cowboys lacked none of the enthusiasm of the miners or prospectors; the cowboys could be just as wild. They were noted for terrorizing local communities with carefree mischief.

The middle of May was roundup time. The cowboys worked 16 to 18 hours a day rounding up stray cattle on the open range. The calves were branded, counted, and again allowed the freedom of the range. Within ten years the original herds had grown and cattle could be shipped out of the area to the east.

Between 1877 and the early 1880's cattle rustling and horse stealing occurred with alarming frequency. Organized bands of thieves and rustlers roamed the Northern Hills at will. Finally after the local law proved unable to cope with the problem, a vigilante group was formed by Spearfish area stockmen to capture and punish the law breakers. The vigilantes were able to stop the flagrant lawlessness without much bloodshed.

The United States Congress had passed the Homestead Act in 1862 and the county farmer was allowed 160 acres if he lived on the land for five years. The farmer fenced his land to keep out the cattle of the open range, built a frame house according to the requirements of the Homestead Act, planted a few trees, and broke the sod to plant his crops.

Early farming methods were primitive. A plow, usually pulled by two oxen, dug the furrows and the grain was sown by hand. Plowing in the Hills had to be done in the spring or fall. A scythe was used to cut the grain and the grain was tied in bundles and shocked. The first crops were wheat and oats, but later corn, barley, and other crops were cultivated. The gang plow replaced the single plow on the large farms before 1880.

Naturally, conflicts between farmers and ranchers occurred over the use of the open range and public waterholes. Not until the decade of the 1880's was a fence and herd law passed that required ranchers to fence in their herds. The days of the open range would soon end.

The Spearfish valley and surroundings proved to be the most sought-after agricultural lands and settlers moved in rapidly, seeing the need in the mining camps around Deadwood and Lead for grain, dairy products and meat.

It is recorded that the first actual attempt to cultivate the soil of the valleys was made in the spring of 1876 by a man named Brown, who broke a few acres of ground in the Whitewood Valley near Crook City. He planted his small tract with oats but when they were ready to be harvested in July of that year, his workers were driven off by the Indians who destroyed the ripened crop.

Hay was cut in the summer and fall of 1876 on Centennial prairie and in Spearfish Valley but those who did the work took their lives

To the Editor of the Times:

The excitement among our ranchmen and villages since the filing of the town plat in the land office, has been at fever heat, everyone trying to get the advantage over his neighbor. Several parties have already located ranches on Spearfish townsite and heretofore laid out by the old town company. The villages have set said company aside, wholly ignoring its claims, and ordered the judge of probate to proceed, Fraserlike, to give them warranty deeds, of course, for a bonus (but you bet your bottom dollar on general principles, they didn't get them. — Ed.)

B H Daily Times
Feb. 6, 1879

A Card from Judge Offenbacher

To the Editor of the Times:

In your issue of Feb. 6 I notice a communication from Spearfish which reflects somewhat upon the integrity of the citizens of the burg. In justice to all parties concerned, I would like to state that no bonus has been offered me, neither has any citizen of Spearfish asked me to take steps not in accordance with the law. Some citizens of Spearfish have conferred with me on the subject of pre-empting their townsite and they were informed that before any steps will be taken in the matter by me, a petition must be presented asking that the lands (describing them) be pre-empted for the use and benefit of the occupants thereof, as provided by the laws of Congress, which petition must be signed by a majority of the occupants or lot owners of said town; but in no case will I attempt to execute the trust created by said act of Congress until authorized so to do by legislative enactment.

J. V. Offenbacher
Probate Judge
B H Daily Times
Feb. 7, 1879

Gardening and farming in the Spearfish Valley is being carried on to a considerable extent this spring. Plowing and planting on every side, the grass three or four inches high, and everything looks lovely.

B H Daily Times
May 17, 1877

in their hands. As a precaution, large parties would go together to where the work would be done, with half of them standing as lookouts and the others cutting the hay.

Some of the ranchers in the Redwater and Spearfish valleys have been induced by the continual snap of warm weather and their pressing needs for groceries, to bring in wagon loads of vegetables. There is one in the market today with a double wagonload of potatoes, selling them for two and a half cents a pound. He said he felt confident he could get six cents a pound for them in the spring, but he was out of "meat" and had to sell. Vegetables of all kinds are scarce in our agricultural belts. The late cold weather nipped all kinds of garden truck extensively. Murphies and scub will be rated the luxuries before the next crop is harvested.

B H Daily Times
**Jan. 24, 1879**

The same dangers were encountered by Robert Evans, Judge Beck and Peter Riley who made gardens in Spearfish Valley. Often they were forced to flee from the Indians to the stockade which had been built where Spearfish now stands.

It was not until 1878 that the first shipment of farming machinery arrived in the Black Hills. A consignment of plows, reapers, and rakes were received by Star and Bullock, Deadwood, who sold them almost as soon as they were unloaded from the bull and mule wagons which had brought them through the hostile Indian country. The same Deadwood firm brought the first self-binders to the Hills as an experiment. Selling for $325 and freight of $100 each, they were disposed of immediately.

In 1876, a small herd of cattle in Centennial Prairie was the first in the Black Hills and later that same year, M. V. Boughton brought 200 head to graze on the Lower False Bottom and in the Redwater Creek valleys, only to be driven off by a band of Sioux.

The first big herd of several thousand cattle, driven over a trail from Texas, arrived in the spring of 1877. Brought in by M. C. Connors, Spearfish, the cattle were guarded by a large band of cowboys and were ranged on the Redwater. However, the settlement of the False Bottom, Redwater and Spearfish valleys in 1879 forced the cattlemen to move their herds farther away from the Hills where they were not disturbed in their possession of the range.

To the editor of the Times:

The quietude of this part of the county has been very much disturbed last night and today. The whole country up and down the Redwater and the lower Spearfish has been visited by one of the most sweeping conflagrations ever witnessed in the valleys. All or nearly all of the ranchmen in the Redwater have lost everything that could be burned — houses, barns, graneries, hay, wagons all have been swept away almost within the twinkling of an eye. The fire, when last heard from in this place, had leaped the Spearfish and Redwater and was bounding away up Falsebottom and down the Belle Fourche, and is perhaps creating considerable excitement in and about "Scupe" town . . . The wind has blown harder today than I have ever known in any country.

B H Daily Times
**Jan. 29, 1879**

Horse breeding followed on the heels of the cattleman and in 1878 Reiley & Son brought into the country several brood mares and a couple well-bred stallions and located them on their ranch in the Spearfish Valley. About the same time J. P. Gammon also imported a number of brood mares and stallions for his False Bottom ranch. Star and Bullock were the first to breed the standard-bred trotter in the Black Hills and located this activity on the Belle Fourche River.

After the gold rush, another community grew because of the farming and ranching activities in northern Lawrence County. In 1876 farmers and hay gatherers, mainly French immigrants from Canada, settled the Whitewood Valley. The farmlands of the valley were settled under the provisions of the Homestead Act. Land and water rights were secured within a few years. In the late 1870's St. Onge was only a post office, a few homes, and nearby farms. The village was named after Michael St. Onge who had come to Deadwood with Sol Star to file for postmaster. St. Onge didn't amount to much until the Elkhorn Railroad stretched its tracks from Whitewood to Belle Fourche in the 1890's.

# chapter IV

# Gold's Melting Pot

**Wild Bill Hickok, like hundreds of other men, came to Deadwood's gold rush to better his lot in life with the chance of striking it rich. Probaby his big mistake, considering his reputation as a "fast-draw deadshot," was mixing his gold ambitions with gambling houses. Regardless of his intent, James Butler Hickok was a marked man.**

**(Centennial Collection)**

It was a diverse mass of humanity that breathed life into the cluster of booming mining camps that overwhelmed Deadwood Gulch in its initial years of settlement. Its component parts consisted of a wide variety of individuals and groups of startlingly different backgrounds and records of achievement. Some had already achieved a measure of fame, or notoriety, "back in the States," as the country outside the isolated Black Hills was known to them. Mostly, though, they were ordinary people with an extraordinary attraction for adventure, however risky or fanciful. What banded them together in common endeavor was a mutual desire to better their lot, whatever their former station in life. They saw unparalleled opportunity in this promising new frontier and they were determined to make the most of it.

Many came with dreams of making a killing in the gold fields and getting out. Others came to seek their fortunes by filling the wide assortment of needs of the free-spending prospectors. Still others were attracted by the unique challenges of fast-developing new towns where the social, political and economic power structures had not yet formed. The most ambitious among them envisioned positions of prominence for themselves in the thriving new communities. The less ambitious were content to just be at the scene of all the excitement. Whatever their motives for coming, they came in ever-growing numbers — the good, the bad and the undefined.

Any objective examination of Deadwood Gulch's earliest inhabitants could not fail to note the presence of such well-known frontier personages as Wild Bill Hickok and Calamity Jane. They were legendary figures before reaching Deadwood in the summer of 1876 and their experiences there added closing chapters to their respective careers. They were not of the stable class that developed Deadwood, however, and the early builders of the community resented the notori-

Madame Lake Hickok, the widow of the late Wild Bill, accompanied by Charles Dalton (Buckskin Charley) and wife, and George Carson, arrived in the city late on Friday evening. On Saturday the widow visited Bill's grave, and proposes, as soon as it is definitely settled that the graveyard will not be disturbed, to erect a fenced monument to his memory, in which kind action Buffalo Bill, Texas Jack, and Buckskin Charley will assist her. Madame Hickok, when she leaves here will proceed to Havana, Cuba, via Cincinnati and New York, in company with her daughter, whither they will take two young horses the Madame has trained this summer, at Cheyenne, for the circus ring.

B H Daily Times
Sept. 4, 1877

**A rough, tough gal was Calamity Jane when she first came to Deadwood Gulch. With her trusty rifle and buckskin garb, she attempted to accompany General Crook's command but was discovered and ordered out. But she came back many times to the roaring gold camp to add to her horrendous reputation and to Deadwood — the town that was just as tough as she was.**

**(Centennial Collection)**

"It is reported from Sturgis City that Calamity Jane wallopped two women at that place yesterday. Calamity can get away with half a dozen ordinary pugilistic women when she turns loose, but she never fights unless she is in the right, and then she is not backward to tackle even a masculine shoulder hitter."

B H Daily Times
Feb. 8, 1879

ety they brought upon the struggling new town. They were a breed apart and epitomized a class of rough characters that was all too conspicuous in Deadwood during its formative period. Yet they, no less than the builders of the community, came seeking a fresh start—a new beginning that their respective destinies would ultimately deny them. They were as controversial as they were colorful and, ironically, they gave Deadwood a lasting legacy — a legacy that the descendants of their contemporary critics were later to exploit to the town's profit. It is doubtful that Deadwood would have attained its national prominence if Wild Bill and Calamity hadn't been there during its boisterous beginnings, however briefly.

Wild Bill's contribution to Deadwood's fame came in being killed there. It was, perhaps, inevitable that the noted gunfighter would be killed someday, somewhere, considering his reputation as the "Prince of Pistoleers" in an era when fast guns seldom went unchallenged for long. Hickok arrived in Deadwood early in July of 1876, a few months after marrying Agnes Lake, a trapeze artist and widow 11 years older than he, and he tried his hand at prospecting in hopes of acquiring a stake equal to his wife's dowry. But he found the gaming tables of Deadwood's many saloons more familiar ground and it was at one of these that his oft-tested luck ran out. He was playing poker with three cronies in Saloon Number 10 on August 2, 1876, when a nondescript drifter named Jack McCall sneaked behind him and fatally shot him in the back of the head. Hickok's cards, black aces and eights, known ever since as the "Dead Man's Hand," dropped to the floor as the famous victim slumped dead. McCall would eventually pay for his cowardly crime, but not in the lawless Deadwood of 1876. Hickok's close friend, Colorado Charlie Utter, buried the 38-year-old murdered gunman on the hillside above Deadwood. Two years later he was reinterred higher on the hillside where his grave has been a leading tourist attraction since.

Calamity Jane, who claimed to have been with the Jenney-Newton Expedition to the Black Hills in 1875, reached Deadwood in July of the following year at about the same time as Wild Bill. She became Hickok's most vocal mourner, even claiming — after Wild Bill was no longer alive to dispute it — that she and the famous gunfighter had been secret lovers. Historians who have researched the possibility dismiss the claim as nonsense. But Calamity probably wrote the truth when she referred to Wild Bill in her diary, candidly confessing that "we both lived a life of lies." At any rate, Calamity had a knack for being noticed and she could usually be found wherever the action was the most exciting on the plains frontier at the time. She had attempted to tag along with General Crook's command when it was ordered into the field against the Sioux in the summer of 1876 — just as she had done with the Jenney-Newton Expedition the previous summer. But her unwelcomed presence was again discovered, despite being dressed like a man, her favorite apparel, and she was expelled from an Army force on the march for at least the second time.

In Deadwood, as in the other boom towns of the Hills, Calamity was a memorable figure as she demonstrated that her reputation as a hard-drinking, gun-toting, foul-mouthed bullwhacker was well deserved. An indication that Calamity had returned to the Hills with the intention of changing the pattern of her life surfaced in 1878. Deadwood was hit by a smallpox epidemic that year and it was reliably reported that she had boldly nursed the sick and dying while other more sensitive women of the community cringed in fear of touching them. But tales of her bawdy behavior overshadow this admirable activity and she did nothing else of record to soften her reputation as "a disreputable harridan." She soon left the Hills for other parts of the West, although she frequently reappeared for drinking bouts with old cronies in the Deadwood saloons. It was on one of these trips that she died in nearby Terry of inflammation of the bowels, an illness often attributed to overindulgence in alcohol. She breathed her last just one day short of the 27th anniversary of Wild Bill's violent death. Her last wish, some phantom friend is reputed to have reported, was to be buried next to Wild Bill. So she was. Their adjacent graves in the Mount Moriah Cemetery mark the final resting places of the best remembered, although not the most kindly, of the Deadwood pioneers of '76.

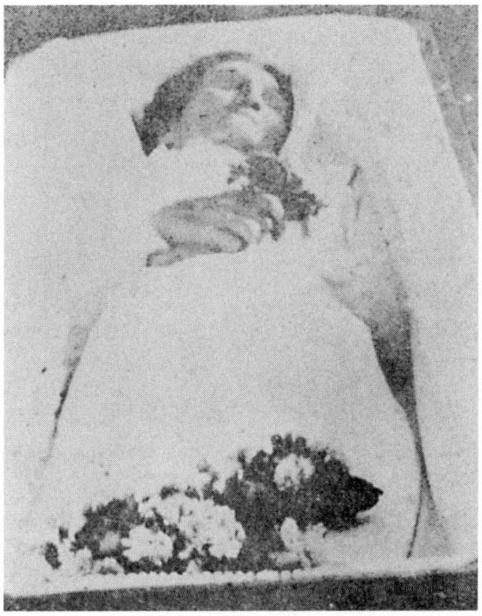

**Finally at peace with the world after one of the most turbulent lives ever recorded by a woman. Calamity Jane is shown in her casket in a funeral parlor on Sherman Street in Deadwood. She died at Terry, a mining camp near Lead on August 1, 1903, one day short of the anniversary when Wild Bill was gunned down in Saloon No. 10 in 1876.**
**(Centennial Collection)**

Representing the higher class of Deadwood Gulch residents during its turbulent first years were such stalwart citizens as Seth Bullock, Sol Star, C. V. Gardner, Peter A. Gushurst, Jacob Goldberg, and Judges Granville Bennett and Gideon C. Moody, among others. Most of them had been men of distinction and achievement before coming to the Black Hills. They were typical of the exceptional individuals who were soon in the forefront of the busy mining center's struggle for respectability. They were industrious, intelligent, generally well educated, highly regarded for their resourcefulness and integrity, and demonstrated progressive attitudes in their individual pursuits. There were others of equal ability and initiative in the rapidly-growing community, but these commanding figures were among the most prominent pace-setters.

**Wild Bill's Headboard.**

The inscription on the headboard of Will Bill's grave, has become a great curiosity among people outside of the Hills, and many of the pilgrims pay the cemetery a visit before returning east and copy it. There were three engaged in this work yesterday afternoon at the same time. For the information of our eastern readers we subjoin the inscription just as it appears on the board, as follows:

"WILD BILL,
J. B. HIKOK,
killed by the assassin
JACK M'CALL,
in
*Deadwood, Black Hills,*
August 2d, 1876.
Pard, we will
Meet again
In the happy
Hunting ground
To part no more,
Good bye,
COLORADO
CHARLIE,
C. H. UTTER."

Both Star and Bullock had been active in the political affairs of Montana Territory before joining the stampede to the Black Hills gold camps. Star had served as territorial auditor and also had been personal secretary to the Governor of Montana. Bullock had been elected to the Territorial Senate at the age of 21 and distinguished himself there by introducing the resolution that urged Congress to establish Yellowstone National Park. He was naturally pleased that Congress quickly accepted the suggestion. Bullock also served as sheriff of Lewis and Clark County before transferring his energies to the new opportunities in the Black Hills. The two Montanans de-

Seth Bullock was one of the first and staunchest pioneers in the gold rush era. He was Deadwood's first sheriff, one of the town's leading merchants, was a close friend of Teddy Roosevelt and was one of his famed rough riders. He is the grandfather of Kenneth Kellar of Lead, former chief counsel for the Homestake Mining Co.
(Adams Museum)

cided to go into partnership in supplying the bustling mining center with needed hardware. They came to Deadwood from Helena, traveling down the Missouri River by boat to Bismarck and then journeying overland with a heavily-laden wagon, drawn by oxen, along the route that would later become the Bismarck-Deadwood stage road. They arrived in Deadwood on August 1, 1876, just one day before the fatal saloon shooting of Wild Bill Hickok.

Bringing with them a large assortment of Dutch ovens, fry pans, dynamite, axes, rope, picks and shovels, and a generous supply of chamber pots, Star and Bullock found a ready market for these goods as soon as they hit town. They established the "Office of Star and Bullock, Auctioneers and Commission Merchants," which also offered "Fireproof Storage," in a building that cost them only $385 to construct. Both men were soon leading figures in the mining district. Their previous experience in government also placed them in major roles in the formal organization of the burgeoning settlement. Star served 14 years as mayor of Deadwood and almost 20 years as clerk of courts when Lawrence County was legally organized. Bullock's background as a proven lawman made him the natural choice for the dangerous position of "de facto" sheriff in the unruly community. He served in that capacity both before and after legal organization of the county.

Gardner, a native of Ohio who had served with the Union Army in the Civil War, was a lawyer who came to Custer on March 8, 1876, to establish a practice. But he soon deserted Custer with almost the entire population when Deadwood became the center of settlement as well as mining activity. His varied activities in the Northern Hills left him little time for his law career. He is credited with building the first frame building in Deadwood in the spring of 1876, establishing the first newspaper, The Black Hills Pioneer, on June 8 of that year, bringing in the first large shipment of freight by ox team, being a partner in the first quartz and 10-stamp mills brought into the gulch, and in the establishment of the first flour mill in Spearfish. It was said of Gardner that "he became at once one of the most active of all the pioneers of the Black Hills. He is credited with being the leader in inaugurating more numerous important things perhaps than any other individual." It appears to be a reasonably accurate description of this diverse individual. He would later serve nine years as a trustee of the Dakota School of Mines and Technology at Rapid City.

Sol Star, a Montanan who came to Deadwood in 1876, proved a staunch citizen by becoming involved in the town's affairs both before and after the dangerous, lawless era.
(Centennial Collection)

Gushurst and Goldberg were pioneer grocers in Lead and Deadwood who typified the enterprising businessmen of their respective communities. Gushurst, a native of New York, was 23 years old when he came to the Black Hills by way of Cheyenne and Fort Laramie. He arrived in Custer on May 24, 1876, but by June 5 was running a grocery store out of a tent in Deadwood. When the Townsite of Lead was laid out he laboriously carried his small stock of groceries on his back and climbed the steep slopes of the canyon to the new settlement. He set up his grocery store there in August of eventful 1876 and continued in business there for many years. He became chairman of the Lead Townsite Company, served as one of the town's first trustees, City Councilman, member of the school board and mayor. Moreover, Mr. and Mrs. Gushurst were the first couple to be married in Lead. Goldberg, born in Germany in 1851, quickly filled the void Gushurst had created by moving his grocery to Lead. Goldberg had been in the clothing business in Helena when the Black Hills boom began. He joined a caravan of 60 covered wagons and in company with about 140 other Montanans reached Deadwood on August 12, 1876. He established the Big Horn Grocery Store and it still is a going concern in the location he selected. It out-lived its founder by a good many years and gained distinction as one of the last of the ill-fated neighborhood grocery stores. Durability was a common characteristic of the pioneer Deadwood Gulch entrepreneurs. Gushurst and Goldberg easily rank among the most durable, and understandably so.

**Peter A. Gushurst was asked by the miners to leave Deadwood and open the first grocery store in Lead. He accepted the challenge and became a successful businessman and one of the town's most civic-minded citizens. After his retirement, his son Albert, who now lives in Denver, took over the business and ran it for many years.**

**(Centennial Collection)**

Judges Bennett and Moody were men of prominence at Yankton, the Dakota Territory capital, at the time of the Black Hills gold rush. They were destined to achieve even greater eminence when their political influence brought them successive appointments to the same important Black Hills judicial post. Bennett had served in both houses of the Iowa Legislature before being appointed an Associate Justice of the Dakota Supreme Court in 1875. Two years later, he was appointed judge of the U. S. District Court for the Black Hills region. He first held court at Sheridan, in the Central Hills, but quickly moved his headquarters to Deadwood when he recognized that it was the real hub of the district's diverse activity. His court decisions, many of them settling rival mining and water right claims involving millions of dollars, made him a central figure in the region. His most remarkable, and easily his most popular decision was handed down in the fall of 1877. It was a ruling that the Laramie Treaty of 1868 had merely assured the Indians the right of occupancy of the Black Hills and had not prohibited the white man from prospecting or owning property there. Not surprisingly, Judge Bennett was elected to Congress the next year — with strong support from the heavily-populated Black Hills mining settlements. His spectacular decision was unanimously overruled by the Territorial Supreme Court the following year, but Bennett's niche in the Black Hills pioneer hall of fame was already assured.

**Jacob Goldberg took over the Big Horn Store in Deadwood after P. A. Gushurst moved to Lead in 1876. For many years he was one of Deadwood's leading merchants. The store was changed to Goldberg Grocery and is still in operation at the same location after 100 years.**

**(Centennial Collection)**

Bennett was succeeded by Moody on the bench at Deadwood when the popular judge went off to Washington as a territorial delegate in 1878. Moody, a native of Indiana, had opened a law practice at Yankton in 1866. He quickly became a leader in the Republican Party that held the reins of power in the territory at the time and

The whites down in Chinatown are making a strong effort to oust the heathen of that part of the gulch, or at least close up their smoke house and other crooked concerns in that quarter. It is a fact, not generally known, that the smoke houses are just as numerous as before the raid was made upon them, but are not so open. Only the initiated have access to the pipes of peace — and death.

B H Daily Times
Sept. 6, 1879

**Wong Yeo had his picture taken to show what the better-dressed man wore in Deadwood's famed, early-day Chinatown.**

**(Adams Museum)**

was elected speaker of the Territorial House in 1868. Ten years later he accepted the appointment as Bennett's successor. Moody's judgeship, like Bennett's before him, was characterized by many far-reaching legal decisions involving property rights greatly complicated by the claim jumping so prevalent in the early years of the mining boom. His court rulings won the admiration of the owners of the dominant Homestake Mining Co. and they induced him to resign his judgeship to become company attorney. He resumed an active role in territorial politics and was soon considered the boss of the Black Hills Republicans. He played a leading role in the prolonged struggle for statehood status for the territory and was rewarded with election to the U. S. Senate when it was finally achieved. Thus the influential Black Hills judgeship proved to be the springboard to national office for both Bennett and Moody. It is perhaps misleading to include them as representative of the upper strata of Deadwood's pioneer society for obviously they were personages of superior ability and ambition. But they serve to illustrate the heterogeneous nature of that frontier society. Ironically, and tragically, it is Wild Bill Hickok and Calamity Jane who are best remembered in connection with Deadwood's early history. There were others far more deserving of public acclaim.

Collectively, as well as individually, the early population of Deadwood Gulch reflected a wide range of backgrounds. Deadwood, Lead, Central City, and all the smaller towns that blossomed into life in the Northern Hills became melting pots of humanity. The most prominent nationalties in the region included English (mostly Cornish), Chinese, Italians, Slavonians, Scotch, Irish, French, Norwegians, Finnish, Swedes, Danes, Jews and Germans. There was also a sizeable number of Negroes in the area in the early years. In Deadwood the dominating ethnic group which played a major role in the development of the restless, boisterous gold camp was the Chinese. The stolid, honest and hard-working yellowmen, loyal only to their own race, built their own city within Deadwood City, the largest self-ruled Chinatown east of San Francisco.

Maybe it was by chance or premeditation, but the bustling Chinatown was located in the most strategic section of long, twisting Deadwood Gulch. All people entering Deadwood from the north had to thread their way through the narrowest section of the gulch, wide enough for only the narrow Main Street and the small creek that babbled over countless pockets of gold that had been washed and filtered down from the mountains for centuries miles above and below the Chinese section of the mining camp. Humming Chinatown proved a profitable stopping place for sightseers and shoppers seeking finery from far off Asia.

Scattered throughout the mining camps were hundreds of Chinese, most of whom had been brought to the United States by labor contractors following the western gold rushes. Some had worked for the

Central Pacific in its race with the Union Pacific for the intercontinental link in Utah. They followed closely the opening of the Black Hills, arriving in 1876-1877, and soon establishing themselves as placer miners, cooks, laundrymen and servants. Two enterprising young Chinese listed themselves as real estate speculators.

Ever a close-knit race, they established their homes and shops within Deadwood in what later became the First Ward. After the old camp burned in the fire of 1879, they rebuilt their homes and businesses, electing their own mayor and council. A Chinese police force and fire department were established. The Chinese Hose Company team won the national championship in hose cart racing, one of the leading sporting events in early-day Deadwood, within a decade of its founding. A Masonic Lodge was built under the guidance of Dr. H. L. Van Wadelstead. The doctor and Sol Star, mayor of Deadwood at the time, were the only non-Chinese allowed to attend the meetings. Respect for the two was instrumental in keeping good relations with the orientals through the many years they remained in Deadwood. Traditions were faithfully observed and "old-timers" tell of the colorful ceremonies. Burial processions to the Chinese section of Mount Moriah Cemetery, high on the mountainside east of downtown, were always preceded by a band. Hundreds of slips of paper punched full of holes were scattered along the route for the Chinese believed the devil had to crawl through each hole before he could get to the soul of the departed and, by that time, they would have the body buried.

Two friends carried a pig on their shoulders, sometimes roasted before the funeral and sometimes at Mount Moriah, where a ceremonial oven was erected. Food was placed on the grave of the departed. Two white men, one day, thinking they would put a Chinaman on the spot, asked, "When does your countryman come up and eat all this fine food?" They got a quick reply, "At the same time the white man comes up to smell the flowers."

The Chinese dead were eventually removed from Mount Moriah for it was written in their labor contracts that their bodies would be sent back to China not more than ten years after their death. They believed they would not enter heaven unless their bodies were at rest in the ancestral homeland before ten years had elapsed. Allowing a sufficient time for decomposition, a Chinese undertaker would arrive at the cemetery, disinter the bodies, separate the bones and wrap each in newspaper and muslin. Each properly labeled package was then placed in a small zinc-lined box, sealed for shipment to San Francisco and thence to China for reburial.

All was not serene in Chinatown, however. Secret societies called "Tongs" fought for control of their people and the opium dens doubtless contributed to much of the lawlessness there. The unsolved murder of "Yellow Doll" was among the most spectacular crimes

**A battered remnant of the glamorous years in Deadwood's Chinatown, is the deserted Chinese Masonic Temple, now the site of a used car lot on lower Main Street.**
**(Centennial Collection)**

**C. V. Gardner did more good and started more important things for the betterment of Deadwood and the surrounding area than any other original pioneer. He came to Deadwood from Custer where he had been a lawyer in 1876.**
**(Centennial Collection)**

The boys who attended the Chinese Masonic celebration Wednesday night and participated in the festivities to the extent of getting on a Chinese drunk on Chinese rice whiskey, have decided that it beats the American or any other drunk all to death, in that it costs less, lasts longer, and makes a harder yet pleasanter drunk, and it is followed by more serious results than anything of the kind ever experienced. We shall, at this writing, mention no names, as it would not look good in print.

B H Times
Sept. 12, 1879

In the midst of the gold rush, numerous Oriental women sought their riches in the world's oldest profession. The Chinese "red light district" was portrayed as "plush but for anyone belonging to it." Along that portion of Deadwood's Main Street that ran through Chinatown, a number of cribs were established. Many of these cribs were operated in conjunction with a laundry business. A traveler noted that Gayville contained "about 20 Chinese laundries, each of which has a female partner who sits in the door evenings and smiles sweetly upon the passerby." Miners wishing to partake of their services merely entered one of the booths and pulled the curtain. No attempt at secrecy was made as such operations were condoned in the 1870's and 1880's.

S. D. History Quarterly

Yellow Doll's Murder

In later years some of Chinatown's old men elaborated on the Doll's exploitation with typical Confucician philosophy. Said the venerable Sing Lee, "In China the woman is servant to the man. In Deadwood the man with the gold becomes the tool of the Chinese girl."

Joe Kollar
Argus Leader,
Sept. 13, 1949

Few Orientals who came to Deadwood had any intentions of settling permanently. Rather, they viewed the Hills as a region of economic opportunity. Profits made here were converted to Hong Kong currency and sent directly to China. All Chinese longed for the day they could return to their native land to live their remaining years in comparative ease. For some like Wing Tsue, Deadwood made the dream come true.

S. D. History Quarterly

committed in the Chinese settlement. She arrived in Deadwood Gulch in 1876, young and beautiful, and lived in secluded luxury until she was crudely chopped to bits with a hatchet in 1877. The leading men of Chinatown gave her an elaborate funeral but her burial site was secretly obscured. The undesirable element immediately left town. Who was she? Where did she come from? Who murdered her and why? All these questions still intrigue historians of early Deadwood. It was reported, though, that the "good" women of the community shed few if any tears at her enigmatic death. Although the Chinese were an integral part of the community for more than 25 years, all evidence of the once thriving Chinatown vanished and only colorful stories make the Chinese a romantic part of the settling of Deadwood Gulch.

"The Chinatown as I remember it was a colorful place, especially at the time of the Chinese New Years," reminisced Violet Gorum, early-day resident. "Lanterns were hung in the streets and other decorations were in windows and doors during the celebrations. The Chinese were very noisy and fired thousands of firecrackers at a time." An oriental sound, an ominous one, that reverberated up and down the gulch, was also remembered as she recalled, "When we

**The Chinese section of Mount Moriah Cemetery in Deadwood, about 1905, is now empty. The bones were shipped back to China. The oven (lower right) was used by the Chinese to prepare food for funeral services. It also is gone along with every other vestige of the once thriving Chinatown era.**
**(Centennial Collection)**

heard the big gong on the porch of the Joss House, we knew a Chinaman had died." The Chinese erected their own house of worship in the form of a log cabin known as the Joss House. Joss himself was represented on canvas but ordinarily he was a large, hideous character carved out of wood. He sat in a chair, or rather on a throne, with two demons supporting him, one at each shoulder, standing beside him. According to the high priest, the Joss would do anything for a Chinaman if he was asked in the proper spirit.

George Hunter, a native son of a pioneer Deadwood businessman, identifies the family of Wing Tsue Wong as the most famed and honored of Deadwood's Chinatown. Wing Tsue came to Deadwood with the pioneers and opened a shop at 596 Main Street. It featured Chinese groceries, imported chinaware, herbs and novelties. Wing Tsue returned to China to marry, but soon brought his bride to Deadwood. They raised a family of three sons and five daughters. Hunter attended school with some of the Wong children. Although the family returned to China before the children reached adulthood, Hunter reports all members of it grew up to be a credit to their race. Most of them eventually returned to the United States and settled in California. Hunter's wife Mame, also a native of Deadwood, long remembered the women of Chinatown. She was most impressed with their "fancy" hairdos, their unique and beautiful oriental costumes and their bound, dainty feet. But there were other features of Chinatown less appreciated by the other citizens of early Deadwood. Heading the list were the opium dens and the prostitutes. The white womenfolk, especially, considered them a curse on the community. Strong feelings about these sordid temptations in the paths of their men led to the demand, "Either the Chinese discontinue these illegal and deadly practices or they must go!" Gradually, the Chinese left and the "city within a city" disintegrated with each departure.

A handful of Orientals capitalized on the miners' hungry appetites by operating restaurants. Ban Wong — known as Benny — managed the OK Cafe whereas the Philadelphia Cafe was operated by another Chinese remembered simply as the "Philadelphia Kid." Susie, as the white miners in Deadwood called Wong Kee, owned and operated the Bodega Cafe. When entering this establishment, Susie would take your order personally. He would never write down any names or ask "did you order this? He simply would bring the food and set it in front of the customer. For dessert, Wong Kee would ask, "What kind of pie do you want?" Then he would answer his question by telling you, "we have apple." In such establishments Deadwood residents could fill themselves with Oriental dishes like chicken rice soup — or if they preferred more common fare — roast beef and pie — for about 25 cents. Home brewed rice whiskey was also abundant and flowed freely.

S. D. History Quarterly

A favorite boyhood prank of George Hunter and his contemporaries was to fill a grape basket with small rocks and tin cans, fasten it to a phone wire extending from Williams Street to Main Street and let it go at the right moment to hit a Chinaman on the head when passing by. "He was so scared, he left his shoes on the spot." Hunter said.

George Hunter
Deadwood Pioneer

**Wing Tsue Wong, as most of the residents of early-day Deadwood knew the venerable Chinese merchant, is shown with his family. Pride in family is one of the characteristics of the Chinese. The family eventually moved back to China but the children returned to the United States to become a credit to their race. (Centennial Collection)**

Anderson Daniels, an old fat darkey friend of ours from Sioux City, is a quartz king now. He was excavating under his house in Lead City a few days ago and struck a rich ledge. He was in Deadwood and came around to tell us about his luck. Said he was staying right with it. "Lor bless me," he continued, "I'se almost quit work to sleep over de hole night and day. I tell you I'se got it." And his eyes bounced out like a brace of scart rabbits."

B H Daily Times
April 2, 1878

News from Lead City: "A lady of color gave birth to a child a few days since, in an uptown hotel, and quite a number of our 'nice' young men are fearful of having a justice's warrant served on them. It is whispered that government officials, millmen, merchants and others are mixed up in the affair, and that lightning is liable to strike at any time. P. S. There is quite a large demand here at present for 'traveling' bags. The reason is obvious."

B H Daily Times
Jan. 13, 1879

**Sidney B. Jacobs established the Hub Clothing Store in Deadwood in 1900. He was an active owner until 1934 when his son Berthald took over and expanded the business to Belle Fourche, Rapid City and Sturgis. He ran the business until 1974 when he retired. Jacobs is an executive member of the Deadwood-Lead '76 Centennial Committee.**

**(Centennial Collection)**

Although very few Negroes remained long in the Northern Black Hills, many of the race succumbed to the lust for gold and joined the stampede in 1876. It is believed the white men, trying to keep the black man out of the plush placering areas of Deadwood Gulch, directed a party of four of them over the mountains to the west of the city on what was supposed to be a "wild goose chase." It backfired. The Negroes found rich deposits in the area still known as "Nigger Hill," just east of Tinton, 17 miles as the crow flies west of Deadwood. Working the area hard, the black men were soon able to load their bonanza of gold dust aboard their burros and leave the area "well heeled," never to return. It is estimated that before the hill's wealth petered out, over a million dollars in gold dust was recovered.

"Aunt Sally," the Sarah Campbell of the Custer Expedition, who had preceded Annie Tallent as the first non-Indian female in the Black Hills by six months, was one of the earliest Negro residents of Crook City. It is not known whether the former cook for the 1874 Expedition's teamsters ever returned to Custer to work the claim she had been given in the abortive mining district organized there during the expedition. Since the district had no recognized legal status, all of the initial claims there were probably "jumped" by the prospectors who later swarmed to the discovery site. At any rate, it is known that Aunt Sally made her living by cooking for various families in the Deadwood area after her return to the Hills. She was living at Galena when she died, and she was buried there.

A political party was organized by Negro men in November of 1877 when there were about 75 of them in Deadwood Gulch. They met at the house of a Mr. Lyon, Sherman Street, elected Henry Watson as chairman and J. C. Stills as secretary. Speeches were made by W. J. Sidway, C. Mix, P. Reynolds, M. Ward and others.

Many prominent Jewish people came to the Black Hills in the 1876 gold rush and stayed on to seek, and in many cases, find the pot at the end of the rainbow in Deadwood Gulch.

Most prominent was Nathan Colman, who, although not an ordained rabbi, officiated at many of the rites, including the first Jewish wedding of his daughter in Deadwood's historic Franklin Hotel.

Prominent Jewish members of the Society of Black Hills Pioneers included Ben Baer, Sol Bloom, Harris and Nathan Franklin, Jacob Goldberg and sons, David Goldbloom, Paul Rewman, Sol Star, Sam Schwarzwald and Charles Zoellner.

In early Deadwood days, the many Jewish residents held religious services on high holidays and the Passover. Colman conducted these rites until his death in 1906 and then Sidney B. Jacobs, a top community leader, took over. As the Jewish population continued to diminish, the Torah, which at one time belonged to Lead, was given to Deadwood and subsequently loaned to the Rapid City congregation where services are held annually.

Enterprising Germans entering the Black Hills, and especially the Deadwood area during the gold rush also had their eyes on the glitter of gold already in leather pokes in miners' pockets.

Instead of rushing to the creeks with gold pans, they quickly built business houses designed to lure luxury-hungry miners into spending their hard-earned gold dust.

The No. 1, gilt-edged business was whiskey — lots of it! Over 100 saloons lined Deadwood Gulch in those first hectic days of the town's birth. Many were operated by Germans who probably were backed financially by distilleries in the East.

One of the first on the scene and one that survived up into the Twentieth Century was a saloon owned by John Treber and John Hermann. Others included Henry Korneman, Chris Bickerham, Jake Schubert. Bickerham's saloon, located on Sherman Street, had a sign on the side of the building going toward Lead which read: "Last Chance Saloon." On the side coming from Lead into Deadwood another sign said, appropriately, "First Chance Saloon."

Other well-known German names in Deadwood included Titus Molitor, who managed the assay office; Ernest Mueller, a jeweler; Charles Sasse, a butcher; John Sohn, a cobbler, and Henry Schnitzel, manager of the Golden Reward Mine.

Fun-loving Germans, enjoying their beer, set up the first bowling alley in South Deadwood at the present site of the Claim Jumper Motel. Although it was mighty crude in comparison to modern alleys, the outdoor one-lane alley was the scene of many hilarious fun fests in the entertainment-hungry mining camp.

Lead was a city of many nationalities from the beginning and quickly became known as a "miniature melting pot." Where the Chinese predominated in Deadwood, in Lead it was the Slavonian people who came, saw and conquered a raw, tough, uncompromising mining town. Nationalities in Lead had their own neighborhoods, more so than in Deadwood and other mining towns of the Northern Black Hills. Most early settlers congregated in the Mill and Main street area of Lead but when the mines started operating in high gear, more hardrock miners poured into the city and spread out — the Finnish on Park Avenue, the English in the Washington section, the Italians on Miners and Prospect Avenues with other nationalities interspersed.

However, stretching the length of Gwinn Avenue in the center of the most gilded gold town in the western hemisphere was Slavonian Alley, which is still in existence today. No finer food, wine or hospitality could be found anywhere, especially during the Christmas

**John A. Treber was born in Germany in 1853. He came to the U. S. in 1874 and to Deadwood on June 11, 1877. He engaged in the wholesale liquor business in the firm of Hermann and Treber. He was a member of the city council for 24 years and the state legislature in 1910. He died in 1936. His son Albert, has lived his entire life in Deadwood and was affiliated with the Black Hills Power and Light Company until his retirement. He celebrated his 94th birthday in Deadwood's Centennial year 1976.**

**(Centennial Collection)**

Judge Nathan Colman came to Deadwood from Denver, Colorado in February, 1877. Although not an ordained rabbi, he officiated at all Jewish rites and ceremonies in the community. He served as a member of the Election Board at the Territorial Election in 1889 when South Dakota became a State. A daughter, Blanche Colman, still living in Deadwood in 1976, was the first woman admitted to the bar in South Dakota. She served as an attorney in the law office of Chambers Kellar of Lead until her retirement.

George V. Ayres was born on a farm in Pennsylvania in 1852. He came to the Black Hills by way of Cheyenne, reaching Custer on March 25, 1876, and Deadwood on May 26. He walked the 60 miles up from Custer. Later he became sole owner of the Lake Hardware Store, later changing it to Ayres Hardware, still a going business in Deadwood. He served in the state legislature from 1927 to 1931 where he was particularly interested in getting new roads. In fact he was called the "father of improved highways in western South Dakota." He was active in the Society of Black Hills Pioneers and the Masonic Lodge. A son, Albro, took over the hardware business. Like his father, he was active in the state legislature and has carried on the family tradition for better roads to cope with growing tourism in the county and the Black Hills.

(Centennial Collection)

Harris Franklin was one of Deadwood's leading businessmen. Prominent in city government, he was a banker, large cattle owner and had an interest in the Golden Reward Mining Company. He was the top investor in the Franklin Hotel, built in 1903.

(Centennial Collection)

season when the custom of "open house" was held. Consumed were countless gallons of wine which the residents made for themselves from California grapes shipped into Lead. The preparation of food for this feast started months in advance and the meals were a gourmet's delight. "It was quite a challenge to make a trip through Slavonian Alley," according to the Chris Krilanovichs, descendants of the first Slavs to settle in the area. "To emerge sober was another thing as the hospitality of the residents knew no bounds," they point out.

Another large single group of one national origin was the Irish. It is believed that they may have been lured to the Hills by Charles Collins' Fenian scheme. This plan to colonize different areas in the U.S. by homesteading the land was presented to the "Fenian Convention," held in St. Louis in 1869. The plan of this Irish organization was to settle the Irish in sufficient numbers so that eventually they would rise up against the British colony to the north in Canada and wipe out their "oppressors," or at least get even with England for oppressing them in Ireland.

To spur interest in this venture Collins wrote a number of articles in the Sioux City (Iowa) Times to attract public attention, stating that an expedition was organizing in that city to explore the Black Hills and find the gold hidden in the "rock-ribbed hills." This was as early as 1872 when the existence of gold in the Hills was but a rumor. However, military authorities got wind of this proposed expedition and immediately issued warnings that any venture organized for the purpose of penetrating the Black Hills would be stopped and the leaders arrested. But evidently some of the Irish took Collins' stories seriously as many later came west on their own to seek the gold.

Among the first groups to come to Lead were the Cornish, natives of Cornwall, a peninsula on the southwest coast of Britain. Known as "Cousin Jacks," they are credited with introducing "pasties," derived from the word "pastries." Made of diced steak or pork or both, onions and potatoes baked in a pie dough shell, they were carried to work in the mines in a dinner bucket made in two sections — the lower part containing hot tea, and the upper half the pastie, with the tea keeping the pastie warm until lunch time.

Noted as musicians, the Cornish had a chorus, glee club and brass band and performed at many parades and other special occasions. Maintaining their own lodge, named the "Sons of St. George" after the patron saint of England, they had their own insurance program and sponsored the brass band which played at all festive occasions.

Coming to Lead with a lot of experience in the tin mines, the Cornish added much to the development of the Homestake Mine. The term "Cousin Jack" was coined back in the hard-time era when they flocked into the Lead area. After one Englishman was fortunate enough to be put on the payroll, he asked the boss if there was a chance for his "cousin Jack" to get a job. All the Cornish, it seemed, had cousins named Jack.

The first white child born in Lead had Finnish parents. This honor was held by Elizabeth Porth, who, as daughter of Mr. and Mrs. William Porth, made her appearance in Lead on August 8, 1877. Her father owned claims in Grizzly Gulch and her brother was an engineer on the first B&M train in Lead. After marrying William Pinske, they moved to a farm near Brownsville which, along with the Custer Peak area, soon became a small Finnish colony. The Finnish, along with the Swedish and Norwegians, were also concentrated in and around Terry, where they added the "Temperance Hall" to the thriving town of two hotels, a Union Hall, saloons galore, numerous grocery stores and a drug store. Many of the Swedish families also settled in South Lead where, noted for their outstanding singing ability, they formed a chorus during the early days.

Most of the Finnish people did not come to the Black Hills directly from Finland, but from the mines of Michigan and Minnesota. They settled in South Lead and along Park Avenue there as well as in Terry, the Crow Peak area, Blacktail and other outlying areas. It was here that they had room enough to pasture cows to provide the abundance of milk they used in their diets and for their operations as dairy farmers.

Most of the Italians settling in the Black Hills, resided in Lead, Central City or Terraville. They lived near each other because of communication problems. They were all of the Catholic faith but because they could not speak English, they were not encouraged to attend church. Hard workers, the emigrants labored seven days a week for 12 hours a day for many years until a priest convinced the Homestake Mining Company it should allow them one day off to attend church. Because of the language barrier, they did not rate the "boss" positions but instead were common laborers in the mine, according to Mrs. Carl Eilers, Deadwood. Julius Street, Lead, was named for her grandfather, Joe Julius, who had come to Deadwood by stage from Sidney in 1876. Each family managed to acquire a small plot of land which was put to good use for gardens; they owned chickens, cows and pigs which they kept in town close to their homes; and the mining town boasted an Italian grocery which imported foods for their native specialty dishes.

Whether American or foreign-born, however, the pioneers of Deadwood Gulch were aliens in forbidden country in the first stage of the region's settlement. The imperativeness of achieving official recognition from the government, whose prohibitions they had so brazenly ignored, was the goal that welded them into a cohesive political entity. Their first opportunity to demonstrate their patriotism and loyalty to the United States, the granddaddy of all ethnic "melting pots," came, appropriately, on the 100th anniversary of the nation's founding. And they made the most of it.

**The Fish and Hunter Company of Deadwood is one of the pioneer firms still in existence in the historic city. John Hunter came from Minneapolis and set up a sawmill between Crook City and Deadwood in 1877. J. M. Fish of Maine set up a similar mill at Two Bit Gulch. In 1883 the two men formed a partnership and two years later E. C. Dickey bought an interest in the firm. Ground was purchased in Deadwood and an office building and a planing mill erected. The firm also entered the mercantile business and added an office in Lead. In 1891 all the interests were incorporated into the Fish and Hunter Co. On December 13, 1953 the company celebrated its 75th anniversary and will be 100 years old in 1978. Gerald Crary is the present manager and a brother Demarest is also a member of the firm. Walter Dickey, Spearfish, is a director.**

**John Baggaley came to Deadwood Gulch in 1877 lured by the chance of hidden wealth in the mountains crammed with gold and silver. He was successful as a major stock holder in the Iron Hill Mining Co. and later left mining promotions for the brokerage and commission business. His son George, carried on where his father left off, specializing in the real estate, insurance and automobile business. A grandson, John became affiliated with the First National Bank of which he was vice president and manager until his retirement in 1975 — a three-generation family covering 99 years in the gulch.**

**Fourth of July celebrations were big events in all of the early mining camps. Central City always went all out with the buildings decorated in bunting and spruce trees. The crowd is shown milling along the business district between races and other holiday excitement. In the upper left background can be seen the Gold Nugget beer brewery and the DeSmet Gold Mine.**

**(Adams Museum)**

# chapter V

# Hell-Bent For Fun

**Deadwood's first newspapers were published in the hastily-built building with the false front on Main Street in 1876.**
**(Centennial Collection)**

July 4, 1876, the Centennial of the nation's founding, was a day of great jubilation in isolated Deadwood Gulch as in the "civilized" sectors of the country. The great day's festivities were well reported in the Black Hills Pioneer which had made its first appearance less than a month earlier. W. A. Laughlin and A. W. Merrick, who had worked on the Denver Farmer and the Rocky Mountain News there, were the publishers. They had left Denver for the Black Hills on Sunday, March 5, 1876, intending to establish their newspaper at Custer City. But when that city was virtually deserted by the stampede to Deadwood Gulch, they hurriedly loaded up their equipment and headed northward too. On June 8, the first issue of the Black Hills Pioneer came off their much-traveled press. "It will be dated earlier than that of any rival sheet so that it will be a pioneer in fact as well as in name," the publishers boasted. At that, it beat out the Crook City Tribune published by X. S. Burk in the expanding mining camp on Whitewood Creek by only two days. Burk, evidently believing that the population in the vicinity would not support two newspapers, ceased publication after his initial June 10 edition. Laughlin and Merrick reported some of the difficulties they had encountered in putting out the Pioneer in time for it to live up to its name. Their historic first edition carried this "local news" item: "Owing to the fact that this first number has been gotten up under the greatest obstacles, and difficulties, there are many important things neglected which we intend to notice. Our material is in four different places, our press in a tent, and everything at a disadvantage; many of our friends have been neglected, but we will try and do justice to all in time."

The Pioneer, however, failed to "do justice to all" in its zealous coverage of the great events of the memorable Fourth of July celebration. It failed to take notice in its columns of two important "firsts" that occurred there that exciting day which, nonetheless, are

Deadwood by Lamplight

In the evening the miners employed on day shifts at the different mines begin to pour in Deadwood City. The streets are thronged, and the multitudes are regularly regaled with music from one or both of the theaters. Fifty cents will buy an admission ticket with a coupon tacked on, redeemable at the bar. The streets are illuminated with various colored transparencies over the many saloon doorways, putting forth in bold relief the names of the various institutions. The card halls are usually crowded with the anxious and delighted throngs, some intent on the progress of the various games, while others are attracted by the music of the orchestra found in these places of amusement. The private boxes in the gallery of the theatres are filled with ladies and gentlemen who quaff their wines, chat, smoke and criticize the performers. Between the acts the performers circulate around their audience and arouse the ambition of the crowd for renewed appreciation of their efforts. All this until the wee hours when out of the gaslight, out of the dazzle, the hardy miner wends his way to his cabin on the hill, there to dream perchance, of loved ones at home and rest himself for the sturdy efforts of the morrow when he will strike it — perhaps.

B H Times
June 15, 1877

B H Pioneer, Dec. 2, 1876 account of sporting event held prior to Thanksgiving. Under headline "Turkey Shooting Extraordinary," the account noted that the turkeys were placed midway up the hillside and the marksmen took their station in front of the Bella Union theatre. The first match was so successful that a second was held! "Turkey shooting became a mania with the approach of Thanksgiving.

That young lady considered to be the handsomest person in Deadwood, who agreed to wait on the ice cream table at Gregory's Restaurant tomorrow at the Sunday feast, sent us the following: Mr. Editor, to see these miners gape and gaze, it really is quite shocking, if one by accident displays, while crossing over muddy way the smallest mite of stocking.

B H Daily News
June 9, 1877

The grand Masonic inaugural ball comes off tonight. Every necessary preparation is being made to make this affair the finest of the season. The new temple in South Deadwood is just completed in structure and ornamental designing. A meeting of A. F. and A. M. was announced for last evening but has been postponed until after the dedication ball.

B H Daily Times
June 13, 1877

well documented. One was the marriage in Summit District, Gold Run Creek, of 16 year-old Anna Card of Colorado to Edward Williams, of Laramie, Wyoming Territory, by Rev. Henry Weston Smith. It was the first and only marriage known to have been performed in the vicinity by "Preacher Smith," a Methodist circuit rider, before he was killed by Indians while walking from Deadwood to Crook City on the following August 20. The certificate of marriage, signed by Rev. Smith and three witnesses, was later deposited in the Adams Museum at Deadwood. The second overlooked "first" was the birth of Revillo F. Robinson, son of Mr. and Mrs. J. N. Robinson, in a little log cabin where the Central School building was later located. He was the first child to be born in Deadwood.

But Publishers Laughlin and Merrick devoted column after column of The Pioneer to the other major events of the day. The Saturday, July 8, 1876, issue of the Pioneer described the celebration as "All Enthusiasm and Pleasantness" and the fact that during one 24-hour period there was no lawlessness, was in itself a memorable occasion for this free and wild settlement. Under headlines that read "Celebrating the Fourth in Deadwood," "300 Guns Fired," "Erection of a Splendid Liberty Pole," "Eloquent Speech of Judge Miller," and "Important Memorial Read," the Black Hills Pioneer account was as follows:

> "The Centennial Fourth was celebrated in Deadwood City in a manner worthy the occasion. The weather was auspicious throughout the day, clear skies above, with refreshing breezes playing through the balmy air, and everybody seemed to enter into the spirit of the celebration with good feeling and enthusiasm.
>
> "The memorable day was ushered in by the firing of 100 guns (anvil artillery) between 12 and daylight and with the rising of the sun there was mingled with the heavy reports a continuous cracking of musketry throughout the town and the gulch, almost every cabin being wreathed in rifle-smoke. If Philadelphia burned as much powder in proportion, the Schuylkill Valley is still glooming in the clouds.
>
> "Hundreds of sturdy miners had gathered into the city the evening before, when a magnificent liberty pole — one of the finest specimens of our grand mountain forests — was erected in front of the platform on the north side of Main Street prepared for the speakers, mounted with a beautiful gilded sphere. In the early morning amid deafening cheers and hill-quaking reports from the anvils, the national colors — the glorious emblem of liberty and a higher civilization — were raised aloft and proudly unfolded their stars and stripes in the clear mountain air; and that banner will ever be furled in the Black Hills — barbarism has run its course here.
>
> "Enthusiasm continued to be manifested by the singing of patriotic songs, anvil firing and bonfires until 11 o'clock

when the program opened with a prayer, the reading of the declaration of Independence and the oration of the day by Judge Miller."

A highlight of the program was a reading of a memorial to Congress by Gen. A. R. Z. Dawson, deputy revenue collector and first clerk of the Black Hills court. The memorial asked the speedy and prompt action in extinguishing the Indian title to and the opening for settlement of the country "we are now occupying, developing and improving. We have now in the Hills a population of at least 7,000 honest and loyal citizens, who have come here with the expectation of remaining and making this their homes. Our country is rich not only in mineral resources but is abundantly supplied with timber and a soil rich enough to produce all that will be necessary to sustain a large population. Your Memorialists would therefore earnestly request that we be not deprived of the fruits of our labor and driven from the country we now occupy, but that the Government for which we have offered our lives at once extend a protecting arm and take us under its care."

The Memorial was signed by everyone to whom it was presented and the following week it was carried to Washington for delivery by Capt. Gardner.

Demonstrations continued until daylight next morning with singing, bonfires and anvil-firing. "Not a single personal altercation, not even an angry word was uttered that we heard of," the news account concluded. "How is that for 'outlaws' in a lawless country?"

Also marking the Centennial celebration in Deadwood was the grand opening of the appropriately named Centennial Hotel. The July 8 paper recorded the hotel opening with the following article:

"Centennial Hotel with Mrs. McKelvey as proprietress, gave a very enjoyable party at opening of her house on the Fourth. A sumptuous supper was served, the music was excellent, and everything passed off pleasantly and to the perfect satisfaction of proprietress and participants. Fifteen ladies were present."

But the big celebration at Deadwood was not the only one in the Gulch by any means. Every little camp put on its own program, each of which was appropriately reported in the newspaper.

At Montana City, two miles below Deadwood, sturdy buckskin-clad mountaineers with Jack Baronett, an early explorer of the Yellowstone geyser region, at their head, took a conspicuous position outside the main crowd with needle-guns pouring volley after volley into the massive mountain walls opposite. The account noted that an elegant dinner was followed with the reading of the Declaration of Independence by Gen. Dawson (who must have been a busy man that day) and a patriotic talk by Judge Maguire.

A Calico Ball will be staged at the General Custer House, where all shades and colors of every conceivable pattern will be seen ranging from five cents to 50 cents a yard, adorning the youth and beauty of Deadwood.

B H Pioneer
Feb. 17, 1877

There was a heap of fun on Main Street Saturday night occasioned by a wheelbarrow race under the direction of Mrs. William Nuttall. The number of miles traveled by one blindfolded boy, between Ludwig's Saloon and the Bella Union could hardly be estimated. He reached the latter place, however, about two hours after starting from the former.

B H Daily Times
Sept. 3, 1877

The Union Park and Brewery in South Deadwood is the finest resort in the Black Hills, with a brass band concert every Sunday afternoon and the park is furnished with fine dancing platform.

B H Daily Times
Oct. 19, 1877

**A peek between the rocks up on the edge of Mount Moriah Cemetery shows Lee Street in downtown Deadwood in 1878. Lee Street had a bend in it before the fire wiped it out in 1879. Rebuilt, the street runs straight from Main to Sherman Street.**
**(Maj. Gen. George Ruhlen Photo)**

Prize fight announced at Cricket Saloon — Johnny Marr, the "Belfast Chicken" and George Latimer, "Cook the Kid." The fight lasted 52 rounds — at this time, by consent of the referee, Billy Nuttall, the fight was postponed until Jan. 28 when it was to be renewed for $250 purse and gate money.
B H Daily Times
Jan. 13, 1877

It was at Elizabethtown that A. B. Chapline delivered an oration which "carried his fellow citizens back to the dark and gloomy days of our forefathers upon their arrival in America." In Gayville there was no public demonstration. Instead the miners, with hardly an exception, left their sluice boxes, forks and shovels in the ditches and each passed the day as fancy dictated. At night "one of the most pleasant dancing parties that ever assembled in the Hills" met at Smeltzer and Reed's restaurant. At midnight a splendid supper was spread, to which ample justice was done. "Those who were present will long remember the first Fourth of July spent in the Hills!" But those on their way to the gold camp were not without their own celebration. Under a headline, "The Centennial in the Wilderness," the Black Hills Pioneer told that those composing Don Stevenson's train, recently arrived from Bismarck, had a grand Centennial celebration on the way, having laid over on the Fourth for that express purpose.

> "Capt. Stevenson manifested both his liberality and patriotism on the occasion by contributing for the dinner every luxury and delicacy which could be found in his large stock of general merchandise, and the professional cooks who happened to be along got it up in the best style of the art cuisine.
>
> "The place selected was pleasant and romantic — a crystal spring enshrined in a lovely little grove of ash and cottonwood, with a verdant flower-spangled landscape and grassy surrounding elevations. The day was ushered in with a salute and the hoisting of the national colors from a 40-foot pole. Just before dining, Col. George May, Montana, delivered an appropriate and eloquent speech, when all the vocalists present sang 'Hail Columbia' and followed by reading of the 'Declaration of Independence.' The participants say they would not have enjoyed themselves as well at Philadelphia."

However, a few of the wealthier citizens in the mining gulches traveled East for the historic occasion and the newspaper made appropriate note of their departure to Philadelphia and the Centennial Exposition. There was no dearth of quality entertainment either for those without the desire or means to attend the Exposition. Dr. Lawrence C. Stine, latter-day professor of opera and director of theater at South Dakota State College, found a fertile field when he made a comprehensive study of the legitimate and variety theater that flourished in Deadwood during its earliest years. He wrote:

> "Deadwood, in its mining camp and formative years, played a role in the frontier American scene. Like the lush and amusement-loving people in other western mining camps, the pioneer Deadwood immigrant hungered for entertainment of any kind and was ready to pay the price, often exorbitant, for an evening's diversion not only in saloon and dance halls, but also in houses of legitimate

and variety theatre and for local amateur entertainment originating with the people themselves.

"Intrepid actors, adventure-loving variety girls, money-hungered managers all soon appeared on the scene where rough and ready miners were willing to pay their hard earned winnings for some amusement. In this world the theatre played its role, though frequently under adverse conditions and with a fare, 20th century sophisticates might look askance.

"The presence of a more genteel society is evidenced by the numerous amusements and celebrations spearheaded by public spirited citizens who had civic interest at heart or simply wanted wholesome recreation. All Deadwood danced on holidays, building dedications and made of them a gala affair on most occasions turning out in most elegant formal attire. There were indoor fairs, social and literary meetings, church suppers, athletic events to while away the leisure hours."

This lust for entertainment matched its counterpart of gold and spread into other mining camps at Lead, Central City, Gayville, Terraville and numerous smaller camps tucked back into the hills wherever gold was sought, fought and dug for by miners of every breed and intellect. Deadwood was the entertainment capital of the Black Hills and had the distinction of having famous theatrical people follow the gold rush to its doorstep. In the period from July 22, 1876 to September 26, 1879, when the great fire swept much of early-day Deadwood away in a roaring inferno, a total of 168 major plays had been presented in Deadwood. Missing newspaper records of the first season would probably have burgeoned the total to over 200.

Jack Langrishe had played all the mining camps from Frisco to Denver and Cheyenne. He arrived in Deadwood in early summer of '76 with his wife and a small company. He had been forced to leave all of his effects in Cheyenne because he owed bills. He soon built a place with a canvas top for shelter on the corner of Main and Wall Streets and opened in July to an enthusiastic and appreciative audience. Not even the heavy rainfall through the temporary canvas roof (no shingles were available) could dampen the enjoyment of the play, "Lillian's Lost Love or The Banker's Daughter." Other plays in July included "Augustin Daly's Divorce" and "Streets of New York," a seven-act play; and in August there were "Flies in the Web" and "The Dutch Lovers."

Because the theatre was not too weather-proof Langrishe leased the use of the Bella Union and tendered that building for the miners' trial held the morning after Wild Bill was shot by Jack McCall. His first season closed in October and he worked for the Pioneer as a reporter. The first musical was presented in January of 1877, a former Denver success of his, "Did You Ever Send Your Wife to Mountain City?" Two more plays were given in '77 but then

**DEADWOOD**

**THEATRE**

**Now Open to the Public,**

--WITH A--

**First-Class Male and Female Comedy Company.**

Manager, - - JOHN LANGRISHE

Treasurer, - JONAS HELLAWELL.

[7-tf]

WM. WALLACE, A. H. RAYNOLDS.

Tom Miller's Belle Union seems to be drawing a liberal share of patronage this past week. Of course the show is of a Vaudeville type, and in addition is a little naughty, but Pete Reed and others sing a few songs nightly that is worth the price of admission, and as for Tom, himself, what with his bone solo and his comic songs, he is a host in himself.

B H Pioneer
Sept. 26, 1876

The talented and popular Langrishe troupe, which has been delighting our theatre-goers for the past three weeks, will to-day take up the line of march northward on a most commendable errand. The troupe goes direct to Deadwood City, where it will open the pioneer theatre of our northern Golconda. Every preparation for a pleasant and comfortable trip has been made; a goodly store of choice provisions has been provided, the huge tent in which the entertainments will be given has been packed, and an outfit most complete in every detail is loaded upon the wagons which are to convey the company direct to Deadwood City, the metropolis of the fabulously rich Deadwood region.

B H Pioneer
Nov. 10, 1876

Langrishe and two other actors, Martin and Gros appeared in special acts at the Bella Union located three doors below where the Fairmont Hotel now stands. Later in the year he organized a company with the talented Augusta Chambers to present "Temptations" and also his very popular "10 Nights in a Barroom." He went to Central City and also Crook City and Lead in 1878 to await the completion of his new theatre which opened on May 9 of that year with Mr. and Mrs. Frank Perkins assisting in "The Poor Gentleman," followed by a farcical afterpiece, "The Obstinate Family."

The theatre has been newly re-fitted, and everything done to render the place attractive. McDaniels has had a number of men at work for the last week putting on a new roof. New scenery has been added, and we can now boast of as comfortable a theatre as any in the west. Langrishe presents a bill for Sunday night full of novelty, variety and amusement, consisting of three pieces, interspersed with songs, dances, choruses, refrains, odd sayings, odd doings, and diversions enough to satisfy the most fastidious. Let everybody be on hand. The new comedy of "The Maid of Munster" will be presented for the first time here, followed by the admirable drama of "Black Eyed Susan," the evening's entertainment to conclude with the new farce of a "Kiss in the Dark."

B H Pioneer
Sept. 23, 1876

Bella Union Varieties

Tom Miller is doing a good business, and presents nightly very attractive bills. He has a good troupe of performers, to say nothing of "Tom," who is a host within himself as an end man, bone and banjo soloist. J. W. Wilson and Johnny Campbell create lots of fun by their witty sayings, songs and dances. The orchestra of the establishment is under the baton of Ross Ingraham, whose reputation as a first-class violinist is enviable, in fact everything connected with the management of the Bella Union Varieties is most satisfactory.

B H Pioneer
Oct. 18, 1876

**The Bella Union was another of the famous or "infamous" theatres that made Deadwood the "Broadway of the West." Famed Jack Langrishe presented many outstanding play performances in the Bella Union's theatre.**
**(Following the Frontier-Freeman Tilden)**

He next starred Fanny Price in "Fanchon and the Cricket," "Lady of Lyons" and "East Lynne" and "Camille." Dr. Stine discovered that in the "East Lynne" presentation Calamity Jane so disapproved of Lady Isabel forsaking her husband and child to elope with Sir Francis, that she strode to the footlights and squirted tobacco juice on the leading lady's pink satin gown. Langrishe produced "Rip Van Winkle" in August and used two child actresses — Maude Dennee (Ogden) and Julie McCutcheon. They also played in "Uncle Tom's Cabin" the next year.

Gulch Hash:
She feels her inmost soul within her stir,
With thoughts too wild and passionate to speak;
Yet her full heart—its own interpreter—
Translates itself in silence on her cheek.
Editor's Note: What a bully girl she would be for a deafmute lover.

In 1879 a rival company, The Metropolitan Theatre, dominated the scene but both companies performed until in September when it was announced the Metro had leased the Langrishe Theatre. On September 26, 1879, the theatre was destroyed in the devastating fire of that year and the site was later leased for construction of a store.

Mr. and Mrs. Langrishe, who were accorded great praise in every city where they performed, went to Wardner, Idaho, from Deadwood and Jack subsequently died there.

One of the largest audiences ever congregated at the Deadwood Theatre was there on Christmas night to witness the performance of "LaTour de Nesle." The piece was well placed upon the stage and the superior acting of Mr. and Mrs. Langrishe and Messrs. Collins, Griffith, Gross, Aiken and Truschses elicited continuous rounds of applause. On New Year's Eve the fine drama of the "Drunkard" will be placed upon the boards.

B H Daily Times
Dec. 30, 1876

Estelline Bennett, in her excellent book, "Old Deadwood Days," described how she had looked down from her lofty home on Williams Street over the raucous section of the town referred to as "The Bad Lands." And "Bad Lands" it undoubtedly must have been with its saloons that numbered 76 at one time, the countless second-story rooms that sequestered "soiled doves" and the variety theatres that encompassed every type of entertainment, music and drink known to man. The variety theatres, it was said, proved a refuge for the talents of every level and age. On the corner of Wall and Main Street stood the popular Melodeon. Later on the name was changed to "The Mansion." Several doors down stood the original Bella Union which was leased for a time by Langrishe while he was building his new theatre. The Bella Union was noted not only for its exciting night life but for featured boxing and wrestling spectacles.

The Gem was one of the most popular variety show places with curtained booths where ladies entertained "hell-bent for fun" miners above the dance floor, bar and stage. Dr. Stine reported the Gem did a thriving business. Crowded audiences were delighted with minstrelry, ballad singing, banjo whacking, bone rattling scenes, sketches and refrains, acrobatic acts, dancers, cancan girls and trapeze artists.

Langrishe's was not the only theatre, the Bella Union, Al Swerengen's Gem, which had occasional sparring matches; the Variety, the Metropolitan, and in Central City, The Senator, Spencer and Ludwig's Variety, and Bonanza Hall, all were popular. In one theatre, unnamed, three comedians fixed up rooms with the wife of each to "dance and sing." It was said to be the only show stopped by the police as being immoral.

The Backlog
Deadwood Pioneer Times

In the middle of July, 1876, a long, horse-drawn wagon train wound its way through Deadwood Gulch. On each side of the narrow streets, buildings were being erected to replace the green log, brush wickiup and tent shanties that comprised Deadwood's Main Street. The wagon train was called the Colorado Charlie Wagon Train. Serving as outriders were Wild Bill Hickok and a buckskin-clad lady known as Calamity Jane. In the wagons were the first "girls" that

# BLACK HILLS PIONEER

DEADWOOD, DAKOTA.

**A. W. MERRICK, Proprietor.**

LARGEST CIRCULATION IN DAKOTA.

The Pioneer Paper of the Black Hills, and from its establishment recognized as the leader, and an authority in all matters of local public concern.

**The ONLY PAPER in the BLACK HILLS**

Taking Full Associated Press Reports.

→AN EPITOME OF MINING NEWS IN EVERY ISSUE.←

The PIONEER has three grades of advertising: Displayed, Special and Local. Rates furnished upon application.

[INVARIABLY IN ADVANCE.]

| DAILY | | WEEKLY | |
|---|---|---|---|
| One Year, by Mail | $15 00 | One Year | $4 00 |
| Six Months " | 8 00 | Six months | 2 00 |
| Three " " | 4 00 | Three Months | 1 25 |
| One " " | 1 50 | | |

Address all Letters

A. W. MERRICK,
DEADWOOD D. T.

**CARPENTER & GALLUP,**

Wholesale and Retail Grocers,

Cor. Sherman and Lee Streets,

**DEADWOOD, - - - D. T.**

came to Deadwood. They were under the auspices of two of the famous "madames" of the west: Madam Mustachio and a madam known only as "Dirty Em." Both madams were expert faro dealers. Some of the girls were known as "dance hall girls," depending on their proficiency at their specialty in the entertainment field. Dance hall girl, a descriptive phrase that delineated a member of the entertainment field from that of the oldest profession, was one of dubious distinction in the early mining camp.

Eleanore Dumont, also known as Madam Mustachio or Madam Mustache, had graced such mining camps as Nevada City, California; Virginia City, Nevada; Silver City, New Mexico, and the mining camps of Colorado. Whenever the miners uncovered new diggings, the sporting population was not far behind. The sporting population of Larimer Street in Denver, could take the train to Cheyenne, get on the stage and be in Deadwood in about ten days. The clean-ups from the sluice boxes of the placer mines were really fabulous that fall of 1876. The sporting population, fully experienced, even more so than the majority of gold seekers, prepared to stay.

**Prairie schooners make the turn onto Deadwood's historic Main Street back in the 1880's. Millions of tons of badly-needed supplies crawled slowly but surely across the prairie into the Black Hills during the 1880 era.**
**(Centennial Collection)**

# chapter VI

# How They Came, What They Brought

Great diversity characterized the people who flocked into Deadwood Gulch and its environs during the region's boom years. It also characterized their methods of getting there. At first they came by horseback, by oxen, mule and horse team on foot. Expeditions were formed "back in the States" and the "live freight," the travelers, were charged for the privilege of walking beside the wagons, providing their own grub and cooking it too. Only the most foolhardy ventured out alone. There was safety in numbers and the heavily-laden freight wagons carrying essential supplies to the mining camps provided the most security. They were generally captained by experienced plainsmen accustomed to the hardships and dangers of the trail.

Probably the most colorful people associated with early transportation were the bullwhackers, muleskinners and wagon masters of the various freight lines. Calamity Jane, sporting buckskins, two Colt revolvers and a bullwhip, was among the most notable.

The life of a bullwhacker was a hard one. The trails they followed were the old bison and Indian trails through streams and gulches. They had to contend with the gumbo of the plains, the thick clay which, when wet, stuck to feet and to the wagon wheels so tenaciously at times the wheels had to be cleared after every revolution. The men had to be prepared to fight off Indians and robbers and, of course, deal with the ornery oxen and mules. Their life was totally unglamorous. Weather conditions tended to be awful, they travelled over rough or non-existent roads and were paid a mere \$50 to \$75 a month. They ate bacon and biscuits and coffee often cooked over buffalo chip fires for lack of real fuel. In order to be prepared for any occasion, they slept on blankets under the wagons with their weapons close at hand. Because the people in the region depended so much on the freight lines, nothing short of an Indian raid, which forced the wagons into a corral or a circle of wagons which sheltered the stock and the men, was excuse for a late shipment.

**The loud snap of the bullwhip and the atrocious cursing of the bullwhacker reverberated through Deadwood and up and down the gulch as long wagon trains arrived and left historic Main Street in the 1876 era. (Centennial Collection)**

Last Monday, Sept. 25, was an eventful day in the history of Deadwood City. The first quartz mill ever shipped to the Black Hills arrived and passed through our city to its destination near Gayville. The first regular coach of the first regularly established stage-line to the Hills arrived that day and brought the first lady passenger in the person of Mrs. R. B. Fay. We record these three events because they may be of importance to the future historians of the Black Hills.

B H Pioneer
Sept. 30, 1876

HAT CREEK — Coach from Deadwood was stopped again last night near Cheyenne River. Both treasure boxes were taken. The passengers were not molested . The Road Agent sent word by the driver to the manager of the stage line to send them a pair of gold scales. They say dividing the dust with a tablespoon is not always satisfactory. They also would prefer to have the box carried loose in the coach. If that can't be done, they want a hammer and hatchet sent up.

Black Hills Pioneer
June 28, 1877

The leaders of the first string of bulls that entered Lead City yesterday, had a little circus of their own. When they were rounding the corner of King's hotel, they became unmanageable, and skipping across the street, they did some grand and lofty tumbling on the sidewalk in front of Kelley's saloon. After a vigorous application of half a dozen "persuaders", they "balanced all," and when they "swung on the corner" they took half-hitch on Key's hitching posting, and leveled it to the ground. A Texas steer is mighty "onsartin".

B H Daily Times
May 4, 1878

Dr. C. W. Meyer met with an accident while returning from Central last evening which came near resulting fatally. In passing down the toll road near Jack McAleer's residence his horse went over the embankment and down the stream. While struggling in the torrent the saddle turned and the doctor was carrier under the animal's feet, and received some severe bruises to his right ankle before he was able to extricate himself from his perilous predicament. W. J. Thornby, who was with him at the time, followed down the stream and found the doctor lying between two logs, unable to extricate himself, and no doubt would have perished had it not been for the assistance rendered by Thornby. He was brought to this city and is getting along very well.

B H Weekly Times
May 25, 1878

In order to keep the teams moving, a bullwhacker used two resources, abusive language and his bull whip. The whip was approximately 20 feet long and was made of buckskin with a four foot stock or butt. This whip was kept rolled up when not in use and could easily be cracked out over the backs of the stubborn animals. Jesse Brown, one of the pioneer Black Hills drivers for a freight line, reported that "the crack of the whip was like a shot in battle and the bullwhackers' perverted language, making a bull team haul through a bad mudhole, created discordant bars of music, and the bulls knew they had to go some." There was nothing cruel in the use of a whip for the drivers were careful not to touch the animals with the end of the whip and make them bleed. The sound was created by a "popper" or broad piece of leather on the end. The bull whip was used more judiciously than the expletives of the impatient drivers, and offended the sensibilities of far fewer travelers. But it was language the animals seemed to understand and it proved extremely effective in motivating them into movement. Bullwhackers without a versatile vocabulary of curse words were a rarity on the frontier.

Besides bulls, mules and often cows were used to pull the wagons. There was some dispute as to which animal, the bull or the mule, was more exasperating. Mules tended to kick when they could but they were a faster animal on the trail. They were also more expensive and more difficult to feed and handle. Oxen were so stupid that if the slightest change in procedure was made, for instance, yoking them with the wrong mate, they would become totally bewildered and unmanageable.

When Deadwood became one of the most populous settlements in the Hills, demands for supplies were answered by the freight lines. However, in the early days, before a more convenient passage to town was discovered, the freighters had to employ the art of "skidding" their wagons down the steep sides of the gulch. This was brought about by chaining the wheels and attaching ropes to the wagons which were wrapped around trees to brake the descent. A single team of oxen or horses kept the wagon moving.

Fred T. Evans, a very substantial man both physically and financially, brought in one of the first supply trains into Deadwood. He formed the Sioux City (Iowa) and Black Hills Transportation Co. in 1875. But his first attempt to carry supplies to the Black Hills that spring was thwarted by the Army which intercepted the train on the Dakota border and burned the wagons. N. L. Witcher and Sons, also of Sioux City, started a freight line to the Black Hills in 1875 too, but the Army also prevented it from reaching its destination. Undaunted, both Evans and the Witchers succeeded in getting supply wagons into the Hills the following summer. J. R. Gordon was in charge of the train that Evans sent to Deadwood in June of 1876. His teamsters cut a wagon trail from Custer, lowered the wagons into Deadwood

**Making way for progress in Lead in the 1870's, the original store built by P. A. Gushurst (first grocery in the city) is being dismantled for a bigger and better building and store. Gushurst is ninth from the left in the group.**

**(Centennial Collection)**

Freighters have been cutting telegraph poles to lift their wagons out of the mud, thus interrupting service, altho' there is a criminal penalty attached to this offense. However, we saw a pole chained to a wagon in Deadwood yesterday.

B H Daily Times
June 29, 1880

Gulch with ropes, advanced through Poorman Gulch to Lead City and gave that mountainside community its first wagon road. Soon other frieght lines were bringing in supplies from Fort Pierre, Yankton, Sidney, Bismarck, and Cheyenne.

The merchandise these lines brought in was incredible . . . furniture, machine and gun oil, hardware, drugs and groceries, including 40,000 pounds of flour by one train the last of June 1876. They brought in machinery for the mines and a 450,000 pound mill from Cheyenne. The smelters were supplied with salt and coke. Goldfish, canaries, safes, pickled pig's feet, oysters and an "eastern luxury" — bedbugs. Whiskey, beer and even champagne were freighted in — in 1878 there were one hundred liquor dealers in Deadwood alone. It was not uncommon for a freighter to carry 500,000 pounds at a time into the Hills at three to five cents per pound. A bull team usually consisted of seven or eight yoke of oxen hitched to an old Murphy or Kern wagon made in St. Louis, Mo. The load generally weighed 7,500 to 8,000 pounds. As a typical flourishing freight line, the Evans Company employed 1,000 to 1,500 oxen, 250 mules, 400 wagons and 1,500 men.

Although not contracted to carry the mail, the drivers of these early freight wagons usually were entrusted with letters addressed to persons known to be somewhere in the Black Hills. It was hoped the drivers would eventually cross paths with the person sought. Sometimes letters were carried in a soiled pocket for weeks before reaching the intended person in tattered, torn and barely legible condition. With the advent of the pony express, letters were carried by swift horseback riders who limited their load to a mail pouch, a rifle and cartridge belt. Through this private mail service it was finally necessary to establish a post office of sorts in Deadwood.

IXL Restaurant installed kitchen range at a cost of $1,000 equal to anything found in any large eastern hotel. Nearly 200 guests are entertained daily and large numbers of rooms have been added.

B H Pioneer
April 7, 1877

Live chickens are sold at Yankton for $2.50 a dozen. In Deadwood they are worth all the way from $12 to $15 a day."
Jan. 14, 1879 — State of our market: One Lee Street retailer, with others about the same, receipts average $175 a day, principally in cash, which is good for the "dead of winter." Butter sold for 50 cents a pound; eggs, 60 cents a dozen; potatoes $3.50 per cwt.; onions, 10 cents a pound; cabbage, 5 cents a pound. Jan. 30, 1879: "A gold mine is a good thing to own in the Hills but we would rather have a big apple orchard near Deadwood than a big lead. Apples are worth from 10 to 20 cents apiece just now, and unsound at that.

B H Daily Times
Jan. 6, 1879

Every mail brings us more or less letters, making inquiries on every conceivable subject concerning the Hills. About one-half of them contain a single postage stamp. Now if these anxious inquirers knew that every letter we receive cost us from twenty-five to fifty cents, and the same amount to send one, in addition to valuable time, stationary and stamps, they would know why their letters are not answered. Now we wish to say, once and for all, that so long as our means of communication with the outside world remains as it now is, no letters will be noticed unless the writer encloses at least fifty cents.

B H Pioneer
June 24, 1876

After many days of busy work our Postmaster is nearly ready to distribute 6,000 letters that have accumulated before his arrival in this city. Those letters not claimed will be sent to the dead letter office.

B H Daily Times
April 27, 1877

Postage stamps for the Deadwood Post Office left Chicago May 10. Twelve days time from Chicago to this place is long for mail matter, and particularly so important as stamps are at this time.

B H Daily Times
May 22, 1877

It costs $12 per day to "run" the Post Office, clerically, outside of the Postmaster's salary.

B H Daily Times
May 15, 1877

The Lead City Telegram asks: "Why is it that our stores cannot give the same inducements to cash customers that the Deadwood stores do, and keep more of the money earned here away from the Deadwood houses?"

B H Daily Times
Jan. 17, 1879

In the summer of 1876 the first Seymour and Utter Pony Express Mail Service was established between Fort Laramie and Deadwood. It later also linked Sidney and Deadwood. Charlie (Colorado Charlie) Utter, the close friend of Wild Bill Hickok, was one of the riders who carved his name in the list of daring young men who raced pell-mell through the Indian-infested plains and mountains to deliver the mail. By changing ponies at each station stop, the mail traveled from Sidney to Deadwood in the incredibly short time of 48 hours.

An unofficial post office was established on upper Main Street to serve as a repository for incoming and outgoing mail carried by the pony express riders. Residents of Deadwood and the surrounding mining camps would line the street in eager anticipation of finding mail for them as each rider dashed into town. The procedure for obtaining the mail was cumbersome and time-consuming. After the arrival of the express rider and the emptying of the pouches, all the mail had to be arranged alphabetically. And only one person's mail could be claimed at a time. Anyone picking up mail for a friend had to go to the back of the line after claiming his own letters, and sometimes the line stretched out a quarter of a mile and more. Adding to the delay was the time it took to weigh up the gold dust for postage. The procedure aroused the ire of the miners, anxious for news from their families, and many of them wrote scorching letters to the editor about their frustrating experiences with it. It was also the subject of a number of pointed editorials.

The pony express service, however, lasted only two months as a contract for carrying the mail was granted to the Cheyenne and Black Hills Stage Co. when it began running stages into Deadwood on a regular basis. On March 14, 1877, the first official U.S. Post Office was established on upper Main Street with Richard O. Adams as postmaster. He held the post until May 28, 1879, when he was succeeded by Solomon Star. The post office was later moved to another site on Main Street that was closer to the business district.

In sister city, Lead, the first post office was located on North Mill in part of the first Hearst Building and its initial postmaster was Giles A. Noyes who was appointed on June 19, 1877. Although the post office was designated for "Lead City" originally, it was later changed to just "Lead." Succeeding Noyes on March 4, 1878, was William H. Faucett, who held the post until May 9, 1883.

The first public highways were actually little more than dirt trails. Toll roads were also built in the late 1870's. The toll roads were no better than the narrow, rough public roads, but the toll roads were located in critical transportation areas to insure profits for the tollkeeper.

Watson Parker in Gold in the Black Hills says that a man with business sense and broke or a miner with marginal claims could set up a toll gate and charge admission for the use of a trail that wound its way through the narrow Deadwood gulches. The owner of a toll road secured the right of way by purchasing mining interests during a meeting of miners, who sold their worthless claims along the toll road route. A few trees were cut down, stumps pulled out, a few boulders moved out of the way, and the tollkeeper was in business. He could relax and wait for the weary travelers.

An early toll road was constructed between Deadwood and Centennial at a $7,500 cost by W. L. Kuykendall and others. A wagon team was charged $1 and 25 cents extra for additional teams for the round trip. Men on horseback avoided the toll gates.

Constant bitterness occurred between the toll gate keepers and the potential patrons of the toll road. Many travelers felt that it was unfair to be charged to use the only road in an area. Furthermore, the toll roads were usually in a poor state of repair. In 1878, a number of men were going to make their own road as an alternative to the Spruce Gulch Toll Road, which was in terrible condition. The toll gate keeper saw the men at work and chased them away. The toll road builders between Deadwood and Gayville would have to continually reconstruct the road due to the undermining of the right of way by over zealous miners in the district.

The county commissioners, aware that toll roads were profitable, set up a committee to investigate the Bald Mountain Toll and Wagon Road. The group advised the commissioners that the toll gate should be located at Silverton, perhaps where more travelers could be charged. As long as the toll roads were profitable, their continuing existence was assured.

Stage lines were established to bring people in — and take some out. The first stage from Cheyenne arrived in Custer City in May 1876 and then ran as conditions allowed. This line — the Cheyenne and Black Hills Stage and Express — was purchased by Gilmer and Salisbury and in 1877 they made arrangements to give Deadwood tri-weekly service . . . this was later changed to daily. When the outfit purchased the line from Sidney the terminus was changed to that town. The first trail to be established by the stage line followed the old Cheyenne trail. It began in Cheyenne, Wyoming Territory, and followed a northeasterly direction to the Hills.

It was early in 1876 that Gilmer, Salisbury and Patrick, previously operating as freighters, attempted to establish their fast passenger service, the Cheyenne and Black Hills Stage Line, into the Hills from Cheyenne. But because of Indian hostilities, it was found impractical. The eastern capitalists backing the enterprise refused to sink more money into the line until the Indians ceased running off their stock and burning their stations. One general agent named Robinson was killed in the early history of the company's operations.

The meeting last evening to take measures towards the elevation of gold dust to its proper staple value, was not numerously attended, but a determination was detected upon the face of everyone present, that they could stand the imposition no longer of taking gold at a rate at which they must lose from $2.50 to $3 on every ounce handled. The agreement will be circulated among our businessmen and ought to be strictly adhered to, and not as was the one of last spring, as advantage taken of a few, to advertise to take gold at $20 to sell their goods and they did not also state that they would advance the price of goods to suit (and probably more too) the advance of gold. Our plan is this: That the agreement state clearly and definitely what was embodied in the resolutions passed, and all businessmen sign it who are agreeable thereto, and have the same agreement to sign kept in a prominent place, that all may see them upon the first violation of any articles in the agreement, the person so violation to be advertised, to which end the Times offers its columns.

B H Daily Times
**Jan. 29, 1877**

Speagle Gap, north of Deadwood on the original road to Crook City, was the scene of an incident involving the pioneer John Hunter family whose son George still lives in Deadwood as this history book went to press in 1976. George's sister, Lillian, just a child at the time, was lost at Speagle Gap where the family had camped before going the rest of the distance into Deadwood in 1877. Over 500 men searched for her and finally found her asleep on a steep ledge. Lillian grew up to become the wife of Dr. Frank S. Howe, early-day doctor, leading businessman and the author of the book "Deadwood Doctor."

Marie Lawler
Deadwood Pioneer

A herd of about 50 Texan cattle passed through town this forenoon to Cleveland. In South Deadwood, a dog ran among them and a general stampede was the result. The herder made an effort to stop the flying bovines and was run down and somewhat injured. The frightened animals took to the timber up Whitewood.

B H Weekly Times
**Oct. 7, 1877**

All restaurants had excellent foods and most specialized in fresh oysters . . . Jan. 29, 1879 . . . Quail are becoming plentiful in the market now-a-days and you can get them served up on toast at the Oyster Bay, in addition to your regular dish of oysters.

B H Daily Times
1878

While we can consistently complain of the scarcity of ready cash in the gulch just at this time, we can't complain of no snow. At the present writing it is showering its weight of wealth down upon us in great white flakes.

B H Daily Times
Jan. 6, 1879

"Deadwood, the metropolis of the Black Hills, contains 6,000 inhabitants, 500 business firms, churches, schools and numerous secret organizations. The assessed valuation of the three counties composing this region has increased from $300,000 two years ago to over $3,000,000 today; without taking the mines into consideration. The Black Hills settlements number about 30 and are scattered over a region 6,000 square miles lying between the south and north forks of the Cheyenne River. There were 15,000 passengers carried to and from the Hills during the past year by the stage lines and the mail which arrives at Deadwood, amounts to 500 pounds daily. These stage lines employ 200 experienced stage men, 1,000 animals, and fifty fine concord coaches and have a capital of about $500,000 invested.

B H Daily Times
Jan. 14, 1879

It wasn't until July, 1876, that the company was able to bring its first coach into Custer. However, it met with ill luck on the return trip. Indians attacked it, chased it several miles, killed the driver and cut the horses loose. The passengers were stranded 12 miles from Custer and were forced to walk the distance back. Once established, the line also transported freight and mail and eventually gold bullion for Homestake. The importance of the gold shipments called for more careful protection and men who were especially brave, determined and reliable. These gold coaches were called "treasure coaches" and were designed by the line superintendent, Luke Voorhees. They were lined with heavy iron plates to resist the attack of robbers and protect the guards within. Many of the robberies and holdups associated with transportation into Deadwood occurred against this company's coaches on their journeys from Sidney to Deadwood. Those interested in following the path of the old Cheyenne and Black Hills Stage Line will probably become a bit confused since the line routes changed several times between 1875 and 1877.

The Northwest Express, Stage and Transportation Co. (successor to the Minnesota Stage Co.) had a stage line from Bismarck to Deadwood in March of 1877 that connected with the Northern Pacific. They later changed to the Pierre route when they bought the line from the Wyoming Stage Co. In 1878 they provided daily mail service as did the Cheyenne route and triweekly from Pierre. The Northwestern could get from Bismarck in 36 to 48 hours traveling day and night the 200 miles or so and in 1878 they were bringing in an average of six passengers a day. The men of the mining gulches were more than happy when a number of these passengers were of the "gentler sex." In the summer of 1876 a stage line between Deadwood and Ft. Pierre was contracted and the first stage carried five passengers and over 500 letters — C. L. Demming had the first stage and in 1877 it was operated by Gardner and Van Tassel.

The stage lines and transportation companies had to contend with bad roads, blizzards, floods, rate wars, Indian depredations and robberies by "knights of the road." Among these road agents were Reddy, Laughing Sam, Modoc Bill, Texas Charley, Long Yank, Doc Middleton and many more — and some of whom ended their lives as the star attraction at a necktie party. The stage and freighting companies fulfilled their jobs admirably in the transportation of the 1876-1880 era. The freighters working for Daughterty and Co., the Merchants Freight Line, Bramble and Co. (later consolidated with Jewett, Dickinson and Co.), Evans, Northwestern and the independent outfits brought in millions of pounds of freight annually, and their prices in the Hills usually compared favorably with those in the States. Not only did they bring in supplies, they took out freight — gold and silver bullion in the treasure coaches and it was not unusual for them to be carrying $200,000 in gold. In fact, one shipment of that value was the production of only two weeks at the Homestake and Father DeSmet mines.

Due to the numerous mine accidents, the Homestake Mining Co. under the leadership of George Hearst and Superintendent Samuel McMaster established a company and community hospital for the miners and their families by the time the mining camps were only two years old.

Homestake's motives for organizing hospital care were not only humanitarian, but also pragmatic. Mine accidents affected the morale of the miners and the efficiency of mine operations.

Undoubtedly, Homestake was one of the pioneers in mining-industrial health care. Hearst, in 1877, hired Doctors D. K. Dickinson for the Homestake Mine and J. O. Gunsolly for the Deadwood-Terra and other Homestake properties to serve as physicians. Temporary medical facilities were provided by the next year.

Early-day hospital facilities were inadequate and the doctors at times inept. Dakota Territory statutes were enacted to discourage incompetent doctors. In 1878 laws in the territory required a practicing physician to file a copy of his diploma with a county's Register of Deeds. The first to file in Lawrence County were Dr. L. F. Babcock, Dr. Joel Haughton, and Dr. J. W. Coombs. During the same year, the county doctors organized a medical society to further the cause of medicine and to promote sound medical practices.

It was also in 1878 that the Sisters of Charity built a hospital on the north side of City Creek in Deadwood. The hospital, built on land donated by James Asterito, was soon forced to close due to financial difficulties. In the same year, the Sisters of the Holy Cross established a hospital on Cleveland Avenue in Deadwood. This hospital, also not self-sufficient, closed. Lawrence County built a hospital in 1878 for the care of the poor near the site of the Sisters of Charity Hospital, but the medical facilities were inadequate.

The first Homestake Mining Co. hospital, located in a four-room log cabin, was established in 1879. Homestake employees during this time paid $1.10 per month as compensation for the physician's medical and surgical services. The hospital funds were given to Sister Mary Edward, who had operated a small Catholic hospital in Lead. The Homestake hospital facilities were insufficient, but Sister Mary did the best she could. An untrained male nurse attended the patients under the supervision of Dr. Dickinson and Dr. Gunsolly and, of course, Sister Mary Edward.

Through the sudden demand for wood products during the frenzied gold rush around the Deadwood and Lead areas, Lawrence County played a major role in the need for establishing the United States Forest Service. The absence of lumber in April and May of

**Homestake's first hospital on Main Street in Lead was in the process of being replaced by a bigger and better facility when this picture was taken. The hospital was first established in 1879.**

**(Centennial Collection)**

An exchange says, "The Black Hills dentists pull teeth with six shooters and fill them with gold dug in the cellar." How ignorant our eastern friends must be of the skill possessed by our accomplished dentists; after loading their revolvers with a fair charge of powder, they insert golden bullets and shoot them into the cavities of their patrons' teeth."

B H Pioneer
Jan. 20, 1877

Don't waste time and money on inferior papers, but become a subscriber to the BLACK HILLS TIMES. By so doing you will get value received for your money, and a paper worth the reading. Bear in mind that the TIMES is the best newspaper of the territory. It contains more reading matter than any other paper in the Hills. Try it and you will never be without the TIMES . . . Advertisers who wish to reach the greatest number of people bear in mind that the TIMES has a larger bona fide circulation than any other newspaper published in the Black Hills.

Circa 1877

1876 in Deadwood Gulch proved a great drawback and was the cause of the most exasperating delay. Whipsaws were used extensively to supply the demand and many sawmills were being rushed to the area by oxen trains.

One of the sawmills enroute was the property of E. G. Dudley who established the first lumber mill in Deadwood. A pioneer, Dudley hired 40 men to escort the mill from Cheyenne, Wyoming Territory as protection against hostile Indian raids. Several times Indians attacked the group and troops were even rushed from Fort Robinson to help the party reach Deadwood. But the demand for lumber was insatiable and the sawmill came through and was set up in Whitewood Gulch, now First Ward, across Main Street from the present Black Hills Novelty Co. building. At that site Dudley sold lumber for $40 per thousand board feet, cut from adjacent and then abundant timber areas.

It was true that forest conservation was not an unheard-of thing. That very year, 1876, Congress approved a study which recommended "means of preservation and renewal of forests." From studies made by the Forest Service in later years, fires and bark beetle infestations destroyed immense areas of forestland prior to the 1876-1880 formative years of Deadwood, Lead, Terraville, Central City and the many smaller mining camps.

Deadwood, being the teeming metropolis of the nation's last frontier, received telegraph and telephone communications before many other areas across the nation. Annie Tallent, in Black Hills, Last Hunting Ground of the Dacotahs, reported that Deadwood, through completion of the Black Hills Telegraph Line, received the service as early as December 1, 1876. "By virtue of the undomitable pluck and the unwavering perseverance of the projector of the enterprise," she wrote, "in the face of multiplied difficulties and dangers and after months of waiting on the part of the expectant people of the Hills, Deadwood, the terminal point of the line, was on that day placed in direct telegraph communications with the outside world. It was a boon to the newspapers of Deadwood and surrounding camps to get first-hand information on the big news breaking around the world."

James Halley, the first operator, flashed his message from Deadwood to the mayor of Cheyenne signifying the line was completed. The telegraph office was located on upper Main Street and was the scene of a boisterous celebration with a huge bonfire along with salutes of gunpowder and anvil artillery. The higher-class people of Deadwood culminated the celebration at the Grand Central Hotel. William H. Hibbard had started the project in June of 1876 and it almost folded due to the extra costs to protect the work crews from hostile Indians. But Deadwood businessmen backed Hibbard to the tune of $5,000 to get the line completed.

COMMITTEE ON STOCK LIST
New York Stock Exchange
New York, Jan. 16, 1879
Official Statement of the
HOMESTAKE MINING
COMPANY:

Incorporated under laws of California, November 5, 1877.

Capital, 100,000 shares, par $100
$10,000,000

Property located in Whitewood Mining District, Lawrence County, Dakota Territory; consisting of Homestake and Golden Star Mines, 1350 feet long by 450 feet wide on the vein; title complete.

Improvements: New 80-Stamp Mill fully equipped, hoisting works, air compressors, tramways, tools, sawmills, offices and houses.

Value .................................... $250,000

Receipts to January 1, 1879 .................................... $175,000

Expended in development, Construction, etc. .............. $387,000

Balance, January 1, 1879 .... $88,500

Present capacity of mill, 175 tons per day; mine can supply 500 stamps; ore in sight sufficient to run present mill ten years.

[illegible] been ordered to be completed in June next; when completed the crushing capacity will be over 100 tons per day.

No debts, liens or encumbrances of any kind or nature.

New York Office, 31 Broad Street.

TRANSFER OFFICE
Wells, Fargo & Co., 65 Broadway

Registered by
UNION TRUST COMPANY

OFFICERS

President .................. Lloyd Tevis
Vice President ... R. P. Lounsbery
Treasurer .................. J. B. Haggin
Secretary .................. J. K. Goodrich
Assistant Secretary H. B. Parsons

DIRECTORS

Lloyd Tevis, J. B. Haggin, R. P. Lounsbery, Thos. Bell, M. N. McDonald, Wm. Willis.

The committee recommends that this stock be placed on the regular list.

AB'H B. BAYLIS,
Chairman

Adopted by the Governing Committee January 22nd, 1879.

Completion of the telegraph line was a boon to the Black Hills Pioneer, published by Merrick and Laughlin, as it gave them faster access to the news of the outside world. But it also brought them their first serious competition. Porter Warner, also a former Denver journalist, launched the Black Hills Times, the first daily in the region, on April 7, 1877. The Pioneer went daily too on August 10, 1878. Numerous other newspapers joined the competition prior to the 1880's, but the Pioneer and the Times were the only ones to survive the rivalry past the first few years. And even they were eventually merged.

"The newspaper starting boom is still in full blast in Dakota territory. Two new papers have reached us during the past 2 days . . . These enterprises are indicative of the great prosperity enjoyed by our territory."

B H Daily Times
June 29, 1880

Other newspapers which began publication in the gulch in 1877 were the Black Hills Miner, the Black Hills Champion, and the Western Enterprise, all at Deadwood; the Black Hills Herald and the Western Enterprise at Central City. The Miner was a resurrection of X. S. Burke's one-issue Crook City Tribune of the previous year. It didn't last much longer than its Crook City predecessor, suspending operations on November 27, 1877, to await a supply of newsprint that never arrived. Charles Collins, a vagabond editor from Sioux City, Iowa, established the first series of frontier newspapers named The Champion in Deadwood on June 2, 1877. But it ceased publication at that location by the end of 1877 too and Collins moved on to short-lived publishing careers elsewhere. Webster and Co. brought out the Western Enterprise at Central City on August 18, 1877, moved to Deadwood the following June and subsequently transformed it into an evening newspaper at Lead City. James S. Bartholomew launched the Black Hills Herald on August 30, 1877, but closed out the Central City publication to become a partner in the establishment of the Lead City Telegraph which issued its first edition on April 7, 1878.

But one dispatch came over the wire yesterday, and that was from the TIMES' special correspondent in Hoop Pole township, Posey County, Indiana, ordering 40,000 copies of the DAILY TIMES of today, and this alone will account for the extra get-up of this issue. We will have to suppress that agent, or employ steam.

B H Daily Times
June 29, 1880

Additional newspapers to make their appearance in the gulch in 1878 included the Lead City Sunday Register, published by Dan Scott, which began weekly publication on January 17; the Black Hills News-Letter which Harry J. Norton brought out in Deadwood on February 8; the Mining and Real Estate Journal which first came out in Deadwood on March 15 as a monthly with Capt. C. V. Gardner as publisher; and the Black Hills Register at Central City. Rev. B. Way Mills established the Central Christian at Central City in 1879 and even Carbonate Camp, a silver mining town northwest of Deadwood, could boast its own newspaper, the Carbonate Reporter, by the end of the year. Dolph Edwards and the Pineo Brothers established the Lead Tribune in 1879 too. Advertising revenue was insufficient to support so many newspapers and most of them disappeared by the end of the decade. The few that survived into the 1880's were eventually abandoned too or consolidated with the more durable Pioneer-Times.

SUNDAY IN DEADWOOD —
One long, rather narrow street, which was practically all there was of Deadwood in the summer of 1876 . . . . bustle and confusion of unloading freight . . . trains, rasping of saws and resounding blows of hammer . . . every business place open and traffic in full blast . . . Sunday was the busiest of the seven . . . hundreds of miners and prospectors in the surrounding camps and gulches threw down their picks and shovels and came to Deadwood to replenish their store of supplies, get their mail and have a jolly time spending their week's earnings.

Annie D. Tallent
The Black Hills or the Last Hunting Grounds of the Dakotas

While in existence only briefly, in most cases, these pioneer publications left a lasting legacy. Future historians would be grateful

**Progressive Hall was a peculiar name for an 1876 saloon. Did it mean progress or progressive deterioration? Anyway, many miners entered the doors of this Deadwood emporium and tossed a poke of dust on the bar to take them away from the grim realities of life with a refreshing drink of whiskey.**
**(Centennial Collection)**

First Directory of Deadwood lists:
Saloons: "Bella Union," J. B. Billings, J. L. Bowman, Wm. Brennicke, G. D. Billings, J. D. Coleman, J. Conway, D. W. Dougherty, H. C. Dunning, "Eureka Hall," Fitzgerald; Healy & Bruce, Al Swearengen, R. A. Goodyear, "Grand Central," Harlow & Co., C. Haserodt, J. Hayes, "Hazen House," "I. X. L.," T. Hanley, "Little Bonanza", W. F. Johnson, Mahen & Connor, H. Maillard, Paul & Wall, O'Neill & Orton, James Ryan, "Red Bird," J. Rosebraugh & Co., L. C. Richards, G. G. R. Sangiovanne, Sigel & Vanocker, George Taylor. J. D. Russell, Wardner & Ryan, Thomas Weaver, Williams & Meskil, Mullen & McReavy.
Theaters: Arcade, Bella Union, Gem, Langrishe, Graves & Martin.

John S. McClintock
Pioneer Days in the Black Hills

for the insights their advertising and news columns provided into the daily life of the gulch communities during their initial years. The plethora of early-day newspapers enabled later researchers to identify who had made local history by doing certain important things first. Some of these "firsts," of course, are open to question in light of recollections told by old-timers who remembered them differently. But their documentation in the newspapers at the time they happened, or close to it, is generally accepted as better evidence than the oft-times faulty memories of old-timers.

At any rate, among the "firsts" reported by one or more of these early newspapers are these: C. V. Gardner and Co. built the first frame structure in Deadwood in June of 1876 and opened "the first completely equipped grocery store" there; George Beemer built the first frame structure on the corner of Main and Mill Streets in Lead City in the spring of 1877, to be followed soon by the first frame hotel, the Miner's, in June of that year; the "first" dance in Lead City took place on July 4, 1877, in the second frame building erected there, and attracted the entire female population of the town — seven women; the first bank was established in Lead City in 1878 with John Ainley in charge; and John C. Ryan, formerly of St. Joseph, Mo., who had brought a shipment of goods by rail to Sidney, Nebraska, and by eight wagons pulled by bull teams to Spearfish in April of 1876, was the "first" dry goods dealer there, using the dry goods boxes for shelves and counters.

Other enlightening facts about the blossoming new communities were also recorded for posterity in these early newspapers. For instance, the Black Hills Daily Times, in its second month of publication, gave a very glowing account of growing Deadwood: "There are five hotels, numerous restaurants, chop houses and lunch rooms. There are about 75 saloons in North and South Deadwood, beside many billiard and card halls. Two brass bands enliven the monotony of mining life, from the principal balconies, and scores of lesser musicians toot the horn or rasp the viol, in the halls of chance, the concert saloon, and in the public thoroughfares . . . gardens loom up around the hills . . . The three banking companies ornament their windows with bullion, bar, retort gold, dust and coin in careless quantities."

In Deadwood, the bath house on Wall Street advertised extensively when it first opened: "Bathrooms on Wall Street now doing business . . . get a bath . . . bathe and keep clean . . . no luxury like a bath. Try it . . . house-cleaning and bathing time . . . " were ads spaced at various places among the personal news items. Credit probably wasn't the easiest to find, "Wanted to borrow, $2,000 on undoubted security Address Box 551, Postoffice." The ad appeared several times. Women's wear required milliners and seamstresses and another ad read: "Wanted — Ten experienced dressmakers and tasty trimmers at Welf & McDonald's opposite McPherson's bank, Main Street, Deadwood. Only the best need apply."

Other items in the Times in 1877 revealed that C. T. Clippinger was operating a circulating library "next door to a newsstand which carried all the magazines," and that "Brown and Thum opened their bank with a ball." Troy, formerly called Gayville, was a rival city of Deadwood, and about the same size in May of 1877 when the Times described it this way: "It has six hotels, eight stores of general merchandise, two clothiers, one hardware, three bakeries, two meat markets, one assay laboratory, two drug stores, two shoe houses, one brewery, two wagon and blacksmith shops, three express and transportation companies, and one news depot . . . From the present outlook there is a bright future for the growth and prosperity of Troy." The attempt to change the town's name did not succeed, however, as the Times editor referred to it as Gayville again when he visited there in September. He reported: "The main street of the town was completely blocked during a portion of our visit there . . . Mule trains, ox trains, express wagons, hacks and buggies were locked in and mixed up in great confusion. It was a perfect jam, and a fearful amount of profanity was breathed upon the air before the entanglement was straightened out."

Another "first" was reported in the Times in 1878 when the Black Hills Telephone Co. opened its operations in Deadwood late in the year. It was an historic event since it was also the first telephone exchange in the territory and it came into existence in the same year that the first commercial switchboard was placed in operation in faraway New Haven, Connecticut, demonstrating that the metropolis of the Black Hills was as progressive as the older eastern community. Paul Rewman, manager for the Black Hills Telephone Co. was the company's first resident and business subscriber. There were 14 telephones in operation in Deadwood by December of 1879.

Progress in transportation, communication and the business development of Deadwood Gulch had been spectacular and swift. Other aspects of frontier life there caused considerable excitement too, forming even greater challenges for the pioneer settlers. There was, for instance, the awesome task of creating order out of chaos and taming the wild elements so active in the gulch in its first years.

**The Deadwood office is the mother bank of the First National Bank of the Black Hills. It holds the original charter, the second oldest in the state, from the Comptroller of the Currency dated July 25, 1878. The bank succeeded the firm of Stebbins, Wood & Post, established in 1877. In 1894 the Deadwood bank took over the Merchants National Bank and Deadwood National Bank. In 1905 the American National Bank, Deadwood, was consolidated into the First National Bank, which is in the same location today as the original bank. An interesting note is the fact that the first bank in Deadwood was established by James Wood in 1876. Wood's only qualification as a banker was that he owned the only safe in the territory! He charged a straight 10 per cent — 10 per cent for exchanging gold dust into dollars, 10 percent for safekeeping, 10 per cent for cashing drafts, certified checks and Wells Fargo money orders and 10 per cent for monthly interest on loans!**

**(Centennial Collection)**

Deadwood City Aug 21st 1876.

Revd J S Chadwick
Louisville Ky

Dr Sir

It becomes my painful duty to inform you, that Revd H. Weston Smith, was killed by the Indians, yesterday (Sunday) a short distance from this place. He had an appointment to preach here in the afternoon, and was on his way here from Crook City, when a band of Indians overtook him and shot him. His body was not mutilated in any way, and was found in the road a short time after the hellish deed had been done His death was instantaneous as he was shot through the heart. His funeral occurred to day from his home in this town. Every thing was done by kind hands, that was possible under the circumstances, and a Christian burial given him. I was not personally acquainted with Mr. Smith, but knew him by reputation, as an earnest worker in his Master's Vineyard. He has preached here on several occasions, and was the only Minister in the Hills. He died in the harness, and his memory will be always with those who knew him, a letter from you which I found in his home causes me to convey this sad intelligence to you.

Yours &c

Seth Bullock.

# chapter VII

# A Need For God And Teachers

Preacher Smith turned down the offer of a revolver and holster the day he left from Deadwood for Crook City to deliver a sermon. He was shot and killed enroute. It was not God's will that he would return home safely.
(Centennial Collection)

The year of 1876 was the crucial period of Black Hills pioneer history. It was a chaotic period, an era of disorder and crime. In the absence of civil law, might struggled for the mastery over right. The year was one of prolonged tragedy. Of all the mining camps of the frontier, Deadwood flared highest and brightest. The struggle of churches and religion in the mining camps and early communities of the Northern Black Hills was as colorful and exciting as the gold rush.

For following the stampede of thousands seeking their wealth were their families and later the schools and churches. The hardship of the times and not the indifference of the people was blamed for the struggle. For the desire for religion to help them through the rigors of the pioneer life was evidenced in the news accounts of those days. The make shift locations by visiting ministers were packed with standing-room only and editorials expressed the need for churches to be built.

The second sound after the woodman's axe in a clearing was the "Halloo!" of a Methodist preacher. The man who brought Methodism to the Black Hills, "Preacher Smith," was of the circuit riding tradition.

Credit for being the first preacher in the area goes to Henry Weston Smith, a Methodist missionary, presumably shot and killed by Indians while enroute from Deadwood to Crook City to hold a service. Preacher Smith did most of his preaching on street corners, while another, a Mark Rumney, slated his in bars and dance halls, including the Bella Union and Melodeon.

Within a radius of two miles, a population of 10,000 to 15,000 souls who would "like to attend Sunday services, but after visiting a few times the present church, crowded as it is every service to almost suffocation, it requires persuasion and often more to induce one to attend.

B H Daily Times
May 2, 1877

However, the first to organize a church was Rev. Lanson P. Norcross, a Congregational minister, who arrived in Deadwood in November, 1876 and held his first services in the Centennial Hotel, December 3, 1876. Organization of the church was completed January 15, 1877 and the building, the first in Lawrence County was located

**The Congregational Church, located at the base of McGovern Hill on Pine Street, was Deadwood's first established house of worship. (Centennial Collection)**

Facts not fiction. In the years past I have noted in the press many statements regarding incidents connected with the man known as Preacher Smith. Most of them are mere romance. The stories related as to how he preached on the way to Deadwood, and how he used to go into the saloons and pray, are pure fiction. I never saw him in a saloon, and I am sure he never was. He preached frequently in Deadwood, generally in front of Bent and Deetken's drug store, or in front of my store. I never knew him to preach in any house in Deadwood but in those days the town had 3,000 to 4,000 people, located mostly on one street, and he had no trouble in securing an audience. He was a man about 6 feet tall, with fine physique and I should say 40 years old. He was very quiet and unassuming in manner. I know nothing of his past life, as he never volunteered to tell me and it was not wise in those days to inquire to closely into a man's antecedents.

Captain C. V. Gardner, Deadwood

at the base of McGovern Hill where services started in June, 1877. This church was credited for the formation of classes for the Chinese of Deadwood, an example which was later adopted by the Baptist Church.

There were many Catholics among the early pioneers and once again the Mother Church followed her migrant sons and daughters to the Black Hills. In 1876, the Catholic population of Deadwood, Custer City, Crook City and Hill City was sufficiently large to demand priests. Mindful of the neglected needs of the Catholic miners, Bishop James O'Connor of Nebraska sent Rev. John Lonergan to Deadwood, where he celebrated his first public mass in a carpenter shop owned by Mrs. Weber on Sherman Street, May 23, 1877. He was the first resident priest of the Black Hills although as far back as 1848, Father Pierre DeSmet, the noted pioneer Indian missionary of the Northwest, visited Indians around the Black Hills. It is reported that he visited the Deadwood Gulch during one of his missionary trips which ended in 1870, and a great gold mine close to Deadwood was named in his honor.

Rev. B. Mackin, sent by the Bishop to assist Father Lonergan, served all the missions of Terraville, Carbonate District, Bald Mountain Camp, Brownsville, Sturgis, False Bottom, Spring Creek, Bear Butte Valley, Crook City, Fort Meade, Pleasant Valley, Alkali, and remained to spearhead the building of the Lead church in the spring of 1878 and one in Central City about the same time. In Deadwood, a small church building was built in 1877 on Williams Street, the same site as the former Catholic Church, used for many years, before the new brick edifice now located on Upper Main Street.

The first Episcopal service in Deadwood followed closely on the heels of the Catholic mass and was conducted by Seth Bullock in August, 1876. Using a borrowed Book of Common Prayer, he read the burial office for Preacher Smith, who was killed while traveling between Deadwood and Crook City. The first organized Episcopal service was held in 1877; over 100 men and three women attended. A year later the construction of St. John's Church building was being planned.

In Lead, the first Episcopal service of record was held over a pool hall in 1878. A year later a Ladies Guild was formed which began raising money to build a church.

In 1878, the Rev. James Williams, a missionary sent by the Northwest Iowa Conference, organized the Methodist Church in Deadwood. The first meeting was in a frame school building which was destroyed when the fire of 1879 swept Deadwood.

Methodism came to Lead four years after the city came into being in the spring of 1876 when placer mining began on Gold Run

Gulch. The Rev. W. D. Phifer organized the first Methodist Society on Nov. 15, 1880. Services were first held in the old log schoolhouse, later in the Opera House and the first Miner's Union Hall.

The first Methodist service in Central City was conducted by Judge David R. Ogden, Anchor City, in 1877. Meetings were first held at Golden Gate, then in a school building which stood on the lot later occupied by the American Hotel, and later in the Opera House. In November, 1878, Rev. James Williams organized the church and an edifice was built in Sawpit Gulch.

In Spearfish, Methodist Services were held in the summer of 1877 by George Read, not an ordained minister, but a blacksmith by trade.

Miners who had come to Deadwood without their families resented paying for educating other people's children, and this was one of the prime factors for the two-year delay in establishing a public school in the gulch. Smaller, surrounding camps, had no difficulty in opening classes months previous to Deadwood, where the first public school did not start operating until April 30, 1878. The first term was held during the spring and summer months in a house owned by the Congregational Church which was leased for $200 with $50 spent for desks and other equipment.

While a school board was elected as far back as July 27, 1876 at a meeting held at the "theatre," it took nearly two years to complete the duties with which they were charged: "Secure a suitable building, canvass and solicit subscriptions to defray expenses, select a teacher and visit the school twice a month."

The selection of a board did not deter others from entering the field of education and during the autumn of 1876, in a small log cabin, a private school was started by William Commode. On Jan. 6, 1877, Mrs. John Callison advertised in the Black Hills Daily Times that she would start a primary school on January 8 on Whitewood Creek at a fee of $1 per week per student — and she was fortunate enough to have 27 register for classes.

Central City has been credited with being the first town in the Hills to establish a school under the public school system of Dakota Territory, having opened a term in the fall of 1877 with several from Deadwood attending, and with Dolph Edwards as teacher. However, Crook City claimed that it had a school two weeks earlier, taught by Mrs. J. S. Bennett. District No. 1, the first organized in the Black Hills, was established there at that time with H. M. Vroman, treasurer; W. D. Wakeman, director and W. M. Anderson, clerk. School was taught in a rented log cabin but soon after a comfortable school building was erected.

A Miss Graham was the teacher for the first classes opened in Lead in the fall of 1876, a tuition school held in a small log cabin on

There is a woman living in South Deadwood who has three husbands. They are all here and it is a small matter to imagine the troubles she has on her hands in consequence.

B H Daily Times
Jan. 6, 1879

Sensational writers have alleged that "Calamity Jane and Kitty Arnold," notorious underworld characters in Deadwood at that time, prepared the body (Preacher Smith) for burial, and that Calamity Jane uttered lamentations and maledictions over the body. This is pure fiction. Best evidence is the the body was prepared for burial by C. E. Hawley, one of the few known churchmen then in Deadwood, later a deacon in the Congregational church, the first established in Deadwood in 1877. Funeral arrangements were made by the only governing body in Deadwood at that time, a public welfare committee of which Capt. Seth Bullock was a member . . .

"Preacher Smith"
By Edward L. Senn

Starting Nov. 20, Tom Miller home on Third Street. Classes will be taught by E. Kermode for three months. All are solicited to send their children.

B H Pioneer
Nov. 10, 1876

Mrs. D. T. Smith, will on Monday, open a select school on the corner of Second and Lee Streets. Her terms are $1.25 per week Also within a few days another announcement in the paper revealed that Mrs. John Callison on Whitewood had opened classes for primary children at $1 per week.

B H Pioneer
Dec. 9, 1876

A total abstinence society was formed through the efforts of Rev. Father Mackin of Deadwood. It is called the 'Murphyites'. On Jan. 13, a temperance rally was called at the Congregational Church. "this is a needed move . . . and it would be a blessing to this community if there were a solid firm temperance organization in every household." A Red Ribbon Club was formed within a few days . . . not to inaugurate a crusade against liquor men but to extend a helping hand to those who have been reduced mentally, financially, and physically by too much fire water." Formed in Lead about the same time was the Lead City Catholic Temperance Society.

B H Daily Times
Jan. 11, 1879

In Deadwood on January 2, 1878, Miss Ann Pichler offered lessons in music, French, German and Italian. Two weeks later the school in Elizabethtown opend with 15 students and another two weeks later, Francis Fallon advertised he would operate a private school on Deadwood Street, starting February 4. Within a week 87 students had registered and an assistant hired for the superintendent, to serve as principal and teacher.

B H Daily Times
Circa 1878

North Bleeker Street with 14 students. In June, 1878, the first school district meeting was held and the first public school was taught that summer in a room over a store by Professor Dean, with 32 students, 16 girls and 16 boys.

And while these classes were springing up to answer the need for educating the young, politics got into the Deadwood school district operation. In answer to many articles in the Times during the summer of 1877, stressing the need for a school, a new board was elected which announced its determination to push for the completion of buildings for school purposes.

By fall, bids were being sought for a one-story school building containing two rooms with a completion date of October 10. The only money available for payment was county script and as could be expected there were no bidders. The two factors trying to control the county then got into the picture and in a general election the Peoples Party candidate for county superintendent won over the Republican nominee.

Under the guise of objecting to the extravagant assessment and high taxes, the board members were forced to resign. After the resignations were declared illegal, other resignations followed and Dr. J. A. Harding was elected district director on March 5.

The first session was financed by a five mill levy with two and one-half mills used for salaries, and one and one half for incidentals and one-half for building purposes.

By August, 1878, the populace was quibbling about the location of the school and some even wanted two schools. The new two-story school, built to accommodate 180-200 students, opened December 16 with only 125 attending out of the 290 of school age.

With no money, the district was faced with a $200 freight bill and payment for the school desks. The students came to the aid of the school and staged an amateur musical entertainment at the Langrishe Theatre, and then later raised money among themselves to buy an appropriate chair for their principal.

The first school in Spearfish was a private one opened in the fall of 1878, and taught by Miss Pettigrew in a private house owned by John Ingersoll.

A flourishing academy was in operation in 1879-1882 in Spearfish, under the management of the Congregational Church. It was located in a two-story building, built of lumber, in the south part of town. Lasting about three years, it closed and the building was used for a hospital, according to the recollection of a Minnie Pettigrew Massie, who came to Spearfish in a caravan in June, 1877, as a member of the famous Pettigrew Party.

# chapter VIII

# Boom In Tombstones

Law and order were unknown in the congested mining camps of Deadwood Gulch as thousands thronged into the Northern Hills in 1876. And matters were not much improved even two years later when one-third of the deaths were attributed to violence caused by murder, suicide or accidents. J. S. McClintock, who authored Pioneer Days in the Black Hills, documented 97 homicides that occurred in the first three years of white settlement of the region. The Indians were blamed for most of them (52), but 34 of the victims were murdered by their own kind. An additional 11 lives were abruptly ended by the work of vigilantes. The early-day newspapers carried unsubstantiated accounts of many more violent deaths that McClintock left off his list. No public record was made of the deaths in those early years so an accurate count became impossible.

There is something wonderful about the power of Deadwood two bit whiskey. One drink will quiet a man so that he is perfectly unconscious, and it is no unusual affair to see them lying as good as dead in barnyards and alleys wherever they chance to fall.

B H Weekly Times
June 19, 1877

While the headboards in the cemeteries identified many of the departed, hundreds of others were buried in unmarked, shallow graves near where they met their fate from Indians, highwaymen or disease. Even deaths by natural causes were not accurately recorded or diagnosed. "Mountain fever" seemed a popular diagnosis for anything that did not fall into pneumonia, smallpox, typhoid or diptheria categories. The Black Hills Times on January 6, 1879, listed a total of 96 deaths in 1878 with 66 from natural causes, 16 from murder, 6 from suicide, and 8 from accidents. Based on a population of 12,000 in Lawrence County, this gave a death rate of 8 per 1,000, which the article stated "proves our Black Hills as healthy as any locality in the world" when it is compared with the lowest rate in the 28 largest cities of the U.S. of 11.32 per 1,000." While news items may have convinced many as to the healthy climate of the Hills, there were the other unspoken testimonials of the hundreds who met their fate before their time in the "unhealthy" gold-crazed atmosphere, who might not have agreed. The Sioux City Journal, which had been investigating the subject of violent deaths in Deadwood since its

It takes $4,000 every week (according to one of the fraternity) to keep Deadwood "sports" supplied with "dust".

B H Pioneer
Oct. 14, 1876

Two soiled doves last night came very nearly having a big pow wow because the one had cut the other out of her darling, but no fight ensued because apparently one was afraid, and the other did not dare.

B H Daily Times
Sept. 7, 1877

settlement, reported that "Bismarck almost double discounted us (Deadwood) in this particular during the first two years of its existence."

John F. Finerty, a correspondent with The Chicago Times who visited Deadwood in 1876, reported "a man or two killed every night." Finerty described the Main Street of the mining camp, the dancehalls and dens of vice, the gambler, their women who operated them, the sacks of gold dust on the faro tables and the ever-present guns. To him it was a cruel and crime-ridden country. While liquor was blamed in most instances, the motivating force was truly greed. Claim jumping, gambling stakes, heart stealing, robbery were paramount causes of the crimes, spurred into actuality by liquor and sudden outbursts of anger. "There is something wonderful about the power of Deadwood two-bit whiskey," states the May 18, 1877 issue of the Times. "One drink will quiet a man so that he is perfectly unconscious, and it is no unusual affair to see them lying as good as dead in barnyards and alleys wherever they chance to fall." The June 19 issue of the same newspaper that year carried the following item:

> "The horse railings along Main Street in Deadwood had a novel appearance yesterday. There were jacks by nature and others by circumstance hitched all along the street. Those by circumstance were unable to navigate even when disengaged from the rail. These men were folded up in the greatest number of queerly organized drunks that have yet disgraced the gutters of Deadwood. One fellow was actually sitting on his head, so completely was he doubled up. Another was spread all over three lemon boxes and a keg of nails, with his head under the walk, while his hat was cautiously being examined by a mule that stood tied beside him. A third was balancing himself across a railing in front of the pawn shop, his head and arms on one side, just equalizing his greasy britches on the other, and, to a casual observer, was comfortable and happy. This is the situation of a drunk in Deadwood. No noise, no talk, but as pliable and stuped as a mopcloth and as easily suspended."

However, not all drunks were as subdued as the news article claims. Many of their disputes were brought to a climax in the joints of the mining camps and Main Street of Deadwood was described as the "Mother Lode." The easy work of fleecing was a regular order of business and also resulted in numerous brutalities but few deaths. Family quarrels were common occurrences and while reported in the papers, they had "no comments to make or names to publish because we consider that an outsider has no right to step in between man and wife except to prevent bloodshed or save life." The Times, September 4, 1877, issue continued: "In fact, it is no one else's funeral." The following day, the Times reflected further on such quarrels with the following item:

Deadwood Street, a thoroughfare connecting Sherman and Main of this city, is being blockaded nightly by travelling campers, to the hindrance to travel and the great annoyance to the citizens of that neighborhood. The officers of the law have been called upon to abate this nuisance, that has become almost unbearable to wives and daughters in that immediate vicinity, and their efforts so far seem to have been in vain. Many of these uncouth travelers came there for several days at a time, pitching their tents across the road, feeding their stock close to the windows of residents, and accomodating nature without reserve or the least degree of modesty. This ought not be tolerated and the rights of people in that section ought to be regarded.

B H Daily Times
June 12, 1877

Shovels and picks are gobbled if left remaining without the cabin during the night. Miners should be cautious and guard against these intruders, as mining tools have been for some time very scarce in the market, and held at unusual prices.

B H Daily Times
May 12, 1877

Among the passengers of the Cheyenne stage last evening was a young woman attired in male apparel. She was from Hat Creek, the home of our Robin Hoods, and immediately on arriving here she struck for a bar. In the course of time she got drunk, drunker than a billed owl, and kicked up a considerable of a rumpus on the streets. The matter coming to the ears of Sheriff Bullock, he gobbled her and lodged her in jail, where she is sleeping off her drunk at last accounts. This is the first case of a woman being imprisoned in the Hills. Her examination has not yet been called for hearing, as she is under surgical treatment.

B H Weekly Times
Sept. 23, 1877

"An Eastern man the other day remarked that if black eyes made beauties, then Deadwood contained more pretty women than any other town, provided a man did not object to the shade of one eye being darker than the other. The remark is true to a certain extent. Deadwood does contain many beautiful black-eyed women, whose eyes are black naturally, but these same rarely appear with one eye of a darker shade than the other, because they won't stand any foolishness of that kind. The fact is there are only three or four women in town with black eyes, given them by nature, but the number of women who occasionally carry black eyes is much more numerous."

The hardships, the privations, the absence from loved ones all took their toll on numerous miners who braved the dangers of their journeys to the Hills only to use up their grubstakes without finding the elusive gold.

"Nearly a case of suicide daily for the last three days." That was the terse statement on May 22, 1877, in the Times. It was this same editor who for a lack of better reasons, in the March 15, 1878 edition, blamed all the killings and fiery tempers on the heavy snowstorms that swept the Black Hills region that year and eventually resulted in a flood that did untold damage to Deadwood and surrounding camps. "The air in the Hills is burdened with dire disaster to man these days. Some are struggling, suffering and perhaps perishing in the great snow covering the hills and valleys. Some are being shot down and others attempt self-destruction to shake their earth-born turbulence. It's an awful state of affairs. An old miner, Rumney, was yesterday found dead in his mine in Two Bit Gulch with a bullet hole in his forehead. The proprietor of a Sherman Street lodging house died this morning from a pistol wound and Charles Mauss, a miner on Claim 6 in Whitewood, attempted to shuffle off his mortal coil at Daman and Mauss' Store in Elizabethtown yesterday with a sixteenth part of an ounce of strychnine."

The first felonious death in the Deadwood area occurred July 9, 1876, according to an account in the Black Hills Pioneer carried the next day. John Hinch, Pioche, Nevada, was killed in his diggings, two miles above Deadwood at Gayville. Hinch was watching his partner, a man named Trainor, gambling with a John Carty and a Jerry McCarty and made the mistake of accusing them of cheating. A ruckus was avoided and Hinch went home and went to bed. Hot under the collar at being accused of cheating, Carty and McCarty went to Hinch's cabin, awoke him and asked him to have a drink with them. Hinch, thinking the offer conciliatory, started to get up but went back down with two shots from McCarty's six-gun. Carty then gave him the "old one, two" with a large sheath knife. Hinch died at 10 a.m. July 10 but his killers escaped. They headed out for the Big Horns, leaving half of their claim to the landlady and half to a friend. They were later captured and brought back to Gayville

Just as we were going to press there is considerable excitement in the lower end of Chinatown over the jumping of a mother lode owned and recorded by Jeff Cleveland. At noon Mrs. Elizabeth Lovell proceded to the mine and ordered the men to desist and leave the mine at the same time drawing a six-shooter to enforce her demands. The men left when she started to cut down the windlass and threw the car down the hill. She was arrested by Sheriff Peterson.

B H Daily Times
Jan. 15, 1878

A serious altercation took place at the Brewery Saloon last evening between the proprietor, Mr. Suchard, and Frank Norton of the Fairview Mining Co. Norton, it seems, was in liquor and created some disturbance when the proprietor attacked him with a heavy beer mug, striking him once over the left eye, fracturing the frontal bone of the skull, and again under the same eye, cutting an ugly looking gash severing a small artery.

B H Daily Times
March 14, 1878

A couple of budge-fatigued miners took a position in Stebbins, Wood, and Post's doorway last night to rest and discuss some important question probably the "Problem of Life." While thus engaged one of them leaned back until he was about halfway into the bank, carrying the large glass in the door with him. The persons inside immediately rushed to the door and upon opening it met the fellow who was mad as a pirate. He allowed that if he had the wealth of the bank proprietors he would put glass in the door that would allow a feller to rest agin' it a little without endangering his life by being cut in two. They didn't ask him to pay the damage. He was too mad to talk business.

B H Daily Times
March 14, 1878

to stand trial, where after an hour and a half of deliberation they were found guilty of assault and battery.

Perhaps the best known crime was the murder of Wild Bill Hickok described earlier. The disposition of the case prompted the following letter to the editor of the Black Hills Pioneer on September 9, 1876:

**Anson Tippie was the bartender in Saloon No. 10 when Wild Bill Hickok was killed August 2, 1876.**

**(Centennial Collection)**

> "The murder trials which have taken place in the past eight weeks in our city and vicinity call to mind the necessity of reminding the citizens that we are living in a part of Territory of Dakota comprising the Second Judicial District and we have at present the deputy United States marshall living in our town, ready to perform duties requiring his attention by virtue of his office. Now in case the jury in the late homicide case had returned a verdict of guilty, what would have been the result? Certainly the jury would not have dared to order the punishment at the hands of the citizens prescribed by the law in such cases. It is a well established principle that private parties cannot take the law into their own hands in any way or manner. That being the case, is it not about time that we cease taking these cases into our own hands? Is it not far better that we proceed at once in a manner befitting an intelligent people, if another homicide occurs in our community, which we sincerely hope will not occur? Let the citizen assist, if necessary, in making the arrest and at once thereafter turn the prisoner over to the U.S. deputy marshall. He will take the offender to Yankton, where he will have justice meted out to him in proportion to the crime."

Two more brief notices in the area papers recorded shootings on August 19 and November 25, 1876. The first reported that an Eddie Geist demanded return of money loaned to a Mr. Gay, founder of Gayville, two miles above Deadwood. Angry words were passed and Gay pulled a revolver and shot Geist in the cheek. "At last accounts the ball had not been extracted." A James Farrell was killed in the second incident which occurred in Cyrus Iba's restaurant on November 18. There was an argument at the lunch counter over an account. A man named Cook shot Farrell after firing some heated words back and forth. Cook apparently beat Farrell to the draw but the story doesn't tell the outcome of the investigation.

The first burglary in the Black Hills was about four nights before the reporting issue was printed. It happened at the dwelling of a Mr. Faulkner in Gayville, two miles above Deadwood. The robbers got away with about $150 worth of swag mostly items of jewelry owned by Mrs. Faulkner. The robbery was not discovered until Mr. Faulkner went to put on his shirt the following morning and found his studs, sleeve and collar buttons missing.

B H Daily Times
March 29, 1878

The first attempt at stage robbery in the Black Hills took place near Deadwood on the night of March 25, 1877, resulting in the killing of Johnny Slaughter, driver of the Sidney and Black Hills Stage Coach. The location was in Pluma, between Deadwood and Lead. The attempt was unsuccessful and happened just before law and order was established in the Black Hills. Seth Bullock was appointed sheriff of Lawrence County and he took prompt measures to hunt down the robbers. Lawrence County made it so tough on highwaymen that they changed their base of operations from the Black Hills to less dangerous areas in the flatlands where they could avoid the tight precautions of county lawmen headed by Bullock. In fact, the surveillance of highway robbers was so secure that the first robbery of a stage in Lawrence County proved to be also the last. The homicides of that same year that warranted a story in the newspapers included the following:

The Black Hills Pioneer on February 3, 1877, reported that Harry Varnes was shot and killed in Hanley's Saloon at Gayville following an argument over a card game which had just ended. Angry words were exchanged with N. Hartgrove, a blacksmith, and Varnes raised a chair as he approached him. However, the fight was delayed but resumed later as the men re-entered the saloon with Hartgrove firing through the door and hitting Varnes. Hartgrove, while waiting to see the marshall, was granted permission to leave to consult his lawyer. Naturally, he disappeared and was never again located. The Pioneer on February 17, 1877, reported a fatal affray at Gold Run where the cabin of Mike Gibbons was the scene of an encounter between James Harrington and Jerry Corty, 37, who was killed. They had been drinking and got into a wrangle. Gibbons attempted to pacify them but Harrington's pistol went off, wounding his friend who died hours later. Stray bullets were the cause of two deaths in March of that same year, according to the Black Hills Pioneer. David S. Lunt was struck in the head by a stray bullet from a gun fired by D. T. Smith who was being "secured" by Con Stapleton, marshal. He apparently was recovering until March 22 when he complained of extreme pain in his head and died. Smith was arrested in San Francisco on orders of Sheriff Bullock.

On March 31 in the Senate Saloon, an argument broke out between Thomas Calder and John S. Goddard. Calder shot when Calder grabbed him. The shot went wild, hitting V. Schuester in the back. The victim had not even been a spectator but had his back turned when the shooting broke out, the account explained. Schuester was a part owner in a meat market in South Deadwood. Under the headline, "The Pistol Again," The Times of April 24, 1877, described how at about 2 p.m. the previous day, a party of a half-dozen men, mostly Slavonians, took possession of a lot on the hillside and were putting up a cabin. In a dispute over the land, Dan Obrodovick was killed and John Blair, Samuel F. May and Al Chapman were taken into custody. All three were held for trial, according to the paper, which noted that this was the first homicide under county organization.

"Terrible Outrage at Troy" was the headline for the following item which appeared in the Times on May 16, 1877:

"On Monday night two human fiends broke into the private residence of William Gay, who was absent at the time. The two men first robbed the house, one of them holding a knife over Mrs. Gay, during the pillage. After plundering the house, they made a violent

Since the shooting outbreak on last Saturday night, the sound of a gun strikes holy terror to the hearts of some of the late arrivals of timid pilgrims. One of them was passing through Chinatown yesterday when an innocent slant-eyed John fired his gun at a rat for his noon potpie. Instantly upon the report of the firearm, the tenderfoot let a cry of terror out of him that echoed from the top of White Rocks, and then ran down the street like a scared wolf. In front of Chas. Stacy's house he fell prostrate upon his face in the dust of the road, and thinking the man was at the end of his run, Mr. Stacy approached him, and as he attempted to roll him over, the fellow sprang to his feet and letting another squawk out of him that was truly frightful, lit out down the street with the speed of parole. The last seen of him he had quit cutting up the dust and was laying straight in the air, going like a meteor toward the foothills and the great plains beyond. He will probably never come within a thousand miles of the Hills again, but will devote the balance of his life to rehearsing to all who lend to him their ears, of how he was riddled with five-pound bullets by a gang of a dozen giant road agents sixteen feet high while the innocent sad-eyed John will keep on shooting and eating rats without ever dreaming of being the cause of a story that will tend to intimidate the children of generations to come.

B H Daily Times
Aug. 23, 1879

Pine Street, Lead City, has more first-class rackets, fires, robberies, dog fights, dances, and opium smokers than any street in Lead.

B H Pioneer
May 4, 1878

and outrageous assault upon Mrs. Gay, beat her over the head and kicked her in a cruel and cowardly manner, Mrs. Gay was at the time enceinte. The brutes left her in an insensible condition. No clue to the perpetrators of this diabolical crime has been found."

There seems to be an erroneous conception prevalent among our local prison authorities. They don't seem to consider the county jail a place of punishment for evil doers. One prisoner, we understand, has the freedom of the city at night, spending his time at the Gem theatre and visiting around among friends. A jail should be made a place of punishment, by keeping prisoners locked up, as the law provides, or work them in a chain gang on the streets. A jailer should not allow his sympathies to interfere with his duties.

B H Daily Times
May 5, 1880

The Times on June 19,1877, reported "Deadwood is fast becoming old fashioned. All the drunks, robberies, murders, etc. if any, are being committed in other localities, while Deadwood moves along as if she was an ancient city plat, plotted over with public flowers." For a town only a little over a year old and expecially for a city with Deadwood's reputation, this was an exaggeration of the actual facts.

Less than a week before the Times ran an account on how F. M. Darling and four other men, three weeks prior, had loaded up a couple of wagons at Cheyenne and started for Deadwood. They reached the city without incident but on the way back home they camped at the mouth of Red Canyon for the night. Darling rolled up in his blanket about midnight but heard a noise where the horses were feeding. He looked up to see a pistol barrel pointed at his head. The robber took his $14 in gold dust, watch, rifle and pistol. The robber and his companions took all of Darling's stock of provisions from his wagon, so he and his partner, whom he believed to be an accomplice of the robbers, had nothing to eat until they reached the next ranch. Darling's partner deserted him there.

Another killing was reported in the Times on September 5, 1877. "About noon today news was received here that a man had been shot in Hidden Treasure Gulch in consequence of the difficulties arising from the dispute to the title of the Keats Mine. Immediately our reporter jumped one of the Travis Bro. best horses and started for the scene of the affray, arriving there, he discovered Mr. J. G. Tuttle was lying at the point of death, having been wounded by a bullet which passed through his body, entering the lower portion of the back." As a result of the fatality, 13 were arrested. Court was held in the Bella Union Theatre on September 19 and ten of the 13 were held for the next term of District Court. Another dispute over a mining claim at Central City prompted the shooting of A. W. Adams by John Bryant, according to an account in the Daily Times on October 4, 1877.

Judge Barnes telegraphs to parties in the city that he expects to leave Bismarck for Deadwood on the 18th inst., and "may hold court a few days." That's rather cool, in view of the fact that our jail is already overcrowded with men charged with the greatest crime known to common law, and who are about as anxious to put a quietus to their troubles as the public is to see them receive simple and speedy justice.

B H Daily Times
May 15, 1878

While the Cheyenne road was the scene of most of the stagecoach robberies, no one and no area was sacred as far as the road agents were concerned, as evidenced by the September 5 issue of the Times:

"A dairyman named Pfrunda, who resides in the vicinity of Crook City, while on his road to Deadwood yesterday morning, in his milk wagon, was coolly told to 'stand and deliver' on the Chase and Vollins road about one mile from the toll gate and about four miles from our city, by two masked, armed men, who relieved him of about $60, then quietly walked into the brush and escaped to parts unknown."

The murderer or murderers of Di Hee, a Chinese woman, were never apprehended. The details of her death were described by the Times in its November 28, 1877, issue in this manner: "The corpse lies in the rear of a small shanty in Chinatown, face and blood presenting a disgusting spectacle. An inquest was held this morning, at which several witnesses were examined but no evidence throwing light upon the crime was elicited. Stabbed with a pocket knife and a fractured skull caused by a blow on the head from a hatchet were the causes of her death. Her effects, consisting of three houses and lots on Main Street and considerable personal property were, upon order of the acting coroner, delivered by officer Johnson to one Hong Gee, who claims kinship." A later account notes that three Mongolians, intent on robbery, were blamed but there was not enough evidence for their arrest.

**Famed stagecoach robbers Collins, Berry, Towle and Farrell are pictured in an "amusing" pose at Deadwood in 1876.**
**(Centennial Collection)**

Just a little over a week later under a headline "All For Love," the Times in its December 6, 1877, issue, described the untimely death of Kitty LeRoy, 28, and the suicide of Samuel Curley, 35, well-known faro dealer. The couple had been married only about six months when the tragedy occurred. The newspaper account noted that Kitty was the legal wife of a Capt. E. H. Lewis, Bay City, Michigan, and the mother of a son. She had left her husband in 1872 and turned to a career of dancing. Before coming to Deadwood Kitty had a theatrical engagement in Texas where she became acquainted with an unidentified man with whom she lived for six years, later moving to California. Several months after that they came to Deadwood where they became estranged and she married Curley. The June 12, 1877, Times announced the wedding under the headline "Surprise!"

"Samuel R. Curley, who arrived in this city last week was very quick to set plans to capture one of Deadwood's fairest daughters. He assembled a select party in the green room of the Gem Theatre about 8 o'clock on last Sunday evening and there and then was united in the bonds of lawful wedlock to Miss Kittie (sic) LeRoy, by Justice Baker. We wish the young couple an unbroken line of fruitful and joyous decades."

A Russian, who could not speak English, was shot in the stomach Jan. 29 near the Gold Run Toll Gate on the Lead City Road. He was sitting on a log. When asked who shot him, he said, "Find out for yourself." He died at the hospital and officials believe he possibly shot himself as his clothes had tell-tale powder burns.
B H Daily Times
Jan. 30, 1878

The article further explained that after Curley left for Denver, she resumed her affair with her former consort and word of this had reached Curley in Colorado, prompting his return. Arriving, by way of Cheyenne, Curley alighted from the coach in South Deadwood and walked directly to the Lone Star where he remained for the day. That evening he went upstairs, where Kitty had allegedly borrowed money from her landlady to give to Curley who was to depart on the morning's coach for Cheyenne. They were engaged in low conversation, witnesses reported, when Kitty suddenly uttered a scream which was followed by two pistol shots.

The Pearl Saloon was the scene of another shooting three weeks later but this time the woman had the upper hand. The Times of December 26, 1877, reported that at about 9 a.m. in the Main Street saloon, Edward Trimpy engaged in a dispute about a $10 bill which Kitty Sparrow, better known as "Tricks," declared he had taken. He denied the charge and threatened to "bang" the girl should she repeat it. She ignored his threats, stepped behind the bar and displayed a five-shooter "bull dog," hoping to check his hostile demonstrations. He started after her and she fired with the bullet going through to the back of his head where it lodged. Doctors deemed it unexpedient to endeavor to extract it. "Tricks" was taken into custody. She had been a resident of Deadwood since its founding and previously lived a "public life" in Montana. Trimpy was a good natured inoffensive sort of person who would not be guilty of assault, particularly upon a woman, unless he was under the influence of liquor — and he was that morning. He exonerated her by saying she acted purely in self defense and the incident terminated in "restoration of the best of friendship."

The highly publicized murder of Kitty LeRoy warranted another article on January 16, 1878, in the Times which claimed that "disembodied spirits were visiting the scene of the death and suicide in the Lone Star Building." It noted that the Lone Star gained its first notoriety from the suicide, by poisoning, of a woman of ill repute early in the spring. A reporter investigating the haunted area of the double phantoms, "who are seen to tread the stairs where once they reclined in the flesh and linger o'er places where they reclined in loving embrace, and finally melted away into the shadows of the night as peacefully as their bodies' souls seem to have done when the fatal bullets brought death and the grave to each."

Deadwood had no exclusive on violence as the Times reported a killing at Lead City on February 26, 1878, as follows:

"About 4 p.m. Monday, 25th, John McTigue was shot by Ben Wadsworth and died about 5:30 o'clock. His wife and four children now residing at Gold Hill, Nevada. McTigue settled labor troubles for mines." The fatal fracas developed when Leahy's lot was jumped by Ben Wadsworth and he came to McTigue for help. On Main Street, near a pile of wood, Wadsworth fired three times at McTigue with a double-barrelled shotgun loaded with navy balls. Three entered McTigue's body. The case was a long one and Judge C. E. Barker ruled Wadsworth was justified in shooting McTigue as Leahy had secured the help of McTigue and went after Wadsworth fully armed. Just about the time the readers of these early-day gun slingings got to feeling sorry for McTigue, leaving a wife and four kids, this item appeared as a letter to the editor from Santa Reasa, California, in the June 8, 1878, issue of the Times:

"Please inform me in as short a time as possible what Wadsworth that is to be hung in Deadwood City? I fear he is a brother of mine. Please tell me what kind of a looking man he is and where he is from."

The Times went on to report "The above note was referred to us with the request 'Please Answer.' There are no less than fifty or sixty villains in this camp who deserve hanging, as general principles, but we know of no one by the name of Wadsworth who is in for it. A young man named Ben Wadsworth killed McTigue early last spring, but was acquitted of the offense on the ground that he had done a good job. That's all we know about it. He looks like Gen. Grant, excepting his whiskers. Don't know where he came from."

On February 6, 1878, the Times reported John McTigue's house on Main Street in Lead had been stolen. The article went on: "I have heard of horse, sheep stealing, stealing from the public treasury, and before the war, stealing niggers, also an ex-Governor of Nevada stealing a set of circular saws and engine, but I never heard of stealing a house from a public street before, and the parties evidently tried to steal the lot too, as there was a large hole on one corner where I suppose they tried to place a lever to raise the lot."

As the period of restlessness was drawing to an end, accounts of murders appeared less frequently in the newspapers of the area — only about one every three months. But the columns continued to be heavy with mining claim troubles and misdemeanors.

As the Daily Times on January 25, 1879, put it: "The shot-gun policy is getting played out in this country and it is thought that a little simple justice meted out to such shooters will have a very salutory effect." The statement followed the announcement that Alex Frankenberg, shot a few days previous on the grade of the new Homestake mill, had died. Angus McMasters, implicated in the homicide and released on bond of $5,000, was rearrested after Frankenberg's death.

One of the last felonies of the four-year period was the death of C. W. Tappan, proprietor of the Sherman Street lodging house in Deadwood, which was characteristic of the minor irritants which so often led to murder in those days. The fatal argument all started over whether Tappan had springs in his beds. Hunt wanted his money back and Tappan tried to get him to leave peaceably but Hunt was hell-bent to argue over the bad sleeping conditions and finally shot Tappan. Hunt was later found guilty of murder after Tappan died following an operation five hours later.

Interfering in the affairs of others could also be a fatal mistake in the violence-prone gulch. Mrs. Minnie Callison, described as the first school teacher in the gulch, was found brutally murdered in her Deadwood home in 1879. The crime was blamed on Martin Couck,

SYNDICATE HOTEL TODAY
Chas. Knight, proprietor

The following bill of fare, the choicest ever served in this city, will be given to the public at the Syndicate hotel, at dinner today. Dinner 50 cents. The public is cordially invited to take dinner today, between 12:30 and 3 o'clock.

BILL OF FARE

Relishes
Celery, Chowchow, Queen Olives
Dill Pickles
New York Counts

Soups
Consomme of Chicken, a la Printanieas,
Bouillion auquineties.

Remotes
Ham, Champagne sauce
Beef,

---

Prime beef
Fricassee of Veal, brown sauce
Leg of Mutton, currant jelly
Young turkey, celery ala cream

Entrees
Spring Lamb chops
Monte Carlo Calves brains,
Salpicon of Mushrooms, sur cossolette
Apple dumplings with cream
Petit polet, ring puff borders

Vegetables
Steamed potatoes, Mashed, Escalloped
Tomatoes, Sugar corn

Salads
Chicken on mayonnaise,
Shrimp with French dressing

Desserts and Sweets
Peach Pie, Vanilla Custard,
Mince Pie, Roman Punch
New York Ice Cream
Merangues, a la cream
Valauvents, Maderia jelly
Angel Food Pound Fruit

Assorted Fruits
Mixed Nuts Eden Cheese
Coffee Tea Milk

Wild Bill Hickok was buried high on the side of the mountain looking down on Deadwood below. His best friend, Colorado Charley Utter stands beside the newly-dug grave. Wild Bill was killed by Jack McCall in Saloon No. 10 on August 2, 1876. He was holding the "Dead Man's Hand" of black aces and eights when shot.

(Centennial Collection)

operator of the Monte Verde Saloon, and Mrs. Mark V. Boughton was indicted as a co-conspirator. Mrs. Callison had apparently learned that Couck and Mrs. Boughton were planning to run off together and she threatened to inform the deceived husband, a prominent citizen of the gulch and the man who brought the first herd of cattle into the region. But her mouth was shut permanently before she could tattle. Couck was convicted of the murder, but Mrs. Boughton was acquitted. The bar owner was later released from prison on the basis of improper evidence accepted at his trial, and he returned to Deadwood to proclaim his innocence. Some years later, however, he was sentenced to hang in New Mexico for another killing and he reportedly confessed on the gallows that he had also "done in" Mrs. Callison. The sordid circumstances surrounding the killing of the school teacher also led to the divorce of the Boughtons.

Crimes committed in the Black Hills prior to extinguishment of Indian title to the region in February 1877 either went unpunished or were avenged by vigilante action. The number of violent deaths dropped somewhat after formal organization of the county and the establishment of legal courts. But not much!

Driving out of Lead today, this road, better known by the natives as "Poorman Hill" is now Glendale Drive. This early-day photo shows these pioneer women and their dog walking past two wood-enclosed graves of white men killed by Indians in 1876.

(Centennial Collection)

# chapter IX

# Hungry For Government

Lawrence County was named after Colonel John Lawrence, member of the Dakota Territorial Legislature in 1875. Lawrence County, Dakota Territory, was organized in 1877.
(L. C. Court House)

Although the Black Hills were still part of the Great Sioux Reservation at the time, and closed to white settlement, the Dakota Territorial Legislature created three counties there in 1875. It did so with the obvious expectation that Indian title to the region would ultimately be extinguished. The new counties were named Custer, Pennington and Lawrence — Custer for the famous soldier whose expedition into the Indian reserve had precipitated the Black Hills gold rush, Pennington for John L. Pennington, territorial Governor 1875-78, and Lawrence for John Lawrence, a Yankton legislator and political intimate of the Governor. The three counties extended eastward from the Wyoming Territory border between the south and north forks of the Cheyenne River. Custer County, where the initial gold discovery had been made, was the southernmost while Lawrence, where the gold boom had centered in Deadwood Gulch, was the northernmost. Pennington County was sandwiched between the other two and stretched into the prairieland east of the Hills. The Act creating these counties, however, merely established their geographic boundaries; it did not provide for their formal organization.

Gov. Pennington, in response to repeated appeals from Black Hills citizens for organizing the three paper counties, asked the federal government about the propriety of such proposals in August of 1876. Negotiations with the Sioux for cession of the region had not yet been completed at the time and the Governor received a negative response. "The white inhabitants of the Black Hills," the Secretary of the Interior reminded the Governor on August 24, "are there not only without authority of law, but in actual violation of law, and so long as that section of country is set apart as an Indian reservation, it would be manifestly improper and unlawful to authorize the setting up therein of any form of civil government for citizens of the United States." Thus self-government was the only avenue open to the Black Hills trespassers in the beginning, and they did the best they could without official sanction of their efforts.

How Uncle Sam can assert that we are here in the Black Hills 'in violation of law' while he at the same time has a Collector in Deadwood City collecting Federal taxes, is a puzzler. But we won't grumble much over the incomprehensible theory, if he will continue to practically ignore it himself. Having now extended the civil functions over us, so far as the revenue department is concerned, we hope he will be consistent with himself, and give us postal routes and regular court sessions without delay.

B H Pioneer
July 8, 1876

Judge William G. Hollins' office on corner of Lee and Main, was first attorney in the Hills, having wended his way here in January, '76.

B H Pioneer
March 24, 1877

Sherman Street is destined to be the principal street of the city. It has the valley for a street of over a mile in length on the level.

B H Daily Times
May 18, 1877

Col. John Lawrence, our county treasurer, informs us that liquor licenses are being pretty generally paid promptly, but a few are still in arrears, and this lays them liable to prosecution for selling liquor without a license.

B H Daily Times
May 24, 1877

**The only known picture of "Crooked-Nose" Jack McCall who sneaked up behind Wild Bill Hickok as he was playing poker in Saloon No. 10 in Deadwood and shot him in the back of the head. McCall was freed by a miner's jury but was later tried for the shooting and was found guilty. He was hung and buried in Yankton, South Dakota.**

**(Courtesy of Old Style Saloon No. 10)**

Included among the thousands of people who were pouring into the Deadwood area in early 1876 were many men who were politically experienced in the running of mining districts and camps. They realized the value of having a well-established government — both for their own advantage and for that of the other Deadwood and Northern Black Hills residents. As soon as white settlers moved into Deadwood Gulch, they began to organize themselves in an effort to govern their life and work in the gulch. On April 28, 1876, several prospectors platted early Deadwood (which did not include all of the current town), but the government of the people was non-existent until the threat of a smallpox epidemic encouraged them to organize. In the spring of 1876 a gambler from Cheyenne brought smallpox to the Deadwood area. Miners called a meeting at Saloon Number 10 and formed a Board of Health to deal with the imminent danger of an epidemic. The commissioners of the board set up a pesthouse to care for smallpox victims, and a large scale spread of the disease was averted. However, the miners recognized that a governing body was needed to at least settle claim disputes and to keep the streets clear of claim jumpers. The Board of Health soon became a Board of Streets also and the commissioners tackled the tasks of keeping side streets clear of claims, settling disputes, and trying murders.

The need for some form of organized government was the subject of an editorial in the first issue of the Black Hills Pioneer on June 8, 1876: "A community as large as this should certainly have some organization, and be governed by a common sense code of laws, agreeable to the majority of the people." Even in a gold rush it was necessary for there to be some fixed rules in order to avoid total chaos. By the time Deadwood was established there was considerable experience to draw upon from the gold camps of California and elsewhere. Most important was the establishment of a procedure for coping with major crimes. The establishment of an impromptu mining district provided a framework for such matters. When a crime of sufficient importance was committed in the area, the miners would either sit in a group as a jury or elect a judge and jury to try the case. The latter procedure was used in Deadwood to handle such cases as the murder of Wild Bill Hickok by Jack McCall.

The miners' court that tried McCall, to the astonishment of the eyewitnesses to the crime, returned a verdict of "not guilty." The remarkable finding, in light of the evidence, may have been based, at least in part, on acceptance of the defendant's self-serving testimony — which later proved to be false. McCall claimed he had justifiably avenged the death of a brother, whom Wild Bill had killed before coming to the Hills, when he fatally shot the famous gunfighter. It was a believable story, considering the victim's well-known reputation, but no effort was made to substantiate it. A more likely motive for the unexpected verdict was a recognition among the jurors that the court was functioning without the authority of law. The jurors probably preferred not to risk being later held accountable for any punishment that might result from a conviction. At any rate, McCall wasted no time in getting out of Deadwood after the unofficial trial, knowing full well that justice had not been fulfilled.

It became clear during the fall of 1876 that a more permanent government was necessary for the ever-increasing population of Deadwood. On September 5, 1876, an election was held to vote for or against town organization. The vote was 1135 for organization and 57 against. At this point the Board of Health and Streets was disbanded and a mayor and five councilmen were elected. E. B. Farnum became mayor and the councilmen were Sol Star, A. P. Carter, Kellar Kurtz, C. H. Philbrook, and Joseph Miller. According to one account, Con Stapleton was elected marshal but another source claimed that he was appointed by Mayor Farnum and was "a tin horn gambler" and no-good character from Montana.

In any case the Council met and adopted several ordinances which were the first laws for Lawrence County even though white settlers and their government were still illegal in the Black Hills. The first ordinance passed provided for revenue to run the city. Anyone engaged in a business enterprise was to be licensed and charged for the license. In late 1876, 172 businesses were liable for licensing. Among these were 27 saloons, 13 places of amusement, and one milliner. Hawkers and peddlers, according to a later ordinance, were required to purchase licenses for $25 that were good for three months. Another ordinance prohibited the burning of hay, straw, or other combustible in streets or alleys. Discharging of fireworks or firearms without permission was also forbidden but "this section is not destined to interfere with mining interests," a newspaper of the day reported. Since everyone could claim "mining interests," this ordinance probably did little to reduce the use of guns in Deadwood. The mayor of Deadwood was also the municipal judge. Farnum held court in the back room of his grocery store, and those who required jailing were placed in an abandoned tunnel in the mountainside. For his efforts, Mayor Farnum earned $100 per year as mayor and judge.

Lead's city government started in a similar fashion. The miners of the Gold Run area needed a form of organization to take care of problems brought by the large number of prospectors in the gulch. On February 21, 1876, a dozen miners met and organized the Summit Mining District. Thomas E. Carey was named recorder and got the discovery claim of 300 feet since he was the first prospector to find gold in Gold Run Creek. The district handled matters pertaining to the size of mining claims, recordings and transfer of claims, but for other matters such as ownership and sale of lots a township government was needed.

Frawley, the lawyer, returned yesterday after a hard ride. Brown, the fellow who was arrested and bound over on a charge of bigamy a month ago, jumped his bonds Monday, and Mr. Frawley went in pursuit Thursday and overtook him 30 miles below the crossing of the Cheyenne. The first day out he rode over 100 miles without rest. That's pretty good for a delicate lawyer.

B H Daily Times
Sept. 22, 1877

Deadwood has not always been in South Dakota. For a very short time, it was in Wyoming. A U. S. surveying party was sent out on July 24, 1877 to establish the boundary between Dakota and Wyoming, according to George W. Kingsbury, in Vol. 1, "Dakota Territory." Kingsbury said, "The survey . . . placed the mining camps of Deadwood, Gap City, Central, Golden Gate, Lead City, Custer, Rapid, Sheridan, Golden, Hayward, Castleton, Hillyer and Crook City in Dakota. Deadwood was located 22 miles east of the boundary line. The mining camps of Sand, Iron and Potato Creeks were in Wyoming.

On Feb. 10, 1877, however, the Legislative Assembly of the Territory of Dakota had approved an Act defining the boundaries of certain counties in the Black Hills. Based on altitude and longitude and metes and bounds descriptions, this placed western boundaries of Lawrence, Custer and Pennington counties at the Wyoming line, and ordered modification and correction of the boundaries of Lawrence and Custer. This was done. County officials were chosen shortly thereafter.

The Backlog
Camille Yuill

**Just a scattering of houses and primitive cabins formed the rare photo of Lead in 1876 before the town mushroomed into a great gold-mining metropolis.**
**(Centennial Collection)**

Mrs. J. J. Finn, Lead, holds a deed to her home located at 15 Park Avenue, which substantiates the location of the early-day road between Lead and Deadwood. The deed, in describing the property, stated . . . 80 feet by 150 feet on the southerly side of the road leading from Lead City to Deadwood . . . The date of the certificate was Oct. 1, 1889. It is believed that the old trail ran up Park Avenue and probably out past the Lead city dump and the old area known as "Cow Flats."

Bert Livingston, the first telephone owner and operator in the Black Hills, yesterday paid a visit to his old stomping grounds, Central City and, it is said, became lost while there. However that may be, he found a different Central City than that of 1877 and 1879 when it was the largest camp in the Hills, and the liveliest in all the west, with every foot of Deadwood gulch occupied or being worked from where the county hospital now stands to a point beyond the mouth of Poorman gulch and all the side gulches in that distance sheltering the habitations of miners, when there were sixteen stamp mills running on custom ore, twenty three saloons and whiskey 25 cents a drink.
Deadwood Pioneer Times
June 21, 1924

A townsite was laid out on the ground between the north and south forks of Gold Run Creek and south of the Homestake and Golden Star mines. On July 10, 1876, the brush was cut, lines were run and lots were staked. The next day the founding fathers met at the later intersection of Main and Mill Streets to organize a government. The new town was named Lead City and two officers were elected — Robert Charles "Smoky" Jones as secretary and James D. Coffin as city recorder. No other officers were chosen since the miners felt that, inasmuch as any civic acts would be without legal status, it would be better to let local unwritten mining laws govern disputes. The miners in Lead were either more scrupulous or more timid than those in Deadwood.

The lots were voted to be 50 by 100 feet without alleys in the rear, and no person could hold more than two lots at one time. All lots were recorded for a fee of $1.25 per lot, and the occupant had 60 days to make improvements. Many people built 25-foot-wide buildings and sold the other half of their lot, which accounts for the narrow frontages that later became a trademark of Lead. The streets laid out at that time were Mill, Bleeker, Gold, Wall, Siever, Galena, Pine, Main, and Saunders. The last street, running parallel with Main, was in existence for only a short time before it was taken over for buildings and other uses. There is not complete agreement that Lead City was the first town in the Gold Run Creek area. A few early sources claim that Washington was laid out in February, 1876, and was, therefore, the first townsite. They also state that Golden, next to Washington, was platted about the same time by a Von Bodingen under P. A. Gushurst's directions.

Indian relinquishment of the Black Hills came in October of 1876 when negotiations with the Sioux were finally concluded, opening the way to lawful settlement and legal organization of the three counties there. The agreement, which included the country between the south and north forks of the Cheyenne River, embracing the entire Black Hills, was hastened by a coercive stipulation imposed by the U.S. Congress. It provided that no more rations would be issued to the Sioux under the terms of the Laramie Treaty unless they gave up the Black Hills. It was an unconsciable condition, but it worked. The Indians simply could not continue to subsist for themselves in a region already occupied by thousands of whites. However, the agreement did not become effective until ratified by Congress and signed by the President, and that did not occur until February 28, 1877.

Meanwhile, confident of ratification, the law, if not order, quickly came to Deadwood Gulch on the heels of the long-delayed cession. The first legal court in the Black Hills opened at Sheridan in October

An article advocates the change of court to Deadwood from Rapid City due to the fact that nine tenths of the cases involve people and property located in Lawrence County. Another article on the same page advocates definite action to induce the Legislature to amend the law so that one term of the Supreme Court should be held each year at Deadwood.

B H Daily Times
Jan. 15, 1879

**Rand & McNally & Co. map shows Lawrence County before its division and the establishment of Meade County.**

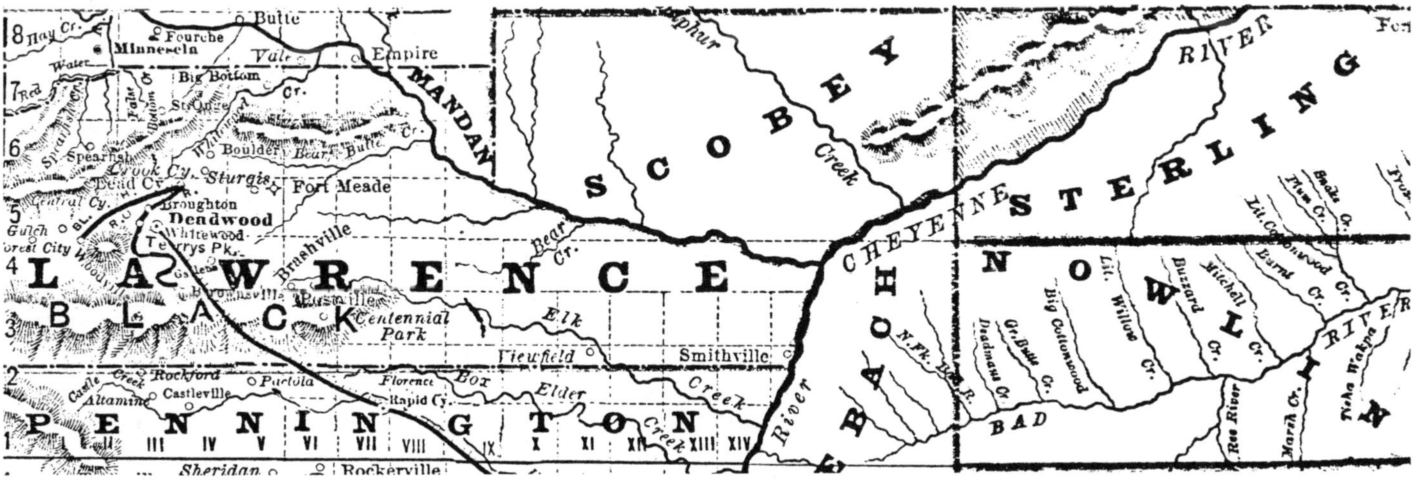

of 1876, but quickly shifted its fall term to Deadwood where a greater number of cases were awaiting adjudication. It convened a grand jury there on October 9 with Hon. G. G. Bennett, one of three territorial judges also appointed to serve as a federal district judge, presiding. The Black Hills Times described the opening session this way:

"The 'Bonanza' (a bar located on Lee Street) by far the most suitable, and best located building for the purpose, in the city, is well arranged, being spacious, light and having ample accomodations upstairs for the grand jury, and a convenient room upon the first floor for petit jurors. The appearance of faro, nut-shell and vingtum tables was a little incongruous at first, but the novelty soon wore away and court settled down to legitimate business by swearing in J. C. Miller and Noah Severs as bailiffs."

Attorney credentials were acknowledged, including W. H. Parker whose son Francis J. Parker, long practiced law in Deadwood, too. The roll of grand jurors was called and included J. B. Pearson, the miner credited with panning out the first gold in Deadwood Gulch in 1875, starting the frenzied gold rush to the area. The opening story stated that "Counsel for prisoners desired the presence of their clients so that they could have an opportunity to challenge the grand jurors. Accordingly the jury dismissed until 1:30 o'clock. Great difficulty was experienced in securing a petit jury, many offering pleas of sickness, either themselves or friends in their care."

In the lengthy news story it was pointed out that "the charge of the court was short and oral. It called attention to the oath taken, and declared that a violation of it was one of the highest crimes known to the law. Attention was directed to the law respecting liquor traffic, gambling, and prostitution, violation of which must go unpunished unless the principals are present by the grand jury."

While no major case came out of this initial session, an historically famous case was being resolved by the U. S. District Court at the territorial capital in Yankton that same month. Jack McCall, the slayer of Wild Bill, had bragged about his infamous deed in a saloon at Cheyenne where he was arrested by a U.S. Marshal and taken to Yankton for trial. He was indicted for murder by the grand jury there on October 18, 1876, and tried under the indictment. The jury, unencumbered by doubts of jurisdiction, returned a verdict of "guilty" on December 6. He was sentenced to hang on January 3, 1877, but appealed to the Territorial Supreme Court, basing his appeal on the grounds that the murder had taken place on an Indian reservation outside the jurisdiction of the court. But the appeal court did not waste much time on the case, affirming the judgment of the district court on January 19, 1877. McCall was hanged at Yankton at 10:15 a.m. on March 1, and justice was belatedly but conclusively served.

To amend chapter 10 of the political code. The bill was defeated by a vote of ayes 5, noes 7. It provides for the holding of a term of the Supreme Court at the city of Deadwood.

B H Daily Times
Feb. 22, 1879

The transfer of the United States Court to Deadwood is a measure that will promote the public interests and is a subject of local pride.

B H Daily Times
Feb. 22, 1879

Denver Times editorial reprint:
One of the queer features of the Black Hills emigration is the large number of unmarried females who are going there. There would seem too much prematureness in their going to the Hills, for the Black Hillers will not be prepared to marry yet a while, and surely these females don't expect to go into the panning-out business. In reply the Daily Times editor said: "So Mr. Times, you had better let them come and assist us in our population, for we are going to be an independent Territory very soon and will then want assistance in the way of population, to help on to Statehood.

B H Daily Times
April 25, 1877

Mark Twain was at the Pioneer Office yesterday.

B H Pioneer
June 26, 1877

While the law had come to the Black Hills, order had not. There was still the matter of formal organization to be resolved. Deadwood residents elected Dr. Carl W. Meyer, leader of the Democrats of the Black Hills, and General A. R. Z. Dawson, a Republican, as delegates to the Territorial Assembly in the fall of 1876 to push for county organization and to "prevent the 'greedy capitalists' from securing legislation in Yankton which would establish a monopoly over the water rights in the Hills." Water was extremely important to mining operations and if any one group controlled the water rights, it could easily control mining as well.

A German who died and was buried in the old cemetery on the hill two years ago, was interred a few days since, boiled down to his bones and sent back to his friends in the old country. The job of reducing him was performed by a couple of men inexperienced in that kind of business, and the trouble they had in doing the work is fearful to relate. They consumed an even gallon of whiskey before they got through.

B H Daily Times
Jan. 6, 1879

The Yankton legislators in February of 1877 provided for the organization of the three counties established earlier. In doing so they rebounded Lawrence County by cutting off the southern part to give to Pennington County and extending the eastern boundary further eastward. This bill also stated how the county government would be organized.

In March of 1877 Gov. Pennington appointed for Lawrence County three commissioners: one from Yankton, one from Deadwood, and one from Crook City. He also appointed men to fill the other offices, including Seth Bullock for Sheriff, James A. Hand as Register of Deeds, for Probate Judge, Charles E. Hanrahan, and Assessor, William James. There soon developed a great furor over Gov. Pennington's appointments. Since there had always been distrust between Black Hills residents and the Dakota Territory government, the Deadwood settlers saw this action as one more example of the "Yankton ring" trying to take advantage of the Hills. Their anger increased when the three commissioners voted to make Crook City, a much smaller town than Deadwood, the county seat. Accusations of bribery spread, and the commissioners, after holding one meeting in Crook City, were "persuaded" to move the county seat to Deadwood.

It must be a consolation to the citizens of Crook City for them to know they cast the greater part of their vote "For County Seat" for Deadwood. There were 202 ballots voted for county seat, of which 31 were for the "Dividing Line," etc. (which was virtually our only competitor) the balance, 171 cast for other places, Central etc, which, had they been cast for "Dividing Line," would have been the only way in which Crook could have thrown against us and thus vent their spite which was with them, rule or ruin. Friends at Crook, thanks for small favors.

B H Daily Times
Nov. 10, 1877

However, the problem of appointees themselves remained. Judge Bennett, the federal judge for the district, held that the appointments were illegal and, therefore, the offices were vacant, and elections should take place as soon as possible. The newly-elected officials would hold office until January, 1879. The campaign that fall of 1877 was a heated and exciting one. Dr. Meyer led the Democrats and Seth Bullock headed the "People's Party." (The word "Republican" was unpopular because it was associated with Yankton control.) Charges of bribery and illegal votes were rife on both sides, but largely because Democrats outnumbered Republicans, the Democrats took most offices in the election held November 5, 1877.

The newly-elected officials were ready to take up their duties but a new problem cropped up. Some people, including the old appointed officials, felt the newly-elected ones shouldn't take office

Lawrence County has more county commissioners than any county in the territory. The old board continues to transact business, and the new board goes on as though there was no old board. In the new board's proceedings carried in the Daily Times that same day, the county commissioners "instructed the county clerk to not recognize the old board." One of the first tasks, the editor suggested that the new board, in the Jan. 11 issue, was to remove the bodies from the old grave yard to the new one.

B H Daily Times
Jan. 9, 1879

Daily Times, Feb. 3, 1879: A bill was introduced in the Legislature at Yankton with a petition of 500 signatures to "divide the county," Crook and Spearfish from the rest of the county, due to refusal to recognize old board of commissioners.

Judge G. C. Moody declares the legality of the election of the new board of commissioners.
B H Daily Times
Jan. 28, 1879

Union Park and Brewery of South Deadwood . . . The finest resort in the Black Hills! Brass band concert every Sunday afternoon. Special arrangement can be made for picnics and private parties. The Park is furnished with a fine dancing platform. Fred Heime, Proprietor.

B H Daily Times
Sept. 3, 1877

. . . A change of programme at the Gem Theater almost every evening. The popularity of this place of amusement is increasing daily. Last night a full house greeted performers with loud applause.

B H Daily Times
Sept. 3, 1877

until the first Monday of January, 1878. Others felt they should assume their responsibilities immediately since Judge Bennett had declared the positions technically vacant. The new and old county commissioners and sheriffs solved the problem by operating simultaneously, but separately, and presumably ignored each other's decisions and transactions. However, the other old officials didn't fare so well. When the new Register of Deeds, Assessor, Probate Judge, etc., went to the courthouse to move in and were refused by the old appointees, the new officials bodily threw the old ones out and settled themselves in the courthouse. The old Register of Deeds, James A. Hand, took the matter to court, but Judge Bennett, and subsequently the Territorial Supreme Court, upheld the right of the elected officials to take over immediately.

Formal organization of the county also legalized the town governments set up by the early residents of the gulch. The miners decided in 1877 to expand Lead City to include both Washington and Golden as well as some other areas. J. D. McIntyre, one of the founding fathers, requested the U. S. Congress to issue a patent for Lead City, a step towards incorporation. In late 1877 the federal government did give Lead a townsite patent, and problems cropped up immediately. Shortly after issuance of the townsite patent, quartz miners discovered that the Homestake vein ran right under the patented area. Federal law forbade townsites on mineral-bearing land, so the mineral claimants brought suit to have the townsite patent revoked. A legal struggle followed which wasn't resolved until 1892 when the federal court decided that mineral claimants would be given patents but would allow townsite claimants title to the surface land.

In 1877 the miners realized the unwritten mining camp laws were not sufficient to settle disputes which came up more often as the city grew. Therefore, they appointed three men as a board of arbitration to settle the usual arguments that developed in all frontier towns — claim jumping, road blocking, etc. One of the biggest drawbacks was the lack of building locations. A big Irishman by the name of A. H. McTeage decided to take matters into his own hands. He erected a cabin right in the middle of Bleeker Street, marked his boundaries with a line of flour, and dared anyone to violate the lines of his domain. Some other people thought he had a good idea and jumped portions of Pine and Bleeker Streets.

However, the more level-headed citizens knew that the town needed streets, and Gushurst came to talk sense to the claim-jumping Irishman. Shortly afterwards, a warrant was issued against McTeage, and he was taken into custody by the Lawrence County Sheriff. The cabin was blown up with dynamite. This ended most of the street jumping but there was another incident of a woman who jumped a claim on the east end of Pine where she pitched her tent. A committee came to talk with her but she brandished such a wicked looking butcher knife that the callers decided withdrawal was the most prudent course of action. She was not bothered from then on, and Pine Street, which no longer exists, stopped at her door.

Such picayune local matters, however, were overshadowed by a serious movement to organize the Black Hills as an entirely new Territory in 1877. The revolutionary idea had been proposed in the Black Hills Pioneer the previous November when suspicions on how the Territorial Legislature would organize the region were rampant. The Pioneer introduced the issue this way:

> "We want a separate and distinct territory which shall comprise all the mineral lands of the Black Hills, a territory which inside of one year will, from the present indication, be entitled to state organization and positive instead of negative representation in the Congress of the United States. The future of such a state can only be speculated upon, but we think, yes, feel assured that it would be a bright particular star in the American constellation."

On April 21, 1877, a convention was held at Deadwood to discuss the matter, and adopted a resolution appointing Senator Chaffee of Colorado and Representatives McGinnis of Montana and Corlett of Wyoming, as "accredited representatives" to secure territorial organization. But there were varied feelings, and on May 22 the following appeared: "The Custer City Herald says that the outcry against Governor Pennington and delegate Kidder and all the strength which the movement for a new Territory possesses, comes from Deadwood, and that other portions of the Hills have no sympathy whatever with Deadwood."

"The Herald man is again wrong about the strength all coming from Deadwood. At the convention Saturday last, nine-elevenths of the entire body were from abroad. The convention consisted of 110 members of which only 20 were from Deadwood."

On May 10, 1877, the Territorial Convention elected H. C. Walker and Dr. C. W. Meyer delegates to Congress in interest of the new territory, to be named "Lincoln." These men agreed to defray their own expenses on the condition that they be appointed agents on Territorial organization. But they "renigged" on their promise. Dr. Meyer later resigned, citing professional duties that interferred with his participation.

The Yankton Press assailed the movement in a vigorous manner, but indiscreetly made the following confession: "The development of the mineral resources of the Black Hills are just what Dakota has been waiting for the last sixteen years in order to secure sufficient population to enable her to ask admission as a State. This has now been accomplished, and Congress can see that the vast agricultural

Considerable trouble is being had with Indians in and around Rapid City . . . Three men were killed on Thursday of last week and two more on Saturday.

B H Pioneer
**Sept. 2, 1876**

The bar is supplied with the choicest brands of wine, liquors, cigars, St. Louis Beer, and all first class articles in our line. Call and see for yourselves. "The Place," next door to the Cheyenne Stage Office.

B H Daily Times
**Sept. 5, 1877**

Newton & Co., on Main Street, are having a fine billiard hall built in the rear and adjacent of their establishment.

B H Daily Times
**Sept. 6, 1877**

ASSIGNEE SALE — Will be sold . . . a bankrupt stock of goods consisting of clothing, hats, caps, boots, shoes, watches and jewelry, guns, pistols, tobacco, cigars, etc. All goods new and first class . . .

B H Daily Times
**Jan. 4, 1878**

section of Southeastern Dakota, with the rapidly growing mineral resources of the Black Hills, give to Dakota inducements that will soon attract to her borders a million of people."

The Black Hills Daily Times published this quote November 15, 1877, and editorialized: "If that isn't an expression of unadulterated selfishness, what is it? Not a word to offset our claims; not a word in refutation of the many complaints preferred by the people of the Hills against the miserable government, which hundreds of miles from this locality, has meted out laws . . . antagonistic to our every interest . . . "

At the request of some of my heaviest debtors, I will postpone my black list until next Monday, the 14th of January. J. Gandolph.

B H Daily Times
Jan. 9, 1878

The March 26, 1878, issue of the Daily Times quotes from the Denver Tribune of March 22: "Senator Chaffee has charge of the bill creating the new Territory of Lincoln out of the Black Hills country. And he seems determined to secure speedy and favorable action upon it. There is already a large population in that section, and it promises to soon become one of the chief centers of population of the far west. Hence its claims to a separate government are not to be ignored. Home rule is as good a principle for the west as for the south."

Our merchants are thinking seriously of putting the price of gold dust down to $17 per ounce. This action is necessitated from the fact that the banks will allow only $17.10 for dust after it has been cleaned.

B H Daily Times
Jan. 27, 1878

Lobbyists for the Union Pacific also backed the movement. But nothing came of all the attempts to establish the Territory of Lincoln.

The newspapers of Deadwood and Rapid City, which seemed to delight in baiting each other, renewed interest in political matters among their readers in 1879. This time the issue was the location of the U.S. District Court of the First Judicial District. It had been placed at Rapid City despite Deadwood's larger population, but a bill introduced in the Territorial Council that winter proposed switching its location. Deadwood's Daily Times on February 10, 1879, editorialized on the controversy:

A couple of thoroughbred Maltese cats was among the freight on the Bismarck stage last night.

B H Weekly Times
Jan. 27, 1878

> "The Rapid City Journal makes a very foolish statement when it asserts that $5,000 was sent from Deadwood to Yankton to secure the passage of the bill to remove the United States Court from Rapid City to Deadwood. The fact is, the matter excited very little attention here, and excepting a few members of the bar, probably no effort was made in its favor, though everybody who knows anything of the court business, knows very well four fifths of it comes from this county. If the future of Rapid City depends upon the holding of the United States Court at that place, its permanency and development will be as precarious and uncertain as Sheridan, where the first term was held."

A Mr. Dorr Heffleman of Central City, D. T., issued one dollar notes; questioned by the Times in connection with the daily handling of notes, our thoughts recurring back to the days of the wild-cat banks of 1860.

B H Weekly Times
Jan. 27, 1878

Despite the infighting, law and order were well established in the Black Hills by 1879. In fact, U.S. troops were permanently stationed there by then to assure that the citizenry could wrestle with the mundane problems of self-government without interference from the previous Indian owners of the newly-settled region.

# chapter X

# Posting The Guard

**Colonel Samuel D. Sturgis, commanding officer of the Seventh Cavalry at the time Fort Meade was established in the fall of 1878, was an investor in the Sturgis City Townsite Company that laid out a town one mile west of the new military post.**

**(Courtesy of Bob Lee)**

Removal of Army troops from the Black Hills in the fall of 1875, following their failure to keep the adventurous whites out, had left the budding mining camps exposed to Indian retaliation. While the early prospectors sought to evade the Army patrols, it wasn't long before they were clamoring for their protection. Repeated demands for military protection against the marauding Indians, who were only fighting to keep what legally belong to them, placed the Army in a paradoxical position. Closing its eyes to the wave of whites swarming into the region in violation of the Laramie Treaty was one thing. Affording protection to the illegal invaders was quite another. But it had little choice. It could not stand idly by while the resentful Indians warred on the interlopers. So the Army moved to safeguard the security of the unlawful trespassers. It did so by launching the now famous Indian Campaign of 1876.

While the Black Hills were outside the field of operations, their illegal occupation by the whites was a major factor in the violence that characterized the 1876 campaign. That violence is best remembered by the tragic engagement on the Little Big Horn on June 25. Prior to congregating along the tributaries of the Yellowstone River in the summer of 1876, the Indians had killed a number of whites around the Black Hills settlements. Reversing its earlier policy of protecting Indian rights the Army succumbed to the frenzied pleas of the settlements for military protection. Consequently, just as a three-prong campaign against the Indians in the Yellowstone country was getting underway, troops were once again dispatched to the troublesome Black Hills.

Early in June troops from Fort Laramie established Camp Collier at the mouth of Red Canyon in the Southern Hills. It was here that the stage from Cheyenne to Custer, "Mother City of the Black Hills," and thence on to Deadwood, passed through a particularly dangerous area. Camp Collier was the first military post of any permanence in the region. The camp was abandoned after one year when the stage company opened a more direct route to Deadwood along the foothills west of Red Canyon. Additional military presence in the Black Hills did not occur until after the major engagements

Messrs. A. A. Abbey, Judge Smith, of Custer, and C. Parker arrived in the city Friday from prospecting tour near Little Missouri Buttes. They had crossed the Red Water and discovered about sundown on Wednesday the 12th, a band of about 20 Indians moving north. Abbey reported trails left by Indians were also moving north.

B H Pioneer
July 15, 1876

The most terrific thunderstorm we ever experienced occurred in Deadwood last Thursday afternoon. For a quarter of an hour the atmosphere appeared to be one continuous blaze with electric discharges, fierce bolts of lightning descending on all sides while the concussions which followed in rapid succession fairly shook the mountains to their foundations. No wonder the Indians have a superstitious dread of the electrical phenomena of the Black Hills.

B H Pioneer
July 15, 1876

**General George Crook, speaking from the balcony of the Grand Central Hotel on Sept. 15, 1876, received a rousing ovation when he assured the citizens of Deadwood that the threat of further Indian raids on the mining settlement were over. In 1878, however, he had occasion to criticize the citizenry there for harboring rustlers of Army horses.**
**(S. D. State Historical Society)**

with the hostiles on the Rosebud and Little Big Horn rivers of Montana.

News of the slaughter of Custer and 225 others of the famed Seventh Cavalry on the little Big Horn did not reach Deadwood until July 21, almost a month after the bloody fight. "There is but one sentiment on the Indian question here," the Black Hills Pioneer at Deadwood editorialized upon receiving the alarming news. "The hostile Sioux should be exterminated and white men engaged in trading ammunition to them should be hung wherever found. Let the government call out the Black Hills brigade and put it in the field."

Relief for the endangered Black Hills mining settlements, however, came from Regular Army forces already in the field. General George Crook's command, defeated by the Sioux in the Battle of the Rosebud, was short of rations after futilely chasing the scattered band of hostiles. The near-starving force set out for the Black Hills on August 26, 1876, for badly-needed supplies as well as to protect the frightened citizenry there. Enroute, troopers of the Third Cavalry destroyed a Sioux village in the Battle of Slim Buttes north of the Hills on September 8. While camped near the Belle Fourche River, after resuming their march, the famished troops were greeted by a most welcomed relief force. It was composed of civilian wagons bringing food and a small beef herd from Camp Crook north of Deadwood. Couriers had informed the mining camp of the command's plight and the needed supplies were quickly gathered up. John Finerty, the Chicago Tribune reporter accompanying the command, reported the condition of the troops at the time the civilian relief train reached them. "With the exception of what had been secured in the captured Indian village," Finerty wrote, "the command, from General Crook downward, had lived upon horse, or pony, meat for more than a week."

William G. Fenton, the sole survivor of the Red Canon Massacre of April 16, writes to the Leader from Fort Laramie that he has nearly recovered from the four wounds he received in escaping from the red fiends, and that as soon as he is able to ride on horseback, he proposes to return to the Hills. He swears that he will have revenge for the blood he lost at Red Canon.

B H Pioneer
Jully 22, 1876

General Crook pushed on to the mining community on Whitewood Creek named for him. Finerty described it as "a rough and tumble place" containing about 250 crude shacks. It has frequently been reported that Crook City had been named for the General because he had camped there during his first visit to the Black Hills in 1875. But there is no evidence that he had been there that year. More likely the settlement, established in March of 1876, was named in his honor because of the sympathetic attitude he had exhibited toward the unlawful prospectors the previous year. It was from Camp Crook, on Rapid Creek in the Central Hills, that Crook had issued a proclamation on August 15, 1875, that ordered the miners out of the Hills until legal title to them could be secured.

. . . There is incessant cracking of rifles and revolvers in the camp — shoot at mark, of course. Save your ammunition boys, until things become a little more pacific in regard to the Indian question."

B H Pioneer
July 22, 1876

Reaching Deadwood on September 15, General Crook and his troopers received a rousing welcome from the relieved citizenry, estimated by Finerty to number over 2,000. "Like Cheyenne," Finerty later wrote, "It possessed a multitude of variety theaters and a crowd of brazen and bedizened harlots, gambling hells, drinking dives and other moral abominations." General Crook and his staff were lodged at the Grand Central Hotel. The general received a tumultuous ovation after assuring the crowd from the hotel balcony that the threat of further Indian raids was over. Crook left Deadwood the next day, leaving a skeleton force behind, and departed from the Hills. The force he left behind, camped in Centennial Valley between Deadwood and Crook City, soon followed him. Jimmy Irons, a herder on False Bottom Creek on the edge of Centennial Valley, was killed by Indians shortly after departure of the troops.

A temporary halt of the Indian attacks on the Black Hills interlopers occurred in the fall of 1876 while negotiations were carried out with the Indians for cession of the region. The separate bands of the Sioux, scattered and harrassed by the Army after their historic initial victory on the Little Big Horn, were too dependent upon the government for sustenance to continue their resistance. One by one the various tribes signed the agreement that relinquished the Black Hills to the covetous whites. The government Commission obtained the last signatures on October 27. The agreement, which opened the Black Hills to settlement and legalized the settlements already there, was not signed by two-thirds of the affected adult male Indians as required for further land cessions by the Laramie Treaty. But what was a technicality the government chose to ignore.

Jubilation in the Black Hills settlements over the long-sought cession, consequently, was short-lived. Consummation of the Agreement did not placate the recalcitrant Sioux who were not signatory to it. They exhibited their resentment over what they logically considered the stealing of their lands by resuming their raiding activities. On January 26, 1877, S. N. Wood of Deadwood sent a letter to the War Department complaining of the Indian depredations. He asked that a military post be established on Spearfish or Redwater creeks or on the Belle Fourch River for the protection of the settlements. No post was authorized, but Army patrols were sent to the Hills from Fort Laramie in Wyoming and Fort Robinson in Nebraska to search out the raiders. Five days before the controversial Black Hills Agreement was ratified by Congress, a party of Indians stole a large herd of horses near Deadwood. Troop C of the Third Cavalry, commanded by Lieutenant J. F. Cummings, pursued the raiders, killed one Indian and recovered the stolen stock. The engagement was a harbinger of an uneasy year in the newly-legalized settlements.

Roving bands of hostile Indians roaming northwest of the Black Hills were persistently pursued by troops under the command of Colonel Nelson A. Mills of the Yellowstone District in the spring of 1877. While the wily Sitting Bull and his followers escaped into Canada, others of the hostiles gradually surrendered. The Indian Campaign appeared to be over when Crazy Horse, the fierce Oglala

Gen. L. P. Bradley, commanding Camp Robinson, Nebraska, telegraphed Gen. Crook on Wednesday last as follow:

"I am sending one company from Laramie and one company from here to the Black Hills tomorrow." The plan was to "render" the Hills country safe, even at the northern end.

B H Pioneer
Sept. 5, 1877

Yesterday afternoon while Mr. H. E. Wentworth, from Omaha, was looking for a quartz lode on Bald Mountain, he came upon a small band of Indians unperceived. They had come to a halt and were holding a pow wow. The noise attracted his attention and upon looking around he espied the "red devils" not two hundred yards distant. The situation was critical as Wentworth slid out of sight, nor did he stop until he had put several miles between them.

B H Daily Times
July 17, 1877

The news of murders committed by the Indians in our immediate vicinity at Spearfish, Yellow Creek, Crook and Crow, call for immediate action of our people. A committee of public safety should be organized to take steps without delay to meet the emergency. Tom Overfelt and the eleven men who went out to fight the Indians are reported to be slaughtered, 20 miles from Deadwood. Wallace Kapinger's house and hay stacks have all burned and his five field men slaughtered not six miles from Deadwood.

B H Daily Times
July 25, 1877

"It seems to me that we should have some protection. The Indians are within three miles of us at this time burning hay and everything before them. I am worn out and other men here are the same. Please call on Senator Spencer and ask him to report the facts to the War Department. Things look checkered here at present. Have had four hours sleep in the last forty-eight."

Yours in haste,
W. L. DeMoss
B H Daily Times
July 25, 1877

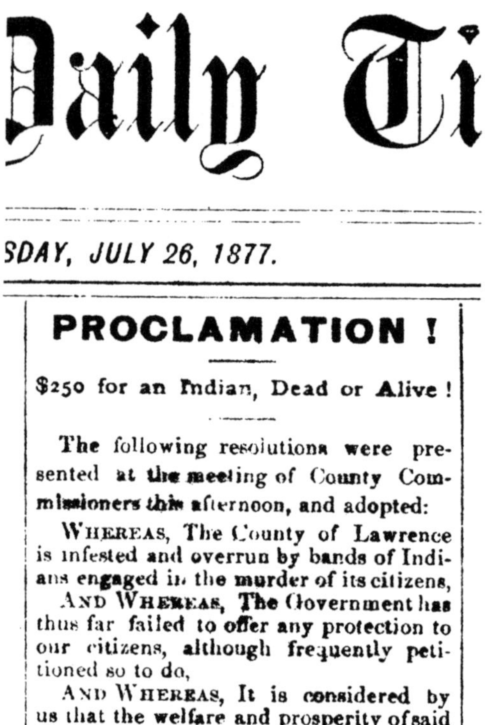

Daily Ti

SDAY, JULY 26, 1877.

**PROCLAMATION !**

**$250 for an Indian, Dead or Alive !**

The following resolutions were presented at the meeting of County Commissioners this afternoon, and adopted:

WHEREAS, The County of Lawrence is infested and overrun by bands of Indians engaged in the murder of its citizens,

AND WHEREAS, The Government has thus far failed to offer any protection to our citizens, although frequently petitioned so to do,

AND WHEREAS, It is considered by us that the welfare and prosperity of said county is greatly affected and much injured by the commission of such cruel and atrocious deeds within its boundaries, and as a result thereof the tide of immigration is checked, business paralyzed, the working of our mines impeded, and more than all, the lives of our citizens imperiled and endangered. Now, therefore, we the Commissioners of said county, in order to secure protection for our cit zens from the depredations of the marauding savages, and to punish them for outrages already committed do hereby offer the sum of two hundred and fifty dollars for the body of each and every Indian, dead or alive, killed or captured, within the boundaries of said county, upon satisfactory proof being given that such indian was killed or captured within said county by the person claiming such reward.

JOHN WOLZMUTH,
FRED. T. EVANS,
Co. Commissioners.
By J. A. HARD, Co. Clerk.
By C. E. HANRAHAN.

Sioux warrior, and 2,000 of his band capitulated in May. But on July 24 Indian renegades attacked a party of government surveyors near the Redwater northwest of Deadwood and three troopers of the military escort were killed. The incident caused a near panic in Deadwood and urgent appeals were made for arms and ammunition for the settlers as well as for additional troops.

Soldiers were again dispatched to the troubled region from Forts Laramie and Robinson. Moreover, the Territorial Governor authorized Sheriff Seth Bullock of Lawrence County to raise six companies of militia. Each company was authorized to enlist 30 militiamen and the County was urged to support the civilian force. On July 26, the County Commissioners issued a proclamation that offered a $250 reward for "each and every Indian, dead or alive, killed or captured" within the county. Demands for a permanent military post in the vicinity were received by the War Department from private citizens and county officials at Deadwood, Crook City and Rapid City. The Indian scare soon subsided, however, and the troops were gradually withdrawn from the Northern Hills. A troop of Cavalry returned in November to assist the sheriff at Deadwood in quelling a civilian disturbance resulting from a strike at the Keats Mine. The troops left after the strike, the first in the Hills, was broken.

It wasn't until December of 1877 that the Indian attacks became so frequent again that appeals for military protection and a permanent post in the area were renewed. On December 3, Lawrence County Commissioner Fred T. Evans wired Washington that protection against the "marauding Indians" was desperately needed. Three troops of the Third Cavalry from Fort Laramie, under the command of Major A. W. Evans, reached Spearfish near the present Wyoming border on December 23. Their presence halted the raids and Major Evans wrote his superiors that "it would be better to establish a permanent post here at once" than to keep sending troops from distant stations at every appearance of Indians around the settlements. The expense of keeping troops in the region was also a matter of concern to General Crook who, on December 31, asked the War Department how long his troops were to be maintained there. "There are no Indian troubles in the vicinity," General Crook advised, "nor have the previous reports of such troubles been corroborated by later information. It is very expensive keeping them in their present position."

On January 6, 1878, almost a year after his earlier letter on the same subject, S. N. Wood of Deadwood repeated his appeal for a permanent military post in the vicinity. His second letter pointed out that previous appeals had brought troops from stations 175 to 300 miles away at a cost that would be "entirely sufficient to build and appoint a post." But this plea, like those earlier, went unheeded too. Perhaps because Major Evans reported on January 15 that "not a sign or token of Indians of any description could be found" in the Deadwood area by his troops. The actions of the citizens of

Deadwood at this crucial juncture might also have been a factor in the Army's reluctance to establish a post in the vicinity. Inadvertently, these actions almost ruined their chances of getting the desired post. A near paronoiac animosity toward Indians, hostile or friendly (seldom was there any attempt to distinguish between the two) created the problem.

It was in January of 1878 that the commander of Fort Custer, established the previous year on the Little Big Horn, reported that some white renegades had stolen a band of horses from there. The herd was driven to the Black Hills where the market for horses was high. An Army scout from Fort Custer, accompanied by a detail of Crow scouts, pursued the thieves. They intercepted them on Spearfish Creek about 15 miles from Deadwood and managed to recover about 50 of the horses after a brisk fight. But the thieves escaped into Deadwood with the remainder of the stolen stock. The Army scout and his Crows followed them there. Rather than aiding the scout and his Indian allies, however, the citizens of Deadwood gave refuge to the horse thieves. "Feeling in the Hills against the Indian scouts was so strong," the Fort Custer commander informed his superiors, "that the commanding officer of the Third Cavalry detachment (Major Evans) had to provide him (the Army scout) with an escort to enable him to leave."

Such ingratitude for past Army favors, of course, naturally irked the military leaders. General Crook, on February 26, reported that "Repeated efforts have been made to recover stolen government animals as well as those lost by Indians in that section without success, owing to the fact that the thieves of such property, it is believed, are sustained and assisted by many people in the Black Hills." This prompted General William T. Sherman, the top Army commander, to inform the Secretary of War: "If these people afford refuge for stolen horses and government property, as indicated by General Crook, they do not merit the assistance of the troops of the United States." In a further communication, General Sherman asserted that, "If the people of Deadwood protect such thieves they cannot expect the U.S. troops to protect them and their property against hostile Indians."

Nevertheless, General Alfred Terry of the Department of Dakota deemed it advisable at this juncture to recommend the establishment of a permanent military post "in the neighborhood of Bear Butte." He wrote: "The occupation and settlement of the Black Hills has created a new frontier, a frontier which, as well as the roads leading to it, needs military protection. Again, when Indians break away from the lower agencies and escape to the northward, their course seems to be well to the west, so far from the posts on the Missouri that it is impossible to send out troops from them in time to intercept the fugitives. With a force prepared to pursue them from the west, the chances of intercepting them would be much more than doubled."

**General Alfred Terry, commanding the Department of Dakota, recommended the establishment of a military post "in the neighborhood" of Bear Butte to guard the Black Hills settlements against hostile Indians.**
**(Courtesy of Bob Lee)**

At the announcement of the reward for captured Indians offered in last evening's issue several companies have secretly organized, and moved quietly away as if in search of some rich quartz diggings. One man was so anxious to earn the $250 prize that he stole a rifle from Leimer and Co. These gentlemen are so willing to do something toward the capture of Indians that they have kindly offered to donate the belt of cartridges that belongs to the rifle of the party who took the rifle.
B H Daily Times
July 27, 1877

"The Bear Butte military camp is becoming a fashionable resort for Deadwooders. Quite a party from this city visited that place yesterday." The party of 12 included six women, three of them single.

B H Daily Times
July 15, 1878

The soldiers at the Bear Butte camp are having a big time. They were paid off Saturday and are now trying to see how quick they can get away with their money. The "girls and the gang" of this city are nearly all there and are reaping a rich harvest. Drunken soldiers with their "earth born turbulence all forgot" are, it is said, laying around all over the prairies and in the woods between Crook and their camp thick as hair on a dog's back. In the language of our informant, "they are having lots of fun," and we reckon, are paying for it dearly.

B H Daily Times
July 22, 1878

A gentleman just in from the Bear Butte camp reports everything quiet out there, and that the "girls and the gang" who have succeeded in picking up about all the money which was disbursed to the soldiers by Paymaster Smith last Saturday, are returning home. The "boys in blue" will now have the opportunity to take a rest until next payday.

B H Daily Times
July 24, 1878

General Sheridan in Deadwood

During our conversation with the General we became satisfied that the military post now located near the Bear Butte will remain there for the present, and when it is moved it will be nearer to Crook City instead of the Spearfish Valley . . . in his opinion, the present location will be the best for the protection of the people of the Hills country from hostile Indians, and give more general satisfaction than if at any other point . . . A military telegraph line will at once be built from Bismarck to the post here and thence to Fort Keogh.

B H Daily Times
July 26, 1878

General Sherman, perhaps reluctantly, concurred in General Terry's views and the Secretary of War endorsed a Congressional act to authorize the post. Congress appropriated $100,000 for the initial construction. Lt. Colonel M. V. Sheridan, aide and brother of the Department of the Missouri commander, arrived in the Black Hills in May to search out a suitable site for the long delayed post. The purpose of his visit was kept secret to avoid sparking rivalry between the communities wanting the post. But officials of the Rapid City Townsite Company seemed to have guessed why the Colonel had come. They royally entertained him when he finally reached their settlement and they boomed their enterprise as the logical place for the new post. It was, they assured the colonel, a future metropolis. Rapid City, not much more than a hay camp at the time, had a population of only about 250 in May of 1878. By contrast, Deadwood, the center of the mining boom, had succeeded the capital at Yankton as the largest community in the territory.

Nevertheless, Colonel Sheridan reported on June 10 that Bear Butte was "too far to the northwest to give this country protection," and he recommended the post be placed on Rapid Creek instead. If his recommendation had been accepted the post would have been in the path of the disastrous flood that killed over 200 persons 92 years later. Rapid Creek, then as now, coursed through the heart of the community. But Rapid City was dropped from consideration when it was learned that Colonel Sheridan on June 1, nine days before making his recommendation, had purchased 12 lots in the center of the townsite for a mere $500. Collusion between the colonel and the Townsite Company officers was suspected. Rather than subject one of its prominent officers to charges of conflict of interest, the Army decided to look elsewhere for a post site. An embarrased General Sheridan, in a telegram to Washington from his Chicago headquarters, wired: "I think I will go out myself and make the selection. It is an important post and should be in the right place."

Troops from Forts Randall and Sully on the Missouri River were dispatched to the vicinity of Bear Butte late in June to establish a summer camp. Their mission was "to afford protection to the settlements of the Black Hills" pending creation of the permanent post. This force was soon joined by rebuilt companies of the Seventh Cavalry from Fort Lincoln. The combined command established a campsite on Spring Creek about one mile west of Bear Butte. It was named Camp Sturgis for Lieutenant James G. (Jack) Sturgis, son of the Seventh Cavalry commander, who had been killed with Custer on the Little Big Horn.

General Sheridan reached the Black Hills in mid-July to inspect prospective sites for the permanent post. He visited the Belle Fourche, Redwater and Spearfish valleys, but avoided Rapid City. He was reportedly impressed with the Spearfish area, but the best ground was already taken up by the settlers of Spearfish. Colonel Dodge of the Jenney-Newton Expedition had predicted that might happen when he proposed that the Army move quickly to locate a post there in 1875. The people of Spearfish asked exorbitent prices for their land when General Sheridan expressed interest in locating the post there and, consequently, the post was lost to them. Instead, General Sheridan returned to Camp Sturgis and selected a site for a 10-company post in the picturesque foothills south of Bear Butte Creek, about three miles southwest of Bear Butte. It was a strategic location as three major trails to the Black Hills converged at Bear Butte and entered the Hills through a gap in the foothills fronting the post site. Moreover, the site was on the route of the Sioux traveling from the agencies to their favorite hunting grounds in the Powder River country. Second Lieutenant Hugh L. Scott of the Seventh Cavalry, who was later to become Army Chief of Staff, was detailed to set the boundaries of the military reservation to enclose an area six miles square.

Following General Sheridan's departure from the Hills, Lieutenant George Ruhlen, regimental quartermaster of the 17th Infantry, was detailed to supervise construction of the new post. He had previously constructed Fort Keogh in Wyoming and several other frontier posts. General Orders No. 1, issued at the site August 28, 1878, designated the construction camp at "Camp Ruhlen." Camp Sturgis was abandoned and the troops not assigned to the construction camp were returned to their home stations for winter quarters. There was lively traffic between Camp Ruhlen and Deadwood, the nearest settlement, during the early stages of construction of the developing post. And it wasn't all one way. The Black Hills Daily Times at Deadwood made frequent reference to "the boys and gals" from there visiting the soldier camp for diverse purposes, especially during pay periods, in the fall of 1878.

Home Baseball Notes

30 to 12, "we scooped 'em again" — the boys in blue played bad from the seventh inning. Deadwood scored 13 runs in the last three innings. The umpire stopped the game to get himself a chew of tobacco . . . our boys had their pictures taken at Camp Bear Butte.

B H Daily Times
July 27, 1878

The liveliest camp in the Hills at present is Camp Ruhlen, on Bear Butte Creek.

B H Daily Times
Sept. 6, 1878

Calamity Jane was a passenger by the outgoing Bismarck coach last evening. Her distination is not known by this reporter, but she probably went down to see the "boys in blue."

B H Daily Times
Sept. 24, 1878

**Camp Sturgis, on the west side of Bear Butte, was established on July 1, 1878, and was the forerunner of Fort Meade constructed later that year south of this site. The temporary encampment was named for Second Lieutenant James Garland (Jack) Sturgis, who was killed with the Custer command in the Battle of the Little Big Horn two years earlier. He was the son of Colonel Samuel D. Sturgis, the Seventh Cavalry commander, who retired at Fort Meade on July 11, 1886, after 40 years of military service.**

**(Courtesy of Bob Lee)**

Jeremiah C. Wilcox, who reached the rank of Major of Cavalry during the Civil War, laid out the townsite of Sturgis City in the early morning of August 26, 1878, "with a hundred-foot rope for a surveyor's chain and the north star for a compass." He was related to Colonel Sturgis, the first Fort Meade commander, and published a newspaper in Omaha, Nebraska. (Courtesy of Bob Lee)

Fort Meade, established in the winter of 1878 just east of a narrow pass leading to the Black Hills gold fields, was laid out by Lieutenant Hugh L. Scott of the Seventh Cavalry, who later became Army Chief of Staff, to encompass an area six miles long, north and south and two miles wide. It was named for Major General George G. Meade, the Civil War hero of the Battle of Gettysburg. Note the stacks of cord wood in the foreground. (National Archives)

A disgruntled Rapid Citian, in a letter to the Chicago Times, complained that General Sheridan hadn't come closer than 40 miles to Rapid City in his search for a post site. The letter writer described the general's selection as a poor one and chided him for failing to "contemplate the advantages of Rapid City." But the Deadwood Times, describing Camp Ruhlen as "the liveliest camp in the Hills," defended the general's choice. "The fact is," the Times editorialized, "that a large majority of the people of the Hills are entirely satisfied with the location of the post at its present place." The people of Deadwood, expecting to reap the benefits of military spending at the nearby post, were delighted that it was sited only 15 miles to the east. It was, at least, in Lawrence County and Deadwood was the county seat. It was naturally assumed, although incorrectly, that Deadwood would be the chief beneficiary of the post's location.

A group of enterprising citizens, however, saw a need for a town closer to the new post than Deadwood to serve the soldier population. So Sturgis City was laid out in August of 1878 one mile west of the post by Jeremiah C. Wilcox, an Omaha publisher, who was visiting the Black Hills at the time to assess their potential for future growth. Wilcox was related by marriage to Colonel Samuel D. Sturgis, the Seventh Cavalry commander, and was encouraged by him to start the new town. In fact, Colonel Sturgis invested in the Townsite Company and received a large number of town lots for his money. His original investment was a $20 gold piece. Sturgis apparently was unconcerned with the conflict of interest fears that had troubled General Sheridan.

Barney Caulfield, a Deadwood attorney who had come to the Black Hills following service in Congress from Cook County, Illinois, filed the Sturgis City plat on October 25, 1878. He also received lots in the townsite for his services. Payment for the 80-acre townsite was made in Valentine Script, a form of legal currency which had its origins in a Mexican land grant in California, that could be used to file on unoccupied public lands. Caulfield had acquired two of the

Script certificates, each good for 40 acres, in December of 1887 and the founding of Sturgis City enabled him to put them to profitable use. While most of the pioneer Black Hills towns were born during the mining frenzy of the 1876-77, Sturgis City came into being with the founding of the adjacent Army post. It wasn't long before the bustling settlement offered the same inducements for the soldier trade as the notoriously wide-open Deadwood. The town name was soon shortened to just "Sturgis." But regionally it became known as "Scooptown" because of the demonstrated skill of the citizenry in "scooping" the pockets of the free-spending soldiers.

On December 31, 1878, the Secretary of War officially changed the name of Camp Ruhlen to Fort Meade in honor of General George C. Meade, the Civil War hero of Gettysburg. Construction of the new post continued during the winter of 1878-79 and civilians of the region, first attracted to the Hills by the lure of gold, found their first big money in contracts for supplying the developing post. Fort Meade was laid out with the officers quarters on the south side of the parade grounds that centered the military reservation. The enlisted men's quarters, stables, guardhouse and other buildings were placed on the north side of it. The fort became regimental headquarters of the Seventh Cavalry when the last of its companies were transferred there from Fort Lincoln in July of 1879.

Sturgis City had a resident population of only 60 when the federal census of Lawrence County was taken in 1880. But the itinerant population swelled considerably during military pay periods when the "boys and gals" from Deadwood would make their monthly visits. The soldier town, for that's what it became, soon rivaled its bigger neighbor in bawdiness as it thrived on the trooper trade. Deadwood didn't seem to mind the competition, though. It was a small price to pay for the military protection the mining settlements had so urgently sought for so long. Fort Meade fulfilled its peace-keeping mission with impressive success longer than it remained in Lawrence County — which wasn't long.

The soldiers at Camp Sturgis will be paid off in a day or two, and the businessmen of Sturgis City are getting ready for the event, and the boys and girls of Deadwood are dusting up preparatory to visiting that place during the flush times which will follow pay day.

B H Daily Times
Nov. 22, 1878

**Military Mismanagement**

Will the War Department hesitate longer to have a post established in lower Rapid valley? Deadwood champagne and laudatory froth induced General Sheridan, when he was at Deadwood last summer, to designate the site of Fort Meade where there are no roads and no settlements to protect. He designated that point in the face of the fact that Colonel Sheridan, his brother, had previously visited this section and reported in favor of establishing the post in Rapid valley where it would result in some benefit. General Sheridan never came here at all. We now look to Judge Bennett to lay the facts before the Secretary of War, and endeavor to have at least a portion of the troops quartered in the Black Hills stationed where they will be of some service.

B H Journal
March 1, 1879

Deadwood had grown so rapidly between 1876 to 1879 it was unbelieveable. Then on September 26, 1879 the disastrous fire leveled most of the town. Even before the embers cooled, the stouthearted pioneers were building again — in spite of the odds.
(Centennial Collection)

# chapter XI

# From Sin To Cinders

**Deadwood was a teeming, gold-mining camp with false front buildings just before the raging fire of 1879 that destroyed most of Main and Sherman streets.**

**(Centennial Collection)**

Four years of uncontrolled growth went up in smoke in the early morning hours of September 26, 1879, when fire wiped out a major portion of Deadwood Gulch so rapidly that it left the populace of the gold-mining settlement completely stunned. The community would rise, phoenix-like, out of the ashes with a new nickname for Deadwood: "City of Sin and Ashes." The sin had been present from the beginning; the ashes symbolized the burned out passions of the undisciplined gold seekers. The disastrous fire was the gold camp's first major tragedy. Others would follow.

Deadwood holds the record for having the first fire department organization of its kind in the Black Hills. The Pioneer Hook and Ladder Company had been formed in June, 1877, and on its roster appeared the names of 64 Deadwood businessmen. Its equipment included 100 canvas buckets and the running gear of an old wagon fitted up as a hook and ladder truck. In January, 1879, the first hose company was organized but it was disbanded before the fire of September 26 that year.

In the first years of its boisterous existence the numerous houses of "ill repute" that catacombed Main and other narrow streets, marked Deadwood as a sinful town. After the September conflagration the cinders lay thick over most of the business district and up the terraced, residential streets of Forest Hill. Subsequent town and forest fires over the years have added depth to the ashes.

A more modern and beautiful Deadwood emerged from the costly fire that destroyed many hastily and improvised business houses and homes, thus proving a blessing in a satanic, brimstone-and-fire disguise. But to future tourists flocking into Deadwood each year expecting to find a sprawling gold camp like the one depicted in moving pictures, most evidence of the early-day town, including the saloon where Wild Bill Hickok was shot and killed, went up in smoke on that fateful day in 1879.

Early-day accounts vary slightly but generally agree that the fire started in the Empire Bakery which was situated on Sherman Street near where the Adams Museum was later located. It was operated by a Mrs. Ellsner. An overturned kerosene lamp set off the

WHERE SOME OF THEM CAN BE FOUND: . . . Farther down the street and near enough to a Chinese wash house "to give them tone," we find Hastie & Plowman, attorneys and notary public; Chambers C. Davis' block is the present headquarters of the First National Bank, Brown and Thum, Andrew Burleigh's law office, VanCise & Wilson's law office, the government telegraph office, Dr. McKown's and S. F. Molitor, assayer.

B H Daily Times
Oct. 2, 1879

The irrepressible Ruggles, of the Oyster Bay, is in full blast again on Upper Sherman Street. He is the only restaurant man who burned out who is on his pins again. His place is open day and night, as usual. Go see him. The fire has not ruffled his temper a bit. He is just as happy as a big sun flower.
B H Daily Times
Sept. 27, 1879

blaze and in minutes it had spread from the frame wooden building to the Jensen and Bliss Hardware Store three doors down the block of tinder-box buildings. Eight kegs of blasting powder in the hardware store exploded with a blast that shook the entire gulch and showered the downtown section with fire and firearms.

Fear-crazed tenants of the upper floors of the business district fled in terror up the steep sides of Deadwood Gulch to safety. The flames spread rapidly to homes stacked like match boxes upon the narrow, terraced streets of Forest Hill.

The Chicago Tribune and Times devoted four columns to the tragic Black Hills fire. The Deadwood Black Hills Times on October 2, 1879, stated that the Chicago paper's "account of our conflagration in the main was correct, but their correspondents evidently exaggerated when they say that a strong wind was blowing at the time. The fact is, not a breeze was in motion at the time the fire broke out and the only air stirring was created by the flames which carried the fire in a northerly direction. Most of the families resided south of the burnt district in South Deadwood, Ingleside and Cleveland. The estimate of our losses is not largely overestimated. It will certainly reach one and one-half million dollars."

"Most destructive fire that ever occurred in the Territory of Dakota destroyed the greater and all the most valuable portion of Deadwood, commercial capital of the Black Hills Mining District," was the way Jesse Brown and A. M. Willard described the catastrophe in their book, Black Hills Trails.

John Hunter, early-day pioneer, had a "corner" on the lumber market back in gold rush days. He started a sawmill between Deadwood and Crook City at Speagle Gap in 1877. When he started up his portable sawmill on the morning of September 27, 1879, he hardly noticed the haze that hung over the surrounding mountains. Out of the haze and into the camp galloped a horseback rider who rushed up to Hunter saying, "I want to buy all the lumber you have right now. He named an enticing price. John, however, not satisfied with the price he was offered, began to dicker with him. Just as he was getting ready to close the deal, another rider came galloping up, "Don't sell any lumber, John," he yelled excitedly. "Don't sell. Deadwood burned to the ground last night."
George Hunter
Deadwood Pioneer

The account added that "in the brief time the fire crossed Lee Street, which runs east and west, and was licking up the business houses with their contents; the people seemed paralyzed or half-crazed and hundreds of them climbed the hills on each side with a few valuable possessions, watching their dwellings go up in smoke. The fire passed down Main Street to Gold and Wall Streets and ran on the hill for three blocks, levelling everything. In other directions it extended along Sherman Street until it was checked by small buildings that were blown up, saving some residences of excellent design on Ingleside and the Cleveland Districts." The observer reported 100 business houses and 75 dwellings were destroyed and estimated the damage at about three million dollars. A later account listed approximately 300 buildings burned and placed the loss at more than a million dollars.

Annie Tallent, in her book, the Black Hills, Last Hunting Grounds of the Dakotahs, gave a stirring account of the fire. After telling of the blasting powder explosion in the hardware store on Sherman Street, she wrote, "in a few minutes the Welch House on Lee Street was ablaze, thence the flames leaped onto Main Street, down which it spread from one inflammable structure to another until the whole of that portion of town from the old courthouse south to Williams Street and to Chinatown on the north was one continuous blaze. Since Deadwood had no perfected water systems for fire, it only stopped at last for lack of material to feed upon."

Mrs. Tallent commented on the fact that "the fire of 1879 was to Deadwood what the fire of 1871 was to Chicago, only the blow fell more heavily on the former in that it was hundreds of miles by wagon train away from its supplies." She also added, "By a singular coincidence a woman was innocently responsible at both disasters." (Mrs. Ellsner's bakery and Mrs. O'Leary's cow.)

The pages of Deadwood's two newspapers, the Pioneer and the Times, as far back as 1877, revealed a premonition of things to come — a fear in the gulch that fire might be the community's greatest enemy and that means to combat it were nil. On January 2, 1878, the Times chronicled an adjourned meeting held at the Bella Union Theatre where Dr. J. H. Harding was appointed chairman and James McPherson secretary. The committee appointed was to ascertain the best location for sinking three wells on Main Street for use in case of fire.

The Times reported that on "October 1, 1879, Chief Engineer Richards received a reply from the chief engineer of Chicago's fire department dated September 25, just one day preceding our great pyrotechnic celebration. The letter was written in reply to one written by Richards to the Chicago chief making inquiries about the latest improved hose and other fire equipment."

The September 30, 1879, edition of the Times stated that the banks resumed business on that day, the First National in the Chambers C. Davis old Army office and Stebbins, Post and Mund on their old site, having hastily erected a temporary building over their vault. (Bank vaults survived the conflagaration without too much damage). The story continued: "All depositors are 'not grumbling' and deposits up several thousand. All waited patiently with the utmost confidence. Not a syllable of distrust in our banking houses was heard even before the vaults were proven to be secure and contents uninjured. It is without precendent in any country that has had our bitter experience."

The same edition of the Times ran columns of loss reports of various business firms. It was surprising how many firms were in Deadwood Gulch only four years after the town's establishment. The newspaper listed 116 firms in one column on Main Street alone. All businessmen expressed determination to rebuild. One item in the midst of business losses stated, "Chinatown, no loss sustained by the heathens. They stole more than they lost in the fire." Another item in the same issue said, "Porter Warner, proprietor of the Times, left for Chicago on yesterday's Bismarck coach, and will return with an entire new outfit for the Times in a few days."

COSMOPOLITAN HOTEL

Main Street, Opposite Post Office.

Everything Refitted in the Latest Style

BEST ROOMS AND BOARD IN THE CITY!

**Rooms with or Without Board.**

JOSEPH KING,
Proprietor.

Headquarters for Photographs!

—AT—

POLLOCK & BOYDEN'S

**ART GALLERY,**

*Corner Lee and Sherman Sts., Deadwood, D. T.*

Branch Gallery Main St., Lead City, D. T.

*We have on hand large collections of Black Hills Views, both new and old. Large views of Mines, Mills, Public and Private Buildings taken at short notice. Call and get our Prices.*

**Remember the Place, Deadwood and Lead City.**

**This is another view of Deadwood's devastating 1879 fire, looking southeast. Many of the remains of buildings caught in the path of the flames had been removed and piles of lumber (right center) signify the rebuilding was underway. The building with the "X" on it was the first Congregational Church at the foot of McGovern Hill.**
**(Centennial Collection)**

A column on current conditions of Main Street after the fire listed post-fire activity. For example: "Ben Baer is selling from his fireproof, D. Holsman is selling his clothes from his fireproof and has a new building started, California George has his chop house running in a tent and will put up a new two-story building."

An October 2, 1879, item in the Times said, "The heat was so intense during the late fire that the lead bushings on which the hose sockets were imbedded in the hydrants of the city water works were all melted out and yesterday Mr. Sacheti was overhauling and repairing them."

Many reports on the fire stated that it was a miracle no deaths were recorded in the conflagration. But a comprehensive story in the Black Hills Pioneer on November 4, 1879, listed one death. The victim was John King, an Englishman known locally as "Casino Jack." The gambler was asleep in his room at the Stone Hotel, believed to be on Lee Street. He was known to be "pretty deaf" and apparently didn't hear the alarm. His death was not verified for several days until workmen found his charred remains when removing debris for rebuilding the hotel on the lot.

Another oddity of the fire was its effect on the canine population of Deadwood. In their fright they virtually stampeded and raced yelping and barking all the way to Crook City before they stopped. A driver of a stagecoach headed for Deadwood said the road was full of canines going at full speed out of the blazing town.

Although only the first of many major fires to plague the timber-lined gulch community, the September 26, 1879, holocaust was the most memorable. Its destructiveness worsened with each re-telling as the old-timers who were there recalled the blazing inferno for their children and grandchildren in later years. Eventually the date of the historic fire was established to identify the real Black Hills pioneers. Only those who were in the Black Hills prior to the fire merited the title; those who came later were tenderfeet. The only difficulty with the test is that the fire also destroyed the official City and County records (to the ever-lasting sorrow of historians) and documentation of residency prior to Sept. 26 of that fateful year is almost impossible to prove. Nonetheless, the number of "true pioneers" of the region who claimed to have seen the cinders, if not the sin, of Deadwood Gulch circa 1879 staggers the imagination. Perhaps it's just as well that the records did burn. There'd undoubtedly be a lot fewer "pioneers" if they hadn't!

Hillary is the most enterprising restaurant man in town. He saved his silverware from the fire, and immediately procured dishes and cooking utensils and rented Wertheimer's hall where he is feeding the hungry by hundreds. No raise in prices.

B H Daily Times
Sept. 28, 1879

# chapter XII

# Courage Against The Odds

**Floodwaters of 1883 carved this scene of tragedy in the heart of the Deadwood business area.**

**(Centennial Collection)**

The decade, 1880-1890, was an extension of the turbulent years following the gold rush. It was a time of Indian troubles, mining intrigues, natural disasters, community rivalries, and quirks of human nature. But populations of the Black Hills towns had levelled off. The 1880 census listed 16,486 people in Lawrence, Pennington and Custer counties. Town populations for the three counties listed Anchor City at 291, Central City 1008, Crook City 100, Custer 271, Deadwood 3,777, Diamond City 30, Elizabethtown 316, Galena 59, Gayville 130, Hayward 38, Lead 1,437, Minneapolis 35, Myersville 103, Pennington 51, Rapid City 292, Rochford 315, Rockerville 321, Sheridan 152, South Bend 209, Spearfish 170, Sturgis 60 and Terraville 775. Thus, Lawrence County was by far the most populated.

The transformation from boomtown mining camp into a stable community was probably difficult for the early settlers. The community leaders were trying to bring some form of law and order into an area still experiencing growing pains. The settlers who wanted to stay and build homes, start businesses, or simply set up tents and work placer claims were contrasted by the "get rich quick" miners and the "get rich any way" train robbers. As the years progressed during the decade, lawlessness gave way to order. Mining proved more difficult than many newcomers had first believed, and the temporary settlers with their dreams of immediate riches moved on. Gradually, a permanent core of settlers stabilized the community.

The science of medicine during the 1880's was still in its infancy, but progress in modernization of mining camp medical facilities was being noted in Deadwood. It was in a March 1883 issue of the Black Hills Daily Times that an editorial appeared suggesting that a new County Hospital and Poor Farm be constructed near Deadwood to care for the poor and needy. The proposal was defeated in a county election because the public did not want higher taxes to pay for the project. So nothing was done.

Dr. McCarty made the acquaintance of a blind man on a street corner. Dr. McCarty escorted the man around for several days introducing him (the blind man) to his friends. The doctor held the hat for the blind man taking in nickles and dimes and spending the last one on liquor. When McCarty became intoxicated and could not walk, the partnership was dissolved.

B H Daily Times
1880

Dr. Meyer attended a seven year old boy, who suffered a skull fracture while being run over by a heavy wagon on Sherman Street
B H Daily Times

Two years later, in 1885, a grand jury was called to investigate the County Hospital. At the time of the inquiry, 13 patients were hospitalized in the facility. The grand jury found crowded sleeping conditions, ten patients in one small room, poor ventilation, dirty bedclothes and filthy rooms. The patients suffering from broken bones or similar ailments were sleeping in the same room with those afflicted by tuberculosis. Interestingly, the kitchen and dining areas were clean. The grand jury recommended that a more suitable place be found for the care of the county poor. Changes had to be made. Dr. D. K. Dickinson, a former Homestake doctor, was appointed to replace Dr. Z. S. McKowan as the County Physician and gradually the conditions at the county hospital were brought up to acceptable standards.

Dr. Bucanan, whose office was over Trebers store, advertises teeth extracted without pain by the use of "Nitrous Oxide Gas or Vitalized Air," the only treatment of its kind in the territory.
B H Daily Times
1885

Progress in modernization of the Homestake Hospital occurred in 1886 when a two-story building was erected. The doctors' offices were located on the first floor and the patients' rooms on the second. This building served the Homestake miners and their families until it was rebuilt during the next century.

The Deadwood hospital, which provided medical care for the community as a whole rather than just the miners, was converted into a school for boys by Father Peter Rosen, a local Catholic missionary, following the flood of 1883. The school, St. Edward's Academy, was reopened under the supervision of the Sisters of the Holy Cross.

The old log cabin had cots, wash stand with crockery basin and water pitcher, a slop jar, and candles or oil lamp. Its furnishings and fixtures came into the Hills by bull train. The early day ambulance was a spring wagon housed at the livery barn. It was succeeded by a horse drawn hearse that doubled for ambulance when the qualms of patrons were overcome by necessity.

The early day doctors had to ride horseback or hike over forest trails to the scattered cabins of patients needing attention. The doctor's black bag was a miniature prescription case filled with essentials to give on the spot service.

Lead Daily Call
Anniversary Edition
Aug. 16, 1959

Although many physicians did the best they could under the circumstances, on many occasions a patient's ailment would be incorrectly diagnosed or a patient might be given the wrong prescription. The Black Hills Daily Times, realizing medicine was a relatively new science, gave its support to the area doctors even though many

**St. Edwards Academy was a Catholic school which later became St. Joseph's Hospital. (Centennial Collection)**

unintentional deaths occurred under a physician's care. Doctors Dickinson and Rogers amputated the leg of Richard Freudenberg who had been injured in a ranch accident. The patient died and Freudenberg's father felt that his son's death was caused by the neglect of the doctors while his son was hospitalized. Dr. Dickinson said his duty had been performed in the case and no charges of malpractice were brought against him. But malpractice suits were not uncommon in the county. The Black Hills Daily Times mentions that three civil suits were brought against a prominent physician, but the civil actions were later dropped and the doctor continued to serve the community. Seldom was a doctor ever found to be incompetent. Doctors were too rare and valuable to lose.

**One of the first signs of a stable community was evident in the new two-story Homestake Hospital constructed in 1886 on Main Street.**

Considering the turbulent period in which the early doctors worked and their limited knowledge of medicine, the first physicians performed their duties admirably. The pioneer doctors were called upon at all hours to deliver babies, perform surgery, and visit patients. Many of their first surgical attempts proved successful. A record was made in the Black Hills Daily Times of a delicate operation successfully conducted by Dr. Dickinson on the arm of a man who had been injured in a sawmill accident. Numerous cases of the amputation of human limbs due to frostbite were handled expertly by Doctors Dickinson, Freeman, and McKowan. As the decade 1880-1890 progressed, the pioneer doctors in the county had established themselves as first rate humanitarians and conscientious physicians.

The dentist, Dr. J. J. Clark, has opened a dental office on Sherman Street. He is well prepared to accomodate anyone in need of fillings, extractions, and any other variety of tooth "carpentery."

B H Daily Times
1880

The newspapers of the period provide insight into the 1880-1890 era of transformation. The Black Hills Daily Times examined the problems and voiced the hopes of a community attempting to mature during a decade of unrest. But the unrest was a particularly complicated problem. An item for the date March 10, 1880, reads: "A gold bullion robbery occurred at Sidney, Nebraska. The treasure in the form of gold bricks was an express shipment from the mines in the Lead and Deadwood gulches. One $1,000 brick was identified as coming from the Esmerelda Mine. The robbery was believed to have been planned in advance. A posse later captured the robbers."

Dr. Dickinson of Deadwood was called to administer to Mr. Newbanks of Rapid City, who was severely injured when the north bound Sidney Stage overturned near Spring Creek.

B H Daily Times
1880

Articles appeared frequently in the old newspapers complaining of the lawlessness and violence. Editorials would demand more law enforcement and yet crime continued. Occasionally, renegade Indians and-or whites intensified criminal activities. In May of 1880, mention is made of a reputed Indian raid in the Redwater and Belle Fourche valleys. A number of horses and cattle were reported taken. The question was whether whites or Indians were responsible.

Pop Nugent, a card dealer in the Gem Dance Hall, was found lying on the street with a badly broken leg. He apparently fell, was run over by a wagon, and was dragged a short distance. He was attended by Doctors J. W. Coombs and Bevans, who had to amputate the fractured leg a few weeks later.

B H Daily Times
1881

The exploits of highwaymen and bandits were often reported. An item for July 25, 1880, reads: "Road agents Jack Campbell and Big Nose George were rounded up after holding up the stage from Sidney, Nebraska." Even embezzlers were not uncommon in Deadwood Gulch. In the September 8 issue, it was written that R. O. Adams, convicted ex-postmaster of Deadwood, was captured at Fort Sully by two soldiers. He had absconded with postoffice funds.

Frequently, warnings would appear in the early newspapers urging future prospectors from the East to be prepared to work hard to find mineral riches since "gold does not grow on trees." Inevitably, prospectors would become disappointed and frustrated. Even though they worked hard, these early day miners sometimes would have little to show for their toil. Disappointment could lead to conflicts with other miners over claims or frustrated miners would turn to illegal means to find the end of the rainbow.

Two cases tried in U.S. District Court at Deadwood during the 1880's have proved the basis for important decisions in similar cases since that time. One involved mining rights and the other the prosecution of Indians for crimes on the reservation.

Galena, with a vivid history which rivals that of any other gold or mining town in the Black Hills, was the site of the mining law controversy. Early prospectors in search of gold, discovered the silver bearing ore in the deep gulches surrounded by high mountains. In two of the claims located was found the vein of galena which gave the town its name.

These claims, the Florence and the Sitting Bull, were centered in the dispute which was settled when the court held that a claim followed the vein of ore horizontally rather than vertically.

Here is the story vouched for by old timers of Galena and Deadwood, court records, accounts in newspapers at the time and from mining law books.

Colonel J. H. Davey, a picturesque figure, wearing the wide hat, flowing tie, trousers stuffed into high boots costume of the period, arrived in the Black Hills from the East in the early 1880's. An expert in the treatment of white metal, he acquired an interest in the Florence mine at Galena, later buying it with some other properties. He went in for extensive development, erecting a completely equipped, ten-stamp mill, said to be the first of its kind in the Black Hills.

It cost about $80 a ton to haul the ore from Galena to Fort Pierre by bull train so Davey needed to operate at full tilt.

Pat Duggan owned the Silver Terra and Richmond properties next to Davey's claims. Duggan and Davey got into an argument over the dip of the ore vein. Duggan accused Davey of dipping into the ore vein on his property and declared that he had the right to follow the vein wherever it led, and that Davey had no right to go over the endline of the claim. Davey contended that he was entitled to follow the vein to its apex, whether the apex was on his claim or some other. In short it must be decided whether the vein was horizontal or vertical.

Lead City News: A singular wager was made last night at McAleer's saloon, a young man betting that he could drink six quarts of beer in 20 minutes. He drank the "lush" but in a few minutes showed symptoms of fainting. Dr. Mike Smith was called, and immediately began the operation of tickling the young fellow's palate with a toothbrush. The doctor is of the opinion he will recover.

B H Daily Times
Jan. 9, 1879

Doctors Hickey and Clark, dentists, and Dr. O'Neal, a physician, had telephones installed in their offices.

B H Daily Times
May, 1883

Several small children were playing along the hillside of City Creek and ate some of the flowers or plants growing on the hillside. One of the children became violently ill. Dr. McKowan was called and administered an antidote that soon relieved the little girl. Other children were similarly affected. Parents should make sure that their children eat only proper food.

B H Daily Times
May, 1883

The center of attraction Sunday morning in Main Street, Deadwood was the carcass of an enormous "silver tip" bear lying in front of the Vienna bakery. It had been brought into the city by a rancher from Castle Creek, who killed it on Saturday. This sort of game had been bothering the ranchmen of that section for some time past, so one of their number set a trap for his bearship. Saturday morning the trap caught the game, and it was immediately dispatched.

B H Daily News
Oct. 24, 1885

The fiery colonel put his men to work on the Silver Terra end of the Sitting Bull claim and they got out the ore as rapidly as possible, filling in the stopes with waste as fast as the ore was taken out. He threw up a bulwark underground and placed an armed guard between the lines. Although the question never has been settled satisfactorily, it is certain that by means of this tactic, Davey was able to extract most of the ore before Duggan could tunnel into his claim from the top and drift toward the ore vein.

Rev. Weston Smith and Charles Mason were re-interred at the Mt. Moriah Cemetery. At the time of the killing of Rev. Smith, Mason had shot an Indian and had gone with a posse to show the body. Mason, in turn, was shot by another Indian, who was shot by the posse. Texas Bill cut off the head of the Indian and in the company of Calamity Jane and Dirty Em paraded through the saloons displaying the gruesome trophy. Seth Bullock took the head and buried it behind the Gem Theater.

B H Daily Times
Sept. 28, 1883

Quarrels were inevitable. Davey's son, Frank and Billy Thatcher, lookout for the Sitting Bull, rode to the Galena Post Office where they met Patrick Gorman, a Duggan man. In the argument that followed, Gorman was killed. The coroner's jury declared that though Gorman carried a gun, he was killed by a bullet from Thatcher's gun. Davey's lawyers cleared Thatcher, claiming self defense and he left the country never to be heard of again.

Duggan's next move was to close all the properties by injunction and bring suit against Davey for damages. The case dragged along for months in the United States District Court of the Territory of Dakota, Judge J. H. Church on the bench. The hearing, in the summer of 1883, took 65 days. The entire court made a trip to Galena to look over the property. One hundred witnesses were examined and the testimony covered 7,000 pages. Finally the jury arrived at a verdict for the plaintiff, Duggan. Davey's lawyers appealed to the Supreme Court of the Territory. The trial court judgment was sustained but before the decision was handed down Davey had exhausted his funds and left the Black Hills.

On Saturday night last there was a raffle in the Bulkhead saloon for a valuable saddle horse, as white as the beautiful snow, as fleet as an Iowa cyclone and as gentle as a Dakota winter. Oscar Waller won the horse and now has one to loan to reporters.

B H Times
Jan. 1, 1884

The legal fight killed the town although it had a brief revival in 1897 when the price of silver was high.

The other now-famous decision involved Crow Dog, who was found guilty of killing the famous Spotted Tail at the Brule Sioux Agency in August, 1881. Crow Dog was tried at Deadwood and sentenced to be executed January 14, 1884.

A Deadwood lawyer, A. J. Plowman, who represented Crow Dog at the trial, contended that no offense was committed under the existing law because both the defendant and the victim were Indians.

Harry Tuttle, horsethief, was taken from the hospital and hanged on Academy Hill in Spearfish. Seven or eight masked men hung him from a tree and left him.

B H Daily Times
Feb. 27, 1884

Crow Dog, of course, was destitute and no arrangements were available in federal courts at that time for the payment of an attorney to defend him. However, Plowman was able in some manner to secure the attention of the United States Congress and an appropriation was made in the Act of March 3, 1883, to advance the sum of $1,000 to cover the costs of taking the case to the United States Supreme Court to test this question of jurisdiction. The high court held that the federal court was without jurisdiction and ordered Crow Dog released.

John Hart forged a check for over $6,000 at the First National Bank. He was alleged to be part of a "slick operation." He was captured, tried, and found guilty. He received ten years imprisonment.

B H Daily Times
July 28, 1884

Prisoners Doherty, Wilson, and Stewart escaped from the county jail by taking Sheriff Knight's horses.

B H Daily Times
March 15, 1889

Charlie Wilson shot his mistress, Kitty Clide, in the Gem Theater. He later shot himself in Lead saying, "Forgive me. I loved her so."

B H Daily Times
Sept. 28, 1883

Pete Mooney, arrested for shooting Noyes, Mrs. Johns and another person at Central, was discharged from custody yesterday, no one appearing against him. He paid the costs. The affair was accidental, caused by too much whiskey.

B H Daily Times
July 7, 1883

The discovery by this decision of the highest court in the land that there was no law forbidding the killing of one Indian by another Indian in Indian territory caused quite a concern in the country and as a result Congress hastened to pass the Act which forbids all Indians in Indian country from committing the crimes enumerated against other Indians, which is the basis of the prosecution of Indians in federal court today.

Being first the hub of the mining in the Northern Black Hills when gold was first discovered, and later designated as the county seat, Deadwood has always been the center for legal actions and lawyers. In fact, in 1881 a pamphlet published by the Deadwood Board of Trade listed a greater number of attorneys than the town has seen recently for some period of time. They included the following lawyers and firms:

| | |
|---|---|
| Burns, John H. | Caulfield & Carey |
| Clagett & Dixon | Chadwick, W.L. |
| Choteau & Bowman | Corson & Thomas |
| Cranston, John | Frawley, Henry |
| Frank, A. E. | Gaffy, Lorin E. |
| Graham, N.J. | Graham, F.C. |
| Harvey & Gantt | Houghton, Dick |
| Haydon & Allen | Hastie, A.W. |
| Kingsley, William C. | Kohn, Edward |
| Liverman, Moses | Martin, Eben W. |
| McLaughlin & Steele | Miller & McGinnis |
| McGinnis, John | Moody, Gideon C. |
| Mullaly, J. S. | Offenbacher, J.V. |
| Parker, William H. | Potter, Daniel |
| Plowman, A. J. | Romans, S.P. |
| Smalley, E.H. | Scofield, G.B. |
| Racy & Hamilton | Van Cise & Wilson |
| Watson, J.F. | Wetmore, E.A. |
| Washabaugh, F.J. | Young, J.M. |

In September, 1882, President Garfield appointed Judge William E. Church to the U.S. District Court where he served until 1886 when he was succeeded by Judge Charles M. Thomas, named by the Cleveland administration, who presided until the end of the Territorial Courts in 1889. That year when South Dakota became a state, Judge Thomas was elected to the bench of the Eighth Judicial District, which consisted of Lawrence, Butte and Meade counties.

More than any other period, this was the time when the law reflected the spirit of its clientele, and consequently was relatively loose and freewheeling. Not yet a state, the Attorney Association, such as it was, exercised little influence over its practitioners, who all carried advertisements in the local newspapers touting their legal expertise in areas such as mining and property rights. This advertising was, of course, a practice that was later banned by the bar association when the attorneys decided that they should not be hawking their professional capacities (or incapacities) in public.

Many of the lawyers first came to the Hills for the same reason as others . . . to pan for gold and strike it rich. Those who didn't, found that the law business was a tricky one that did not readily supply them with a living source of income. The practice of law, like the times, was precarious. In the Black Hills Trails by Jesse Brown there is recounted the early experience of a well-known Lead attorney by the name of Tom Harvey. This pioneer lawyer first settled in Custer during the original rush, more to seek gold than to practice law. Drifting up to Deadwood, he was fortunate, as his story goes, to be engaged by a bank there for some legal work. Upon the successful completion of the work, he was paid in six new ten-dollar bills. Satisfied with his days work and his fee, he bedded down in the IXL Hotel for a good night's sleep only to awake in the morning to find his clothes scattered and his money gone. With not another cent to his name, he borrowed some money for a fare to Custer on the stage that was leaving later that afternoon. While waiting for that vehicle, he was hailed by a fellow who was being hauled off to jail by the local sheriff.

Two well-known gentlemen of South Deadwood had a slight misunderstanding yesterday which culminated in one rebuking the other with his fists. The rebukee started to file a complaint against the rebuker, but before he could reach the justice's office the latter had already been there and plead guilty to an assault and paid the fine provided by the statute. The one chastised felt considerable crestfallen.

B H Daily Times
July 15, 1883

The fellow identified himself as Jack Rhodes, a person Harvey had successfully defended in Cheyenne some time before. Rhodes pleaded with Harvey to defend him once again. He was reluctant but stated that he would do so if Rhodes paid him a $100 retainer. Whereupon, Rhodes pulled out a huge wad of bills and promptly pealed off the money. Included in the retainer were six new ten dollar bills, the very bills that had been stolen from Harvey the night before. Taking Rhodes aside, Harvey told him in no uncertain terms that he was a no-good reprobate and that if he didn't turn over all of the money stolen from all of the guests at the hotel the previous night, he would really be in trouble. Surprised, Rhodes gave Harvey all of the rest of his ill-gotten money, whereupon Harvey marched him to the judge where charges were dropped, money returned and case completed. Harvey had matters settled quickly enough to be able to board the Custer stage and be gone.

Frank P. Jackson, well-known in this locality, formerly a deputy United States marshal and more recently as deputy sheriff, is in jail charged with stealing upward of $1,800 in certificates of deposit, cash, mining stock from Edward Majors, carpenter employed at Deadwood-Terra, yesterday.

B H Weekly Times
April 14, 1888

During this violent era, murders were common. In a December issue, it was reported that James Layton Gilane was publicly hanged for homicide. An article appeared in the paper deploring the barbaric use of capital punishment. Lynchings also occurred. The old paper reports that on August 24, 1885, Dr. V. P. Lynch was assassinated in Sturgis by Corporal Ross Hallon of Fort Meade who was, in turn, lynched by an angry mob.

Chris Henley, one of the fire laddies, on Thursday night was on a lumber pile at the rear of Star and Bullock's store trying to break a gorge that had formed in the current. He slipped from the lumber, and fell into the stream, passed under two buildings, around and between the posts, under water all the time, until he arose below. He then struck for the shore, passed behind the Gem Theatre building and landing on Conway's building.

B H Daily Times
May 20, 1883

Fires and natural disasters occurred with disturbing frequency in the Deadwood gulches and surrounding region during the 1880's. The Black Hills Daily Times reports that after the fire of 1879, 50 new buildings were in the course of construction. A positive outlook for the Hills was forecast. However, fire bugs were cause for alarm up and down the gulch in Lead, Central City and Deadwood. Such people were "too mean to live in any community," the local newspaper stated.

These buildings, located approximately where the new highway and Sherman Street merge today, really took a beating in the 1883 flood that ravaged the Deadwood business district. (Centennial Collection)

In 1881, a fire destroyed a drug store and a variety shop on Deadwood's Lee Street. Fire departments from Lead, Deadwood and Central City kept the fire from spreading. The Black Hills Daily Times mentions that many comments came from the people on the sidelines, but little help was forthcoming from them. A better system of fire alarm was necessary and a bell was installed on the Congregational Church.

On a day in 1881 when the air was heavy and sultry, a cyclone, accompanied by torrents of rain and hail, swept down City Creek as far as McGovern Hill and turned back up City Creek. One woman was killed and several people were injured. Houses were flattened and people took refuge in mine tunnels. "This destroying force appeared like a gigantic column a thousand feet high and one hundred feet in diameter," exclaimed the Times. A tremendous flood occurred on May 16, 1883, and hailstorms of huge proportions devastated 20,000 acres of farmland in Butte and Lawrence counties the next year. Another hailstorm in 1884 despoiled 50,000 acres. The hail was alleged to be as big as a man's fist. Crops were wiped clean and the agricultural loss was set at $200,000.

The night of March 10, 1883, near Brownsville in Elk Creek Valley, 11 men died in a fire. Buried in a mass grave at Mount Moriah Cemetery in Deadwood on March 13, 1883, were Albert Tunnicliff, Raisha C. Rice, James Chalmers, Samuel Haines, Fred D. Peters, Thomas Finless, Charles Hammontree, Peter Hanson, Louis Hanson, Harvey Woods and W. H. Andrews. The men were employed by Hood and Scott at a nearby lumber mill. They were sleeping in the second story of a rough boarding house, provided by the company, when the fire started, presumably in the kitchen, and sent clouds of smoke into the sleeping quarters. Some of the men were overcome by the smoke and tried to escape. Some who got out, for some reason, went back into the building and they too were overcome by smoke and died. Four other men were badly burned but escaped. Little was known of the men whose ages ranged from 22 to 50 years. Relatives of Rice and Tunnicliff erected monuments to them at the cemetery.

A lady living on the south side was on Main Street when the bridges all went out. She was compelled to stop at a hotel and the Times saw her yesterday on the bank opposite her residence trying by signs to make a neighbor friend understand that she wanted her to look after her canary bird. To this she flipped her arms and hopped around on one leg and succeeded in seeing her bird cage in the hands of her friend.

B H Daily Times
May 20, 1883

Best reported among the natural disasters of the 1880's was the devastating flood of May 16, 1883, that brought Deadwood to the edge of extinction for the second time. The community had suffered its first flood damage in the spring of 1878 when a late season snowstorm piled huge drifts in the gullies and gulches of the mining camp. A sudden downpour of rain melted the snow and sent Deadwood and Whitewood Creeks over their banks, seriously undermining buildings along their edges. Nevertheless, when the waters receded, building continued along the two streams that yearly merged forces in the center of town. The populace was to pay a terrible price for its neglect of the obvious threat.

Conditions in the spring of 1883 were identical to those that had caused the 1878 flood, but this time the damage was far more extensive. Big snows set the stage in mid-May and the heavy rains that followed forced the destructive flood waters into motion. Debris came cascading down every littered gulch and smashed into the Lee Street bridge. Soon the flood waters flowed over and around the bridge and many buildings were washed away. It was estimated the rampaging waters caused over $300,000 in damage and a number of lives were lost.

"The Great Flood," as it became known, was thoroughly reported in the May 18 edition of the Black Hills Times, two days after the deluge. It gave this account of the disaster:

> "On Wednesday noon, the 16th, the barometer took a downward tumble, and it kept going down, down, until a lower point than ever before had been known was reached. Yesterday afternoon (16th) it commenced raining, a steady pouring down rain, that increased in volume with time. The snow that had been lingering in the lap of spring, on the mountain tops, soon yielded to the softening embrace and came rushing down, in rivulets at first, then in torrents. As the stream began to swell, the mayor and city marshal were to be seen with such force as they could procure, clearing out the channel that was clogged up with buildings, bridges and floating debris. At 4 o'clock in the afternoon Dan Rathbun telephoned from Ten Mile ranch that the snow was all leaving the mountains, water was belly deep to a horse everywhere, and to look out for a big flood.
>
> "Soon after this Sam Cushman's building, and the Oyster Bay, on Lee street, began settling, and the citizens then realized that they were in danger. The houses were emptied of their contents, fire companies called out, hose attached to hydrants, and with water coming from the clouds in torrents, the Cushman building was saturated with coal oil and fired.
>
> "Lee street was thronged with men rushing in every direction, doing everything they could, which was nothing. As a section of firemen were running across the creek in front of the Oyster Bay, the sidewalk went down, carrying James Northey, a Lead City fireman, and Will Warner (now of the Whitewood Sentinel) with it. At that point the water was twelve feet deep, and running with the velocity of a cannon ball, through and under the bridge and between the innumerable posts that were planted everywhere in the creek. Hundreds of men witnessed their entanglement, and a hundred hearts ceased to beat. It seemed that no man could go thro' the maelstrom and live, but in a few moments they came up below the bridge, swimming like ducks (mallards), and very soon landed all right. Northey lost his hat, was slightly cut on the head. Warner had a damaged leg.

They Knew the Ropes

At 10 o'clock yesterday morning Evans Transportation company rigged up an inch rope across the creek, to which was attached a pulley and seat, and from that time until dark a continuous stream of people passed back and forth. A Times reporter took passage, and made the middle of the stream without any mishap, but at that point he came to a standstill, occasioned by the men pulling the rope refusing to do so any longer until he swore he would never lie to them again. To show that he regards that oath as sacred he will now state they were all gentlemen.

B H Daily Times
May 20, 1883

**Two women residents of lower Deadwood sit and console each other amid the debris of the 1883 flood. It was another of the many catastrophes that hit the town following the fire of 1879.**

**(Adams Museum)**

From Lead the word came that no flood damage had occurred, other than the flooding of the mines. The Highland mill stopped at noon. The railroad track has been washed badly, and the bridges across Nevada and Whitetail gulches are in tolerable good shape.
B H Daily Times
May 20, 1883

At 11 o'clock Thursday morning in Spearfish the rain poured down in torrents and continued unabated until 2 p.m. Friday. By 5 o'clock Thursday the whole bottom of town was submerged, commencing at the flouring mills and following the east side of the rise of land upon which the town is situated and following north to the front of Main Street.
B H Daily Times
May 20, 1883

The recent flood has destroyed the work of seven years and almost every trace of man's empire over savage nature, especially in the roads and highways of this county. We have heard it stated and believe it to be literally true that there is not a public bridge standing in Lawrence County, neither is there a public highway that is passable, or which can be entirely passable, or which can be made practical, except at considerable expense.
B H Daily Times
May 23, 1883

The flood of 1883 washed out the two bridges along with the school, Methodist Church and everything else along its path. The loss was estimated at one-fourth million dollars and the school was rebuilt on higher ground. The businessmen raised $10,000 to put in the bulkheads to protect the bridges from future floods. The timbers were joined together by special long arm spikes and the back of the bulkhead was filled in with boulders.
Deadwood Atlas
1884

"Late in the afternoon the water broke out from the channel at Cleveland and came down through Sherman Street deep enough for a steamboat to float. After night set in all was excitement and confusion. Men and women running in every direction, each trying to do something for their own or the community's good. Back of Star & Bullock's, on Sherman street, the chattels and effects of the girls were being removed from the buildings; pianos, with men and women carrying them, could be seen wading through water up to their knees; firemen detailed for special duty could be seen all along the stream.

'Ben Garr, a fireman, at the H. and L. Co. house on Sherman street, in attempting to save the house went down with it into the flood, but by pluck, perserverance and luck, landed not far from Harry Damon's, alive, but nearly gone.

"At 10 p.m. William Henley telephoned from Gayville to the Times that within an hour Bobtail had increased in volume four fold, Deadwood Creek a fourth and had only commenced to rise, the road washed away and John Alien's dam gone. At this hour a Times man went on to Deadwood street and found three feet of water in Patsy Boliver's house, and neighbors carrying out the traps; Tom Manning's livery barn from which he had at an earlier hour removed the horses and carriages, afloat, bobbing around until it brought up against the bridge, and at this point he saw Fred Fredericks of the Vienna bakery tackle it with an axe. He stood up like a hero and pounded holes in the siding; said he would make it come down and go under the bridge.

"Hurrying around to Lee street he was just in time to see the Oyster Bay rear up behind, groan and disappear in the flood, and as the debris went down stream it was for a moment resisted by the H.&L. house that stood on stilts, but it soon succumbed and went out. It was here that Ben Garr went in. This house had previously been fired . . . No one who saw him fall in ever expected to see his lifeless remains, but strange as it may seem, with a tenacity born of desperation, he made a brave fight for his family and his life, coming ashore at the Northwestern company's barn, with a badly contused head and an exhausted body. Harris Franklin's stable on Sherman street quietly arose and quietly sailed down stream, as did Jacoby's marble shop and Butler's shop on Lee street.

"Merchants on Main street were busy that night moving goods from the basements. The bridges on Lee, Deadwood, Wall and Pine streets went off and all communications with South Deadwood was cut off. In the way of incidents the record shows that Sam Cushman, with a spirit that has always actuated him, seeing that his building on Lee street if left standing would endanger the whole city, requested Mayor Steele to have it burned. Frank Ickes was standing on the bank of the stream; it caved in; Frank caved with it, and but for a colored man who was near at hand and yanked him out, would have been drowned.

"At 2 o'clock when going to press, Deadwood street was being cut away at a fearful rate, the current making for the Vienna building on Lee street. At 3 o'clock a.m. the danger was so imminent that the fire bell was rung to call the people to the rescue."

In the issue of the Times for May 19, the flood report continued.

"The city water right; continuation of the doleful story of the destruction of Deadwood; the new high school has disappeared in the waters; the Methodist church has gone to join the general wreck and ruin; a wide swath cut zig-zag through the heart of the city; Chandler, the toll-gate man, his wife and hired man gone; the water going down.

" . . . Sherman street below the Pioneer office two doors has been taken out, all of Lee street up to Headquarters building gone, all buildings on Bull Flats are gone and an apparent clean sweep made through to Cleveland. The $12,000 school house with furniture, and the Methodist church are no more. So imminent is the danger to Main street that all the merchants on the east side have removed their goods to places of safety. Every conceivable article and animal were seen passing through the city on the debris of houses from up-gulch, cats, dogs, chickens, hogs, horses and cattle, pianos, organs, wagons, buggies, stages and a hearse on their way to the sea.

"An inch cable was thrown across the gulch, made taut, and in a chair suspended thereto communication has been established with the other side of the creek. The water main that supplies South Deadwood with water was broken where it crossed the gulch. This deprived them of water and when at noon a fire was seen to be raging in Christie's saloon, opposite the court house, a good many of our people became discouraged. The roof of the court house, caught fire and for a time it seemed from this side of the gulch that everything must go, but the heroic exertions of a few men who had nothing to fight fire with but water carried in buckets, it was extinguished and the fire kept from spreading.

"In all probability they would not have succeeded had it not been for the encouragement they received from a hundred or more able bodied, lazy loafers, who sat on the hillside above them and never raised a hand.

"Dr. Myres and Frank Peck who were mourned as lost, have turned up, the Dr. spent the night on Hebrew Hill astride a stump. G. W. Chandler, wife and hired man were seen to set down to dinner, and a moment afterwards, the house and contents went into the flood and disappeared. All of them are known to have found a watery grave. Sam Cushman's safe weighing 800 lbs. has gone, two other large safes are also missing, one of which belonged to the Times, reported loaded with Golden Eagle stock, is no more. At 9:30 Mrs. Chandler's body was found below Harry Damon's.

**Another scene shows the damage back of the Bullock Hotel in the 1883 Deadwood flood. The Bullock Hotel was later changed to the Ayres Hotel and Hardware Store. In 1976 the building was restored as the Carpetbagger Hotel as part of Deadwood's restoration plan for historic Main Street.**

**(Centennial Collection)**

Mr. C. H. Wagner, of the Parlor Billiard hall, (Merchants Hotel) having repaired the damage by the flood, will reopen on Saturday evening for the pleasure of those who desire to enjoy themselves. Grand free lunch will be served to excel any heretofore offered in the Hills. All invited.

B H Daily Times
May 25, 1883

**Sherman Street was this sorry mess after the 1883 flood. The long building at the far end of the street is the first court house and the same site as the present expanded county buildings.**

**(Centennial Collection)**

Numerous suggestions as to the feasibility of changing the channel of the creek through Deadwood, and confining the same, have been made and among them is thus: That the creek be made in a straight line from the junction of Whitewood and Deadwood creeks, to or near the point of rocks just in the rear of the Northwestern Stables and left 150 to 200 feet in width; that the property inside the limit be condemned and paid for by the city, and an ordinance be passed prohibiting the obstructing, by buildings, or otherwise, of the aforesaid property.

B H Daily Times
May 24, 1883

"In conclusion, we will add that the remains of Chandler were found soon afterwards and later the body of the hired man, Gustaf Halhusen. The Pioneer issued no paper for several days and the first anyone knew of its being alive, was when Keller Kurts appeared on the streets asking for subscriptions to a mammoth sheet that would be issued in a few days with every particular of the flood, damage to property, etc. It was at the time designated as the "sublimity of gall.' "

During the 1880's, the Black Hills Daily Times also carried stories about the mines, the Board of Trade happenings, religious news, the fight for statehood, social activities, and the "Fire Laddies," who were highly politically oriented. The railroad extension into Deadwood was a favorite topic. News about the several lodges, including the Masons, Knights of Pythias, IOOF, Knights Templar and the G.A.R. frequently appeared in the papers.

Many community social events were organized during the 1880's. In September of 1881, the second annual Black Hills Fair was held at the Park Association Grounds. Horse races with $6,000 in premiums, a drill by U.S. soldiers, baseball games and wheelbarrow races were some of the events. Also agricultural and mining exhibits were shown. Plays, circuses and operas were also provided for the enjoyment of the public throughout the decade. However, the greatest celebration of the year was the Fourth of July.

The rivalry, bordering hostility, between Lead and Deadwood was apparent in the early paper. The rivalry entered into everything from sports to economics. Prior to the Fourth of July, 1882, a heated controversy ensued over which town should stage the festivities, Lead or Deadwood. No compromise was found, and little celebrating occurred.

Politics was another sensitive subject in the Lead-Deadwood communities. During the aldermanic elections of May 1882, great interest was shown by two local political factions, the Solid Six and the Fireman's Citizen Ticket. In the election of May 2, the Fireman's ticket headed by Kirk G. Phillips, won every ward. The proposition of building a new jail and a poor farm for the county was soundly defeated in the election. The public did not want the increased tax burden.

Life in the 1880's in the Lead-Deadwood gulches provided a variety of experiences: some humorous, many frightening and a few tragic. The ability of the first settlers to establish a growing community despite numerous obstacles is a tribute to their pioneer spirit.

# chapter XIII

# From Ruts To Rails

**The best of roads were none too good is evidenced as Harris Franklin and his wife rode out of Deadwood for a Sunday outing in the 1880-90 era.**

**(Centennial Collection)**

The decade, 1880-1890, was the beginning of changes in the county highway system. In 1881, a Board of Trade was organized in Deadwood for the purpose of encouraging business expansion. The most important subject considered was to promote highways to replace the toll roads. Deadwood was isolated without a major highway link to regions outside the Hills.

Little progress was made on converting the toll roads into public highways until the great flood of May 1883 washed out the toll roads. Prior to the flood, the main roads, ordinarily in fair condition in May, were submerged in mud and difficult to find. When the flood came, a wide path was cut through the city damaging or washing away many of the buildings. Included in the massive destruction were the toll and public roads.

The Deadwood-Gayville toll road was destroyed by the flood of 1883 but repaired at a cost of over $4,000. Thirty-six bridges were washed out on a 10-mile stretch of Whitewood Creek. Loss of the placer gold brought the demise of placer mining years earlier than it should have done. The owner of the Gayville Toll Road planned to allow free passage on a temporary road until his road was repaired. But miners, who had jumped claim on the toll road owner's property, refused to allow the proprietor access. Further objections were raised concerning the rebuilding of the Gayville-Deadwood Toll Road. Due to the tremendous losses suffered during the flood, no one wanted to pay tolls. And, after the loss of the Lead City Toll Road, Homestake officials began looking for another road without toll charges.

News from Lead City: Considerable complaint is made about the bad condition of the toll road between this city and Deadwood, especially about the width of it, as it is impossible for two teams to pass in a good many places. When large trains travel over it, which has been the case quite frequently of late, it is entirely blocked up . . . .

B H Daily Times
Jan. 17, 1879

The toll roads were not meant to withstand the great floods that occasionally roared down the gulches. The community leaders realized that the need for good roads in the flood area was essential if Deadwood was to successfully recover from the flood. The population, usually very sensitive about any new tax increases, was receptive to the idea of raising taxes to build new county roads instead of paying tolls to use poor roads.

News from Lead: A petition is being circulated in this city for the purpose of getting a free road between this place and Deadwood. It is receiving a large number of signatures and our citizens hope they will succeed in their endeavors, as it is a want long felt.

B H Daily Times
Feb. 10, 1879

The flood of 1883 was the beginning of the end for the toll roads in Lawrence County. The county, encouraged by the public, soon started its own highway system, little better than the toll roads.

Toll-road gates were a thing that embroiled the innards of wagon drivers going through Deadwood back in the gold rush days. This one was located opposite the present Deadwood Amusement Park on Lower Main Street.
(Centennial Collection)

The Boulder Park toll road is sustaining considerable travel since its opening. It is nine miles shorter than Crook City road and the grade is very light.

B H Daily Times
Feb. 11, 1879

An accident occurred last evening on the Central road about three-fourths of a mile from Deadwood, which came near resulting seriously for several parties, and was the cause of a painful injury to one of Central City's hack men. Fred T. Evans, accompanied by his wife was coming toward town driving a pair of spirited horses, and coming around a sharp curve where the road was narrow, met a Mr. Fruin from Sturgis driving a single horse and buggy. Mr. Evans had the outside and as the passing was close the driver of the single horse got scared and backed into Evans' team and crowded them so near the bank that the rocks giving way under them, they went over the bank where it was about ten or twelve feet to the creek bottom. Mr. Evans and lady both succeeded in getting out of the buggy in time to save themselves from going away with the team. Dan Leo, who was coming down with his hack, leaped over the bank to stop Mr. Evans' team, and in doing so badly sprained his ankle. He was taken to Dr. Leonard's office and well cared for, the doctors reporting no bones broken, but the ankle was badly sprained and very painful.

B H Daily Times
June 29, 1880

To carry gold out of the mining country, the various firms used steel-line "battleships on wheels," like the Black Hills Stage and Express Lines' "Monitor" which had steel plating five-sixteenths of an inch thick with portholes through which guards could fire. Wells Fargo and Company hired Wyatt Earp, the renowned gun fighter, to "ride shotgun" on its heavily armored stagecoaches.

Challenge, the South Dakota Story
Robert Karolevitz

The public demand for better roads forced the Toll Road Commission, established around 1880 to supervise the collection of the tolls, to dissolve two years after the flood, in 1885. A small number of toll roads such as the Lead City Toll Road lingered on for a few years, while others like the William Harmon and Co. Toll Road were so severely damaged by the flood that they were virtually given to the county. About 1890 the county began to purchase the old toll roads.

Early transportation in the Hills had been hazardous and difficult. Throughout the 70's the nearest railroad points were Pierre to the east, Bismarck on the north, and Cheyenne and Sidney, Nebraska, to the south. From there passengers came by stagecoach and freight by bull teams. Merchants had to replenish their stock twice a year — once in June and again in the early fall; any other time of the year was too risky because of the weather. Bull teams were also an extremely slow and costly method of freight transportation; the first stamp mill brought in by Homestake cost $30,000 to transport from Cheyenne and took several weeks to deliver. It is no wonder, then, that there was so much interest in the 1880's in railroad development and the approach of standard gauge railroads toward the Hills. In 1881 there was already discussion in the Dakota Territory Legislature about encouraging the expansion of railroad service to the Hills.

In the meantime, railroad speculators were busy developing their prospects for further expansion, including the Black Hills. Up until the discovery of gold, railroad developers weren't interested in the Hills, seeing them as merely geographical obstacles, but once long-term economic possibilities for the area became apparent, several companies began planning to build lines into southwestern Dakota Territory.

It was a local company, however, that first brought in railroad transportation. As the Homestake Mine grew larger, the managers realized that the area around Lead would not supply a sufficient amount of mine timber for the current operations and future development. So, in 1881, Samuel McMaster, the superintendent of Homestake, supervised the grading and laying of rails for a narrow gauge line about 14 miles out into the timber south of Lead. Meanwhile, a locomotive was being brought by bull team from Pierre, the closest rail point at that time. The locomotive arrived Nov. 29, 1881, and service began shortly thereafter on the Black Hills and Ft. Pierre Railroad. The length of the line was gradually extended. In 1887 the Fremont, Elkhorn, and Missouri Valley standard gauge railroad built a line from Rapid City to Whitewood, so the BH&FP by 1890 extended its line to Piedmont on the edge of the Hills, an additional 21.57 miles, in order to connect with the standard gauge line. This event was heralded by the Black Hills Weekly and Daily Times whose editors were enthusiasts of railroad development in the Hills.

Returning from Carbonate, a TIMES reporter came over the route of the new Carbonate road, and, as is the case with all who examine the route, was surprised at its feasibility, and the great reduction in distance. A large force is at work on the construction, and by the end of the month the road will be open for travel. From Main street to the head of City creek, the road takes an easy grade along the west and south side of the hills, insuring freedom from snow in winter and thorough drainage at all times. At the head of City creek, the new road to Spearfish descends by a scarcely perceptible grade to Polo gulch and the valley, while the Carbonate road turning to the south, follows the divide until opposite Garden City, where it descends by a grade of eight feet to the hundred, continuing for a mile and an eighth, to False Bottom, thence up Elkhorn gulch to an intersection of the old Carbonate road. Heaviest work, including the grade from False Bottom, up City creek and along the Spearfish road is, nearing completion.

B H Daily Times
July 22, 1886

The little BH&FP had quite a winding journey up and down the gulches of the Northern Hills. When the editor of the Black Hills Daily Times first saw a map showing the railroad's route, he wrote:

> "It (the line) looks like an angle worm in excruciating torture. An one point in Whitewood gulch the bend is so sharp as to enable the brakeman on the rear car to receive a chew of tobacco from the engineer of the locomotive."

Although this editor was stretching the point a bit, it was true that the grade from Brownsville to Woodville was so steep that the engine had to make several trips bringing one or two loaded cars up at a time until the entire train was at the top and could continue into Lead. In all its years of service, the BH&FP remained primarily a timber train, stopping at many camps and sawmills along its line in order to keep the ever-expanding Homestake supplied with wood. However, the line did run a few passenger cars, and there was one time when the railroad performed a life-saving service. A big fire in 1886 ran through an area two to four miles wide and about 15 miles long, burning 23 railroad bridges and warping the rails. But the train ran along over the burning bridges, picking up the people living along the line and carrying them to safety.

"My father, who was a member of the original Russell-Gordon party said that he always impressed upon his employees, who drove the Deadwood Stage, that they could drive as they thought best when out on the road, but that they must come into town and up to the stage depot at a dead run. And no matter how depressed the camp might be in the long winter months, they always kept up their spirits by the slogan, 'There'll be a boom in the spring."

Laura Russell Sentman
Deadwood Pioneer

The BH&FP had other exciting moments in its 40-year history. Homestake sent a $12,000 payroll for its employees in various logging camps along the line the 12th of each month. Since this fact was well-known, in 1888 three different holdups were attempted. All three were foiled, although only one ended in a shoot-out.

Working on the railroad was an exciting and often dangerous occupation, not only on the BH&FP but on all railroads that ran in the Hills. Locomotives on the narrow gauge lines were called "hogs" because of the large amount of wood needed to run them; engineers were consequently referred to as "hoggers." There were many steep grades and sharp curves on these lines so brakes were often in use. The first brakes were worked by hand, although crude air brakes eventually were used. In winter the "brakie" sprinkled sand on the tracks in order to get a gripping for the brakes. Since the only fire was in the caboose — called the waycar or crummy — and the engine cabs were open to the wind, winter was not the most pleasant season to work. All railroads in the Black Hills had a fair number of wrecks.

The Black Hills Daily Times reported on October 28, 1888, that, "As train No. 1 (of the BH&FP) was coming from Brownsville to the lake yesterday morning two flat cars loaded with wood jumped the track and turned bottom side up. Ben Bell, conductor of the train, was on one of the cars and went over with it. He found himself sitting on a big rock some distance below the wreck, with his backbone driven up at least a foot." Fortunately, he soon recovered and returned to work.

In 1888 construction began for another narrow gauge railroad. The Deadwood Central (DC) was to run from Deadwood through Pluma to Lead via the narrow Gold Run Gulch. There were also plans to build spurs to some of the mining camps around Lead and Deadwood for a total of 344 miles. In spite of financial problems, a law suit by the owner of the Gold Run Gulch toll road and bad weather, the railroad made its first run on February 26, 1889. The run between Deadwood and Lead was primarily for passenger service and was used a great deal since the wagon roads were still pretty rough. However, the railroad continued to have financial

The tax levy for 1882 was 25 mills . . . "One thing is certain, the want of railroad communication is keeping thousands of dollars out of the county and retarding progress in a most exasperating manner."

B H Daily Times
August 18, 1882

A petition was circulated that demanded the unfair toll road fees be reduced from 40 cents to 25 cents. Citizens had frequently complained that Dakota Territory law had no provision for toll fees and the tolls were illegal. The fees were reduced, but the toll road commission was still allowed to operate.

B H Daily Times
January, 1880

The Northwestern Express, Stage and Transportation Company had a through train to the East which made connections at Pierre and saved thirty hours. The stage with buffalo robes in every coach left Deadwood every day at 7 a.m. for Pierre. The Sidney and Black Hills Line could take a person to St. Louis in four days, Chicago in four and a half, and New York in eight and a half.

B H Daily Times
Jan. 21, 1883

**In the late 1880's the railroads were working feverishly to be the first to reach Deadwood. The Fremont, Elkhorn and Missouri Valley work train is seen edging its way toward lower Deadwood. It was the first standard gauge railway to reach the Historic City.**

**(Centennial Collection)**

difficulties and was unable to build spur lines as planned. In 1890 the Grand Island and Wyoming Central Railroad was pushing up through the middle of the Hills with a standard gauge line. The GI&WC bought the DC's right-of-way from Englewood to Deadwood for $75,000 with the DC having the right to lay a third narrow gauge rail from Kirk (which is as far at the DC had gotten) to Englewood and the GI&WC reserved the right to lay a third standard gauge rail from Kirk to Deadwood over the DC's line. Thus the DC was able to extend its service to more mining camps and the GI&WC was able to bring a standard gauge line to Deadwood with a minimum of construction. With the financial boost this transaction brought, the DC was able to build a line up into the Ruby Basin area west of Lead where there were several mining camps.

The DC, even in the short, three and one-third mile run between Deadwood and Lead, had a fair number of wrecks and accidents. One occurred in May, 1890, when a boulder, weighing about 1,000 pounds according to the Black Hills Weekly Times, rolled down the side of Gold Run Gulch and struck the locomotive. Fortunately, no one was hurt and the engine wasn't badly damaged. But the accident proved a good example of what could happen in the narrow gulches where the DC ran.

There were two more railroad companies that built lines into Deadwood by the end of this decade. One was the Burlington line. On Dec. 1, 1888, the Black Hills Weekly Times reported that the Burlington and Missouri River Railroad was conducting surveys and beginning to grade for a standard gauge line up through the middle of the Hills to Deadwood. Actually it was the Grand Island and Wyoming Central Railroad, a branch of the B&MR, that was constructing the line with the backing of their parent company, the Chicago, Burlington, and Quincy Railroad. The GI&WC intended to go directly into the Hills in order to pick up mining business from the Harney tin belt up to the gold mining district around Lead and Deadwood. It turned out to be a highly successful enterprise with a branch line eventually built to Spearfish in the 1890's. Construction progressed very rapidly in spite of bad weather. While still grading and laying rails in the Southern Hills, the GI&WC completed the purchase in May, 1890, of the Englewood to Deadwood right-of-way from the Deadwood Central which meant the company would only have to lay a third standard gauge rail from Kirk to Deadwood once the line got that far. On January 25, 1891, the Black Hills Weekly Times noted the excitement of the GI&WC's arrival in Deadwood with the laying of the final rail.

The other standard gauge line to reach Deadwood about the end of the decade was the Fremont, Elkhorn, and Missouri Valley Railroad, originating in Fremont, Nebraska. The FE&MV was one of several small railroad companies in which the expanding Chicago

**Deadwood and Lead had their own railroad before the big standard gauge lines arrived in 1890. It was known as the Deadwood Central, making its first run in 1889 from Deadwood through Pluma to Lead. One of the early-day coaches is shown.**
**(Centennial Collection)**

Snow three feet deep in the Hills has hindered the building of a wagon road from Galena to the Salt Springs, near Cambria, Wyoming, a distance of 44 miles. Captain Willard, road engineer, reported that progress is being made.

B H Daily Times
May 13, 1883

The Marquis de Mores of Medora, North Dakota, was entertained by a citizens committee in Deadwood. He had travelled over 200 miles on horseback and was escorted through the Homestake Mine and several of the Hills towns.

B H Daily Times
April 18, 1884

and North Western Company held a controlling interest, although it wasn't until 1903 that the C&NW purchased the FE&MV Railroad outright. In 1885 the Elkhorn, as it was called, turned north from Chadron, Nebraska, and began to build a line up through Southwestern Dakota Territory skirting the eastern foothills of the Black Hills and reaching Rapid City in 1886. By 1887 the railroad arrived in Whitewood on the northern edge of the Hills, only ten miles from Deadwood. Deadwood residents were still waiting for a standard gauge railroad to come to their city but it wasn't until 1890 that their wishes were fulfilled. In the spring of that year the Elkhorn and the Burlington (GI&WC) began racing to see which company could reach Deadwood first. The rivalry became fairly bitter at times. At one point the GI&WC obtained an injunction against the Elkhorn to stop it from condemning right-of-way over land the Elkhorn needed to cross. But both railroads kept pushing along anyway. The Elkhorn was slowed up for awhile because it had to construct a 1300 foot tunnel through a hill between Whitewood and Deadwood, but on Dec. 29, 1890, the first train on the FE&MV line steamed into Deadwood, the first standard gauge line reaching that city. It was greeted with a great deal of excitement on the part of Deadwood's residents. The Black Hills Daily Times reported:

> "Yesterday, Dec. 29, was a historical day for Deadwood, the metropolis of all the Black Hills. The first passenger train from the outside world arrived in our city promptly on time, 8:45 a.m. over the Fremont, Elkhorn, and Missouri Valley RR and was greeted at the depot by fully 2,000 people. Even at that early hour, men, and women, carriages, horsemen and people on foot crowded to the depot and lined the street and walks for a quarter of a mile, awaiting the arrival of the train that gladdened the hearts of thousands . . . and there it was rounding the curve in full view, the black coal smoke in the sky marking its trail, and its shrill whistle screaming and answering response to the shouts of the people and waving of handkerchiefs. There she is! There she comes! What a glorious sight! were the frequent ejaculations heard on every side. And what a gratification to the officials who were on that train . . . "

Deadwood celebrated with bands and a parade to escort railroad and city officials to a banquet hall where many triumphant speeches were made. Although there was another celebration when the Burlington's GI&WC reached the city, it wasn't quite as exuberant as the Elkhorn's arrival, so the Burlington men must have been sorely disappointed to have the second railroad to arrive.

There was always a rivalry between the Burlington and Elkhorn men, but they did find one point of agreement shortly after both trains began making regular runs to Deadwood, and that had to do with the narrow gauge "hogs." The Black Hills Daily Times of Jan. 31, 1891 noted:

The main street is clogged with traffic. Everyday large shipments of machinery, household goods, and miscellaneous articles from the east are being unloaded in Lead.
Lead Daily Tribune
Sept. 27, 1886

The freighter Fred Evans has retired leaving a great gap in freight haulage system that has to be filled. Hopefully, the railroad will be in Deadwood soon.
B H Daily Times
Jan. 14, 1887

The first eastern mail via Whitewood arrived in Deadwood. If Deadwood had a railroad, the mail delivery would be much faster.
B H Daily Times
Feb. 19, 1888

President Marvin Hughit of the North Western Railroad assured Mayor Sol Star of Deadwood that the railroad will be built as soon as the survey shows it to be practical.
B H Daily Times
June 14, 1887

"Trainmen of the Elkhorn and B&M are inclined to sneer at the diminutiveness of the Deadwood Central. 'Betsy,' engine No. 1, has been designated as 'peanut roaster', 'dinkey', and 'wheelbarrow'. Which if any of the names will stick is not known. The DC boys fortunately were not around when their pet was so alluded to, or a sensational column with scare head might have been furnished."

Unfortunately for the pride of the standard gauge men, both the Elkhorn and Burlington employees began working on narrow gauge lines by the mid-1880's, and the 1890's and early 1900's saw Deadwood become a very busy railroad center.

The stagecoaches, freight wagons, and horseback riders, using the toll and public roads, provided the only transportation links to the outside region until the Elkhorn and Burlington Railroads were built to Deadwood in the early 1890's. The only railroads in the Northern Hills were Homestake's railroad, the Black Hills and Ft. Pierre, and the Deadwood Central, both local narrow gauge lines. Not until 1884 did a stage line, built by the Marquis de Mores of Medora, Dakota Territory, give the Black Hills its first route to the north. Other stage companies were organized in the county. In 1887 a stage ran between Deadwood and Galena and between Deadwood, Central City, and Carbonate. In the 1880's public transportation was at best inadequate.

Wells Fargo's express wagon arrived very heavily loaded yesterday, the greater part of the matter being several hundred baskets of grapes for Deadwood dealers.

B H Times
Oct. 15, 1888

The Deadwood Central company has fitted up the old McCoy carpenter shop, Sherman street, for temporary quarters and will be used, pending the completion of the road to Lead, as an accommodation for passengers desiring a comfortable place to wait for the street cars. There is ample time to reach the car at the Sherman street switch during its necessary wait there.

B H Times
Dec. 31, 1888

**Deadwood celebrated with a gala parade in 1888 the coming of the horse-drawn street railway. The intersection (upper left) is Main and Lee Streets.**

**(Centennial Collection)**

Central City was virtually wiped out in the disastrous fire of 1888. In true pioneer spirit, a new building in the center of the burned-out area has gone up and piles of lumber along the road shows the residents are preparing to rebuild.

(Centennial Collection)

# chapter XIV

# Civilizing Sociability

**All set for a social afternoon these three typify the women of the 1880 era.**
**(Centennial Collection)**

When Deadwood was rebuilt after the fire of 1879, the gold rush was over. With the construction of a majority of the new buildings out of brick and stone, the wild mining camp assumed an air of permanency and progress as well as a more dignified appearance. Many gold seekers had come — and many had left. But those that remained had either sent for their families, or had married and set up housekeeping. These two factors — permanent buildings and family life — were the prime civilizing influences. And not far behind were cultural and social activities.

By 1900, Lead had more fraternal, religious, civic and social groups and societies than any town of comparable size and Deadwood was running it a close race. For example, by 1886, in Lead there was a highly successful amateur theatrical group known as the Lead City Dramatic Club; a rifle club was active two years later; and for the first annual Labor Day picnic, September 3, 1888, attended by 2,000, there was a free train ride to the site, where dancing, eating, speech making and the playing of games were the major activities.

The social club will give the first of the series of parties at Kiemer hall this evening. All members are expected to be present and help to make it a success. Invitations have been issued to a number of persons in Lead, Central and other outside camps. Those who have not secured their certificates of membership can do so by calling on C. F. DeMouth, as, according to the by-laws, no one will be admitted without their cards.

B H Daily Times
Jan. 3, 1884

The first woman's club organized in the Black Hills was the Round Table Club of Deadwood. This took place, February 14, 1887, with a charter membership of five. Following, not far behind, were the Thursday Club, the Culture Club, Twentieth Century Club, all of Deadwood; the Mothers' Union, Woman's Club and Fortnightly Club in Lead City; Twentieth Century and Fortnightly Clubs in Spearfish; Twentieth Century Club in Terry and the Ladies' History Club in Whitewood, not to mention the various other clubs in other towns of the Black Hills, most of which were united under the Black Hills Federation in 1897. This organization grew out of a meeting called by Miss Clara D. Coe of the Deadwood Round Table Club. Deadwood was also the site for the organization of the State Federation on January 16, 1900.

A number of the clubs did philanthropic work and notably among these was the Lead Women's Club, which brought about the organization of a kindergarten and financed the addition of organs to the public schools in that city. The Thursday Club of Deadwood during its early years contributed pictures for the schoolrooms and influenced the City Council to bring about better sanitary conditions in the city.

Eighteen Eighty-three
Thou Art Forever Gone From Me.
Eighteen Hundred and Eighty-Four.
Thou Art Welcome at Our Door.

B H Daily Times
Jan. 3, 1884

Churches also played an important part in the social life of the newly-founded communities. Each church had its "Ladies Aid" or "Ladies Guild" which performed many charitable acts, sponsored fund-raising dinners and ice cream socials featuring homemade ice cream and strawberries. The Sunday School picnics were looked forward to by the small fry. Sometimes these picnics were held at Brownsville when teachers, kids, mothers and perhaps some fathers would board the train and ride to the picnic spot, have an all-day outing, then return by the same mode of transportation.

The numerous friends of Max Fishel, headed by Mrs. Harris Franklin, marched into his residence in Ingleside on New Years night, taking them completely by surprise, and from that time until 3 a.m. yesterday morning had a glorious time dancing, feasting, music and pleasant conversation.

B H Daily Times
Jan. 3, 1884

This same method of travel was also used by fishermen, picknickers and "berry pickers" in the summer when people would go to Spearfish Canyon on the train, stay all day, then when the train would come back from Spearfish it would toot a warning whistle and everyone would scramble back to the station at Elmore to ride home with their loot, or empty baskets. Some would get off at Bridal Veil Falls to spend the day.

The rectory of Christ Church in Lead, which was at the rear of the church, served as a recreation center for the city. Included were billiard and pool tables. When the first church was to be built, a ladies guild was formed and its fund-raising drive began in 1879. The women sponsored the first dinner and dance ever presented by a church organization in Lead and raised $175 from the event held in the old Miners Union Hall.

Miss Bogle is a professional music teacher. Last Saturday a number of her pupils and friends gathered at her residence to enjoy themselves by singing, music and recitations, in which all participants are deserving of praise. After the music, etc., refreshments were served. Miss Bogle picked some very beautiful presents from the Christmas tree.

B H Daily Times
Jan. 1, 1884

The Congregational Church, one of the earliest in Deadwood, had a school for the Chinese children. Religion was taught and hymns sung. The children were also taught to speak English, how to write and were introduced to some arithmetic. The minister organized this school and the young women of the church were teachers. Later the Baptist Church had one such school. As a cultural benefit the Ladies Aid of the Congregational Church raised money to give books to the children of the Sunday School as a Christmas gift.

There were also several flourishing women's Christian temperance clubs in the Hills, with the publication of the state paper at Rapid City by Mrs. Alice Gossage. Even the famed woman suffragist, Susan B. Anthony, came on the Northern Hills scene on November 5, 1890, to speak at the City Hall in Deadwood, accompanied by Miss Rev. Anna Shaw. The next day's newspaper reported that it was as fine an audience as ever assembled in Deadwood. "We do not believe a single convert was made by either of these speakers," the article noted . . . "The American mother, family and daughter have not asked for, (nor will they ever ask so long as that home and family exist in its happiness and content) ever desire or demand, the ballot for women." Newspaper items reveal that there were also several card clubs in the two cities, also 5 o'clock teas, which were more like dinners, after which cards were played.

Dancing played a major part in the social life of the communities and the newspapers were filled with notices like the following: "A social hop at Jack Gary's Hotel;" "A select dance at the French Hotel, July 3, no lewd characters will be admitted." The Miners Union had a grand ball on July 5, 1880, at its hall in Central City. There were "dancing clubs" enjoyed by young and old alike. A nice ballroom was located on the third floor of the Phoenix Building where the New York Store was later established. According to the news reports the ladies were dressed in their very best and it was quite a social affair. After the dance many would go to the "bakery down the street" for oyster stew and-or raw oysters. Quite a contrast to the first dance in Lead on July 1877, when only seven ladies were in attendance.

Sleigh riding was practically an institution in the winter. The young men would take their best girls on a ride around the belt (from Deadwood to Lead by way of Pluma and back down by Central City) in a "spiffy" cutter, or perhaps a group would have a party and climb in a sleigh with four-horse power. Almost all of the kids had a sleigh of some sort, whether homemade or store-bought and there were a few bobsleds in operation too. One of the most thrilling and hazardous runs was from the top of Mill street in Lead, bumping over the tracks, then down the hill to Pluma.

Bands were an important part of any civic function or holiday celebration and each town boasted at least one, even outlying mining camps like Cambria. Most lodges also had their own bands and choruses, with the Clan Stewart, a Scottish group, featuring a bagpipe and drum troupe.

Many excellent singers were found in the community, including the Cornish, Scotch and Italians, who shared their talents at numerous gatherings. In 1889, a newspaper article reported, "A Sangerfest in the City Hall attracted a large crowd on the sidewalk."

Spearfish shared many of the talented entertainment acts with Lead and Deadwood, according to the Queen City Mail of February 6, 1889, which reported that The Spearfish Hose Company No. 1 was to have a ball on February 22 at the Opera House with the "well known Hattenbach orchestra of Deadwood" to furnish the music. A follow-up story reported it as "one of the most pleasant and successful social events of the season." The Queen City newspapers reported that the

A molasses candy hop is to come off next Thursday at a private residence on Main Street. The principle feature of the affair is to pull little nuggets of gold out of a saucer of molasses with the teeth, and then donate the nugget to kiss the prettiest girl at the party.

B H Daily Times
June 12, 1887

"On Mon. eve. Miss Anthony and Miss Shaw spoke at the City Hall to a packed full house. It was Jammed! Miss A- is a tiresome old lady — but Miss Shaw was fine — everyone was charmed. One would suppose she must have made some converts to the Womans cause — Mama was invited to tea with those two celebrated W. S. speakers at Mrs. Morse's. Mrs. Mirdy, Mrs. Gaston, Mrs. Paddock, Mrs. Flynn, Mrs. King were the other guests. Tea was very fine . . .

. . . Papa came up on Sat. from Rapid City, stayed to vote and went back yesterday noon. Accompanied the Hon. Susan B. Anthony and Miss Anna Shaw (Rev.) on their way east via Lead and Piedmont. Showed them the way down — the sights of the road."

Irene Cushman's Diary
November, 1890

The season of society banquets has about passed, and will long be remembered both for its number and character of gastronomical entertainments. Few cities of the land are as well equipped as Deadwood for public entertainments, which has the Vienna, an establishment of wonderful resources and very attractive features generally. The Vienna is indeed a household word with everyone.

B H Daily Times
Jan. 10, 1889

**The "hot spot" in early-day Deadwood was the Gem Variety Theatre and Dance Hall. There was plenty of variety including gals for lonesome miners. The owner, Al Swearengen and his wife, are in the carriage on the left. (Centennial Collection)**

GAR met every Saturday afternoon; there was a chapter of the Woman's Christian Temperance Union; the Good Templars hosted dances, the Masonic Lodge and Odd Fellows had good sized memberships; and numerous surprise parties were held. In addition, there were shooting matches and hay rides. Sleigh rides were also popular in spite of the fact that the plans were sometimes interrupted by "chinooks," warm winds that melted the snow.

86 *Premium List of the*

# GEM THEATRE

AL. SWEARINGEN, - - - Proprietor.
IRVIN T. BUSH, - - - - - Manager.

OPEN EVERY NIGHT.

20 SPECIALTY ARTISTS 20

Minstrelsy,
Variety,
Comedy.

The performance to commence every night with the Character Comedian,

**John J. Riley,** supported by **Miss Lizzie Smith,**

In their Great Comedy,

**OLD SI SALEM:**

| | |
|---|---|
| Uncle Si | John J. Riley |
| Amelia Claire | Lizzie Smith |
| Harry Wilson | Billy Parant |
| Dick Martin | Irvin T. Bush |
| Bob Jones | Geo. Thornton |
| Ed Clark | Josie Bright |
| Little Katie (with song) | Ollie Evans |
| Mrs. Jones | Kate Mauri |
| Maud | May Mouri |
| Bessie | Vergie Varney |
| Lillie | Maggie Mauri |

**6 New Specialty Artists. 6**

Much of the social life centered around the Normal School at Spearfish where on February 8, 1889, a concert was slated featuring Charity Martin, Deadwood, "a musical prodigy whose history is familiar to people of the Black Hills." A lecture on the geology of the Black Hills by Dean Carpenter of the Dakota School of Mines at Rapid City, packed the Hall and a review of the Jubilee Singers reported that "several of the company were once children of bondage" and that their concert was . . . "enchanting, soul-inspiring music."

The Gem Theatre in Deadwood sported a band as part of its entertainment, playing to the crowds in the street from the balcony each evening. Mrs. Horace Clark, pioneer Deadwood woman, recalls that although not allowed to go to the theatre, she and her friends would stroll along the street above Main and listen to the concerts. The Gem band played for celebrations as well as for theatre performances. On July 4, 1880, the members played over an hour at the City Creek Water Works in Lead, after which they marched in the parade at Central City.

Central City was slated to have the main celebration that year; however, all three towns — Lead, Deadwood and Central City — decorated their main streets with evergreens, flags and Chinese lanterns. Many hours were consumed making flags and putting up flag poles. By June 29, the newspaper reported: "Four cases of fireworks for the grand pyrotechnic display on the eve of the 5th on the hill between Central and Terraville, arrived at Barnes' and the rest is enroute."

Deadwood citizens didn't wait for the celebration in Central City but had "pre-holiday doings of their own." After church the Gem Theatre Band tuned up and ended playing a concert in Lead. That evening Madam Evans walked a wire from the ground to the top of the courthouse on a rope made slippery by a sudden shower of rain. This exhibition was not staged until she walked through the crowd with a cigar box to defray expenses of her trip and meals, etc. In addition, there was a rifle match and glass ball contest for shotgun artists, plus billiards at Hirem's Billiard Hall.

On the 5th of July the big doings at Central City started off with a parade including the Knights of Pythias, Seventh Cavalry of Fort Meade, Lead City Miners Union, the hose companies, General Custer Lodge No. 4, all the other lodges, young ladies to represent the Goddess of Liberty (riding on a wagon), as well as several bands and other organizations marching or riding in all available rigs. The speakers were honored by being transported in a double buggy. On arrival in Central from Lead, the thirsty firemen ran into the saloons and were treated to a quick beer. A large display of fireworks at night with 7,000 to 8,000 watching on the streets was an exciting event. The streets were aglow with many bonfires. The grand ball at the Central City Miners Union concluded the day's activities.

Just prior to the big three-day affair, the Deadwood Driving Park Association was formed to build a track in the city where races could be held for the Fourth of July. Sandy loam was spread on top of clay and a grandstand to seat 720 people was built. Sixty feet long, with a roof overhead, the grandstand featured pool rooms and a saloon under the seats. The Hook & Ladder Co. was out in force in uniform to keep the crowd off the track where the races were held with a purse of $1,300 for the two races.

Furnishing lots of excitement and interest were the hose companies which marched in all the parades in their uniforms. Many bets were placed on a "favorite" company to win. The fact that they were also participants in many other functions was evidenced by a news note that the "Hook and Ladder Co. sold 200 tickets to Deadwood citizens for a theatrical performance." While the main function of the fire departments was the protection of the towns, their social activities played a major part in the lives of the members and their families. These included potluck dinners and dances, lasting far into the night, with the children finally giving in to sleep, scattering themselves around on the floor in one of the adjoining rooms, with coats for pillows and covering.

Contests were staged regularly between the various departments and with fire departments from nearby towns. Races with the hose carts and other fire-fighting paraphenalia, with all the crew on foot, and tug-of-war contests were exciting. But the biggest and best were the hose fights that took place on the bridge on Bleeker Street in

The Deadwood Athletic Club was organized with A. E. Frank, president. Frank said, "The club should be of special benefit to clerks and others, who are prevented from having sufficient exercise conducive to hardness of frame and development of physique so much admired in human kind."

B H Daily Times
Aug. 16, 1882

Lead, with the losers sometimes landing in the creek. Strong, fast runners were much in demand in those days of man-powered fire fighting.

The reception given by the South Deadwood Hose Company was the grandest ever before seen in this city. The reception room on the first floor was crowded with gentleman friends from 4 until midnight and during the entire time the greatest decorum and good feeling prevailed. (large table on first floor for men) Upstairs the parlor was elegantly arranged, and a table heavily laden with refreshments, occupied a central position . . . Messrs. Bonham, Decker and Jacoby received the ladies who called, and for hours they were kept busy dispensing hospitalities to their visitors. In all over 200 called, and each one we think was pleased with the attention shown . . .

B H Daily Times
Jan. 3, 1884

Lead soon had the largest and best equipped volunteer fire department in the state, and its citizens were proud of it. It was composed of six hose companies with the full fire fighting equipment of carts, hoses, hook and ladder, lanterns, and helmets; and each had its own main building as well as auxiliary structures to house the horses and carts.

In 1888 Central City was practically destroyed by fire. The blaze started at 5:30 a.m. in Velliveau and Jensen's restaurant in the heart of the community's business district. The loss was estimated at $175,000 with 140 buildings destroyed. The fire was believed to have started in the cafe stove, still warm from the evening's business. In one-half hour, one-fourth of a mile of businesses were a ball of flames. A relief meeting was held to organize temporary housing in Deadwood for the fire victims. Rebuilding started at once and Homestake furnished the lumber. Although all of the business owners announced their intentions to rebuild, Central City was never the same — no longer was it a mining center.

The Gem Theater was denounced as an "infamous den of prostitution under the guise of being a dance hall." Several unsuspecting and innocent girls from Chicago, who had been engaged by misrepresentation, had been arrested and then set free by the Marshall.

B H Daily Times
Sept. 3, 1884

Central City, Golden Gate and Terraville had a hose company which held the state championship in the 200 yard hub-and-hub race with a time of 21:25 seconds. Its splendid bronze fire bell that hung atop the Central City hose house was preserved by placing it in the Central City school yard. It bears the inscription "C and G Hose No. 1, organized Central City, Dakota, April 25, 1889, one year after the great fire."

Smith & Fletcher's bowling alley, Main and Gold Streets, was recently re-equipped with new alleys, pins and balls, affords facilities for healthful exercise and pleasure as nowhere else presented. Every attraction is first class.

B H Daily Times
June 30, 1880

A Chinese Hose Company was named the champion Chinese hose team of the world as result of a Fourth of July celebration race staged in Deadwood in 1888. The event was unique in the history of the world due to the fact that there were only two Chinese teams in existence!

Within three months after the September 26, 1879, conflagration, the South Deadwood and Homestake companies were organized and joined the Deadwood department, which by 1898 consisted of five companies with a total of 156 firemen, eight hose carts, over 4,000 feet of hose, a hook and ladder truck, a chemical engine, as well as banners and regalia for service and display.

The hot-house at the head of Bobtail gulch is driving a good trade by furnishing the ladies of the up-gulch towns who wish to beautify their homes with a fine assortment of flowering plants in full bloom, and at moderate prices.

B H Daily Times
June 30, 1880

The Gem Theatre, destroyed in the great fire of 1879, arose out of the ashes in a larger, more luxurious structure to hold the spotlight on Main Street from 1880 into the turn of the century. Topping the big touring companies that came to Deadwood in the '80s and 90's was the Montague Company. It celebrated its 200th consecutive program at the Gem in 1887 (February 24) with a lavish production of the "Mikado," (complete with pink silk souvenir programs) which ran for 130 nights. In 1880 Red Cloud's Indian Dancers proved another popular show at the resurrected Gem. Dr. Stine reported this famed night spot, "for nearly a quarter of a century was a clangorous, tangling, insidious part of Deadwood's night life. The raucous sounds of its ballyhooing brass bands in the street outside threaded through the peeling church bells like an obligato."

The Gem-type life lived on spasmodically in saloons with new names such as the Green Front, The Mansion and The Combination, in the block below the present Ayres and Fairmont Hotels. They remained in the vaudeville circuit era with excellent traveling shows.

Gambling became the main attraction. After the "lush" days of the first "company" theatres, business declined rapidly and Lead and Deadwood were forced to rely on local entertainment and amateur plays. Railways and communication lines with the outside world brought troupers to the towns as a "side stop" on their tours across the nation. At that time the two cities were seldom entertained by nationally known artists but still attracted on occasion many actors and actresses with fine New York stage experience.

In the 1880's, after the great fire, Nyes Opera House and Vincent's Theatre were built. Vincent's opening show was "H.M.S. Pinafore." Wertheimer's Hall, between what is now Lee and Shine Street on Main Street, had other outstanding attractions such as magicians, exhibitions and wax works. From 1881 to 1885 roller skating became a craze and many halls were stripped to make spacious arenas for the new fad. Fannie Price, an actress originally with the Jack Langrishe Company, married Lorin E. Gaffey, a local attorney, and was the moving force behind many fine plays until she moved to Pierre. "Uncle Tom's Cabin" was her final production.

(February 3, 1898)

Next
MONDAY NIGHT the

JOSSEY - MARVIN
Company.

Commence a return engagement of the Beautiful Four-Act Drama:

"A Southern Rose"

On Monday evening one lady and one gentleman or two ladies admitted on one reserved seat ticket.

If the walls of the Gem Theatre could talk, many of the "goings on" in this famous early-day Deadwood fun spot would be censored. The Gem was in the center of the area referred to by more discreet society of the town, as the "Bad Lands."

(Adams Museum)

This panoramic view of upper Deadwood Gulch shows the homes and mills of Terraville (upper left), Central City (upper right), and Blacktail (lower right). The circular track heading into the cut (lower left) carried the Chicago, North Western train into Lead from Deadwood. Part of the famed Open Cut is visible to the right of Terraville.
(Centennial Collection)

# chapter XV

# Loose To Hard Gold

**An entire mountain was eventually mined away at the site of the rich Homestake lode site. Scene shows early mining operation in the "Open Cut" at Lead in 1880.**
**(Centennial Collection)**

By 1880 placer mining by prospectors on a number of Hills streams had faded away. Even the gold panners that worked in nearly every gulch to find the particles of the precious metal had for the most part left. All the loose gold was found. The problem was to find the gold beneath the surface.

Homestake's first mining interests were centered around the Manuel brothers' discovery of the Homestake Ledge, or Lead, in 1876. After Homestake purchased the early claims, the mine was developed as an open cut. Then the Homestake, under the management of an early mine superintendent, Samuel McMaster, began lode mining. The development of an ore body using the lode mining method required that shafts, tunnels, and drifts be built for access to a vein of ore. The rock of the ore body was broken and brought to the surface for processing.

Shafts were constructed as early as 1878 for underground mining activity. Hoisting equipment and the heavy machinery for a stamp mill had to be transported by oxen teams into the Hills from Sidney, Nebraska, where the closest railroad was located. Nevertheless, the mill was completed and mining accelerated. A flat rope hoist of a capacity of 100 feet was installed at the B&M shaft to lower and raise men and materials in and out of the mine. Ore was hauled out of the mine by the same hoist.

The B&M shaft was ready in 1880 and ore was soon taken from the stopes or underground mining areas at intervals of 100 feet. In the stopes, the square set timbering method was employed. As the ore was taken out, little square compartments were constructed to prevent a mine cave-in. Since the mine wasn't very deep, this method worked rather well.

Miners of the era used candles to light their way in the darkness of the mine. Leather boots, a hat to ward off dripping water, and

Alex Street was arrested for taking crude gold bullion from the Homestake Mine. Street was tried, found guilty, and sentenced to four years at the penitentiary in Sioux Falls. The paper editorialized that Grier's efforts to recover the gold shows that he is more than an "ordinary mortal" in the high position he holds.
Evening Call
July 10, 1895

Mining Stock was the order of the day. With just an entrance showing a drift into some remote hillside, mining stock was printed in Gold Scroll and proximity to the Homestake Lode a sure fire promotion.

An explosion of powder on the 300 foot level of the Caledonia Mine in Terraville killed four miners and injured many more. Blood, dust, and powder were everywhere.

B H Daily Times
Oct. 6, 1886

Miners of the Black Hills in the Dakota Territory were paid $3.50 per day, a very good salary. Foremen and skilled miners made between three and six dollars a day.

B H Daily Times
June 8, 1889

a comfortable shirt and pants were worn by the early miners. Their equipment consisted of a pick and shovel, a drill rod, a hammer, blasting gelatin; and, of course, many, many candles.

In the beginning, almost everything was done by hand. Even the drill bits were forged by hand. Miners used the double jack technique of breaking ore. By candlelight one man turned the drill steel and his partner would strike the rod with a sledge hammer to bore a hole for the explosive. When a miner performed this tedious job alone, it was called single jack drilling. During the late 1880's a contraption — the mechanical dry drill — was tried. But it proved ineffective since the ore of the Homestake Lode was unusually hard.

As the mine enlarged, horses and mules were used to aid the men who pushed the ore cars from the stopes to the shaft. On the surface steam-powered locomotives hauled the ore from the mine to the mills. The ore in the early mills was crushed by batteries of weighted stamps or small battering rams, which would run continuously in pulverizing the ore. Steam engines powered the stamp mills. After the ore was crushed, the amalgamation process was used to extract the gold from the ore. Mercury or quicksilver was added to the pulverized ore and recovered as a gold amalgam. When the amalgam was heated to a high temperature, the quicksilver boiled off and liquid gold remained.

Numerous inventions accelerated the growth of the gold mining enterprise. In the 1880's a better telephone system was added to the few telephones Homestake already had. McMaster made use of the electric generators and electric lamps, recent inventions of the times, as soon as they became available. Expansion of early mine holdings continued throughout the decade. Homestake acquired controlling interests in the Highland, Caledonia, Deadwood-Terra, and Father DeSmet mines, but did not officially include these properties in the Homestake corporation.

Homestake's operation in the beginning was dominated by legal battles and water rights disputes. The fledgling mining company was attempting to organize and simply survive. Many prospectors of the gold rush era did not believe that Homestake would be able to continue. Fortunately, they were proven wrong by 1889. After Homestake became a stable mining operation, new mining methods were introduced; larger, more efficient ore processing mills were bought or constructed, and numerous mining claims were acquired.

Other mines in addition to the Homestake workings were developed after the gold rush. Some of the more important were the Portland (later the Bald Mountain), Golden Reward, the Carbonate group, the Galena group, and the Clover Leaf (Uncle Sam).

The Bald Mountain area west of Lead was the scene of feverish mining activity in the 1880's. The Portland Mining Company had consolidated the Empire State group and lesser claims, becoming the largest mine on the mountain. But the ore mined by the Portland was difficult to treat. Various types of ore processes were tried and none proved adequate. Development at the Portland continued slowly until a satisfactory treatment process could be found.

The Golden Reward, two and one-half miles west of Lead in the Ruby Basin mining district, was formed in 1877 by combining the holdings of several mining groups. A treatment plant for the processing of difficult ores, an important mining advance, was built by the Golden Reward in 1889. The Golden Reward soon became second only to the Homestake in gold production.

The silver, lead, and gold ores of the Carbonate district, northwest of the Bald Mountain region and Lead, were developed in the 1880's. The production of lead and silver declined after 1889, but the production of gold continued on and off into the Twentieth Century. The principal mines were the Iron Hill and the Seabury-Calkins. The Iron Hill, basically a silver mine, began in 1883 and only lasted eight years. The Seabury-Calkins also began in 1883, but outlasted the Iron Hill by a couple of years. It was abandoned soon after.

In the Galena district, southeast of Deadwood, three major silver properties — the Richmond, the Sitting Bull, and the Branch Mint — produced great amounts of silver in the early 1880's. Another mine in the Galena district of some importance was the Clover Leaf, or Uncle Sam Mine, at Roubaix The Clover Leaf showed little promise as a major gold producer until 1883 when a fairly rich ore vein was discovered. The rich ore find, unfortunately, played out quickly. Mining activity at the Clover Leaf languished for the next ten years.

Early day mining operations had their share of difficulties. Explosions and natural disasters made exploration and mining dangerous. Before safety regulations were established by the federal and state governments, the safety records in the mines were atrocious. An explosion in the High Lode Mine in Bobtail Gulch killed three men. Three more men were killed in a cave-in at Gayville's Esmerelda Mine, and in 1885 a succession of five non-fatal accidents occurred in the Homestake Mine. In the name of progress, the Black Hills Daily Times editorialized, "mining accidents must be expected."

In the 1880's Homestake was only another mining company competing with other companies for control of mining interests in the Lead-Terraville-Deadwood area. Homestake had a few advantages the others lacked. Under the management of some unusually shrewd men and with consistent financial backing, the Homestake Mine could keep going while other mining ventures floundered. Homestake's promoters gambled that untold mineral wealth was in the Homestake Ledge and their gamble paid off. They had found the Mother Lode.

Samuel McMaster was an early-day Homestake superintendent. An article taken from the Sturgis Record of January 4, 1885 said: "Thus passes away one of the best-known men in the west, and certainly the central figure in Black Hills matters. Mr. McMaster's death came of an overpowering strain on a once strong constitution, and the result, probably of excess in his younger days. The cause of his death was simply this: He knew no man in the immense Homestake business but Samuel McMaster, and entrusted the details of the giant workings to no brain but his. He knew every foot of ore that was extracted; every pound that was milled; the result of every cleanup; the woges of every man, and in fact, the details of probably the largest business over managed by one man. He died with its weight on his mind . . . He was a peculiar man. He knew no friend — he didn't want to."

Deadwood's street railway tracks are conspicuous in this 1888 scene, showing sturdy brick buildings on the east side of Main Street in the block between Lee and Wall Streets. Wooden buildings with false fronts were being replaced rapidly.

(Centennial Collection)

Lead's first Christ Episcopal Church was located at the corner of Wall and Addie Streets. Meddaugh Photo (Deadwood Carnegie Library)

# chapter XVI

# An Air Of Permanency

**The city hall was a proud addition to Deadwood in 1889 and a half slice of the city's first opera house is visible on the right. The lot in the foreground later housed the Franklin Hotel, completed in 1903.**
**(Centennial Collection)**

Building activity was bustling during the 1880's. New buildings and businesses changed the appearance of the main streets of Deadwood, Lead, Central City, and Spearfish yearly. The buildings made from logs, the shanty huts, and the tents were replaced by solid, permanent structures of wood and brick. A company in Deadwood manufactured the bricks used in many of the buildings, including churches, constructed in Deadwood in the 1880's. The Syndicate Building and the City Hall, financed by a bond issue of $18,000 voted by the citizens in 1888, were also made of local brick.

However, wood, as a building product, was still in great demand and because of this, in 1886, the Division of Forestry showed concern over the vast amounts of timber being used and warned against exhausting the supply of wood through wasteful cutting.

The period from 1880 to 1890 was a flourishing one for established religion, and handsome houses of worship were constructed, several of which are still in use today. The cornerstone of St. John's Episcopal Church, Deadwood, was laid in 1880 with the first service held in the spring of 1881. St. John's Church is the Episcopal "Mother Church" for all the Black Hills region. It remains the oldest standing monument still in constant use in the area.

Christ Church, Lead, was officially designated as a Mission January 1, 1881, with services being held in the Opera House. By 1887, the cornerstone for the church was laid for the building, located on the corner of Addie and Wall Street. It was also not until 1887 that the first Episcopal service was held in Spearfish. A Spearfish woman, Susan Weare, was a delegate to the Episcopal Church convention in New York City a year or two later and it was there that she interested the granddaughter of Alexander Hamilton, first Secretary of the Treasury, in the start of the Sunday School in Spearfish. Eventually Miss Hamilton provided funds to build the church which now stands in Spearfish.

To the east of the city, and but a short distance away, the celebrated White Rocks, like "Guardian Angels" rear their heads above all surrounding objects. To visit Deadwood and not climb the summit of the peak, is to go to Egypt and not visit the pyramids. When once there, the immense distance the eye can reach, the distinctness with which objects far away appear, can scarcely be comprehended by our eastern friends. On a fair day, from the top of these rocks, in looking toward the plains, the first object is Bear Butte, a sugarloaf shaped mountain, standing alone near the foothills, a conspicuous land mark and grim sentinel, guarding the gates to these gold mines. The plains for a hundred miles and perhaps more, can be distinctly seen until they fade away into the misty distance.

Deadwood Board of Trade's
Black Hills of Dakota, 1881

2391

THE

# First National Bank

OF DEADWOOD,

United States Depository

AND

Financial Agent of the Government.

Capital, - $100,000.
Surplus, - $125,000.

OWNS U. S. 4½ PER CENT BONDS, $125,000.

O. J. SALISBURY, Pres't.
D. A. McPHERSON, Cashier.
B. P. DAGUE, Ass't Cash'r.

DIRECTORS:

O. J. SALISBURY, T. J. GRIER, P. E. SPARKS,
D. K. DICKINSON, D. A. McPHERSON.

Principal Correspondents:

| | |
|---|---|
| NEW YORK | Fourth National Bank. |
| NEW YORK | Kountze Bros. |
| CHICAGO | First National Bank. |
| SAINT PAUL | First National Bank |
| OMAHA | First National Bank. |
| SAN FRANCISCO | Wells, Fargo & Co. |
| LONDON, ENG | Baring Bros. & Co. |
| LONDON, ENG | Melville, Evans & Co. |

It has direct correspondence also with the banks in Lead City, Central City, Sturgis, Carbonate, Rapid City and Custer.

With ample capital and with its business connections, it has every facility for the prompt transaction of every kind of banking business.

Electric lights were turned on for the first time. "Deadwood is the only city without a railroad that has electric lights."
B H Daily Times
Dec. 25, 1883

The Deadwood Methodists constructed a church in 1883 on Water and Pine Streets but the May flood destroyed the building two months after work on it had begun. The present church, located on the corner of Shine and Williams Street, was dedicated May 12, 1885. A Methodist church in Lead was nearly complete in early 1881 when a violent storm blew it down. Undaunted, members began again and the building was dedicated August 11, 1881, and the parsonage in 1889.

Spearfish Methodists, who attended services conducted by a blacksmith until 1883, did not have a "regular preacher" until 1886 when Rev. A. E. Griffith was assigned and then it was another three years before their church was built.

The first Baptist church in Western South Dakota was organized in Deadwood in September, 1888, but the first house of worship was not dedicated until three years later. Located in the vicinity of the present elementary school, it was built at a cost of $7,000. Changes of pastors were numerous due to the rugged frontier life.

After the gold rush era, the growth of area businesses was phenomenal. The Deadwood Board of Trade, organized in 1883, reported that business was flourishing in the gulch. The Black Hills Daily Times characterized Lead as a growing community with many important mercantile and banking institutions. Many banks were thriving in the Lead-Central City-Deadwood area. The Lead City Bank, built of brick, opened in 1883. Deadwood had at least two banks, the Merchants National with a branch office in Central City and the Deadwood National. During the 1880's, Spearfish had a new bank built of brick. Lending institutions were also common in the area.

Other businesses were prospering. Star and Bullock of Deadwood with branch houses in Custer, Spearfish, and Sturgis advertised in the Black Hills Daily Times numerous items including mining and mill equipment, hardware, wagons and buggies, agricultural supplies, glass, and silverware. The Star and Bullock firm was a complete general store. In the 1880's, the Hearst Mercantile Company's "Brick Store," located in Lead, was one of the largest department stores in the territory. The Brick Store handled everything that was needed in a mining community.

Transportation companies doing business in Deadwood and the area were the Northwestern Express, Stage and Transportation Company, the Evans Transportation Line, the Wyoming Stage Company, and the Miles City and Deadwood Stage Line. According to "Andreas' Atlas," the total estimated amount of frieght and goods hauled by the transportation companies and others was at least four million pounds. During the summer and fall of 1886, the transportation companies, in conjunction with the Chicago and North Western and the Elkhorn railroads, advertised the sale of through tickets to "all points of the compass."

Numerous newspapers were started in the late 1870's and early 1880's. The Black Hills Miner, Western Enterprise, Deadwood Press, Evening News, Deadwood Post and Journal only lasted a few months or years. The Black Hills Daily-Weekly Times and the Black Hills Pioneer served the city of Deadwood for a number of years. The Lead City Tribune and the Belt City Herald started in 1881 but were later absorbed by the Lead Daily Call. Spearfish had three different newspapers. Only one, the Queen City Mail, survived. In Central City three newspapers were temporarily established. Terry was served by the Bald Mountain News which lasted 15 years.

No city of the size of Deadwood in the United States can boast of so perfect a telephone system as we are enjoying. In October, 1880, the first move was made with A. S. Livingston, manager. Since that time there has been some changes, but all the time the system has become more popular with our people, and today, under the management of Livingston and Baird Bro's., we have forty miles of wire connecting us with all the towns of the upper camps.

Black Hills of Dakota
Deadwood Board of Trade, 1881

The Black Hills Telephone Company, established in Deadwood late in 1878, was sold to J. L. Baird in 1881 and he extended phone service to Spearfish, Sturgis, Rapid City, Galena and Central City before selling the company to E. D. Dyar in 1883. Dyar, a Minnesotan, incorporated it that year as the Black Hills Telephone and Telegraph Company. The following year it was purchased by the Nebraska Telephone Co. and at that time there were only 235 subscribers, 120 of which were in Deadwood, 22 in Lead, and 10 in Spearfish. The residence rate was $5 a month for local service but for $2 more, the customer was entitled to unlimited calls to any phone in any of the company's exchanges. By 1888, the company listed 165 telephones in Deadwood, Lead and Central City. The Black Hills Electric Light Co. was started in Deadwood in 1883 and for a brief period Deadwood was the only city in Dakota Territory without a railroad that could boast electric lights.

Building activity was also increased by the need for enlarged educational facilities to handle the constantly growing enrollments. By April of 1880 it was reported that the Deadwood school was too small and that another room and more teachers were needed. As a consequence classes were started a month late with 216 enrolled. Along with becoming an organized town in March, 1881, a new board of education was elected. One of its first tasks was a find a better location than the Whitewood Creek site, where grounds had been flooded, and to submit a $20,000 bond issue for a new building.

By September, 1881, classes were operating in various public buildings until the new school could be completed. Enrollment by November reached 249 and it was that month that the board gave permission to the superintendent to buy one copy of Webster's Unabridged Dictionary! It wasn't until September 4, 1882, that the new school opened with a registration of 300 students.

The following spring, the schools were closed because of epidemics of scarlet fever, typhoid and diphtheria, and because of muddy roads. Then the May 16 flood destroyed the school, resulting in a special election in June at which a $8,000 bond issue was approved for a new school in a better location, above flood level. Opening of the classes was delayed until the epidemics were under control. Mean-

J. F. IRWIN. J. H. BECKMAN.

VIENNA RESTAURANT

AND COFFEE HOUSE

Oysters Served to Order. All Kinds of Game in Season.

CONDUCTED FOR THE PURPOSE OF SERVING FIRST-CLASS MEALS AT FIRST-CLASS PRICES.

SHORT ORDER BILL OF FARE.

| | |
|---|---|
| Broiled Sirloin Steak, and Eggs, | 50 |
| Veal Cutlet, plain or breaded, and Eggs, | 50 |
| Pork Chop, and Eggs, | 50 |
| Mutton Chop, " " | 50 |
| Sausage, " " | 50 |
| Ham, " " | 50 |
| Breakfast Bacon, " | 50 |
| Calf Liver and Bacon, and Eggs, | 50 |
| Mackerel, " " | 50 |
| Sweet Breads, " " | 50 |
| Scrambled Brains, " " | 50 |
| Tenderloin of Beef, | 65 |
| Porterhouse of Beef, | 75 |
| Extra for Spanish Style or with Onions, | 15 |
| Extra for Mushrooms, | 25 |
| Chicken, Stewed, | 75 |
| Chicken, Fried | 75 |
| Chicken, Broiled, | 75 |
| Breaded Veal Cutlet (Tomato Sauce) | 75 |
| Griddle Cakes, with Pure Maple Syrup, per plate, | 15 |
| Waffles each, | 25 |
| German Pancakes, | 25 |
| Cold Meats, with Bread, Butter and Coffee, | 25 |
| Cold Roast Chicken or Turkey, with Coffee, | 50 |
| Welsh Rarebit, | 40 |
| Soured Pigs Feet, | 25 |
| Fried " " plain or breaded, | 50 |
| Tripe, plain or breaded, | 50 |
| Two Eggs, fried, boiled, scrambled or shirred, with bread, butter and coffee, | 25 |
| Two Eggs, poached, with bread, butter and coffee, | 35 |
| Each additional Egg, | 10 |
| Omlette, cheese, ham or jelly, | 40 |
| Brunswick Omlette, | 40 |
| Oat Meal and Cream, | 15 |

One cup of Coffee, Tea, Milk or Ice Tea served with each Meat order. Chocolate, per cup, 20 cents.

FULL LUNCH 25 CENTS.

while, teachers out of work opened their own schools with rates of 50 cents a student per week.

In January, 1884, the new school building was completed on Main Street with such a large enrollment that another teacher had to be hired to augment the grammar department. Her class was located in the basement of the Congregational Church until an addition could be made to the new school. A fourth year was added to the high school and the first class graduated in 1886 with six students awarded diplomas. Of a total of 2118 school age children, 1139 attended classes at an average cost of $2.67 a month per pupil. Employed were 41 teachers with the average pay per month (including board) of $88.88 for males and $52.90 for females.

By 1886, 57 school districts had been organized in Lawrence County some of which were transferred to Butte and Meade Counties when they were formed. As the school census expanded, so did the tax levy. Ten to twelve mills was the average levy, according to the book of records in the county superintendent's office. Woodrow Forrest Hall in his "Education in the Black Hills before 1900" describes the early years of Black Hills Normal. In 1883 the Legislature of Dakota Territory passed a resolution establishing a school for the training of teachers at Spearfish. A small building was constructed and the next April the school began classes. The first principal was an Easterner, Van B. Baker, who was also the only teacher. Baker was found to be incompetent and students avoided his classes. He resigned after a nine-month tenure. However, the Normal School was opened again in September, 1885, under the supervision of F. L. Cook, who taught many years at the college.

When Cook first came to the school, he found its curriculum disorganized and the school building was poorly planned. The classrooms might have been made for giants, since the blackboards were too high for the students to reach. The students bought their own books, if available, but the school had no library and no books. The only desks in the building were ready to collapse and these did not belong to the school. Cook was the only teacher for a year and due to sparse funding he also became the janitor.

Though the obstacles seemed overwhelming, Cook reorganized the school. He bought or borrowed books and loaned his own books for a makeshift library. The blackboards were lowered and the desks were acquired for the 17 hopeful students who enrolled the first week. By the end of the semester, almost 40 had signed up for classes.

The Normal schools in their early years were primarily used to train elementary teachers. The curriculums were very similar to a high school course of study. The curriculum at Black Hills Normal was designed to correspond to four years of high school and one year at a university. As academic standards were revised, the curriculum at Black Hills was upgraded.

**The Main Building at Spearfish Normal was erected in 1887 following a $25,000 grant by the Territorial Legislature.**

The Deadwood Board of Education was criticized by the public for removing Superintendent Conant. At a community meeting, a resolution was drawn up that the Board either reconsider or resign.

B H Daily Times
July 10, 1885

The first graduating class from Deadwood High School contained six girls, including Irene Cushman, Estelline Bennett, and Marie Phillips.

B H Daily Times
May 24, 1886

Extensive tree planting began in 1889. Before the white man came, a few trees grew along Spearfish Creek and other streams entering the larger river. A hundred trees were set out on the Spearfish Normal campus. Cottonwood trees were planted extensivley because of their quick growth.

Queen City Mail
Jan. 26, 1939
Historic Edition

During the first school year, 1885-1886, there were more students than space in the classrooms. Although enrollment qualifications were as high as other state Normal schools, over 100 students were attending classes in a two-room building with only 80 desks. A new building was needed.

The Territorial Legislature appropriated $25,000 to be used for the school building constructed in 1887. The amount was much less than requested by the Board of Trustees, but they used the funds wisely. The product of their efforts was a thoroughly planned and well-made building, one of the best school buildings in Dakota Territory. A few years later a new dormitory and dining hall for women were needed because most of the students were women. Funds were forthcoming and the campus at Spearfish began to expand.

The biggest school event during the late 1880's was the commencement exercise. The 1889 commencement of the third class to graduate from Black Hills Normal was truly a community affair. Many local people filled the Normal hall to witness the graduation program which included music, art presentations, orations and speeches. Rather than being called seniors, the graduating class was classified as AI's. The years, 1883-1890, were a period of growth and future preparation for Black Hills Normal and its eager young students.

S. P. Allabaugh, chairman of the committee on advertising, immigration, statistics, etc. for the Spearfish Board of Trade, is planning a folder for promotion of the city.

Queen City Mail
1889

**A firemen's convention in Spearfish in 1887 prompted this parade at the intersection of Main and Hudson Streets. The building in the background has a history of brimstone and fire. The original Spearfish Hotel, a simple log cabin, dated back to the 1870's. It went up in smoke in 1880 and was replaced by a larger structure, the one shown in the photo. The new Spearfish Hotel was also a fire victim in 1884 and was rebuilt and modernized in 1946. On October 24, 1975, the structure which housed Kelley's Motor Inn, burned to the ground.**

**(Black Hills State College)**

Early-day parades were handy occasions to show off the hose cart teams of the various towns. This one was held in Lead at the upper end of Main Street.

Heading down Gold Run Gulch out of Lead is this eight-mule team freighting outfit back in the 1880's. This road is now U. S. 85 going toward present-day Pluma on the way to Deadwood.

(Centennial Collection)

# chapter XVII

# Pride In Progress

**The original Bank of Spearfish, completed in 1886, makes a backdrop for a band concert on Main Street.**

In the 1880's Deadwood and Lead were shaking the rough frontier image and each was becoming a "solid-citizen" type of town. Entering the decade Deadwood was still the leading city in the Hills but without any of the niceties of eastern towns. It didn't have paved streets, a street railroad, electric lights or gas — but it did have handsome women. Boulder Ditch, a water canal, hung over the town reaching from cliff to high hill to cliff. A visitor in town commented that looking out of his window he could see 27 saloons, four to five gambling dens and six girlie houses. Hard telling if this included the ten saloons running in lower Deadwood — called the Bad Lands because it was the most unsavory part of town. There were opium joints in Chinatown and periodic attempts were made to close them down. They were patronized both by the Chinese and the whites.

The new assay office on Lee street is now in full blast and Mr. Bomeisler is rushing things. Those who wish to know exactly what their ores contain would do well to give him a call. ADV.

B H Daily Times
June 29, 1880

Lead had its share of opium dens (one source said 30) and there were faro games running full blast. The narrow streets had mudholes and cows and pigs ran all over the place. At times the thoroughways were blocked by horse, mule and oxen teams and one individual complained that you took your life in your hands crossing the street by being kicked by a contrary mule or gored by an ox. The Mile High City did have a stable economy, thanks to the Homestake Mining Co. There were other companies operating too, mainly the Greenback Mining Co., but the outfit that had the water rights gained all the mining properties and inch by miner's inch of water the Homestake became king pin.

Senator Pettigrew introduced a bill into Congress to establish an assay office in Deadwood at a cost of not over $50,000.

B H Daily Times
January 17, 1882

In the 1880's the main topic of conversation was railroad building. Deadwood constructed a horse railroad that went through the town and connected with the Deadwood Central Railroad that tied Deadwood and Lead by rail. The Homestake's Black Hills and Ft. Pierre railroad was popularly known as the railroad that ran from a hole in the ground to a saw log. In 1890 they added passenger cars and

Deadwood has three daily and two weekly newspapers. The Herald Express, a daily and, an evening paper. The Pioneer and the Times are published in the mornings. All have power presses and are thoroughly equipped. The Pioneer was started as a weekly in 1876 and the next season came out as a daily. The Times was the first daily, and has been issued since April 7, 1877. Neither of the papers at the time of the fire missed an issue although their entire material was destroyed.

Black Hills of Dakota
Deadwood Board of Trade, 1881

Why do you buy stale crackers when you can get them fresh from the factory? Ask your grocer for them and see that they are Deadwood crackers. Factory on Sherman Street.

B H Daily Times
1880's

Mr. Herancourt's pen and ink sketch of Deadwood, will receive a few additional touches today, and tomorrow will start for Boston, where the plate will be prepared and the pictures made. It will require about six weeks time for the work to be done and the picture returned here for delivery to subscribers. It is an elegant picture, and stamps Mr. Herancourt as an artist of high rank.

B H Daily Times
Jan. 1, 1884

The Western Investment company, Jas. Carney, president, and F. W. Hamilton, secretary and treasurer, are now open for business in their handsome office on Lee St. in the Syndicate block. County and city securities purchased at the highest market price. School bonds negotiated, mining stocks and real estate bought and sold on commission, rents collected and assessments paid. Correspondence solicited.

Ibid

The year 1883 is of the past, and will soon be forgotten; 1884 has come, like its predecessor, with bright promises and alluring smiles, but it, too, will go, and be remembered only as a period of time that brought death, suffering and disappointment to countless millions of people. Allabough and The Cosmopolitan, however, are here, and they have come to stay, and their mission is to make glad the hungry multitude. Today chickens, that would make the mouth of a circuit rider water with delight, will be served.

B H Times
Jan. 1, 1884

transported people to and from Piedmont where it connected with the Fremont, Elkhorn and Missouri River Valley line.

With the approach of the '90's Lead and Deadwood were justly proud of their progress. It was noted that in Lead six-shooters and bowie knives were no longer commonplace. The streets were lined with solid brick blocks, there was a school with 303 pupils — most of any school in the Hills. The people were bright, neat and enterprising; there were many new houses (the miners doted on good homes) and many of the buildings had red roofs — more than any other city in the Hills. The new hospital had hot and cold running water with the faucets conveniently located and the operating room could be hosed down easily. The Brick Store was building a second floor and had installed incandescent lights. Not that there wasn't a vestige of the old days — in one of the saloons there was a free-for-all fight and two men were arrested and jailed; however, friends stormed the bastille and freed them. Deadwood was a cosmopolitan city of 4,000 people representing all nationalities — Africans, Scotch, Spanish, French, Ethiopians, English, Irish and Germans. Houses were renting from 10 to 40 dollars per month and there was a new jail. Town lots were selling for $400. They now had electric lights, phones, a water system and some of the streets were macadamized with gold and silver pulp (tailings).

Things looked bright for the 90's. Homestake and associates and the Caledonia were sending out $250,000 a month in bullion by Wells-Fargo to the railroad at Whitewood. More railroads were coming in (and a couple on paper) and survey and work crews were swarming over the hills and gulches. And best of all, a method of processing the hard blue ores of Ruby Basin and Bald Mountain had been discovered and a reduction works was built in Deadwood. It burned down shortly but was re-built. Before long the city had a pyritic smelter as well as chlorination works. The future looked rosy indeed.

In 1880 Lead had a population of 1,500 and by 1890 the mining town had 2,580 inhabitants. The town grew steadily during the years the Homestake Mining Co. consolidated its early holdings and soon the mine began to have a considerable influence on the community. Lead's growth extended to both sides of Gold Run Gulch and beyond. Of interest was the fact that Lead had a cigar factory; weather flags were furnished to the post office where they were hoisted for convenience and information of the public; and the Homestake had a store at Piedmont, where the railroad hauled wood to the sawmill.

Lead was known at this early date for its peculiar sound, characteristic of a mining town of the '80's, the roar of the stamps in the mills. It was also known for its appearance. Lead in the early 1880's looked like a mining town that could disappear on short notice. All the buildings with the exception of Homestake's surface works were constructed mainly with wood. No one knew how long the town would last. As the decade progressed, a few brick buildings were erected and Lead began to resemble a community that would be around for a while.

A center of attention in Lead during the early 1880's was the Homestake's narrow gauge railroad, the Black Hills and Ft. Pierre. The railroad was built to carry timber for underground mining activities and cordwood for the steam boilers that powered the stamp mills. A landmark in Lead in the 1880's was three huge chutes. The train cars of cordwood would be dumped down these chutes which led to the boilers. The railroad was used not only for business but also for pleasure. On special occasions the railroad was taken for excursions into the nearby hills for picnics and sight-seeing.

In the 1880's Deadwood changed gradually from a rough and tumble gold rush town to a fairly stable commercial and wholesale center for the Northern Black Hills. It seemed a natural place for such a center. For most of the 1880's, stagecoaches and freight wagons from Cheyenne; Sidney, Nebraska; Fort Pierre and Bismarck, D.T., terminated their daily trips at Deadwood, bringing people, supplies and news of the outside world to the community. By the end of the decade two standard gauge railroads had reached Deadwood, increasing significantly the speed of transportation and communication. The gulch was also by then connected to most of the Northern Hills mining camps by several narrow and standard gauge local railroad systems.

In the early 1880's prospectors eager "to get rich quick" were still pouring into the gulch but by the end of the 80's the local residents for the most part were engaged in more or less stable mining or other business careers. The rowdy lawbreakers of the '70's didn't find Deadwood quite as attractive. McClintock listed 66 murders and suicides in the Northern Hills from 1876 to 1879 and only seven from 1880 to 1890 — a telling statistic which points out the growing stability of the area. However, Deadwood still remained wilder than many peaceful Eastern towns. Gambling and prostitution continued in full force throughout the decade and arguments were still sometimes settled with guns or fists instead of through the developing legal system. The streets were not yet quite safe for everyone. In 1881, a Sturgis resident whose wife was apparently about to take a trip to Deadwood, wrote the following to the Black Hills Daily Times:

"Watch her kindly, stars
"From the sweet protecting skies
"Follow her with tender eyes:
"Look so lovingly that she
"Cannot choose but think of me;
"Watch her kindly, stars."

Sol Star was removed from office as Postmaster of Deadwood on the charge of "complicity with star route carrier (contractor) "in arranging arbitrary arrival of mails." Star was probably not guilty, but the victim of a sinister plot. J. A. Harding was appointed postmaster in his place.

B H Daily Times
Sept. 29, 1881

A mixup in the first names in the 1880's resulted in the wrong man being named postmaster of Lead. T. D. Edwards, long-time owner and publisher of the Lead Tribune, had been endorsed and slated for the position, but the commission was finally issued to Dolph Edwards, who published the Lead newspaper in 1882-83. According to accounts carried in the newspapers that year, the matter of the appointment of Edwards had been dragging in the Post Office Department at Washington, D. C. One day, during a lull, a clerk in the Washington office remarked that they might as well dispose of the appointment "out in Dakota" and asked what Edward's first name was. Another clerk said he didn't know but he had heard someone speak of "Dolph" so the commission was issued to Dolph Edwards instead of T. D. Edwards for whom it was intended by his political backers. Both men were surprised at the outcome. T. D. Edwards was later appointed consul at Juarez, Mexico.

Circa 1880-1883

The county commissioners assured the public that there will be a new jail.

B H Daily Times
Feb. 18, 1886

The Merchants National Bank closed its doors. The closing was caused by a heavy withdrawal of business and lack of confidence. The Deadwood National and First National Banks survived the run. The mayor closed the saloons and gambling houses as a preventive measure in case of panic, but there was none. "Statements of condition" for both banks appeared in several issues of the paper.
B H Daily Times
Feb. 12, 1887

A committee from the Board of Trade was appointed to present a bill to the state legislature for the appropriation of $50,000 to build an insane asylum in Deadwood.
B H Daily Times
Feb. 9, 1889

The city clerk is in receipt of letter from the McShane bell foundry, Baltimore, stating that the 1500-pound fire bell ordered for Deadwood's new city hall, would be cast and shipped at the earliest possible moment. Harry Damon having kindly volunteered to haul the bell from Whitewood, free of charge. The manufacturers deliver at Whitewood, freight charges paid.
B H Daily Times
Aug. 30, 1889

The newspaper's comment was that "we have great respect for the stars and have faith that they will watch her if she goes gadding around after sunset. Everybody knows Deadwood is a very moral town, but we still recommend our Sturgis City fellow-citizen to fix things so that he may be able to accompany her and watch her himself. It will be safer than to entrust her to the stars."

A major event of the decade for the residents of Deadwood Gulch was the incorporation of the City of Deadwood in 1881. There had been pressure for some time to organize a formal city government. A Revision Committee made recommendations to the 14th session of the Dakota Territory Legislature in January, 1881, complete with names of people to be appointed as mayor and councilmen. On February 12, 1881, the Legislature passed the incorporation bill. The city was to consist of Deadwood, South Deadwood, Ingleside, Cleveland, Elizabethtown and Fountain City and was to be divided into four wards. Each ward would be represented by two councilmen and a mayor would preside over the city government. Both the mayor and eight councilmen would hold office for two year terms. Among the many powers and duties given the municipality was the obligation "to prevent horse racing and immoderate driving and riding in the streets." Daniel McLaughlin was appointed mayor but the legislators appointed only three of the councilmen recommended by the Revision Committee and chose five other men to complete the roster. By mid-March the mayor had received a copy of the incorporation law and appointed men to the positions of city marshal, city attorney, police justice, engineer and city clerk. The position of treasurer was forgotten briefly by the mayor and council but soon filled once someone reminded them of the vacancy.

The Legislature had provided that there would be an election for four aldermen on the first Tuesday of June of 1881 and thereafter

**By 1886, Deadwood was becoming a well organized town. Main Street (lower part of photo) was mostly brick, fireproof buildings. Sherman Street formed a V-shaped outline in the left side of the picture. The railroads which would change the looks of the town, would not arrive until 1890.**
**(Centennial Collection)**

each year on the first Tuesday of May, four council positions would be up for election as well as other city offices. Thus there would be a rotation of half of the councilmen each year. On June 7, 1881, the first election was held with 492 men voting, and four councilmen were chosen. The newspaper reported the results by ward on June 8 with the comment:

"The above is the vote and if any of our readers desire to know the majorities of the different candidates they have our consent to figure them out. We haven't interest enough in the result of the contest to do so."

Apparently the editors felt that once the government was established, there was no reason to be interested in it. There was no doubt, however, that organization of the government was an important step in the stabilization of Deadwood. The Black Hills Daily Times pointed out that City incorporation would considerably help local real estate interests because "no eastern capitalist will loan money on property in a western mining camp" but they would in an incorporated city.

Spearfish during the 1880's became an important agricultural and cultural center for a large area north of the Black Hills.

The last outpost of civilization for hundreds of miles in 1880, it was a crossroads between East and West. Prospectors on their way to the gold fields from Montana would pass through Spearfish before moving on to the mining and agricultural areas of the Hills.

Hindering Spearfish's development as a transportation and mining center was the lack of rail connections with other area communities. Not until the 1890's did the village have a railroad route via Spearfish Canyon to Deadwood. City fathers in 1889 had hoped that Spearfish would become another Denver. However, plans for Spearfish as the metropolis of the Northern Hills didn't materialize.

Although Spearfish didn't develop as a major agricultural, financial, and industrial center like Rapid City, the town had other possibilities as a tourist and cultural center. Spearfish civic leaders in the 1880's had to settle for the town becoming the educational center of the Northern Hills when the Black Hills Normal School was established.

Unlike the cities of Lead and Deadwood, Spearfish did not have the boomtown burst during its beginning. Spearfish grew gradually and steadily and by 1890 it had a population of about 670. At times boom possibilities appeared but little became of them. Spearfish in the 1880's was never as large as Lead or Deadwood. Consequently, town development there occurred at a slower pace.

The most important events occurring in Spearfish during the 1880's were the establishment of Black Hills Normal and the in-

We regret very much to announce the intended departure of our artistic photographer, J. C. H. Grabill. As previously mentioned, he intends locating in Chicago on or about Feb. 1st next. He wishes to dispose of some views of Black Hills scenery, and for an inducement offers them at 20 per cent discount.
B H Daily Times
Jan. 10, 1889

Patronize home industry by smoking "Selection, Imperial Private and Pubb" cigars. ADV.
B H Daily Times
Feb. 8, 1889

Sol Star was elected mayor of Deadwood for the sixth time.
B H Daily Times
May 1889

From the Ottawa, Ill., Republican, Dec. 7: "Degan Brothers on Tuesday last shipped to Jones brothers, Deadwood, Dakota Territory, a fine lot of their Norman stock, consisting of three imported stallions, two imported mares, and one high grade mare. They go via Pierre, and thence overland 200 miles. Some of the animals brought as high as $2,500. Tom Jones, one of the brothers, and everybody knows Tom, one of the first men to locate at Lead City, arrived here Monday night with the stock above mentioned, and we can only hope that the speculation may prove a successful one, as it is a move in the right direction.
B H Daily Times
Jan. 1, 1884

A cholera epidemic killed a number of pigs in Lead. The affliction abated, but pigs continued to die. Humans were not infected.
Lead City Tribune
August, 1886

## Gentle Women

**Who want glossy, luxuriant and wavy tresses of abundant, beautiful Hair must use LYON'S KATHAIRON. This elegant, cheap article always makes the Hair grow freely and fast, keeps it from falling out, arrests and cures grayness, removes dandruff and itching, makes the Hair strong, giving it a curling tendency and keeping it in any desired position. Beautiful, healthy Hair is the sure result of using Kathairon.**

---

## Charles Karcher,

Manufacturer and dealer in

## BOOTS AND SHOES

**Leather and Findings.**

**BURT'S GOODS, SPECIALTY**

DEADWOOD. 24tf

---

## AUSTIN MABBS

**Moves and Raises**

## HOUSES

I will attend to raising and moving buildings in any part of the Hills. Moving heavy machinery a specialty. Address post office box 50, or call at my office at the bridge, Sherman street, Deadwood.

corporation of the City of Spearfish. On March 12, 1885, Spearfish was incorporated under a special charter granted by the Dakota Territory Legislature and a Board of Trustees was selected. The board replaced the old Spearfish Townsite Company as the legal municipal corporation. Three years later on June 7, 1888, the City was re-incorporated under a new Dakota Territory statute. The Queen City Mail described the reorganization of the city government by reporting " . . . the town was organized under the general incorporation laws into the City of Spearfish and divided into three wards to be represented in the City Council by two members for each ward. The first officers of the city were M. C. Connors, mayor; John A. Clark, clerk;" and six aldermen. The reorganization signaled the beginning of rapid growth in Spearfish.

From its beginning as a stockade and a few log cabins, Spearfish became a thriving town. The small town retained its distinctive frontier look throughout the 1880's. Many of the buildings were merely log cabins, but a few wood frame and brick buildings were erected near the end of the decade. A private banking company, Stebbins, Fox and Co., in 1883 provided the first banking service to the community and in 1887 the bank became the Bank of Spearfish headquartered in a new brick building. In 1889 a school building was completed to replace the log cabin school. The same year, 1889, a sawmill was built on Spearfish Creek near the town. A stucco mill, brick factories, and machine shops were also operating in the late 1880's.

During that decade churches were built, lawyer offices established, a flouring mill was constructed by the Spearfish Milling Co., the Spearfish Daily Bulletin began to publish, furniture and dry goods stores opened, and all other businesses characteristic of a prospering community could be found in the picturesquely-sited community.

The agricultural industry continued to grow in Lawrence County during the 1880's. The Deadwood Flouring Mill and the Spearfish Milling Co. manufactured flour from grain grown in the area. The cattle ranchers and horse breeders were prospering. Even after the gold rush, raising cattle to supply the immediate area with beef was an important business. Locally, the Jones Brothers and the Bullock Ranch specialized in horses.

Improvements in farming methods were made by county farmers during the decade. The McCormick reaper and threshing machines began to replace farming done by hand. Harvesting in the area was done bv hand with a scythe until the reaper was widely used. Since the farmer could harvest more efficiently, he could plant more crops. Innovative county farmers introduced threshing machines, pulled by six teams of horses, to replace the tedious job of threshing by hand. The threshers were ungainly and cumbersome machines, but vastly improved farm operations in the county.

In 1884 the first apple trees were set out in the Black Hills on the Joe Wells farm in Spearfish Valley and ready sale was found for this fruit as well as for the prunes, plums and cherries grown in orchards in the Whitewood valley. The names of Jesse L. Driskill, Henry Weare, Milton C. Connors and Henry Frawley were synonymous with the growth of the ranching business in the foothills during the 1880's when several large companies drove their herds to the Hills. Tom Matthews Sr., of Spearfish also had one of the largest herds in the area.

Everyone who had any money invested it in cattle in the early 1880's and as a result the range was overstocked. Money was made, however, until the hard winter of 1886-87 when the over-grazed range provided little food for the herds and up to 75 percent of the cattle were lost. It was a severe setback to those in the business.

Historic firsts for the area recorded Neil P. McArthur of Spearfish Valley as having the first reaper and binder; Rasmus Anderson, the initial blacksmith shop; and the first sizeable acreage of corn was credited to Albert Christensen.

The pioneer dairy operators in the Northern Hills lacked refrigeration and the dairymen had to rely on the next best thing, the spring house. The spring house was made of stone and located near a cold spring. If a spring was not nearby, a well was dug and water pumped to a building that served as a spring house. Dairy products could be stored in the spring house until market time and then butter, milk and cream would be shipped in a spring wagon to Deadwood or another town to be sold.

The Hills ranchers, concerned about the problems caused by homesteaders and cattle rustlers, formed the Black Hills Livestock Association in 1880 to protect and promote the livestock industry. In the county the homesteaders and farmers that followed the prospectors built fences to keep the range cattle from trampling their crops. Soon barbed wire fences of many homesteaders or "nesters" as they were called by cattlemen, blocked off access to waterholes and the range.

The ranchers, who had their hands full with rustlers, used threats, wirecutters and guns to force the nesters off their homestead claims. The homesteaders were just as stubborn and would not give in. In order to quell a threatened confrontation, the Legislature passed a Herd Law in 1885 that required the ranchers of Dakota Territory west of the Missouri to fence in their animals or be held responsible for any damage caused by roaming range cattle. The days of the free grass and water of the open range were over.

When the gold rush ended and many prospectors left the hills, the county stockmen realized that the big cities in the East were markets for area agricultural products. Farmers and ranchers in

**The most important and popular cowboy out on the range at roundup time is the cook. He is shown here trimming the crust edges off a pie, a special treat for the hungry crew. All the necessities of good cooking are visible in his chuck wagon pantry plus all the sanitary cooking utensils on the ground.**
**(Centennial Collection)**

The winter of 1886-1887 will be remembered as the worst winter in the county. Snow was heavy, blizzard conditions occurred continuously, and the temperature was frequently way below zero. Cattle losses were great.
B H Daily Times
March-May, 1887

A "sea of fire" destroyed grass and timber south and east of Boulder Park. Hundreds of men fought the wind swept fire without success. Many homes were burned and also the Jeffries saw mill. Galena was threatened.

B H Daily Times
Sept. 12, 1889

Wind, rain, and hail created much damage in the Spruce Gulch area. Two houses were destroyed and several people injured.

B H Daily Times
June 12, 1885

The Deadwood Reduction works near Spruce Gulch was destroyed by fire. The fire started in a dry room and the building was covered by insurance. The Works were rebuilt.

B H Daily Times
March 2, 1889

The principal business block of Gayville near Central City was destroyed by fire. Nine buildings were gutted including a brewery, stable, and residences.

B H Daily Times
May 22, 1886

A fire occurred in Chinatown at one a.m. in ten below weather. The fire started in an opium and gambling place and destroyed ten old buildings. Chinatown will be rebuilt.

B H Daily Times
Feb. 12, 1885

the county knew that their future depended on a railroad built to a town in the region. Near the end of the 1880's, the Fremont, Elkhorn, and Missouri Valley Railroad, seemingly in response to the hopes of local ranchers and farmers, extended its tracks to a point in the county nine miles northwest of Deadwood. The Elkhorn Railroad and land speculators saw an opportunity for land development and possibly a town.

The townsite of Whitewood was originally an orchard owned by William Selbie, one of the early settlers in the Black Hills. The Pioneer Townsite Co., an adjunct of the Elkhorn, bought the orchard and the surrounding land for a townsite in 1887. The area was surveyed by the townsite company and lots were sold at an auction on Thanksgiving Day 1887, the same year the first train arrived in Whitewood. The townsite company gave the town the name of Whitewood, which comes from the Indian Teton Sioux, "Wak Pala-Snow-Ska" or "Running Water-White-Wood." The next year Whitewood became an incorporated town.

The nearby residents of Crook City were joyous over the coming of the railroad. The Crook City settlers moved their homes and businesses the one and a half miles to Whitewood and Crook City gradually faded to extinction.

The railroad operations of the Elkhorn and later the Chicago and Northwestern employed many local residents for a number of years. Until the Elkhorn built lines to Deadwood and Belle Fourche, Whitewood for a few years became a shipping center for agricultural equipment, mining supplies, mail and livestock.

In the 1880's St. Onge in the northern sector of Lawrence County was only a post office and a few homes. The St. Onge school district was organized in 1883 and a school was built. The valley was an excellent place to raise horses and horse racing became a popular pasttime. Betting on horses by local sportsmen was a common occurrence during the early years of St. Onge.

**Early-day cowboys at roundup time in the ranchland near the Black Hills enjoy a picnic like meal in the prairie grass. In the background are two chuckwagons.**
**(Centennial Collection)**

# chapter XVIII

# County Divides, Statehood Is Won

**Judge Gideon C. Moody was the second federal judge to be assigned to the Black Hills. He succeeded Bennett in 1879. After dominating territorial politics for ten years, when South Dakota was admitted to the Union he was elected to the U. S. Senate. For many years he was chief attorney for the Homestake Mining Co.**

As originally organized, Lawrence County encompassed the territory that makes up Lawrence and Meade counties today. The division of the territory into two counties was accomplished in the same year as statehood for South Dakota, 1889. The primary cause of the separation was the extreme distance of the county seat which created a travel hardship on those residing in the eastern portion of the county when they had legal business to transact. There also were complaints by those in the agricultural districts about being taxed for the maintenance of the courts, which handled mainly mining cases and were of no benefit to them.

Although they had labored hard for such a separation, when the time came and they had set up a county government of their own, they found they were burdened with a heavy debt. While Lawrence County hated to have her agricultural residents leave, they could not be dissuaded and Meade County was created and named after Fort Meade. In the adjustment of credits and debits of Lawrence County, the commissioners, in a joint meeting, apportioned to Meade County, twenty two and one-tenth percent of the total indebtedness of Lawrence County based on the assessed valuation of the county in 1878. As a guarantee of payment, Meade County issued bonds to Lawrence County. It was then decided that the commissioners had overstepped the limits prescribed by law, and litigation ensued. The issue continued in the courts for several years and was finally settled by the U.S. Supreme Court, holding Lawrence County for the full face of the bonds.

In the July 10, 1887, issue of the Black Hills Daily Times the following article appeared:

'The long threatened move for a division of the county has finally taken definite shape, after everybody other than those directly interested had forgotten all about it; and it would seem from the

It was noted that several colored people were in residence in Deadwood. They were all Republicans — 'the party of liberty.' If it wasn't for the Republican Party these people would still be slaves.

B H Daily Times
September, 1882

The first session of the Supreme Court and Grand Jury was conducted in Deadwood with a calendar of twenty cases. Chief Justice Edgerton and Associate Justice McConnell from Medora presided.

B H Daily Times
October 6, 1885

*Premium List of the*

"Zipp's for Boots and Shoes."

F. ZIPP,

Manufacturer of and Dealer in

BOOTS AND SHOES,

Deadwood, Dak.

FRANK X. SMITH'S

Saloon

AND BEER HALL,

Corner Main and Lee Street, - DEADWOOD.

ST. LOUIS KEG BEER ON TAP.

*Fine Stock of Wines, Liquors and Cigars Kept Constantly. Cold Lunches whenever you want them.*

timidity, not to say secrecy, characterizing the action of the ones having the matter in hand, that it is thought best that interest should not be restored."

The article goes on to state that the petition that was presented to the county board had the signatures of 457 people who were residents of Deadwood, Sturgis and other localities within the county. The proposed division would give new Meade County the largest portion of the territory, taking 43 townships and leaving 23½ to Lawrence County. The Times reacted later that month to an article that was printed in a Sturgis paper, finding its article "amusing." The Sturgis Record had printed the following account of the presentation of the petition to the Lawrence County Board:

"Monday morning the matter came up, and Commissioner Frank Allan moved that an election be called in accordance with the terms of the bill, under which segregation is desired. There was, however, a petition presented, signed by residents of the county seat, asking for delay, and its presentation to the board by one of the king bees of the script gang was eagerly watched by a crowd of those speculators in county paper and men who have been supplying Lawrence County with various things — merchandise and 'services.' It would be good reading to vote the big bugs and butterflies, the carrion moths and millers, as they asked for more time — even a two weeks delay in giving up jurymen and witness script from this end of the county. Some of those that thronged to see that 'justice' was done are even under indictment for irregularities (that's mild) in county script but the force of habit was so great that they couldn't bear to see an attempt to segregate without a choking sensation."

The movement for division proceded, however, and eventually was successful. By remaining in the hands of the territorial Governor, although not signed, the bill dividing the two counties became law on March 7, 1889. The only comment from the Times was:

"The Governor, it seems, did not give the houses the supreme satisfaction of over-riding a veto, whereat, we opine, the members were greatly disgruntled. The bill differs from the one of two years ago, only in county boundaries, the 'jog-in-the-timber' and other 'jogs' being so cut as to give Tilford the worst of it as a candidate for county seat."

By the time the county division fight had been settled the pioneers of Lawrence County were swept up in another major political issue — the battle for Statehood — and a number of its most prominent citizens were destined to play leading roles in it.

As the last Fourth of July for the Territory of Dakota was planned to its final stages in Deadwood, the people who wished statehood had great reason to celebrate. Many obstacles in the previous years had proved the undoing of other statehood movements for the Dakotas. For example, national politics had played a role for a while with the Democrats opposing the admission of North and South Dakota for the reason that four sure Republican votes would tip the balance of power in the Senate. Another factor was the independence of the people themselves who seldom pulled in the same direction. For instance, in 1877 a territory-wide vote was taken concerning division and statehood. The people in what was to become North Dakota voted by an overwhelming majority of 18,000 to 8,000 against division of the territory. But in South Dakota, the voters favored division by a plurality of 14,000, although fully 15,000 declared against division. The people had also been to the polls in 1883, 1885, 1887 for votes on statehood, a state constitution, or division. But the vote was light, the people of the south showing more interest by casting double the vote of the north on the average.

As a major mining area in the country, Deadwood during the year of statehood admission of 1889, was in the thick of state politics. It was estimated that less than 200 men achieved statehood for North and South Dakota in that year and only a dozen possessed any true political popularity. All of those twelve were from southern Dakota and two of the most eminent, Judge G. C. Moody and Judge D. Corson, were from Deadwood. In spite of the fact that the Black Hills area was effectively cut off from the rest of the territory by the large Indian reservation to the east, it played a substantial part in the state politics of the day. An indication of this influence is the fact that Lawrence County had 24 delegates to the Republican Convention of 1889, an amount equal to the other two biggest counties of Brown and Minnehaha. Thus, it was natural for the editor of the Black Hills Daily Times to effuse on the coming Fourth of July Celebrations. The people were about to be set free!

> "No one not a resident of a territory, before the dawn of emancipation had awed the federal authorities into a degree of respect theretofore unknown, can conceive the galling situation because of the humiliating conditions under which we have been placed. Happily such are passing away, and long before another national day of the nation, South Dakota will be in touch with the great sisterhood marching to the music of the Union, and not mere onlookers of a glorious pageantry. Dakotans should rejoice, and do rejoice with great vehemence, and have abundant warrant therefore."

The major issue of the day, besides statehood, was prohibition. The issue had been one of which the people of the territory had agreed at an earlier election should be submitted to the people for decision when statehood came. The betting on which way the state would go was fast and furious but it appeared on Independence Day 1889 that the "drys" had the edge, in spite of the furious and vitrolic editorials against the same that the Black Hills Daily Times was pumping out.

The issue of the selection of the first representatives of the state on the national and state level was also of high interest and spec-

*Premium List of the*

**AYRES & WARDMAN,**

Wholesale and Retail

**HARDWARE**

**And Mining Supplies,**

DEADWOOD, DAKOTA

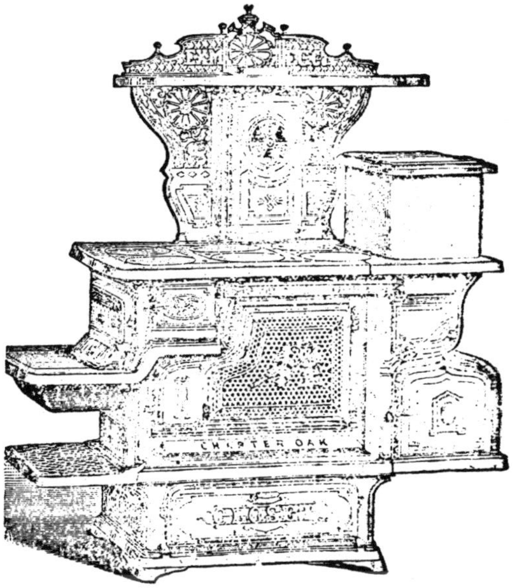

THE CELEBRATED

**CHARTER OAK STOVES.**

A citizens meeting is organized to discuss revelations of the mismanagement of county affairs. A committee of fifteen is appointed to investigate and take necessary action.
B H Daily Times
Oct. 22, 1885

President U. S. Grant died. The city of Deadwood was in deep mourning with all flags at half mast. A public assembly was arranged by Mayor Sol Star.

B H Daily Times
July 23, 1885

**MAX FISHEL,**

Wholesale and Retail Dealer in

STATIONERY,

BOOKS, TOYS,

FANCY GOODS.

**Jobber in Fine Cigars.**

Sole agent for the Black Hills for the genuine
*Singer Sewing Machines.*

*Machines rented by the month. All kinds of needles, oil and extras for sale.*

*Machines Sold on Monthly Installments. Send for Catalogue & Price List.*

I carry the largest stock in the territory, and parties can be easily suited in anything for Wedding or other presents.

**Main Street, - - { Deadwood, Sturgis.**

ulation. One of the more eager candidates for senator was Judge Gideon C. Moody from Deadwood, an ambitious attorney who had long fought for statehood and who was backed by the Homestake Company. He was not without his enemies, however. But the Times never missed an opportunity to back him up by knocking anyone who had anything bad to say about him.

"Those democratic pin-head editors egged on by a few straggling sorehead ex-members of the Republican Party also attempt to send the impression abroad that Judge Moody unduly exercises authority over the constitutional franchise of employees of the Homestake company. The only reason they have for this absurd assertion is that Lead City renders a republican majority on election day. The very minute organization of 'corporation and capitol' cannot imagine how Lead City is made up of republicans largely, although they are willing to admit that every other town in the Hills but the sheep ranch town of Hereford bring in large republican majorities at every election. Judge Moody has clear sailing in his ambition to become the first United States senator from South Dakota and such pestiferous sources are not liable to cloud his way."

Another issue in the politics of the day was the opening to settlement of the plentiful land of the Indian reservation to the east of the Hills. As Judge Moody put it in a speech on July 10, 1889:

"The extinguishment of the Indian title to so large an area of our state must be insisted upon and that speedily. If the red man refuses to accept the terms so considerately tendered him, the right of self preservation manifestly requires that Congress must legislate in the interest of the white man. Treat the Indian with all proper consideration and kindness, but yield him no more privileges than properly belong to the white man. With this accomplished and railroads permitted to traverse longitudinally throughout this great domain, the problem of cheap fuel will be solved. Compact and continuous settlement will accrue, and this state will assume the proportion in which the law of nature and nature's God has placed it, one of the brightest stars in the great constellation imprinted upon the emblem of American Liberty."

As the summer of '89 wore on, arguments for and against prohibition were dredged up. Surveying the scene, the Times decided that prohibition would not only mean bootlegging, but would also mean that Lawrence County would be short on revenue.

"If prohibition would bring a compensating advantage, there would be no great objection to such willful deprivation, but the history of prohibition in every state wheresoever tried, demonstrates that liquor drinking is not suppressed, and that the only effect upon the liquor traffic is a relief from financial burdens imposed by a license law. Prohibition means the freest kind of free liquor of the vilest quality. It means a multitude of dives, holes-in-the-wall, obscured establishments and surreptitious transactions. High license, on the contrary, signifies a handsome revenue to the county and city; a limited number of regularly and decently conducted establishments and an absolute supression of the hell-holes from which four-fifths of all iniquity chargeable to liquor, now proceeds."

At the close of the constitutional convention, Judge Moody came back to Deadwood to prepare for his campaign for senator. Shown a copy of a Tilford newspaper attacking him, Moody was asked if he had any reply:

> "No," replied the Judge: "Dawson (the editor) is too small fry to waste my time over. I am too busy. I have read part of his rabid abuse of me, but I cannot stop to answer all the lies such whiffets may feel called upon to publish. However, his publications in such papers as the Tilford Times and Lead Tribune won't do me any harm. I am not seeking the support or friendship of such cattle. I am a republican and expect such abandoned rascals will lie about me to their heart's content. I cannot afford to stop and notice them. Abuse from such a source is far more to my credit than praise would be."

The big and exciting issue of statehood, however, did not deter the good citizens of Deadwood from dealing with the day-to-day problems of existence in the Hills. The following letter to the editor found on the front page of the Black Hills Daily Times, September 15, 1889, attests to that:

> "Please print the following notice that the guilty may take warning. Having organized a woman's vigilance committee, we have resolved to rid our town of the would-be respectable prostitutes that have in the past, are in the present or will in the future try in any way to make trouble in any of our Deadwood families, by separating the husband and wife and disgracing the innocent little children, or by trying to cause trouble between husband and wife. We will introduce the woman to the cowhide or a dose of tar and feathers. We will leave the man(?) in the case to the mercy of his wife. We will begin with - - - - - - - - - We will give them one month in which to leave our town. Any time after that they may expect an interesting call from us. Our city officers are very careful to drive all the tramps and vagrant persons from our town, but they leave worse villains than tramps unmolested. Therefore we have resolved to rid the town of the would-be-respectable villainous women that are a disgrace to their sex. DEADWOOD WOMAN'S VIGILANCE COMMITTEE."

Almost as a harbinger of things to come, the Times displayed for several days before the important election of state and national officers, the following slogan, in black headline form, interspersed between articles and columns: "IF A KNOWN REPUBLICAN ASKS YOU TO VOTE FOR A DEMOCRAT, SPOT HIM AS A TRAITOR, AND REMEMBER HIM FOR ALL TIME TO COME." But the election was held and some Democrats were elected. The Times

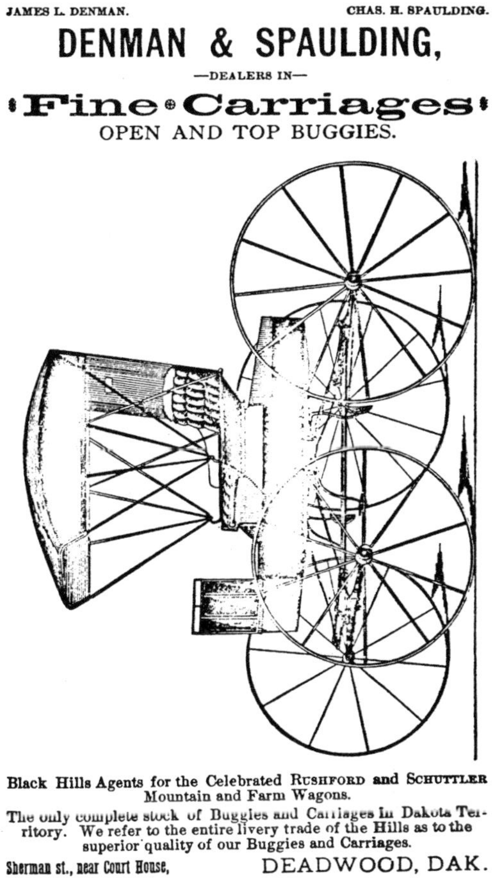


Judge G. C. Moody received a great ovation upon his return from his senatorial campaign in Eastern Dakota. Accusations have been made about his war record at Buffalo Mountain during the Civil War. Moody was exonerated of any guilt or acts of cowardice.
B H Daily Times
Sept. 28, 1889

took it hard, as the headlines evidenced: "A SLAUGHTER: An Important Portion of the Democratic Ticket Elected. Mr. Hastie Butchered in the Camp of his Friends; the Legislative Ticket Under the Black Shadow of a Grave Doubt; Pennington County Elects an entire Democratic Ticket."

The election enthusiasm in the cities of Lead and Deadwood was varied, however.

At Lead:

"It was one of the liveliest elections known to the town, resulting in 1,013 votes, against 800 last fall. The day shift was given time to vote, and with the night shift at or near the polls, gave a very animated appearance to the streets. Here it was that the great knifing act occurred, consequently a great variety of tickets and posters in unlimited quantities appeared. Saloons were apparently closed, but the condition of many individuals indicated that a back-door or two was conveniently ajar. At this writing it is uncertain that returns will reach us in time for this paper. Hastie was unmercifully slaughtered, and Parker and Wolzmuth badly cut, in the interest of Thomas and Cox."

At Deadwood:

"Many a city election has occasioned more interest and excitement, and every county election has drawn out a larger vote and occasioned more concern. For instance, at the election last fall, a total of 793 votes were polled, while yesterday's total amounted only to 657 . . . this too with a larger population than a year ago. Such apparent apathy is not easily explained. It is true — and to their shame be it stated — that a certain element understanding or suspecting that, in the aggregate, a large sum of money had been sent to the Hills by capital boomers, declined to vote because not offered money therefore. At first they were very stiff and offensive in their demands, but as the closing hour approached they relaxed, and finally dropped to a nominal sum, but that even was refused, and almost before they knew it, the polls closed. For such proceding the prohibition element is very grateful, as otherwise the 'wet' vote would have been increased the full strength of the saleable class.

"Indifference largely explains the small vote. Many persons even when sent for with carriages, declined to leave their work, and several instances were observed where they passed the polls and refused to stop.

"Meteorologically it was a delightful election day. The sun shone brightly from morning till night, while a light breeze maintained agreeable temperature. Banks and all public offices were closed continuously, and all saloons were under lock and key till after 5 o'clock. As a result, no intoxication was anywhere observed, and no disorder reported. During the forenoon the streets were deserted like unto Sunday, save at the polls where at no time any-

Seventy-five of McDonald's men employed on the Elkhorn Tunnel, quit work Wednesday evening, on account, they said of poor and inadequate grub . A Burlington runner, offering $2.50 a day induced the greater number to accompany him to the grade near Rochford. The party reached Deadwood at an early hour yesterday morning and, pending the arrival of transportation, proceeded to do the Bad Lands in "Bad Man" style. After several unsuccessful encounters with saloon and store owners, Dr. Freund rushed to the aid of an officer of the law who was being attacked and they collared four of the leaders and escorted them to the lockup .

B H Daily Times
June 27, 1890

This is the last day of grace. Tomorrow the penalty bill will be in force, and as for a month even druggists cannot dispense alcohol, or a compound of which alcohol is an ingredient, theoretically, at least, absolute prohibition will prevail. "What are they going to do-" is a question involving liquor men often heard. It is safe to reply they will abide by the law. No one, however, will suffer from the lack of stimulants, inasmuch as during the last month wholesalers and retailers have been doing a rushing business filling bottles, demijohns, kegs, etc. to meet the demands of families and individuals. Scarcely a habitation in Deadwood is without a sufficient supply to withstand a siege of at least six months, at the end of which time a method of supply from points beyond the state will be devised. John Treber is planning on moving his mammoth stock to Beulah, just over the line in Wyoming from which he will fill orders for original packages.

B H Daily Times
April 30, 1890

thing like a crowd assembled. No challenges and no wrangling occurred at either poll. The W.C.T.U. opened a free coffee booth in the old Franklin & Baer building, but it was poorly patronized save by ladies and gentlemen of prohibition proclivities. The only approach to a spirited contest was over capital location. Pierre money paid for the Lead band, which made a tour of the belt and Deadwood. It was easy work for the Pierre boomers, however, as their town at all times has been the favorite. Watertown was well represented, and Watertown checks for $20, payable in the event of that city capturing the temporary location, were plentiful last evening. At noon only 245 votes had been polled . . . "

The election results made Pierre the capital of South Dakota.

On November 3, 1889, Secretary of State Blaine sent the following dispatch to the Dakotas:

> "To Governors Mellette and Miller, North and South Dakota: The last act in the admission of the two Dakotas as states in the union was completed this afternoon at the executive mansion at 3:40 o'clock by President Harrison signing at that moment the proclamations required by law for the admission of the two states."

On November 18, 1889, Gov. Mellette issued a Thanksgiving Proclamation that called for rejoicing that the state had achieved statehood. He urged that business and labor be suspended on the 28th after 10 a.m. for thanksgiving in each one's own religious way. The final act in the long battle for Statehood fueled a brief controversy between the two states over their priority of admission to the Union. President Benjamin Harrison, after signing the admission documents, purposely shuffled them. So it wasn't known which of the twin states was the 39th to be admitted and which was the 40th. Eventually the dispute was settled on an alphabetical basis by mutual agreement.

A week or so ago a party of strangers visited the city ostensibly in the interest of the Pioneer Press of St. Paul. They were glib talkers and chaperoned by a gentleman well known to this community, and persuaded our people to contribute over $600 spot cash in consideration of honest, impartial and a fair write-up of the locality. The result is at hand, one of the cleverest swindles . . . The Pioneer Press of April 11 to arrive last evening entertains two pages purporting to be a "general description of the famous Black Hills, and what they contain." It is nothing of the sort. On the contrary it is the boomiest kind of a boom article in the interest of Rapid, so replete with falsehood and so studiously avoiding reference to Deadwood and its environment that great harm and no good possibly can result.

B H Daily Times
April 14, 1888

**This map shows Lawrence County after it was divided with a portion forming Meade County Circa 1897**

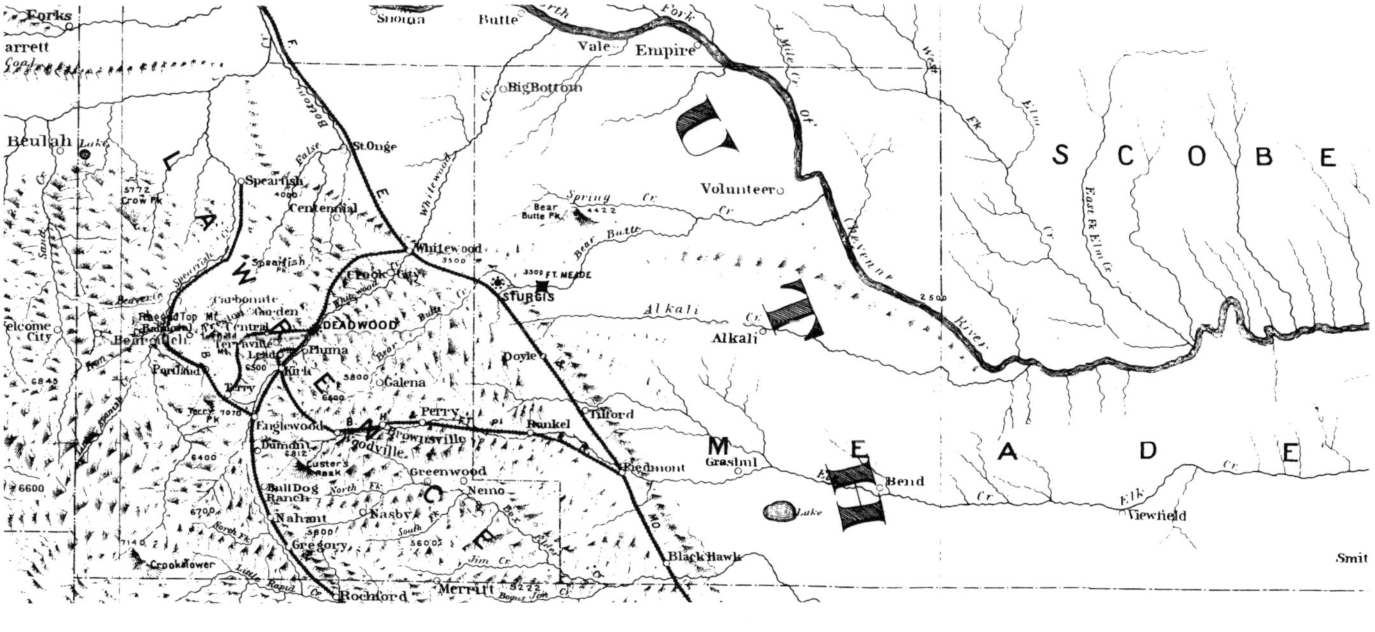

The Aurora Borealis Club is shown in 1893 at a social gathering. Charlotte Cushman, later Mrs. Horace Clark (second from left) now living in Lead, is the only survivor. She celebrated her 100th birthday in 1975. Edna Ford (on the right) was a grade school teacher in Deadwood for many years.

(Courtesy of Cushman Clark)

Charles Brown had the leading role in a drama of death on July 14, 1897 beside the county courthouse in Deadwood. Everyone had a ringside seat for the hanging of the convicted murderer. The Hattenbach building (visible top center) is still a landmark on Sherman Street.

(Centennial Collection)

# chapter XIX

# The Good Life--
# And The Bad

Life, as a whole, was good in the Northern Hills during the 1890's. Family and social activities were dominant and women were enjoying some of the luxuries offered in those years.

(Adams Museum)

The period of 1890 to 1900 was the end of an era for the gold rush communities but it was the beginning of finc living and enjoyment of life. Social activities took the spotlight. Where in years before most of the entertainment was supplied by traveling theatre groups, now it was being furnished by local talent, of which there was a good supply, both in music and sports.

However, the numerous theatres were still competing for customers by bringing in professional troupes which put on light operas, comedy, song and dance acts and various exhibitions of skill. Raffles were also popular and the prizes were attractive. The Oyster Bay offered a gold watch for the lucky number and Allen's Saloon in Central gave a silver tea set to the winner.

The ladies organizations of the churches were wasting no time in attracting the populace to their form of entertainment for pleasure and profit, with members of their congregation and some borrowed from "outside." "The Two Golden Lilies" was presented at the Methodist Church in Lead with tickets at 25 cents for this "service of song." Lawn socials were at least once a week affairs. The Lead Baptists had several at the J. S. Freeman residence, with one advertising "A program of guitar, piano, singing by Miss Ferrie, Jones children and W. R. Dickenson." A cake contest was held and the winner decided as follows: Everyone buying a lemonade was given a lemon and the person finding the most seeds in the same was awarded the cake. The Congregational Church had a "pound" auction in which things weighing a pound were sold.

Benefit dances were often given for someone who had met with misfortune; a game of cribbage to decide who would have undisputed possession of a young lady's affection drew a large crowd and every point was watched; home talent entertainment in the Miners' Union Hall at Terry was packed to the doors.

The ladies of the Congregational Church will give a bonnet social at the residence of Mrs. S. Koenigsberger, Ingleside, on the 19th inst. An amusing feature of the evening will be the trimming, by the gentlemen present, of a hat or bonnet from materials furnished by them at the house, each being required to depend entirely on his own taste and skill, no suggestions from the ladies being permitted. While it is not expected that any of the work will rival a Chesney or the art of a Beebick, those present may at least be assured of seeing some startling effects in the millinery line. The finished bonnets will be worn to supper by the ladies to whom they may be presented. A committee will give their decision as to the merits of the work. A light but bountiful supper will be served, for which a charge of 25 cents will be made, which will entirely cover the cost of the evening's pleasure.

B H Daily Times
April 19, 1895

**Houses of prostitution in Lead were concentrated in the Mill and Bleeker Street area during the 1890's. They featured a dance hall on the main floor from where the miners were enticed upstairs. The most famous house had Fannie Hill for its madam. She advertised for gals and musicians through Omaha newspapers for her "Fannie Hill's Dancing Academy."**

**(Adams Museum)**

Cook-Culbertson — at Winona, Minn. Thursday, Aug. 25, 1892. Prof. F. L. Cook and Wenona Culbertson. Prof. Cook, as will be remembered, is and long has been the head of Spearfish Normal school of which Miss Culbertson was one of the teachers. "At home, Spearfish, after September 15th," says the card.

B H Daily Times
Aug. 30, 1892

CONCERT

....MUSICAL
Miners Union Hall and LITERARY

Monday Evening August 21

BY TERRY'S BEST TALENT

Mrs. Crow, Mr. A. Richards, } Directors. CHILDREN 15 Cts.

New secret societies and lodges were being formed as well as ethnic groups. A national organization known as "Improved Order of Red Men" was started in the area around 1899. It was social in nature and used Indian names and terms in its bylaws and records. The Lead tribe was "Sitting Bull No. 3" and Deadwood, "Lakota No. 1." Although very secret, the lodge helped its members when they were financially in need. The Matrimonial Society of Central, a once-famous organization, was reported by the Lead newspaper as preparing to reorganize and regain its former place as "the" popular society. At one time they held a large membership and gave dances and entertainment in the Hills. When members married they were presented with $100 and a nice present by the Society.

There was an Italian society known as S.I.M.S.C.C., an English League comprised of all residents born in England, Slavonians organized for social and political purposes with 125 names on the roster and a Scandinavian club and an Anglo-American League were two more. The Lead Daily Call reported that the lodge rooms over the Miners' Union in 1894 accommodated many lodges, including the Miners' Union, Masonic, IOOF, AOUW, K of P, Mine Workers of America, and various temperance, literary and national organizations. Illustrating the enthusiasm of the members was the Lead Knights of Pythias group which rounded up a delegation to attend the annual encampment held in Washington, D.C., with the round trip fare only $49.15!

Study groups continued in favor with the ladies and equal suffrage was a popular topic for club meetings as it was eyed as an improvement to the tone of both social and political life.

Black Hills Normal, Spearfish, served as the cultural center for that city and supplied orators and speakers on nearly every subject for the surrounding communities. In fact, the Black Hills Weekly Times of February 22, 1896, reported that Dr. J. W. Hancher, president of Black Hills College, delivered a speech, "Our Daughters," on February 19 at the M. E. Church in Deadwood. The one and a half hour talk dealt with the equality of girls to boys and the benefits of a broad liberal education for women. By 1890 teachers of Latin, reading, history, science, math, art and gymnastics had been added to the faculty. The Spearfish Weekly Register praised the capabilities of the faculty and the high standards set for the students. As the college student population grew to over 300 in 1900, new teachers were constantly added to the faculty. Indeed, the services rendered to the Spearfish community by the school were immeasurable in the years before the turn of the century.

Numerous hose companies were organized during this decade as each community strove to eliminate fires which had proved so costly since the gold rush days. As they organized, each company planned its own social activities. Every town and village also had at least one band and they all kept in practice for special musical programs, parades and picnics. Lead had three first-class bands and several theatres in Deadwood, as well as the lodges, had their own. In the summer of 1894, Lead was promoting the idea of a band tournament, sponsored by several Hills newspapers. Hot Springs later in the summer sent an invitation to all bands to be present at a band carnival with expenses paid by Fred Evans, the pioneer freighter and entrepreneur of that community.

A prettier sight than the city hall, without and within last evening, has seldom ever been presented in Deadwood. The spacious windows unscreened permitted a flood of light to fall upon the streets beneath and to illuminate the city for a long distance round. The council chamber became the dancing pavilion. Seventy five couples participated in the grand march, which was led by Arthur Simpson of Lead, the Deadwood orchestra furnishing the music.

B H Daily Times
Feb. 14, 1890

If a holiday picnic wasn't being planned, the bands would organize one and put up the dance pavilion as well as serve all the refreshments. One Labor Day there were two such doings, one in Bender's Park and one at the City Park. Besides, the Knights of Pythias band of Terraville went to Spearfish on the early train to entertain the crowd at their Labor Day celebration at Powers Grove and Jefferson Park. It was at the latter event that J. W. "Buc" Driskill donated two fat cows for a barbeque.

Yesterday was the opening day of the regular fall meeting at Deadwood Driving Park. Early in the morning the Knights of Pythias Cornet band, with the wind blowing through their new linen dusters and their new white stiff hats shining in the sun's sarcastic blare mounted a band wagon with streamers flying and started out on a tour of the belt, literally drumming up an attendance for the races.

B H Daily Times
Sept. 12, 1892

Baseball teams were starting to be formed. One early nine went over to Fort Meade and scored a victory. Shorty Moran's Colts and the Kickers from Deadwood staged a ball game at Hiawatha Park and this eternal rivalry between the uphill and downhill clubs went on for the rest of the summer.

Foot races were an interesting part of every celebration and sometimes were held as a separate event. Ben Rathbun and Rod Murray, according to the Lead Daily Call, ran a foot race of 100 yards before a large crowd, with the winner receiving $25. However, Labor Days and celebrations on the Fourth of July were really the place to go to enter every kind of track event and other competitive contests. There were sack races, greased pig race, fat man's race, tug of war, and even a bronc riding exhibition by the Jolley Bros., which netted them $25. Tug of war winners received $25 and the losers 20 bottles of beer! A contest, which could hardly be classed as a sport, was arranged between two of the fastest whisker butchers in South Dakota, according to the Lead paper. The match was to take place during the Business Men's Carnival, and the paper predicted that "considerable will be bet by friends of both parties."

A pretty trial run was made by the South Deadwood running team on Main street last evening. The boys got over the ground at a very rapid rate, and the connections at the plug were made without a hitch. Lynch and Higbee, who did the coupling, worked like a unit and made the coupling with incredible quickness.

B H Times
July 1, 1892

Kiemer's Opera House, later known as the Deadwood Opera House, was in existence from 1886 to 1890 and was located next to the present site of the Masonic Temple on Main Street. Originally built for a theatre, it opened, however, as a skating rink. When interest in that entertainment ebbed it reopened on June 11 in the same year with the Grace Hawthorne Company in "The New Camille" followed by 11 other productions. The lease was not renewed the following year but the firemen used the structure to prepare for an immense Fourth of July celebration and plays were produced. Reopened again

In the Gem Theater, Deadwood, Jack Fassold slapped a dance hall girl. Charlie Large came to the aid of the girl and pushed Fassold aside. Fassold pulled a gun and a struggle ensued. The revolver fell to the floor during the struggle and discharged striking Large in the chest. John Byrnes, manager of the Gem, attempted to stop the commotion, but Fassold struck Byrnes on the head several times. Fassold was arrested and held for $300 bond.

Evening Call
April 23, 1896

**Phoebe Hearst was the wife of George F. Hearst and the mother of William Randolph Hearst, millionaire newspaper publisher. She was a widely-known philanthropist throughout the United States. Hearst made a good share of his fortune as the major stockholder in the Homestake Gold Mine at Lead. Mrs. Hearst maintained the free kindergarten and library in Lead. A reception was held there in her honor early in the century when she returned for a visit. Thousands attended the reception held at the home of T. J. Grier, Homestake superintendent, to pay their respects to Mrs. Hearst and her contributions to the city.**

in 1888, the blizzard and severe winter of that year and 1889 brought a lull in the activity. However, it gained momentum and theater lovers continued to enjoy productions there until it burned in the early part of the new century. Many of the same troupes or similar casts played at the Miners' Union House in Lead, situated where the present First National Bank of the Black Hills now stands.

But perhaps the main cultural event of the decade was the establishment of the Hearst Free Library. "The city of Lead and all of the citizens have cause for rejoicing and remembering the Christmas of 1894, for all time to come." So says the official record concerning the origin of this public enterprise. The library was a Christmas gift to the city of Lead from Mrs. Phoebe A. Hearst.

The Lead Woman's Club started the kindergarten and so entranced with it was Mrs. Hearst on a visit to that city that she took over its financial responsibility and every year she came back to inspect the facilities and the eager young pupils. The library was first installed in the Miners' Union Opera House with Mrs. Ferrie (later Mrs. T. J. Gier) as the first librarian. Only a reading room where musical entertainments were given in July of 1896, the library was moved to the Hearst Store on North Mill. The loaning of books had not begun until that year.

Thanks to another woman's club, Deadwood's first library was opened in March 1895 in Room 5 of the Syndicate Block. The great cultural achievement was through the efforts of the Round Table Club which incorporated the Round Table Club Library Association with capital stock of $5,000, represented by 1000 shares of stock at $5 each. The club secured what books they could, gave entertainments to raise money to buy more and later that month published their first catalogue consisting of about 1,000 volumes.

The automatic organ recently ordered by the Deadwood Masonic order of Deadwood, which was ordered through agent Hawley, arrived in the city yesterday. The organ is almost identical with that now in use at the K. of P. hall and is equipped with music rolls suitable to the order.

B H Times
July 8, 1892

This was not a free library. Memberships were sold at a cost of $1.50 per year to stockholders and $3 per year to non-stockholders. Transients were given the use of the library on a deposit of $1 as security and a fee of 10 cents a week. Later the library was turned over to the City of Deadwood to operate and in 1899 it was moved to a room in the Smith Block, later known as the Wagner Hotel building, and the name was changed to the Deadwood Public Library.

About this same time the Thursday Club and other women's clubs became interested in the library project and through their cooperation, aided by influential citizens of Deadwood and the efforts of Mrs. Marie Gaston, librarian, a grant was obtained from the Carnegie Foundation. Land was obtained, the ground broken and construction of the present Deadwood Public Library was started and carried through to completion.

The members of the Round Table Club with their husbands and gentleman friends, assembled at the home of Judge and Mrs. G. C. Moody on Wednesday evening the 13 inst, to celebrate the eighth anniversary of the organization.

B H Times
Feb. 15, 1895

The Society of Black Hills Pioneers, organized in 1889 in Deadwood, had as its reasons for existence the creation of a fund for helping indigent pioneers; the collection and preservation of information on the early settlement of the area; and the gathering of biographies of Black Hills founders. In the beginning, only those coming to the Black Hills before 1877 could be members. This created animosity on the part of many who had come later, and an organization called the Black Hills Pioneer and Historical Society of 1877 was formed in 1895. Very little is known of its subsequent activities. It quickly faded from public notice.

By 1891, the original 1876 organization had an enrollment of 220 members. Annual meetings were held each January 8, with a picnic arranged for during the summer. The first president was Captain Tom H. Russell, a member of the Gordon Party that came into Custer in 1874, and he was succeeded by Captain Seth Bullock, the first sheriff of Lawrence County.

Along with civic advances, vestiges of Deadwood's violent beginnings remained. Two hangings at the Lawrence County jail yard in Deadwood were high-interest incidents during the decade. The first was the legal execution of Cha Hopa Uhan, alias Chief Two Sticks, which took place at 10 a.m. December 28, 1894, after his conviction for the murder of four young men at one of Stinger and Humphrey's cattle ranches on White Clay creek on the Pine Ridge reservation in February of 1893. The Black Hills Daily Times reported that on the day of the execution, people arrived as early as 8 o'clock in the morning and were admitted to the jail courtyard only by ticket and invitation. Those who were without tickets mounted the stable and sheds adjoining. In his last statement, Two Sticks continued to deny any part in the killing and named four other Indians as the murderers. The account of the event also described how the condemned man watched the work on the scaffold outside his jail window on the previous day; was baptised by Father Digmann, his spiritual adviser from the reservation, and repeated his innocence, saying that he did not fire a shot. A telegram from the President arrived on the last day, refusing the application for pardon or commutation of sentence to life imprisonment.

The second to pay the penalty in this manner was Isadore Cavanaugh (also known as Charles Brown) who was found guilty of killing Mrs. Eva Frances Stone at her apartment in the basement of the Syndicate Building on the night of May 15, 1897. Mrs. Stone ran a boarding house and was accustomed to taking her cash box and keeping it under her pillow while sleeping. Cavanaugh had been employed by her and, according to a statement made to Jailer William A. Remer just prior to the prisoner's death, went to her room with the intention of robbing her. Her little pet dog barked when he entered the room and awakened her. Cavanaugh became frightened and hit her with a meat cleaver in the head, killing her. He then also killed her dog. Cavanaugh fled but was soon captured and brought

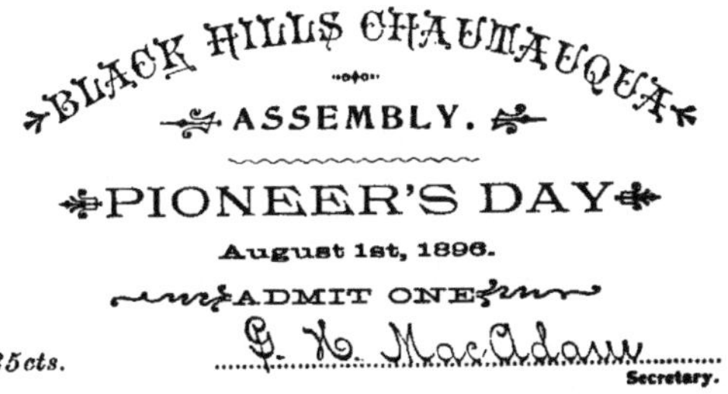
BLACK HILLS CHAUTAUQUA
ASSEMBLY.
PIONEER'S DAY
August 1st, 1896.
ADMIT ONE
35cts. G. H. MacAdam
Secretary.

Both of the railroads have made a fare of one and one-fifth for the round trip to all who attend the annual meeting of the Black Hills Pioneers in Deadwood next Saturday. Tickets will hold good to return Monday.

Pioneer Times
Jan. 7, 1898

**Deadwood's first jail, located on the corner of Washington and Monroe Streets, was the scene of the first legal execution. James Layton Gilmore went to the gallows for murder on Dec. 15, 1882. The jail was more escape-proof than it looks on the exterior. Steel walls and bars lined the inside. The Sundance Kid and Kid Cassidy were jailed here in 1897 following a bank robbery at Belle Fourche. The Belle Fourche jail had burned down, necessitating the removal of the famed bank robbers to Deadwood.**

**(Centennial Collection)**

The excursion to the Elk Creek crystal cave yesterday was attended by over one hundred persons, as jolly ones as could be found. At 7:30 a.m. a train of two observation cars and coach left the B. H. & Ft. P. depot with Chas. Lavere (Lavier) in charge of the train, while Fred Walters was at the throttle, and his fireman, Roy Emerson surely earned his day's salary, as he was kept busy putting in fuel . . . The excursionists arrived back in Lead at 7:30 p.m.

Daily-Pioneer-Times
July 6, 1897

The ice skating rink on upper Sherman street this city, of which E. V. Hatch is the proprietor, is the most popular place of amusement in the Northern Hills. Considerable experience has been entailed in fitting up the rink . . . and embraces such facilities as comfortable reception rooms, cloak rooms, etc. There is no more healthful nor elevating amusement than ice skating and it is growing rapidly in popularity.

Daily Pioneer-Times
Jan. 2, 1898

**William Jennings Bryan, on one of his trips to Deadwood, is shown in front of city hall speaking to a crowd from a buggy. Note the muddy street, prevalent before brick pavement became a blessing to the town.**
**(Centennial Collection)**

back for trial. He was defended by one of the leading attorneys of the community, William L. McLaughlin, convicted and hanged on a scaffold.

One of the greatest days in the year of 1899 for Deadwood and Lead was the visit of the Hon. William Jennings Bryan who, according to the Pioneer-Times, addressed an immense throng of citizens of Deadwood and vicinity August 24, 1899. Presidential candidate of the Populist party the fall of 1888, Bryan talked on the subject of Bimetallism and other political questions.

"Mr. Bryan held his vast audience as if by magic power while the sun's rays were shriveling hot, and not a breath of fresh air could be had."

The audience was estimated at from 5,000 to 15,000.

Bryan brought with him his wife, three children and his wife's sister. The party was met in Edgemont by Populist Gov. Andrew Lee and a delegation of prominent citizens consisting of Congressman Freeman Knowles, Mayor Sol Star, Capt. Russell and daughter Miss Laura, A. H. Oleson and C. A. Hornberger, Deadwood, who accompanied him to Deadwood where he arrived on the Burlington at noon, August 23. The Deadwood band played a lively air from the cemetery hill, directly above the depot a salute of giant powder was fired, which fairly shook the city. It required a strenuous effort on the part of the chief of police and a squad of police to clear a space through the crowds. The procession of carriages passed across Lee Street, down Main to the U.S. Assay Office, back up Main and to the home of Congressman Knowles on Ingleside.

Bryan spoke from a stand in front of the opera house, which was located across from the site later occupied by the Franklin Hotel.

Bryan said: "Of all the great questions before the American people, the financial question is paramount. If free coinage means the detriment of the nation's credit and honor, then what question can approve it; if the gold standard means the servitude of the people, what question can approach it. It must be settled and by the people."

Leaving Deadwood by the 7 o'clock Deadwood Central train, Bryan went to Lead, accompanied by his wife and Congressman Knowles and escorted by Mayor Jenkins and the reception committee of Lead, where he spoke at 8 o'clock, also on bimetallism. He was met by two brass bands and a procession was started with a band in front and one in the rear. The procession, highlighted by fireworks, went to the Palace Restaurant to eat. It was a memorable event, and long remembered by the old-timers of Deadwood and Lead.

# chapter XX

# Growing Pains

While Lead and Deadwood communities were expanding, the schools in both cities were also experiencing growing pains. This is the First Ward School on Burnham Hill in the 1890's. (Centennial Collection)

Mining and timber were important industries in the economic base of Lawrence County before the turn of the century. In 1890 net gold production in the Black Hills was $3,904,160 and by 1900 it had increased to $7,250,000. The Black Hills Weekly Times of August 22, 1896, noted that Homestake's annual report revealed that "the mine has twenty years of ore in sight." The three mills crushed 245,220 tons of ore and the net returns were $1,158,457 with the net product for the year at $1,171,190.

Timbering was vital to supply the needs for building, the Homestake and other mining enterprises as well as for fuel for homes and businesses. Because of this need, in the summer of 1897 Homestake built the town of Nemo, about 25 miles southeast of Lead, to house its employees and their families who worked in the timber operations. The Homestake railroad, officially named the Black Hills and Ft. Pierre, stopped at Nemo to pick up timber for hauling to Lead.

There were three operations at or near Nemo: lumbering, sawmilling and transportation of the timber to Lead. The school census taken from 1890 on showed a sizeable population in the area before the town was actually founded. It was a town without City officials, but along with the Homestake families, the countryside surrounding Nemo was populated with farmers and ranchers who, with their families, made up the community. Their children attended school there, the parents traded there and enjoyed the numerous social activities of the closely-knit community.

Ruthless waste of timber was evident in the forest of the Northern Hills and the concern which grew during the 1880's over the massive consumption of lumber was alleviated when the Black Hills Forest Reserve was created in 1898. However, it brought the bitter resentment of everyone in the Hills. Frank Thomson, Sundance forest ranger from 1906-1908, recalls that a large number of men were thrown out of work as the sawmills shut down and some mill owners lost heavily. People were amazed that this timber was to be held out of use and as a result business was stagnated, according to Thomson.

Thomson also recalled the Black Hills pine beetle destruction started in about 1897 and from then until 1900 numerous tie camps

This morning two hundred men began work on the extension of the Black Hills and Fort Pierre Railroad, they will have the lines graded and rails laid before snow flies. The extension started one mile and a half below the Sam Mine, on Elk Creek, and will continue until the country around Jim Creek has been penetrated by the line, where there is a very heavy growth of thick timber. The extension is for the purpose of supplying the mines of the Homestake Company with timber. The work will employ the present force for at least three months but it is thought that before that time the road will be in shape to operate.

Rapid City Journal
Sept. 21, 1897

Rapid City Journal says: The suit of the United States against the Homestake Mining Company and the Black Hills and Fort Pierre Railroad company will be tried in Deadwood commencing the first of next month, and will consume fully a months time. This action is brought by the government to recover for the timber used by these companies since 1878 to the present time, the value of which is estimated at nearly a million dollars . . .

B H Weekly Times
Jan. 18, 1896

The ordeal, excitement and strain which Deadwood has passed through in the past twenty four hours, has been intense in the extreme. Glib tongues and easy pens cannot describe it; no artists's brush can paint it. This is the second serious conflagration our city has had, though not so destructive as the one of September 26, 1879, yet its effect is quite as hard to bear. When Deadwood's business district was entirely destroyed in 1879, few there were who predicted it would ever be rebuilt. It was, however, with better buildings. We have suffered a great loss again, but the energy and pluck of our property owners will again assert themselves, and by the close of the year 1894, scarcely a vestige of yesterday's conflagration will be left . . . Within two hours of the start, the entire west side of Main Street, from Gold Street to the bluff, a distance of 1000 feet, had been reduced to a mass of smouldering embers and ruin, with the exception of Dr. Hardings, Gib Stone & Co.'s, Parker's and Fink's fireproofs . . . (saved) brick building occupied by Croghin & Allen, across Wall Street from Star & Bullocks, and saved the property, as also the row of frame buildings below it, including the Gem Theatre.

B H Daily Times
March 6, 1894

A fire nearly started at the Homestake Mine. The night watchman, John R. Curnow, discovered timbers burning on the tramway and the fire was quickly put out.

Lead Daily Call
August 26, 1894

were established at about five-mile intervals along the Burlington Railroad for 80 miles, where bug-infested timber was cut and sold to the railroad company. It was part of the great effort made by the government and private enterprise to stop the beetles and save the infested timber to use before it rotted. It was to be a recurring problem.

In 1899, a "Christmas Time" cutting started on Jim and Este Creeks in the Black Hills, the first activities on "Case No. 1," the first timber sale from public lands in the United States. T. J. Grier, superintendent of the Homestake, had submitted an application to purchase all of the timber of a diameter of eight inches on the Jim and Este Creek district. Through its final approval, Grier and the Homestake were instrumental in the nation's first timber sale.

Forest fires proved to be the major problem in the era which was launched by the 1890 blaze of over 3,000 acres occurring in the Dumont-Hanna area, as well as the Savoy burn which destroyed another 1,000 acres. Both of these fires took place before the 20,000 acre Roubaix holocaust in 1893. This was a disastrous year with big burns in the Elk Creek country and on French and Squaw Creeks.

The Black Hills Times for September 21, 1893, left out none of the horrendous details under the heading "Merciless Flames . . . Terrible Fire in Centennial Prairie . . . Narrow Escape for Lead and Terry . . . Deadwood Nearly Surrounded by Raging Fires Fanned by a High Wind." The last big fire before the turn of the century was at Iron Creek in 1898. Fire was not confined to the forest as the headlines in the Deadwood newspaper disclosed, March 5, 1894, when the "Fire Fiend Again Visits This City, Destroying Two Blocks of Buildings." The reporter predicted that by the close of the year, "scarcely a vestige of yesterday's conflagration will be left." The $100,000 blaze destroyed two blocks of buildings, starting in a boarding

**Fires plagued Deadwood throughout its first 100 years. The above holocaust in 1894 swept over part of the area which was destroyed in the great fire of 1879 when most of Deadwood went up in flames. The 1894 fire destroyed most of the downtown area on the west side of Main Street from Lee Street north past Wall Street.**

**(Centennial Collection)**

house by a "drunken man with a lamp." Among those rebuilding immediately was J. H. Schubert who had a loss to his building and saloon fixtures of $7,000 and only $1,500 in insurance.

Shortly after the fire of 1894, that block of buildings that had again comprised the "Bad Lands" of lower Deadwood were completely replaced by solid structures of brick and stone. The Mansion House contained game rooms and a marble swimming pool in the basement. Across the street the large native sandstone Bullock Hotel was completed. It was a period of hectic mining activity in Deadwood. The government assay office was located in what is now known as the Ranger building. The Adams Brothers grocery on the corner of Wall and Main across from the Mansion House became the Topic. This had been the site of the Centennial Hotel and the Marble Hall before the fire of 1879. The Topic was known as the "Combination" — a combination of saloon and gaming rooms with a famous bordella on the second story known only as the Topic — complete with ballroom. The Nye's Opera House on the corner of Gold and Main Street, the Keimer Hall, and the Wertheimer Hall, had all presented everything from roller skating to legitimate theatre.

**One of Deadwood's most notorious theatres, the Green Front. It was built on Main Street where the used car lot for the Deadwood Ford and Mercury firm is now located.**
**(Centennial Collection)**

For 18 years, the schools had been conducted under the district township system, but on April 26, 1895, Lead Independent School District No. 6 was organized. By the time the district was established there were two school buildings in Lead, one on the present Central campus and the other in the Washington district. In 1895, a $35,000 bond issue was approved and the first high school building on Central campus was constructed and completed a year later. The basement floor housed a few of the lower grades. In the first commencement, held June 23, 1895, six students were graduated. Kate Kemper, who was elected county superintendent in 1894, stated in a report at the end of her four-year term that 56 teachers were employed in town schools and 35 in rural schools and that there was no over-supply of educators at any time. Most districts were on a cash basis and only a few had to issue warrants! On April 4, 1896, the Black Hills Weekly Times reported that school facilities were inadequate in Deadwood. The newly-built Ingleside school accommodated 60 pupils, a new addition was needed for the First Ward school which accommodated 50, and every seat was filled in the high school and its annex.

Queen City Mail: The meeting of the Black Hills Educational Association at Deadwood was pronounced by all present the most successful ever held in the Hills . . . Prof. Garrett, when in Lincoln last week, met Col. Francis W. Parker, the noted educator, who said that he had heard of the excellence of the schools of this region and expressed his determination of visiting in the Hills during the coming summer.

B H Weekly Times
Jan. 11, 1896

Other segments of the community also felt growing pains. The town's telephone system, for instance, began to have serious problems as its customer ranks swelled. Abuse of the phone services by subscribers and non-subscribers led the Nebraska Telephone Co. in 1895 to establish a new schedule of rates and toll charges. As a result, many subscribers abandoned the service and finally forced the discontinuance of all exchanges in the group except Rapid City which had lost 16 customers and Deadwood where 24 customers also dropped out. According to the Black Hills Weekly of February 8, 1896, second

Since the city has received good service from the Belt Power and Light Company, the electric light contract will be extended six months.

Lead Daily Call
Sept., 1894

circuit telephone lines were being installed linking Lead, Central, Terraville, Terry, Deadwood, Sturgis, Rapid City and the Southern Hills. A main office was proposed for Deadwood with exchanges at Lead, Sturgis, Spearfish, Rapid City and Whitewood. Four wires were coming into Deadwood, two from Spearfish and two from the Southern Hills with the work being handled by the Harrison Telephone Co., that offered service at rates lower than those charged by the Nebraska Telephone Co. A very competitive situation arose and all service rates offered by the Harrison Co. were duplicated or even bettered by the Nebraska Co. As fast as the Harrison Co. extended its toll lines, the Nebraska Co. gave free service to these new points.

Never in the history of the Hills and in fact the whole state, has male help been so scarce. Railroad contractors complain that men are very scarce, farmers come to the city daily for help to garner their harvest but are compelled to go without it. The same condition exists all over the state. Wages $3 to $5 and even to $8 per day have been offered for help but none is to be had.

B H Daily Times
Aug. 19, 1892

Congressman John R. Gamble was busy in Washington securing federal funds for buildings in the Northern Black Hills. On March 21, 1896, he filed an appropriation bill for a public building in Deadwood to contain an assay office "for the convenience of the Black Hills region which last year produced over $5,000,000 in gold." On March 28, he followed it with a bill for $25,000 to be appropriated for a government building at Lead and within days another bill appropriating $10,000 for a fish hatchery at Spearfish.

Marie Van Dobeneck of Germany, is name of grantee, and M. D. and C. Muller names of grantors in a warranty deed filed for record yesterday. The property transferred is that known as the "Otterbine Brewery" and Deadwood baseball park, containing about three and two-thirds acres in the extreme southern limits of the city. Consideration named in the instrument, $4,000.

B H Daily Times
March 18, 1892

By the end of 1897, the Pioneer-Times reported that the year had brought from 100 to 300 building improvements to Lead, highlighted by the construction of six business blocks and the completion of the Episcopal Church at a cost of $20,000. Leading the list of buildings was the large addition adjoining the Brick Store, erected at a cost of $27,000. The building, erected by Mrs. P. A. Hearst, had its basement and part of the first floor occupied by the Brick Store. The remainder of the ground floor was occupied by the post office and on the second floor there were rooms for the Hearst public library and free reading rooms. The post office, which moved to its location in the Hearst Library on June 1, 1897, was reported by the newspaper as doing a larger money order business than any other city of like size in the United States. "An average of twenty-five money orders are sent out daily and receipts from these approximate from $800 to $1,000." The Hearst Library, which had opened on Christmas Eve, 1894, had achieved 2,500 volumes and averaged 160 patrons for each day it was open during 1897.

In another column of the Times appears a call for proposals of the A. F. and A.M. society for site of the proposed Masonic temple. Several sites are in view, all of which are desirable; sufficient to say the building will be centrally located. Money has been secured sufficient to assure the enterprise and we are assured it will be completed ready for occupancy before January 1, 1893.

B H Daily Times
July 13, 1892

For the same year, Deadwood boasted that it had 125 new houses; its First National Bank, which had been in existence 23 years, and the American National, which had opened in January, 1895, had a combined total in deposits of $1,116,731. The Deadwood Post Office had moved to quarters in F. D. Smith's new three-story building fronting on Deadwood Street and located one-half block from both passenger stations.

Hon. Theodore Roosevelt, one of New York City's civil service commissioners and aldermen from the "tenderloin" district unceremoniously dropped into Deadwood yesterday from his cow ranch in the northern part of the state, having driven the entire distance in his buggy.

B H Times
Aug. 29, 1892

By the end of 1898, Deadwood claimed construction for the year had totalled one half million dollars. Included were the Deadwood and Delaware Smelting at a cost of $150,000; the Carr & Berry business building on Main Street at $30,000; W. E. Adams' four-story building adjoining his grocery on Sherman Street; the Deadwood High School, a two-story brick and stone building, scheduled for completion in March of 1899 at a cost of $25,000; the two-story Fish & Hunter building on Sherman Street at $8,000; and a new water system from Gayville with new tanks built on McGovern Hill at a cost of $25,000.

By 1898 Deadwood had 11 restaurants and seven of these were operated by Chinese proprietors. In addition to the other businesses there were 22 saloons, a cigar factory, seltzer and soda water company, Western Union telegraph and the Black Hills Steam Laundry, which had branches in all Hills towns, built on Sherman street above the light plant occupied by Hattenback Bros.

In the 1890's toll roads on the Deadwood-Central City and Deadwood-Sturgis routes were still operating, but they didn't last long. As the toll roads gave way to the slightly improved public roads, progress in a county highway system was delayed by the need for a more efficient form of transportation, the railroads. The County Commissioners were well aware of the disadvantages of roads. The local roads were expensive to build, hard to repair, and no one knew what condition the roads would be in from one day to the next. In the spring, for instance, the roads would be submerged in mud, hindering the movement of freight wagons and stage coaches. Although the roads were bad, they were neglected until the Twentieth Century when much better roads were required for the horseless carriages.

Some old stage and freight lines did not last until the Twentieth Century. In 1890 the Northwestern Transportation Co., an important area freight carrier, ceased operations when the Elkhorn Railroad was built to Deadwood. At least one stage line did last beyond 1900, though. John McClintock, owner, and Harvey Fellows, stage driver, ran the Deadwood-Spearfish Stage Line until 1913 when the horseless carriages began to hurt business. The automobiles were simply more comfortable than a rough riding stage.

A committee was appointed by the Business Men's Association to consider abolishing toll roads between Central City and Lead . . .
B H Times
Jan. 18, 1896

The D. C. (Deadwood Central) will lay off one train crew today and hereafter the ore train crew will be required to assist in the Lead City service. Travel is light and officials of the company claim the road has not paid actual expenses.
B H Times
Jan. 18, 1894

The climax was reached yesterday by the county commissioners in the Gayville toll road controversy. The owners of the road refused the $1,000 offered by the board, and the board ordered Tony Bartolino, road supervisor of that district, to remove the toll gate, which he did. Mr. Brennan, manager of the road, offered no resistance, and Tony was very gentlemanly about executing the order. There will probably be a law suit over the matter.
B H Weekly Times
July 18, 1896

The Bodega Cafe has changed hands. A. Sprando, the new proprietor the well known restauranteur of Rapid, assuming charge last evening. This cafe, which has always borne the name of the being the best in the city, will lose none of its prestige under the new management.
B H Daily Times
Oct. 3, 1892

**On a rainy day the road between Lead and Pluma must have been a "dilly" back in 1890 when this photo was snapped of two, two-horse-powered vehicles.**

**(Adams Museum)**

Growing pains even affected the original boot hill on Ingleside in Deadwood. The cemetery where Wild Bill Hickok was originally buried is the area in the center of the picture with the fence around it. Individual graves had wooden fences also. As Deadwood grew rapidly after the gold rush, the cemetery was moved up the hill in 1879.

(Deadwood Carnegie Library)

Lead's spacious Chicago and North Western Railway Depot was on the southeast corner of Mill and Main Streets. This view was looking up Main Street before the streets were paved.

# chapter XXI

# Prosperous '90's

**Bridal Veil Falls was a main attraction on railroad excursions through Spearfish Canyon in the early 1900's. Today a modern highway follows the roadbed of the scenic rail line.**

Spearfish, the Queen City, in the early 1890's was a boomtown built on rumors, the closest Spearfish ever came to a boomtown like Deadwood or Lead in 1876. Rumors of a railroad extension, an ore treatment plant, and a fish hatchery were heard throughout the early years of the decade. It was also believed that the town would become a great mining and industrial center. Some of the rumors materialized; others didn't. After the "boom" ended, Spearfish still remained an agricultural and educational center for the Northern Hills. The town had definite possibilities as a tourist center with the scenic attractions of nearby Spearfish Canyon and the Hills, but that would wait until the next century and the advent of the horseless carriages.

Spearfish's population grew rapidly during the "boom" period. Many of the inhabitants were land speculators, mining investors, businessmen, and itinerant railroad workers. The town only had a population of 670 in 1890 but the population almost doubled by the end of the decade. In 1900 Spearfish was the third largest city in the county after Lead and Deadwood. City officials had hoped that Spearfish would become the mining and industrial center of the Black Hills. Large deposits of minerals were believed to be located in the Hills near Spearfish. Real estate and mining promoters, investing heavily in land in and near the town, were betting that Spearfish would become a large industrial center. But without a railroad, the chances of the town becoming industrialized were nil.

During the early months of 1890, the community leaders constantly asked for a railroad extension. The January 8, 1890, issue of the Spearfish Daily Register, established in 1889 to publicize the coming boom, reported that a great deal of time was spent by the Spearfish City Council discussing days to bring a railroad to Spearfish. In a later issue, the paper mentioned that the citizens of the town started a bond issue and donated land for a railroad right of way. Then the rumors began. Rumors of a railroad, whether the Elkhorn or the Burlington, to Spearfish were as numerous as the bets by local citizens on the date a railroad would reach the town. Finally, in November of 1890, work began on the Burlington Railroad route from Deadwood via Spearfish Canyon to Spearfish. A site for a new depot in the town

Eight couples of our young people went over to Spearfish last evening for the drive and a few hours of dancing. They had engaged an orchestra and Lown Hall was awaiting their arrival. A large number of their young friends in Spearfish were invited to the festivities and were at the hall waiting the coming of the visitors. The party was as follows: Misses Fox, Dickson, Power, Kemper, Phillips, Cushman, Pease and Russell, and Messrs. Cable, Miller, Zink, Cushman, Murphy, Richards, Ford and Mosher.

B H Daily Times
Jan. 10, 1895

**The crowd gathered to greet the first train into Spearfish on December 11, 1893. Expected in September, the railroad completion was delayed by rough terrain through Spearfish Canyon and the 13 bridges required for tracks.**

**(Centennial Collection)**

Farmers of Centennial Valley are plowing and putting their fields in shape for seeding and we were informed Tuesday that one farmer was seen sowing wheat. There is little or no frost in the ground and it is in splendid condition for working . . . .

B H Weekly Times
Feb. 1, 1896

Farmers of Centennial Valley have organized an irrigation association. A meeting was held on Saturday evening, Feb. 29, when J. W. Thompson was elected president and John Cashner, Spearfish, secretary. The association purposes to sink a number of artesian wells if possible.

B H Weekly Times
March 14, 1896

Railroads have brought about a wonderful change to Deadwood, where only a year ago stood the frame shack and log hut now can be seen the two and three story stone and brick structure, a marvel of beauty in its design and workmanship. Deadwood is now and always will be the metropolis, as well as the railroad center of the Black Hills. Sixty-four trains arrive and depart daily from their respective depots, bringing merchandise to our doors and taking our ores from the mines to the mills.

B H Daily Times
May 18, 1892

was selected. The Elkhorn decided to build its line from Whitewood northwest to St. Onge and Belle Fourche.

Burlington Railroad officials planned to haul ore from the numerous mines along the proposed rail route to an ore processing plant in Spearfish. A chlorination ore treatment mill was built by numerous investors in the Queen City. The plant was later destroyed by fire and quickly rebuilt. The ore processing facility treated some ore from the Bald Mountain and Ragged Top mining areas but the dream of Spearfish as a great mining and ore processing center soon vanished. When the railroad was completed during October 1893, the mines along the railroad route had already begun closing. The lead, silver, and gold mines of the Carbonate district, the tin mines of the Tinton region and the numerous gold mines of the Ragged Top area shut down operations one by one. Nevertheless, the railroad enabled Spearfish to become the commercial center for the farmers and ranchers in the Northern Hills. Spearfish grew steadily and perhaps the growth was aided by the numerous rumors circulated during the 1890's.

The vision of Spearfish as an ore processing center attracted other investors developing the Hay Creek coal mines across the border in Wyoming. Rumors were heard in 1894 that a number of railroad companies intended to build branch lines to Spearfish from Hay Creek. The coal was believed to be valuable for the ore treatment plants built or proposed in the Queen City. But these plans for coal shipments by rail to Spearfish didn't materialize. When it became apparent in 1894 that the boom would not develop, the Spearfish Daily Register, a publication of the weekly Queen City Mail and instrumental in promoting the boom rumors, was unable to continue due to rising costs and ceased publishing. The "boom" ended.

In the 1890's the residents of Spearfish realized that nearby Spearfish Canyon, known even then for its scenic beauty, would attract visitors to the area. In 1897 Spearfish citizens petitioned the County Commissioners to build a highway through the canyon. Until roads were built for the horseless carriages, other forms of transportation were used by visitors to Spearfish. The railroad line through Spearfish Canyon was converted to passenger service for area residents and later tourists as the mines continued to close along the railroad route. The railroad line became famous for its steep grade down Crown Hill into Spearfish Canyon. Extra train cars had to be chained at the siding near the top of Crown Hill or they could make the trip to Spearfish alone. In addition to the Burlington line, Spearfish was served by the Deadwood Stage Line, operated by McClintock.

Citizens of Spearfish in 1889 had asked the federal government to locate a fish hatchery in Spearfish. Since the white man came to the fertile Spearfish Valley, the streams and lakes had been filled with undesirable "suckers." Two years later a shipment of trout from Colorado was freed in the nearby streams and thrived so well that Spearfish and Rapid City were named as proposed sites for a fish hatchery. The Queen City was considered in 1893 as an excellent location for a fish hatchery by the Federal Fish Commission. In March 1896, legislation for a federal fish hatchery was introduced in Congress. The bill later passed and a Commission official arrived in Spearfish the following December to select the site for the proposed hatchery. Three years later, in 1899, construction began on a fish hatchery consisting of three buildings and numerous hatching channels. The fish hatchery soon provided millions of trout for the streams and man-made lakes of the Black Hills.

Unlike Deadwood, Spearfish in 1890 didn't have a Police Chief or City Marshal. It had a reputation as a quiet town but the new temperance law which went into effect in May of that year attempted to make it even more law-abiding. The City Council voted to dispense with the services of a Marshal and its members and the Mayor became the self-appointed custodians of the peace. The City Council later decided to appoint a Chief of Police. The reasons for this change of heart are not clear, but it can be assumed that enforcement of the new temperance law was not an easy job. An ordinance providing for a Police Chief was passed in December 1891. Alderman John Bell, a member of the Town Council, voted for the new law and then resigned so he could be appointed Police Chief by Mayor J. F. Summers.

The notorious Ray Taylor, at whose dive near Sturgis Ed Green recently died, and who bore such an unsavory reputation at that place, she was not permitted to remain there, came up to Deadwood on Monday, bag and baggage, with a couple of wagon loads of old furnishings, secured a house on lower Sherman Street and moved into it. She intended to conduct an assignation house, probably on the order of those heretofore run by her, but Chief of Police Diltz, with the support of the executive, ordered the woman to decamp, that she cannot run a house in Deadwood. She expressed deep regret, but went, we do not know where, probably to the next town. Many eastern communities know but little about Deadwood and what they do know is not complimentary. Why is it that Deadwood has such an unsavory reputation throughout the country, we cannot understand, for there is very little crime in this place as compared with many others, that profess a great deal in a moral sense. Visitors are surprised to see how little disorder and crime there is here and volunteer to speak about it.

B H Daily Times
Jan. 1, 1896

A young man of Lead, who of late has been leading a high life, made a record for himself a few nights ago by knocking one of the demi monde (sic) over a bannister. He became so disgusted with his own actions that he left town.

B H Daily Times
March 18, 1894

Officer Donovan, at 11 o'clock last night served a warrant of attachment upon Eugene Ecker, proprietor of the Green Front, and took possession of the place. The attachment was issued upon the judgment obtained a few days ago by J. P. Laffey for $180 for legal services rendered.

B H Weekly Times
June 30, 1895

A meeting was held on Jan. 23 organizing the Black Hills Improvement Association which was attended by the mayors and representative citizens from all the towns in the Hills. The goal of the group was to advertise the Hills and its resourcements to induce capital for development, as well as attractions as a summer resort.

B H Daily Times
Jan. 25, 1896

**From the rim of Spearfish Canyon, the scenic railroad line can be seen far below. Floodwaters forced the abandonment of the railroad through the canyon.**

Committees from the M. E. Church of Lead were around yesterday securing signatures to a petition which will be presented to the mayor and city council asking that all saloons in the city be closed under the state law. A large number of signatures were secured.

B H Daily Times
Jan. 16, 1894

One of the largest companies ever gathered in a private house in Deadwood thronged the home of Stewart Thompson on Williams Street last evening at the W.C.T.U. Social, 200 was a conservative estimate of those present. There was a fine program made up of Lead and Deadwood people which furnished excellent entertainment. The refreshments were fine though the crowd overtaxed the committee just a little. One of the most pleasant features of the evening was the large number of Lead people present.

B H Daily Times
Jan. 18, 1894

Some eight years ago Ben Welf deserted his family, leaving an invalid wife and a small boy to what at that time seemed to be at the mercy of the charitable public. Before leaving he mortgaged their little home on City Creek and started out on an extended tour of the Pacific Coast. Artie, the seven-year-old boy, was taken in by A. C. Hornberger, the grocer, and set at work in his store. The little fellow soon developed aptitude for the business, was honest and faithful and Mr. Hornberger saw such determination in the boy that he retained him and from time to time raised his wages. Yesterday was Artie's birthday and also the turning point in his eighth year as a clerk for the grocer. During these eight years the little lad has paid off the mortgage and back taxes on his mother's home, besides supporting her and himself during that period and has a small amount of money on hand. Mr. Hornberger yesterday called all of his clerks together and when they were assembled presented the boy with a handsome gold watch, chain and charm in behalf of himself and Artie's associates. It was a pathetic scene, when the manly little fellow, with great tears in his eyes, portraying unmistakable evidence of gratitude, thanked his employer and fellow clerks for the gift. Artie is now drawing $40 per month.

B H Daily Times
Jan. 15, 1897

While Spearfish complied with the law, its local newspaper reported that the saloons in Deadwood "have scarcely made a pretense of closing up." Because liquor was still legal in Wyoming, the trail from Spearfish to the little town of Beulah was well traveled. In the fall of that year an injunction was issued to close every establishment where liquor was sold in original packages. Reportedly 31 saloons were closed by the Sheriff in Deadwood while Lead and Central City dealers got wind of the trouble and closed their doors without the aid of the Sheriff. When the City fathers found that they could line their coffers with monthly "fines" or voluntary contributions from the establishments, liquor continued to flow. By 1893 when construction crews arrived to work on the railroad, the number of Spearfish's saloons had grown to seven. When the Spearfish City Council raised the monthly "fine" to $50 in 1895, the city saloons went "on strike," and closed their doors. Injunctions ordered the saloon keepers to pay up or be closed for good and they complied. Moonshiners, who had their stills carefully hidden in dugouts, canyons, and even root cellars throughout the Northern Hills, kept the liquor available even when the supply was cut off by the prohibition enforcement.

The Queen City Mail launched out at violators of the prohibition after a raid on an opium den in Deadwood's Chinatown in February, 1895. It criticized laws which prohibited the use of opium and the arrest and imprisonment of the Chinese who violated that law, in contrast to the prohibition laws which the white men were permitted to openly ignore. Within two years the Salvation Army arrived in the fruitful fields of Deadwood and delivered its temperance lectures in front of many saloons. But by 1897, the prohibition, which had been adopted eight years prior, was returned to the voters and repealed by about 7,000 votes. Following on the heels of the repeal, however, was a new liquor license law setting the fee at $400 per year. Spearfish hiked its fee to $600, and if chairs and tables were allowed in the room another $600 annual license had to be paid. The second license was required in an effort to discourage gambling, which was also illegal, but instead it moved the gamblers to another room in the saloon.

Spearfish in the 1890's was a quiet and peaceful town with its citizens hoping for another boom. If Spearfish wasn't destined to be a mining or industrial center, it became an agricultural and educational center instead. The numerous Burlington workers in town were responsible for some new building activity, especially saloons. During the early 1890's, a number of homes and at least one hotel was built. The town had two hotels to accomodate the railroad workers and the many business promoters and land speculators in the city. The construction and lumber industries were thriving. About 1900 the brick factories, a sash and door factory using local lumber, and six sawmills within five miles of Spearfish, each producing 10,000 to 25,000 board feet per day, were operating at full capacity.

Other industries in the town manufactured flour and processed gold ore. The Spearfish Milling Co. produced 75 barrels of flour a day. It milled both corn and wheat and produced animal feed from corn, oats, and barley. At one time, the mill ground 2,000 pounds of feed barley per hour. Around 1899 the Spearfish Cyanide Co. began building a cyanide plant for the treatment of gold ores from the Ragged Top area. The company leased an unused stucco mill and the building was remodeled and equipped with the most modern machinery available.

The Bank of Spearfish continued to prosper in the 1890's. Its deposits in 1900 were more than $150,000. Around the turn of the century, Spearfish had a creamery, four department stores, three drug stores, and two furniture stores. It also had retail outlets for groceries, clothing, and hardware. The Spearfish Electric Light and Power Co. owned by a group of Chicago investors was organized in 1893. A hydroelectric plant was built two and a half miles above the city on Spearfish Creek to generate electricity. The cost to the city was $1,260 per year.

Although Spearfish didn't boom like Deadwood or Lead, it was assured of steady growth by the Black Hills Normal School and the fish hatchery.

Two other communities, Whitewood and St. Onge, in northern Lawrence County were continuing to grow during the 1890's. After the Elkhorn Railroad was extended to Belle Fourche, Whitewood remained an important cattle shipping center. In 1892 a grain elevator was erected by two Whitewood businessmen and two years later they built the Whitewood Roller Mills. The mill produced 60 barrels of flour a day. Around the turn of the century, the town of 500 population had a bank, the Whitewood Banking Company; two general stores, a hardware company and a furniture store. Whitewood also had three hotels that mainly served the itinerant railroad workers.

The first building, a railroad depot, was constructed in St. Onge in 1890 by the Pioneer Townsite Co., a subsidiary of the Elkhorn Railroad. The depot was used only a few months during the busiest part of the cattle shipping season. Two years later the railroad built stockyards for livestock shipments. A small building boom occurred in St. Onge between 1890 and 1898. A general store, a post office, a new school building, a creamery and numerous homes were built.

The City of Lead experienced its most rapid growth between the years of 1890 and 1900. The Homestake Mine was expanding operations and hiring new workers. The mining town had a population of 2,580 in 1890; two years later the population doubled, and by 1900 the town had 6,200 inhabitants. Lead became the second largest city in South Dakota after Sioux Falls with a population of 10,000 in the

On Thursday night Ambrose Lester came very near going to the happy hunting grounds as a sporting girl, known as Ella King, with whom he had been infatuated for many months, got into a fracas with him, and after throwing a lighted lamp at his head, which set fire to things behind the store, attacked him with a four-tined fork, and succeeded in cutting his face severely and inflicting a wound which required six stitches to sew up. Lester, who bled freely, was taken to the hospital, where Dr. Freeman dressed his wounds after sewing up two veins which had been severed. Ella King, who did the carving, has the reputation of being the toughest prostitute in Lead, and was locked up in the quay by officer Rube Miller . . . .

B H Weekly Times
**Jan. 11, 1896**

Sturgis Record: John Scallard is in receipt of a letter from Calamity Jane, who is now in Butte, Montana. Calamity wants to come back to the hills, where she will reside indefinitely, claiming that Butte is too slow. She has one child now. Incidentally she suggests that Scallard send her fifty dollars or so to help pay transportation. Not wishing to become a general ticket agent for the numerous parties who have gone hence heretofore, the unchristianlike Scallard has lost Calamity's letter.

B H Daily Times
**May 4, 1895**

Miss Shallabarger, who had a narrow escape from death early Thursday morning by taking an overdose of morphine, is up and about again as usual. But for the timely arrival of Dr. Torrence and the good affect of heroic methods brought into requisition, Miss Shallabarger would no doubt be floating around with the angels at this writing.

Pioneer-Times
**Jan. 7, 1896**

The person who was going around Lead Sunday night, dressed up as an Indian, got a little too flossy with some gentleman, on whom he raised his war club, which was taken from him and he in return received a blow over the head, which laid him out.

B H Weekly Times
Jan. 18, 1896

early 1900's. The population growth was due to the influx of immigrant workers or miners and their families, the "new immigration."

The early Homestake workers, prospectors who failed to make a strike or others seeking employment, were a mixture of nationalities. After the gold rush, most of the miners were of Cornish descent. The Cornish were famous as expert miners. They were known for their ability to endure the difficult working conditions of mining. The large number of "Cousin Jacks" in Lead meant that Homestake was a stable gold producer and Lead was a stable community.

In the 1890's, various nationalities and racial groups of the new immigration — Canadian, Scandinavian, Russian, German, Cornish, Dutch, Spanish, Italian, Slavonian, Negro, and even Chinese, merged to make Lead a cosmopolitan city. The Negroes and Chinese, the non-European ethnic groups, did not work for the mine. They were mainly servants or small businessmen. The Chinese operated many of the numerous restaurants and laundries in the mining town. Segregation of the numerous nationalities and racial groups was difficult because the mountainous region around Lead compelled city inhabitants to live in Gold Run Gulch near their place of employment — the Homestake. Although most of the new Homestake workers did not speak English, language and cultural differences did not hinder the assimilation of these diverse people into a growing community. Many of the present residents of Lead are descendants of the "new immigration" of the 1890's.

The different nationalities brought with them diverse cultures, ideas, and ambitions. The mixing of different cultures and many intermarriages made Lead a unique city in the 1890's.

After South Dakota became a state in 1889, the civic leaders felt that Lead should be incorporated as a town. Many legal entanglements dating back to 1877 made incorporation of the city a lengthy and complicated process. The legal question in the 1890's was who actually owned the Lead City town lots? Homestake owned most of the mineral rights and land, but who legally owned the non-Homestake buildings on the lots? The controversy between Homestake, the principal holder of the mineral claims, and the representatives of the townsite continued on and off in the federal courts until an agreement was made in 1892. The Agreement of March 18, 1892, was signed by the parties involved at the Deadwood courthouse. Homestake received title to the land and, in turn, the mining company gave surface rights to occupants.

The actual incorporation of Lead City on September 12, 1890, as a township was not difficult. The first mayor, Cyrus H. Enos, and councilmen from four wards were elected. The word "City" was dropped from the name since Lead really wasn't a city. After the incorporation problem was settled, the new Town Council turned its

Lead is truly a cosmopolitan city. Nationalities from all over the world are represented.
Evening Call
June 5, 1895

Lead has a voting population of 1,500; school attendance of 950; an electric fire alarm system, electric lights, water works, an excellent fire department, and 1st class hotels and restaurants; two daily papers, the Evening Call and Lead City Tribune; six churches, two public and one parochial schools; and is an aggressive candidate for the permanent location of the county seat of Lawrence County, with bright prospects of success.
Lead Evening Call
Aug. 14, 1894

Miss Daisy Hulling, an erring colored girl, residing at No. 8 Pine Street, Lead, made a New Year's resolution Sunday night and kept it. Miss Hulling had been unhappy for some time and concluded this earth held no peace for her and so took a large dose of morphine. She was alone at the time and concluded that this earth held no peace for her . . . Miss Hulling was 28 years of age.
Pioneer-Times
Jan. 3, 1899

The residents on upper Main Street complain daily of the kids who congregate on the street in the locality every evening and make life a burden to them. The chief of police will have a round up almost any night now. Parents should see that their children are not allowed out after a reasonable time in the evening.
Lead Daily Call
Aug. 17, 1894

The city council met to consider the acquisition of a lot to build the proposed new city jail and city hall, which are badly needed.
Evening Call
Jan. 25, 1897

Since the city of Lead was incorporated in September 1890 one police court docket has been used up and it shows there had been 640 cases docketed . . . .
B H Weekly Times
Feb. 22, 1896

attention to improving City services, the collection of the property tax, and the writing of City ordinances.

Some of the ordinances established by the Lead City Council were unusual. It was illegal to shoe horses in the streets, drive cattle through town, swear, and serve females at the local taverns. Other ordinances outlawed gambling, slot machines, and houses of prostitution. A law directed primarily at the Chinese of Lead declared opium dens illegal. The mining community was still a tough town and the influx of immigrants did not make law enforcement any easier. A uniformed police force was established in 1897 consisting of at least five officers. The local police did not strictly enforce the gambling and prostitution ordinances and Lead was a wide open town.

**Homestake superintendents were literally surrounded by their work in the early days of the company. The mansion in which they lived (left) was in the center of the milling area. A special guest or a holiday probably prompted the flying of four flags on top of the ornate home.**

**(Centennial Collection)**

Lead was a strange city. A visitor seeeing the city for the first time was usually stunned. In Lead the streets followed the zig-zag contours of the hills and the streets meandered in every direction. Because of the terrain, Lead had no organized system of city blocks. The narrow streets in many areas of the town abruptly ended at the foot of a stairway leading to houses perched high on the hillsides. Houses of all descriptions were piled one on top of another up the hillsides in crazy quilt fashion. The Main Street, the symbol of a community's vitality, could easily give a visitor the impression of poor planning, but the wooden sidewalks were built with occasional crooked steps because of the steepness of the terrain.

Lead also had a strange sound. Throughout the decade of the 1890's, Homestake enlarged its stamp mills and added numerous stamps. The pounding of the stamps over the hill in Terraville and in Lead became a familiar sound in the mining community. By 1900 Homestake had about 900 stamps pounding continuously day and night. Few complained about the noise. Homestake expansion meant growth in Lead and the mining town in the 1890's was experiencing a building boom. The immigrant workers needed homes and places to stay, businesses were established or enlarged to serve the influx of miners, and the City had to expand services to meet the demand of a rapidly growing population. Homes and hotels seemed to be constantly under construction. The local brick and construction industries were thriving. Almost two million bricks were produced by the large Phillips and Barlett Brick Plant at Pluma for the building boom in the mining community. Homes were constructed wherever there was room, but the hotels, of course, were built with more planning. The hotel business in Lead during the 1890's enjoyed its golden years.

Deadwood in the 1880's had been the commercial center for the Lead-Deadwood area and by the end of the next decade Lead's business district became as large as any business district in a city of

New steps were badly needed on the corner of Main and Siever Streets.

Evening Call
April 23, 1896

Some of the parties who travel over the hill from Lead to Terraville have struck a novel way of getting over slippery places. Some of them yesterday were seen crawling on all fours.

B H Daily Times
Jan. 1, 1895

Some of the merchants in Lead are going to turn over a new leaf commencing today, that of selling their goods for cash only. It will be hard to educate some of their customers up to that, but it will be far better for the merchants for their goods to remain on the shelves than to have so many bad accounts in their books.

B H Daily Times
Jan. 7, 1894

comparable size. Lead was a gold mining town and everyone paid or was expected to be paid in gold coins. The financial institutions prior to 1890 had done a tremendous business in gold dust and nuggets exchanged for greenbacks or deposited in the banks by prospectors and placer miners. After the prospectors left the Hills, dealings in gold dust and nuggets became rare. The custom of using gold coins continued in Lead until the Federal Reserve Act was passed in 1913. Soon after paper money began to be cautiously accepted by the citizens of Lead. The big bank in Lead was the Lead City Bank. In 1891 this financial institution became the First National Bank of Lead. The bank was able to survive the financial panic of 1893 and grew until it was one of the largest in the area.

The Hearst Mercantile Company, or the Brick Store, and other Lead businesses had a flourishing trade with the immigrant workers, other Homestake employees and the local inhabitants. During the decade of the 1890's there was a large number of different retail and wholesale outlets; grocery stores, butcher shops, hardware companies, and clothing stores. Carriage and cigar factories, iron works, quarries and jewelry handicraft were some of the local industries that didn't last long. Thorpes of Lead made Black Hills gold jewelry in the 1890's but later moved to Deadwood.

Unions for nearly everything from miners to barbers were organized in the mining town. Even the cigar workers had a union. The unions like the Lead City Miners' and the printers were more social than labor oriented.

In 1893 the Belt Power and Light Co. began electric service to homes and businesses in Lead. The power company, which built a large electric generating plant at Pluma, continually improved service and updated equipment. Three years later construction began on a city-wide telephone system in the mining community. The local telephone and telegraph companies expanded operations to offer better service to their customers.

Lead had changed considerably during the 1890's. The Lead Daily Call described the growth of Lead as "phenomenal." The boom town mining camp had become a settled, prospering city. The "get-rich-quick" prospectors left and a stable mining industry developed. The citizens of Lead eagerly looked forward to the promise of the new century.

Commencing with tomorrow the price of all meats with the exception of pork will be advanced a few cents by the butchers in Lead, who have taken this step to protect themselves from loss, as they now have to pay from $8 to $10 more a head for stock than during the past score of years.

Lead Pioneer-Times
Jan. 1, 1898

At present there are only three vacant store rooms in the two principal streets of Lead, which is speaking good for a town that size.

B H Times
Jan. 5, 1894

Raspberry wine, fresh, sweet and delicious for sale at all saloons. Excellent for family use, delivered free. Henry Maillard.

Lead Daily Call
August, 1894

R. H. Driscoll, formerly clerk of the court at Deadwood, has been appointed cashier of the First National Bank of Lead . . . The directors could not have made a better choice.

B H Daily Times
Jan. 31, 1894

Residence houses are very scarce in Lead at present and a number of persons who have wished to move to that city have had to postpone doing so on account of not being able to get houses to live in.

B H Weekly Times
Jan. 11, 1896

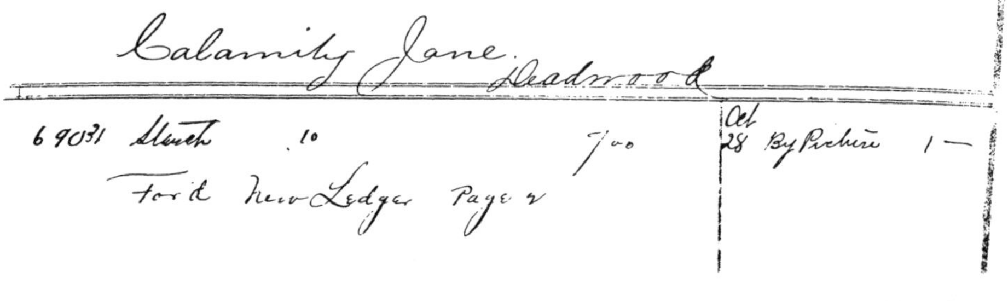
3
Calamity Jane Deadwood
Oct
28

**Calamity Jane had many troubles and paying her bill at Goldberg Grocery Store was one of them. The bill of October 10, 1895 was written off as a bad debt in 1901. The store is still doing business in the historic city.**
**(Courtesy Goldberg Grocery Store)**

# chapter XXII

# Gold Fingers Reach Out

**Horses were used in the Homestake Mine to haul ore cars. "Old Smokey" who spent a lot of his life underground, hauled ore to the dump chutes on the 400-foot level. Horses were rapidly replaced with more efficient steam engines.**

**(Centennial Collection)**

The economic realities of gold mining can be just as harsh as any other business. Mining is a gambling proposition. Mineral wealth can be discovered and exploited quickly, but at any moment financial troubles, labor difficulties, or the lack of high grade mineable ore can end the venture. During the years 1890-1900 Homestake officials, rather than exploit the Homestake ore body for its immediate wealth, decided to plan for mining activities far into the future. To ensure the continuance of the mine and the prosperity of Lead, Homestake began to buy other mines in the area with apparent ore reserves. The gold mine in the 1890's was able to extend its known gold reserves for 20 years well into the next century.

Another problem confronting Homestake officials in the 1890's was the necessity of discovering an efficient technology to mine and process gold ore that was constantly decreasing in value and still keep the mining operation financially sound. Expenditures were made during the decade for new mining equipment such as pneumatic drills and a new ore processing method, the cyanidization process.

By 1900 Homestake had joined together all phases of mining activities to make the company more efficient. Foundries, stamp mills, electric plants, a water system, a railroad, timberlands and sawmills were combined into one organization. The mining company had about 2,000 employees and a payroll of over a million dollars a year by the end of the 1890's. The consolidated Homestake mines had produced $60,000,000 worth of gold and paid $15,000,000 in dividends between 1877 and 1900. Homestake wasn't the only gold producer in the county but it produced more than the other mines combined.

Expansion of early mine holdings characterized Homestake progress in the Black Hills during the 1890's. The mine, managed by Supt. Grier, consolidated all the mines in the Lead-Terraville-Central City district into a single operation by 1901. Under the ownership of

The Times is boycotted by five of the trades unions of the Hills consisting of Central City, Miners' Union, Terraville Miners Union, Lead City Miners Union, Deadwood Barbers Union and Deadwood Knights of Labor. The reason given for such is as they claim, that the Times Is antagonistic to the interests of labor and use the article published in these columns of Dec. 14 in proof of such claim.

B H Daily Times
Jan. 7, 1894

DRIVEN FROM THE WORK — A Mob of 300 and 50 Men March Out to the South Dakota Company's Grading Work and Force the Workmen to Leave — They are Marched to Lead, Where the Rank was Broken and the Men Headed for Deadwood — Superintendent Lock and E. W. Martin Knocked Down with Clubs.

B H Daily Times
Jan. 11, 1894

Homestake, the Highland, the Caledonia, Deadwood-Terra and the Father DeSmet stamp mills became the Amicus, Monroe, Pocahontas and the Mineral Point mills, respectively. Improvements were gradually added to make the stamps more productive, but the stamps were a part of the gold recovery process well into the Twentieth Century.

The progress of the Homestake Mine at Lead parallels the development of advances in all phases of mining activities, making Homestake a pioneer in the gold mining industry. The introduction of modern, efficient machines to supplement or replace work done by hand was the most important innovation in the 100 years of Homestake at Lead. During this decade of innovation, new shafts were built, compressed air (pneumatic) drills were introduced, and a modern hoist was erected at the Ellison shaft.

The main shaft of the Homestake Mine in the 1890's was called the B&M shaft, located next to the Open Cut. The elaborate and delicate hoisting machinery of the B&M was powered by steam. Directly across the gulch from the B&M, construction on the new Ellison shaft and hoist building began around 1895. The next year, 1896, a 900-foot tramway was erected across the gulch from the Ellison to the Star Mill, Homestake's largest stamp mill at that time.

Homestake officials experimented with various ore treatments to find a process that would remove more of the gold from the ore. The amalgamation method of ore processing, based on the affinity of gold for mercury, was not adequate. Finally, a sufficent cyanide treatment was developed in the early 1900's by Charles Merrill to supplement the amalgamation process. Expansion, experimentation and mining difficulties did not interrupt the production of gold bars. By the turn of the century, Homestake was the largest gold mine in the Black Hills and one of the largest in the nation. Gold ore reserves were estimated to last another 20 years and the future for the Homestake Mine at Lead looked very promising.

The future for other area mines, the Portland, Mogul, Golden Reward and the Ragged Top group, appeared promising in the 1890's. Ore bodies were believed extensive and financial stability was assured by many investors. No area showed more promise than the Bald Mountain and Ruby Basin districts. The Portland Mining Co. found an adequate process for the treatment of its ores and mining activity accelerated. Mining soon sprawled all over Bald Mountain. The Portland no longer had to ship its ore by wagon to the Golden Reward treatment plant in Deadwood since the Elkhorn Railroad continued its line to the Bald Mountain mining areas. Later the Portland erected its own mill in Deadwood.

Not far from the Portland, the Mogul and Golden Reward appeared to be possible major gold producers. Developmental work began at the Mogul in the 1890's and by 1897 a 300-foot shaft was sunk.

Mining news — The Deadwood-Terra stamp mill began operation with 160 stamps. An explosion occurred at the Perry Mill when one of the stamp cylinders blew out. No one was injured.

Lead Daily Call
Aug. 22, 1894

A strike of cigar factory workers occurred in Lead. The workers wanted $1 or more per week, but a man was hired to replace the young strikers.

Lead Daily Call
Aug. 22, 1894

Terry, South Dakota, is a lively mining camp and continues to boom.

Evening Call
April 25, 1896

A group of distinguished visitors from the East, including Ex-Governor Pattison of Pennsylvania and his wife, visited the Yellow Creek mining district and the Homestake surface works.

Evening Call
April 24, 1896

City of Lead: Its population at the present is 5,200, easily holding 2nd place among cities of the state. It has two railroads; the Black Hills and Ft. Pierre, connecting with the North Western system at Piedmont, and the Deadwood Central, connecting with the Burlington system at Pluma. It is connected by hack lines with Terry Peak, Welcome City, Central City, and all mining districts. It is the home of the Homestake and Highland Mines, the largest gold mines known to the world today, employing about 1,000 men and handling 1,500 tons of ore daily. The total shipments of bullion for 1893 from these mines alone amounted to $2,200,000. The ore is free milling and is handled through three stamp mills, the Eighty, the Star, and the Highland, dropping a total of 360 stamps.

Lead Evening Call
Aug. 14, 1894

The Golden Reward built an experimental cyanide plant in Deadwood in addition to the treatment mill. The property of the Deadwood and Deleware Co., including a smelter, was added to the Golden Reward in 1899. The Portland, Mogul, Golden Reward and the Homestake all seemed to be important mining ventures. Only one, the Homestake, endured.

In the 1890's mining in the Carbonate area was declining and exploration continued elsewhere for precious metals. Gold ore was accidently found near Ragged Top mountain northwest of Lead in 1896. The Balmoral, Spearfish Gold, Dacy, and Ulster mines became noteworthy producers of gold. The Ragged Top mining activities reached a peak around 1900 and then started to decline.

The Galena and Tinton area mines also were possible big time producers. Southeast of Deadwood in the Galena mining district, the Golden Crest was an active mine during the decade of the 1890's. The Clover Leaf (Uncle Sam) Mine at Roubaix remained closed until a group of investors reorganized the company. Mining activity was followed by the building of a new mill and the introduction of new equipment in the mine. The mines at Tinton, northwest of Lead, worked mainly pegmatite ores since gold placers had been mined out during the gold rush and 1880's. All these mines were producers. Unfortunately, the lack of high grade mineable ore, financial difficulties, and numerous mining problems forced these mines to close for months or years at a time. Finally they were closed for good.

Many mining camps had started during the period of the 1890's. Near Ragged Top Mountain, Balmoral and Preston were boomtowns but gradually became ghost towns after the mines in the area began closing. When the Iron Hill Mine closed, Carbonate Camp north of Ragged Top faded away. However, Roubaix, located south of Deadwood, experienced a rebirth after renewed activity at the Clover Leaf Mine.

Homestake branched out into other commercial ventures during the decade. The mining firm controlled the Hearst Mercantile Store and the First National Bank of Lead. The stable economic base provided by Homestake allowed and encouraged other businesses to develop in Lead. Other mines in the area provided a stable economic base during the 1890's. The development and growth of the communities of Terry and Portland near Lead depended on the success of the local mines.

Terry, a few miles west of Lead, was a thriving little town in the 1890's. The Golden Reward Mining Co. was expanding operations near Terry and hiring new workers. The Golden Reward acquired numerous mining claims and the Deadwood and Delaware smelter to ensure future profits. The investment by the Golden Reward helped make the mining company the second largest gold producer in the county after Homestake. Terry in the 1890's was one of the largest towns in the Black Hills with a population of over 1,000.

A number of Slavonians arrived in Lead yesterday direct from their native land.

B H Daily Times
Feb. 14, 1894

It is a nice thing to have an electric light system in any city, but where there is one, the public at large expects to have the same burning on a dark morning but yesterday they were disappointed in the city of mills (Lead) for there was not a street light burning out of the eleven paid for.

B H Daily Times
Jan. 17, 1894

Some persons in Lead imagine that the death rate has been far larger during the past year than it really has. In looking over S. R. Smith's death register we find that since June 1st, '96 to September 1st, this year, that he had buried 165 persons. The largest number of funerals that Mr. Smith had in any one month was 26, which was during September last year, at the time the fever epidemic prevailed in Lead.

Daily Pioneer-Times
Sept. 12, 1897

Dickinson and Faust, the prosperous and well-known druggists of Lead, were in Central yesterday making an inventory of the latter's branch store in that city. Since the two stores have been consolidated they make the largest in the Black Hills.

B H Daily Times
Jan. 18, 1894

A diphtheria outbreak was contained to only two families. The danger is believed past.

Evening Call
June 23, 1895

A Labor Day picnic was planned at Bender's Park for those who could not attend the celebration in Spearfish . . . . A rumor that gold was found on Yellow Creek may be true . . . . The superintendent of the South Dakota Mining and Milling Co on Annie Creek could not pay his miners. Operations have been temporarily suspended . . . . The new shaft at the Father DeSmet Mine at Central was completed.

Lead Daily Call
Aug. 17, 1894

Rapid City Journal says: "Lawrence County is threatened with a lively county seat fight this coming year. Lead city is of the opinion that there are enough votes in that city to move the seat of government from Deadwood to the city of mills." These threats of county seat fight above referred to count for naught to us in Deadwood. They are as idle as the wind, for first of all Lead City should not be bamboozled into the idea that they can get even a majority of the votes of the county to vote for a change of the county seat, to say nothing of what they must have. The law upon removal of county seats says that the vote must be a two-thirds majority. Does Lead or Spearfish think this possible?

B H Daily Times
Feb. 8, 1894

The county seat fight between Lead and Deadwood continued the local rivalry. The Lead paper states: "Deadwood is tumbling fast. Its people are torn up by internal dissensions, distrust, jealousies and petty spites. Its real estate is largely owned by eastern capital and the tenants dissatisfied with the burdensome monthly rents. Socially, the place is demoralized, and morally it is a subject for missionaries."

Lead Daily Call
Aug. 14, 1894

Lead city fathers are still optimistic that Lead will be the new county seat even though most of the county's political power is centered in Deadwood.

Lead Daily Call
Sept. 11, 1894

Portland (Trojan), four or five miles west of Lead, depended on the Portland Mining Co. for its existence. The Portland Mine was forced to make expenditures on new ore processing techniques to keep the mine profitable. The mine was hiring as many new workers as possible and Portland's growing population required new homes, businesses and schools. Another mine near Portland, the Mogul, was also expanding mining operations and hiring workers. The acquisition of nearby mining claims enabled the Mogul to become one of the largest gold producers in the county. With all the mining activity in the area, the town of Portland prospered throughout the decade of the 1890's.

Mining activities directly affected the economies of other communities. During the 1890's, many mining companies built ore processing plants in or near the communities of Deadwood and Spearfish. Deadwood and Spearfish had the rail transportation and water supplies necessary for ore processing. Deadwood, the railroad center of the Hills, was the site of at least three different ore treatment mills and Spearfish, on the Burlington route, was the location of a chlorination treatment mill.

The labor strike against the South Dakota Mining Co., which was constructing a flume on Annie Creek, set off one of the most heated controversies in the Lead-Deadwood areas and posed a real threat of removal of the county seat to the City of Mills. The union claimed to be seeking just wages and wanted an established pay of $2.50 per day for ten hours of outdoor work which they stated was "as low as present prices for necessities will permit men to live and support families."

Deadwood business men's objection to the work stoppage brought united opposition from the labor union men and Knights of Labor, joined by a group of Lead and Spearfish businessmen who indicated their intentions to wrest from Deadwood its right to the county capital. The group claimed that the town was "owned by foreigners, syndicates and that $20,000 would not cover amounts of monthly rent, while residents of Lead owned their own homes and business houses." Meanwhile, the Black Hills Times questioned the belief that Spearfish and Lead could agree on where the county seat would be located or could garner two-thirds of the vote for its ratification.

However, Deadwood businessmen organized themselves as the Business Mens Protective Association on January 14, 1894, after the union voted to boycott all Deadwood firms. The effect of the boycott was apparently so strong that by March 4 of that year, the Protective Assn. declared it had never been in favor of reduction of the standard scale of labor. Realizing that the higher the wages paid to labor, the more prosperous will be the county, they pledged to maintain the existing scale in Lawrence County.

At a Lead delegate convention, $35,000 was raised and Lead won the vote as the new location for the county seat by questionable means. Spearfish won on the first ballot but Lead carried it on the second vote by securing three extra votes from the Lead Barbers Union.

A headline in the Black Hills Times on August 7, 1894, announced that the hearing on the county seat removal was "Short and Sweet" and that the Lead efforts "ran up against opposition they cannot cope with." Objections filed by the committee of 11 prominent Deadwood businessmen named to oppose the removal action, listed point after point of legal technicalities and irregularities in the 2,447 signatures on the petitions. And so on August 10 the petition was rejected on grounds that the county seat was regularly located at Deadwood in an election held in November, 1877, and that the petition was insufficient.

Following the November election, the Lead Daily Call, new to the publishing field, noted that Lead had more voters than any other community and therefore should rightly be the county seat. It is believed that the efforts to stir up the controversy was primarily to interest new readers in their publication and nothing further developed on the quarrel. Although there were no published charges it was generally believed that the Homestake power structure had amply rewarded Deadwood's opposition to the union by throwing its support to the sister city in the legal battle.

That the power structure of Lawrence County starting in 1890 rested with the Homestake Mining Co. is indisputable. To anyone who is cognizant of the economic and physical influence of the company on the area the conclusion is irrefutable. But the power and influence of the company was not as pervasive, monopolistic and all-powerful as it could have been. It would be fair to say that the company exercised beneficent paternalism.

An illustration of the early and less refined power plays of the company can be found in the great water issue that involved the City of Deadwood in the late 1870's. At that time there was great competition between two companies which had been formed for the specific purpose of obtaining and carrying water in flumes down the gulches for possible use of the miners there. One was the Boulder Ditch that came from Lead down to Deadwood via a route just around Brown Rocks overlooking the City of Deadwood. The other was called the Foster ditch and originated above Central City in Poorman's Gulch and came down to Deadwood via Central City.

At this time there was great competition between the Homestake and an early rival called the Father DeSmet Mine which was located in Central City. Shortly after completion, both ditches were in rather tight financial straits. Knowing this, the superintendent of the Homestake, Sam McMaster, quietly bought the Foster Ditch which ran

Political fevers ran high during the election of November 5, 1894. Lead had the majority of voters. This "demonstrates beyond a shadow of doubt that Lead is the largest of the two towns by several hundred population. It is apparent that we will have the county seat located here where it belongs. The wicked city (Deadwood) always was a social wreck and now it is both a social and financial wreck.

Evening Call
Nov. 8, 1894

The silverites declare that the gold dollar is a 200-cent dollar and assert it must be put back to its place as a 100-cent dollar. That is, that its purchasing power must be cut in two. In the face of this assertion they are asking the wage-earners to support this policy. It is not very often that workingmen ask that their pay be reduced one-half, yet that will be the effect of free coinage.

B H Daily Times
Aug. 22, 1896

Judge A. J. Plowman Monday called the attention of the county commissioners to the miserable condition of the court room and requested them to put the room in a suitable condition for holding court. It has been impossible to heat the room with one stove and as for ventilation there has not been such a thing . . . .

B H Weekly Times
Jan. 18, 1896

The county commissioners yesterday made requisition upon the U. S. Fish Commissioner for 500,000 young mountain trout, which they propose to plant in the streams of this county.

B H Daily Times
Jan. 11, 1894

The receipts of the county treasurer's office so far this month have been about $95,000 which is the largest amount by considerable ever received for a like period. Deputy Treasurer Grimshaw informs us that the month's receipts will exceed any month in the history of the county and he says it is a good indication that times are improving when taxes are paid promptly . . . .

B H Weekly Times
Feb. 29, 1896

The board of county commissioners appointed Sol Star, clerk of courts, to fill the vacancy caused by the death of General Dawson.

B H Weekly Times
July 18, 1896

The prolonged controversy between Lawrence and Meade Counties in which the latter endeavored to repudiate her portion of the floating debt ($24,500) of Lawrence at the time of the segregation of Lawrence and creation of Meade, has been settled by the Supreme Court, who declared the debt valid and Meade County responsible to this county. States Attorney Hayes received a copy of the Supreme Court decision.

B H Daily Times
Feb. 16, 1895

A mine accident at Terraville injured two men who were ready to blast and the dynamite went off too quickly . . . . A rich gold ore vein at the Durango Mine near Lead has been discovered . . . . Several Hills miners are contemplating going with Charlie Price to South Africa's new gold fields.

Evening Call
April 22, 1896

right by the DeSmet mine. Late in awakening to this master stroke in geographical power plays, the superintendent of the Father DeSmet, A. J. Bowie, promptly marched out and bought the Boulder Ditch which passed close to the Homestake. Opening the battle, Bowie brought suit to enjoin the Homestake from polluting the water that went into Boulder Ditch. The Homestake, on the other hand, pointed out that if the water was not put to use, the Father DeSmet would lose its legal right to use it. Thereupon, Bowie offered a pure supply of water to the City of Deadwood, free for one year. Not to be outdone, Homestake made virtually the same offer and convinced the City that a vote should be held on the issue. A vote eventually was held and it is said that both sides liberally acquired all the votes that could be bought with all sorts of inducements. However, in the opinion of local observers, the Homestake was the better organized of the two companies as far as vote-getting was concerned and won the election.

In retrospect, the election was really rather bizarre. But it amply illustrates the effect of mining politics on local politics. The issue, of course, wasn't related at all to philanthropic motives of either company. The battle was for power and control and the City of Deadwood came into the scene only as a useful pawn in the water issue. Eventually the matter was settled in court with the judge ruling that the Foster Ditch should revert to the original owners and Homestake, getting the Boulder Ditch for the price of $30,000, paid off the DeSmet. While the decision was recognized by the legal authorities as an excellent decision in riparian law that was to be followed in later years, it is also interesting to note that the judge in the case, Gideon C. Moody, soon after resigned his position and became chief counsel for the Homestake.

As the area moved toward the Twentieth Century, it was clear that the growing economic power of the Homestake led to an equally great political influence on the county, state and to some extent national level. It was aided, to a degree, by the political aspirations of its people. The company was not shy in indicating to its workers the people it wanted in office, and the policies it wanted in effect. The shift bosses could be and were used to set the men straight as to the "right way" to vote. But the company was sometimes beaten on local issues when the workers could see no rationale for the position that the company wished to see in force. The GOP influence grew and remained strong in the county. However, it should be noted that the position of Lead as a "company" town did not hurt it under the auspices of the beneficent Homestake. The workers obviously felt that what was good for the Homestake was good for them. And, generally, it was!

Lead was fortunate not to have major fires during the early years of its existence. The first scare was on June 24, 1893 when fire broke out in the huge woodpile Homestake maintained to keep the boilers at capacity performance. For years Homestake had chutes that slid the wood down from the top of the mountain to the stockpiles. The town was not threatened by the blaze. The fire occurred where the Open Cut is now located.

(Courtesy Harold Ludeman)

Deadwood despite its turbulent past of devastation due to floods and fires, took on a cosmopolitan look by the 1910 era. Most of the downtown area featured attractive brick buildings. In the center of the picture the central school buildings, the Franklin Hotel, City Hall, Deadwood Theatre and Masonic Temple made an impressive nucleus.

(Centennial Collection)

# chapter XXIII

# Potpourri

After the turbulent gold-discovery days in the Black Hills, time edged gradually but serenely into the new century. With thorough planning by the U.S. Forest Service, the future of the ponderosa pines was assured. The scars of overcutting, fires and bark beetle infestations began to heal. But it was again just a matter of time before new quirks of nature had to be reckoned with. On June 21, 1968, a huge Ponderosa pine was cut in the Case 1 timber sale area near Nemo, representing the second billionth board foot of lumber cut in the Black Hills. The 203-year-old giant tree had been left as a seed tree to reforest the area. When the tree was cut down, forest officials pointed out that controlled timber management was evidenced by the fact that one and one-half billion board feet were available when the first official timber sale was made at Case 1 in 1898. "We have cut two billion since then and there is still two billion left in the Black Hills," it was pointed out.

Big freezes and various storms destroyed 17,500,000 board feet of timber. In July, 1928, a hailstorm felled 90 percent of the trees northwest of Roubaix. On June 22, 1940, a tornado blew up Riflepit Canyon in the Limestone area, destroying 1,500,000 board feet of timber. On January 15, 1943, the famous Chinook, a unique warm wind, destroyed countless acres of trees. A twister on May 17, 1944, cut a swath near the Hardy Ranger Station 20 miles long and three-fourths of a mile wide.

After the turn of the century, timber losses from fire fell in the Northern Hills due to Forest Service suppression efforts. But two big losses occurred in the Rochford fire (20 miles long covering 21,600 acres in 1931, and the McVey fire (21,857 acres) which started on July 8, 1939. In the Northern Black Hills alone, 82,025 acres burned between 1909 and 1941.

Far greater losses than fire were caused by the Black Hills bark beetles. The first outbreak in epidemic stage was reported in 1895 in the northwest part of the Hills. But by 1901 it was estimated 226,896,000 board feet of good pine timber was destroyed by beetles. In 1906 beetle infestation was heavy near Elmore in the Northern Hills where damage had resulted previously. In a 14-year invasion, the Black Hills beetle had killed between one and two billion board

**A trolley car would create a traffic jam today along Lead's Main Street. One is shown at the intersection of Main and Mill Streets with the old First National Bank Building as a backdrop.**

**(Centennial Collection)**

The greatest variance in temperature, according to the Guinness Book of World Records was recorded at Spearfish, S. D. on Jan. 22, 1943 when the thermometers rose from 4 degrees below zero at 7:30 a.m. to 45 degrees above zero at 7:32 a.m., a matter of 49 degrees in two minutes. The National Weather Service at Rapid City reports that at one time, the same day, Lead had a reading of 52 degrees above zero and Deadwood was recording a minus 16. At 11:15 a.m. that day in Lead, it was a minus 12 degrees. In the following 15 minutes, the temperature recording equipment at Montana-Dakota Utilities rose to 30 degrees above zero. The sudden hike in temperature caused several plate glass windows in town to crack. Other freakish variances were reported in various portions of the two cities, with some areas recording below zero readings and others enjoying above freezing weather. The Chinook did not hit portions of Deadwood until late in the afternoon. There a 5 p.m. reading was 10 below zero and by 6 p.m. it had warmed to 35 degrees above and had risen to 44 above zero by 7 p.m.

Deadwood — One of the most remarkable orders ever received by the local forest service office has just come from Washington. Supervisor Hamilton has been requested to have his rangers kill and dress two dozen woodpeckers, selected from different parts of the Black Hills national forest. The stomachs of the birds are to be preserved and after being detached and given temporary treatment with an embalming fluid, labeled and forwarded to Washington, where they will be analyzed and tested to find if the birds have eaten any of the bark beetles that have proved so destructive in the hills.

Rapid City Journal
Feb. 13, 1908

A forestry official who has received special recognition was Tom Gill, who was assigned to the Deadwood office following World War I, at an annual salary of $1,600. Deadwood residents recall him as a quiet, unassuming man, dedicated to forest management. In 1922 he was transferred to Washington, D.C. where he climbed the success ladder quickly, becoming editor of forest publications. In 1926 he headed the Charles Lathrop Park Forest Foundation. Gill led a double life; although he was devoted to the advancement of forestry, he was a prolific writer and several of his books were made into movies. He wrote of cowboys, forest rangers and frontier characters. Before he died at the age of 81, he donated $500,000 toward the erection of the Gifford Pinchot Forestry Building in Washington, D.C.

Journal of Forestry
November, 1973

**Thinning was done at the time of Case No. 1, by horse logging and cross-haul method.**
**(U. S. Forest Service)**

feet. Heavy beetle damage is presently ravaging large areas of the Northern Hills, especially in the Deadwood-Lead areas. Every effort, including the removal of the beetle-infested trees from the steep canyons by helicopter, is being made to stop the scourge.

The Black Hills National Forest Supervisor's office remained in Deadwood until 1954 when the Black Hills Forest was combined with the Harney National Forest. At that time the main office was moved to Custer. The first supervisor of the Black Hills Forest was H. G. Hamaker, who served from 1898 to 1901 and was followed by Seth Bullock, who held the post from 1901 to 1906; John Fremont Smith, 1906-1907; Edwin M. Hamilton, 1908-1909; Paul D. Kelleter, 1909-1918; George A. Duthie, 1918-1930; Theodore Krueger, 1930-1939; Clarence C. Averill, 1939-1941; Arthur F. C. Hoffman, 1941-1948; and Clarence Averill again from 1948 through 1953.

When the Black Hills and Harney National Forests combined, Jack C. Kern was supervisor in 1954 and 1955. He was followed by Grant A. Morse, 1955-1958; Howard Lee, 1958-1963; Theodore Schlapfer, 1963-65; Kenneth Scholz, 1965-1972; David Johns, 1972-1975 and his successor James Overbay.

The three foes of a forest — fires, insects and weather — were not the only troubles experienced by the U.S. Forest Service in the Northern Hills. There were management problems that knew no end. One of the major controversies resulted when sheep growers petitioned to use the national forest land for grazing. Gifford Pinchot, Chief Forester, visited Deadwood in July, 1909, to see for himself how matters stood. After two all-night open air mass meetings with cattlemen, small settlers raising crops for a living and the sheepmen, Pinchot held with the majority and ruled that sheep were to be excluded from all parts of the Black Hills National Forest. Apart from the fact that the sheep would do untold damage to the forest land by destroying the young growth, Pinchot realized that homes are the sustaining life of a community and that his decision would encourage settlement of the Hills as well as conserving its resources.

Since it beginning, the Black Hills National Forest came into prominence as an outstanding proving ground and demonstration area for scientific forest management. Proof that forestry, as practiced in the Black Hills, has been practical is the fact that there is more timber growing here today than there was 75 years ago, in spite of the continuous cutting of forest products. During the trying period of World War II, great pressures were put upon the supervisors of the forest to cut timber beyond the limits of sustained yield. Their job was not easy; but they did not yield, for they knew that by so doing, the future economy of the Black Hills would be disrupted for many years.

Actually, the beginning of intensive forestry in the Black Hills was made possible largely by the work of the Civilian Conservation

Corps. The first camp in the Northern Hills was established May 18, 1933, on the site of the old Este Logging Camp, where the lumber was sawed from Case No. 1, the famous first timber sale on a national forest. The most extensive job done by the CCC was the thinning of thousands of acres of ponderosa pine. It was the largest thinning project in the national forests of the country. The reputation of the Black Hills as a recreation center can be credited largely to the work of these camps.

The Homestake Mining Co. has had a real stake in the Black Hills National Forest, which has supplied over 12 million feet of timber annually for ground support in mine workings. Nearly all of this, through the years, has been processed by Homestake's lumber and timber department from ponderosa pine cut by Homestake on the national forest land. Homestake has owned extensive holdings of timber land in the Northern Hills, and, in addition, purchases stumpage from the Forest Service. In the busy days of Nemo, the train would arrive from Lead in the morning, hitch on carloads of wood from the Homestake sawmill there, then leave for Lead where it would arrive in the afternoon. However, on January 13, 1930, the narrow gauge railroad, the Black Hills and Ft. Pierre — the Homestake railroad that never made it to Fort Pierre — was abandoned as well as all of the stations along the line. Lumber was then hauled by truck and in November 1940, the sawmill at Nemo was abandoned and dismantled and a new modern electric sawmill plant was located on a 211-acre tract west of Spearfish where all of the milling activities for Homestake were established. So Nemo, having served it purpose, was sold by Homestake to private individuals and now is a guest ranch with a post office, store, cafe and grade school.

At Spearfish, in addition to milling mine timbers, the slab or edging is used for commercial lumber, as well as the trees which are smaller and not usable for mine posts. Recently the Spearfish sawmill output of commercial products has been 80 percent of its production total. In 1962 a market opened up for pulpwood chips recovered from sawmill waste for use in the manufacture of paper products. This necessitated major alterations at the Spearfish sawmill and a giant debarking machine was installed, adding a new dimension in the use of thousands of tons of once-wasted wood chips for added profit.

In August, 1972, the Homestake sawmill at Spearfish became the property of a wholly-owned subsidiary of the mining company and is now known as the Homestake Forest Products Co., managed independently from the mining operations in Lead, and employing about 150 workers.

In the Lead-Deadwood area, which in its early years was dependent on the forest for its construction supplies, lumbering has grown to be one of the most important industries in the county, with a pay-

**June 20, 1914**

Burlington Route

**BETTER SERVICE EAST**

*Electric Lights*
*Dining Cars*
*Pullman Sleepers*
*Tourist Sleepers*
*....on....*
*Through Trains*

*Leave Deadwood 2:20 p. m.*
*Leave Lead - 2:10 p. m.*
*Ar. Hot Springs 7:50 p. m.*
*Ar. Denver - 8:25 a. m.*
*Ar. Kansas City 8:40 p. m.*

*J. L. BENTLEY,*
*Commercial Agent,*
*DEADWOOD*

"The change of water quality standards would reclassify Whitewood Creek from I-90 at Whitewood to the Deadwood city limits as cold water marginal and limited contact recreation rather than cold water permanent, emersion recreation and limited contact recreation as it is now classified."

Lead Daily Call
July 18, 1975

. . . . Toscano pointed out that the lowering of standards may allow the district to build a sanitary treatment facility that individual households can afford. Cost of a facility has been the biggest stumbling block in the path of construction for the past two or more years. More than $1 million has been expended in engineering and other costs over the last six years in a vain effort to find a solution to the sanitary problem.

Lead Daily Call
Aug. 16, 1975

roll second only to Homestake. Approximately 20 years ago only nine percent of the 40,000 cords of pulpwood and pole timber, available in a 20-mile radius, was being utilized. Today, as the giant logging trucks wheel through the Northern Hills, residents are well aware that the industry is coming into its own. Officials of the Nemo District, U.S. Forest Service, report that for the fiscal year ending in July, 1975, the combined Spearfish and Nemo districts sold 43,545 million board feet and cut out of the forest were 17,772 million board feet used for posts, poles, wood chips and paper products, as well as saw timber for lumber. A decline in building activity due to inflationary interest rates throughout the nation has caused a corresponding drop in the demand for the product since about 1972 when a peak was hit. However, the decline is believed to be only temporary and with the return to normal construction, the logging industry is expected to boom again.

It is understood that electric motors will shortly be installed by the North Western railroad on its line between Deadwood and this city. For some years past the company has been running the regulation steam engine. The grade is one of the steepest on the whole North Western system, and it is declared that the motors can do more effective work. The cars, it is said, are now being constructed and the change will be made in several weeks.

Lead Daily Call
Feb. 19, 1909

Nationwide concern for cleaner air and water has affected many communities in Lawrence County. Control of environmental pollution has focused on the Homestake tailings, cyanide solutions, and mercury discharged into Whitewood Creek; the Lead-Deadwood sewage disposal system; and open burning at the local dumps. For nearly 100 years the Homestake Mine and the cities of Lead and Deadwood have deposited waste materials into Whitewood Creek. In the 1970's the Environmental Protection Agency ordered changes in these practices. James O. Harder, a former manager of the Homestake Mine, in a statement presented to the EPA in Rapid City in 1971, explained local pollution must be controlled in a way that does not jeopardize the future of the Homestake Mine at Lead or the economic stability of the Lead-Deadwood area.

Prior to the 1970's, the amounts of toxic cyanide and metallic mercury discharged by Homestake into Whitewood Creek were minimal. Homestake had conducted experiments on animals and humans subjected to diluted cyanide solutions that showed no harmful effects. Mercury was the more controversial issue. At the insistence of the EPA, the Homestake Mine discontinued the use of mercury in any way that would allow the metal to be discharged into local streams. Henceforth, the mining company depended on the cyanide process to remove gold from the ore. The mercury pollution problem was resolved without forcing the mine to close.

Lead, S. D. — Unless the city council agrees to fix a higher rate for gas charges here, the Lead-Deadwood Gas company threatens to go out of business in Lead. President Smith of the company appealed to the council declaring that his company daily was losing money here, and unless permitted to raise their rates here at once he would quit. Inability to procure Colorado coal, he claimed, was responsible for the additional cost to the company. The present rate for gas in Lead is $1.60 per 1,000 feet for fuel and $1.80 for light.

Sioux Falls Argus Leader
Dec. 6, 1907

Lead and Deadwood voters passed a resolution in 1968 to form a single sanitary district. An area engineering firm was asked to study local environmental problems. The firm recommended that the Homestake Mine and the Lead-Deadwood Sanitary District build a nine mile pipeline to a dam site in Centennial Valley near Whitewood. The pond would be designed to settle Homestake tailings and to begin the treatment of municipal sewage. The cost at that time was estimated at six million dollars. Plans were tentatively made for the settling pond, funding for the project was arranged, and Homestake began to acquire the land for the dam site in Centennial Valley.

In 1971 farmers and ranchers in the Centennial Valley area formed a Save Centennial Valley Association and later filed suit against the Lead-Deadwood Sanitary District (including Homestake) and the EPA in Washington, D.C., disputing the proposed settling pond and waste disposal project. The people in Centennial Valley did not like the idea of a sewage treatment and sediment settling facility in their backyard. They objected to possible settling pond leakage contaminating underground water supplies, the odor caused by the sewage, and damage to the valley environment and scenic beauty. Over a year later an agreement was reached by the parties involved in the dispute. The EPA and the Sanitary District decided that the objections of the Centennial Valley Association and rising costs made it imperative that an alternative site be found. The Centennial Valley project was abandoned.

The Lead-Deadwood Sanitary District in July 1975 asked the EPA to lower the water quality standards of Whitewood Creek from the Deadwood city limits to the I-90 bridge. The revision was necessary since the higher costs would be paid by fewer households in the Lead-Deadwood community, an area of declining population. High taxes and inflation were other reasons cited by the Sanitary Board. The Homestake also objected to the high water quality standards as unrealistic. The project appeared to be threatened financially unless water standards were lowered. Over one million dollars had already been spent and no definite plans had been made. The South Dakota Environmental Protection Agency finally lowered the classification of Whitewood Creek. The Lead-Deadwood Sanitary Board was hopeful that a new plan within cost limits could be made quickly.

In October 1975 the Lead-Deadwood Sanitary District representatives revealed tentative plans to build a two-part waste treatment facility to process sewage from Lead, Deadwood, and surrounding communities and to settle Homestake's tailings beginning in 1976. Lead's sewage and Homestake sediments would be piped to a settling pond north of Lead in Grizzly Gulch. Deadwood's waste would be piped to a tentative site for treatment near the Deadwood fairgrounds. Many loose ends had to be resolved and cost estimates finalized before the project could be submitted to local voters for approval. Meanwhile, the Homestake started its own pollution control program and scheduled it for completion by July 1977. The Homestake project was designed to be flexible enough to include sewage disposal for Deadwood and other area communities if found to be feasible.

NEW SHORT LINE TO THE BLACK HILLS !

R. BLAKELY, President, St. Paul, Minn. C. W. CARPENTER, Sec'y & Trea., St. Paul, Minn.

The Northwestern Express, Stage & Transportation COMPANY.

Chartered under the Laws of the State of Minnesota.

CAPITAL STOCK, - - - $500,000

—IN CONNECTION WITH—

THE AMERICAN EXPRESS COMPANY

Does a regular Express Business in all its Branches between the Black Hills and all points in the East and South.

IN CONNECTION WITH

CHICAGO & NORTHWESTERN RAILWAY,

Passengers can buy through tickets from New York, Chicago, St. Louis and all Eastern and Southern Cities to Deadwood,

VIA PIERRE.

Time, 44 Hours from Chicago to Pierre, no Change of Cars.
Stage, 36 Hours from Pierre to Deadwood, Excellent Meal Stations.
Only 28 Hours' Stage Ride from the Missouri to the Hills.

—o: SLEEPING CARS ATTACHED TO ALL TRAINS. o:—

FREIGHT

Through Bills of Lading to Deadwood can be obtained from

L. F. BOOTH, 415 Broadway, New York City. C. H. WISE, 5 State Street, Boston, Mass. THOS. S. RATTLE, 60 Clark Street, Chicago, Ill.

WILLIAM SELBIE,
Agent, Deadwood, D. T.

Infernal "gas buggies" were crowding horses off Deadwood's Main Street in the early 1900's. Looks like a three-lane, one-way highway with autos all over the street heading south. The blotches on the brick pavement, however, are evidence that "horse power" hadn't been completely obliterated.
(Centennial Collection)

Along with the autos of the early 1900's — came their advertising and H. S. Clark, first Ford dealer, took advantage of a circus parade through Deadwood to get the word across.
(Centennial Collection)

In the 1970's the Lead, Deadwood and Spearfish waste disposal dumps were no longer allowed to use open burning. The Lead and Deadwood dumps were closed and waste hauled to a land fill site near Sturgis.

Another critical environmental issue in Lawrence County during the past few years has been the proposed taconite mining development near Nemo. A Minnesota mining firm has planned a large scale surface mining operation for taconite, a low grade of iron ore. To handle the taconite ores profitably, a treatment mill would have to be built to process the ore for shipment, creating a large pile of mine wastes or tailings. Initially, the greatest concern of the local residents was the effect of taconite mining on the water resources of the area. Nemo residents quickly discovered that water would not be the only problem. The mining operation could disrupt the natural environment, damaging the recreation and scenic values of the area. How the people and government of Lawrence County react to the possible taconite mining in the Nemo area could influence the future of strip mining in the Black Hills — a future characterized by increasing industrial pressure to develop the natural resources and increasing public pressure to protect the environment.

And one of the most recent attempts to keep the Northern Black Hills environment in its natural state was the adoption of a comprehensive zoning plan in 1973. An interim plan was drawn up in 1972 by the Lawrence County Zoning and Planning Commission and formally adopted in 1975. However, a move is underway to have the plan ratified by the voters in the June 1976, election. If rejected at the polls, the State will take over the work or the Zoning and Planning Commission will start all over on a new plan.

The Twentieth Century was a time of startling changes in transportation in Lawrence County. Improvements in the county highway system were made gradually until a new invention, the horseless carriage, began to appear on county roads. A virtual transportation revolution occurred when the automobiles attempted to negotiate the mud roads around Lead, Deadwood and Spearfish and found tough going. New roads were needed! John McClintock, a colorful Deadwood pioneer, called the Deadwood-Spearfish public highway via Deadwood Hill a mud hole of a road. This road was repaired and efforts to maintain it were made every summer. But every spring the road would turn to mud. After 30 years of neglect, the automobile changed everything. Since the horseless carriages were unable to move in the mud, the Spearfish-Deadwood road in 1911 was rebuilt into an excellent graveled highway, one of the best in the state at that time. More money was spent on this highway in two weeks than in the 30 years it served as a stagecoach road.

The reconstruction of the Deadwood-Spearfish highway signaled the beginning of a comprehensive road building program in the county. During the next ten years, the county spent over $600,000 on road improvements. Lawrence and Meade Counties around 1919 were each building a section of the Boulder Canyon road to their respective county lines as an alternative to the road up Whitewood Hill. By 1929 this road was covered with limestone chips. The automobile continually made people conscious of the poor road conditions in the county. The road from Deadwood to Spearfish and roads to other communities in the area were constantly upgraded. New roads were built and the state began to modernize their highways in the county.

Other important highway developments have occurred in the Twentieth Century. In the 1940's and 1950's, the major gravel roads were widened and covered with asphalt. The most recent phase in county highway development was the construction of Interstate 90 near Whitewood and Spearfish.

After the Elkhorn Railroad reached Deadwood in 1890, railroad progress moved quickly forward. The Elkhorn continued its tracks to Central City, Lead and the Bald Mountain mining areas. The Elkhorn was eventually sold to the Chicago and North Western in 1903. The Burlington Railroad, another major carrier, purchased the Deadwood Central in 1893 and the Homestake's Black Hills and Fort Pierre in 1901.

Higher freight costs, trucks and bus lines have forced the county railroads to cut back on freight and passenger service. In the 1960's the Chicago and North Western abandoned its tracks, used mainly to haul Black Hills pulp wood, between Deadwood and Whitewood. Freight is still delivered to the Homestake Mine and Deadwood by the Burlington Northern Railroad. However, Burlington passenger service to the Lead-Deadwood area has been discontinued for over 25 years. The trains have been effectively supplemented by trucks and buses.

The invention of the flying machine also revolutionized county transportation in the Twentieth Century. Art Smith made the first flight over Lawrence County to Deadwood in 1912 less than a decade after the Wright Brothers' flight at Kitty Hawk. The biplane that landed in the Deadwood Amusement Park was shipped to the Black Hills in crates and assembled near Mountain Ranch not far from Deadwood. Because of bad weather conditions, Smith had to wait three days before he could make the flight. The next flight over Deadwood was not made until 1921 when a World War I "Jenny" performed acrobatics for the local 4th of July celebration. Charles Lindbergh after his Atlantic crossing to Paris in 1927 flew over Deadwood as part of an aviation promotional tour. He was visiting state capitals by air and on his way to Cheyenne, Wyoming, from Pierre, South Dakota, he passed over Deadwood and dropped an autographed note about his Atlantic flight.

A young aviator named Art Smith was the first to land a plane in narrow Deadwood Gulch. He brought this early-vintage plane down in the Deadwood Amusement Park on August 12, 1912.

(Centennial Collection)

Lead — After several months of agitation and public controversy, the city council turned down the proposed new ordinance granting the Lead-Deadwood Gas company a twenty year franchise at increased rates. The company some time ago threatened to withdraw from the field here unless permitted to raise their rates to what they considered a fair figure and what action they will now take remains to be seen . . . .

Sioux Falls Argus-Leader
Feb. 15, 1908

Most of the merchants had started out with the three phones but finally decided that the Bell was the best and now the independent phone company is dealing with the "trust" and wants them to take over the junk that was at one time their pride and which was also thought to be the road whereby they were to make a large fortune.

Deadwood Pioneer-Times
Nov. 30, 1906

Announcement Monday of the sale of the Lead Daily Call to Fred Seaton of the Seaton Publications of Manhattan and Winfield, Kansas and Hastings, Neb. brings to a close 31 years of continuous publication of this newspaper by the Stanley family.

Lead Daily Call
Oct. 1, 1945

The Lawrence County Airport was established in the 1930's near Spearfish on Highway 14. The airport has been used for general aviation, commercial stops, and slurry bomber runs during the Deadwood fire of 1959. The building of I-90 forced the airport to move north and today the facility serves local aviation. Changes in transportation in the 100 years of Lawrence County have occurred rapidly. From the toll roads of the late 1870's to the modern interstate highways and from the wagons of 1876 to the modern automobiles, trains and airplanes, the changes have been profound.

Utilities in Lawrence County during the early 1900's grew their own "family trees." Many of the small companies were acquired and consolidated under new names until August 27, 1941, when the Black Hills Power and Light Co. became the parent organization. Both the Black Hills Electric Light and Belt Light and Power Co. were acquired in 1905 by the Consolidated Power and Light Co. of South Dakota (Wyoming Corp.), with Harris Franklin, Deadwood, as president. This company, in turn, was acquired in 1908 by the Consolidated Power and Light Co. of South Dakota (Maine Corp.) which served the area until 1935. It was on that date that the General Public Utilities, Inc., took over; two years later it acquired the Tri-State Milling Co. property; and within six years was incorporated into the BHP&L.

Spearfish had a small plant and in 1908 the Homestake of Lead started its water power plant which supplied the town until 1915 when Consolidated Power and Light purchased it.

A similar history was recorded by the telephone companies. At the turn of the century an exchange with 45 subscribers was opened at Spearfish on February 21, 1903, by the Nebraska Co. And in Lead, a new 300-line common battery board was installed in March, 1904, with the exchange serving 239 customers. Improvements were also made at Deadwood where a new 400-line switchboard was installed as well as underground and aerial cable.

In 1904 a firm known as the Home Telephone Co., which also had offices at Deadwood, took over the property of the Harrison Telephone Co. Two years later all of the company's properties were sold to the Nebraska Telephone Co.

Independent companies continued to own the majority of the South Dakota exchanges; however, the Black Hills exchanges remained subscribers of the Bell system. In January, 1921, the properties of the Nebraska Telephone (in Nebraska and South Dakota) and of the Northwestern Telephone Exchange Co. (in Minnesota and North Dakota) merged with those of the Northwestern Bell Telephone, which had come into existence in 1920.

One of the outstanding milestones in the field of telephone switchboard operating took place in 1923. For the first time in telephone history, the person who placed a telephone call in Baltimore, Maryland, was answered by an operator using the same phrases and methods as did the operators in Deadwood. The dial system was introduced in 1962 and in 1964 direct dialing was initiated in the county, with even long distance calls dialed without operator assistance.

While most homes in the county were heated with coal and wood, the Lead-Deadwood Gas Co., which was located at Pluma, between the two communities, supplied gas for lighting. Mains for the system were laid in Lead in 1903 and the same year a large plant for the manufacture of gas was built in Deadwood and its pipe lines laid through every street and alley of the city. Old-timers recall that the system was used mostly for lighting because of its high cost for cooking and heating and as a result most meals were prepared in homes on old wood stoves.

When the firm appeared before the Lead City Council in 1907 seeking permission to hike its rates the Council agreed only if the company would improve the quality and quantity of their product and "show the people that they can supply something of a commercial value." The Council also stipulated that there be an examination of the company's books by an expert accountant to determine if it was operating at a loss. As the use of electricity increased in the area, the gas companies, with their increasing costs, finally bowed out of the competition.

However, natural gas came to the Northern Hills in 1928 when Montana-Dakota Utilities incorporated a new subsidiary, Black Hills Utilities Co. in May. During the summer and early fall a 12-inch natural gas pipeline was built from Cabin Creek, Montana, to Whitewood, together with a 10-inch extension from Whitewood to Rapid City and branches to Spearfish, Lead, Deadwood, Sturgis and Belle Fourche.

Colorful journalism continued on into the Twentieth Century and newspapers continued to come and go. Willis H. Bonham, a pioneer of the Black Hills who began his career in 1878 by running a hand press on the Pioneer, became its sole owner in 1885. He later purchased the Black Hills Times from Porter Warner and with its consolidation, the Pioneer-Times became the mouthpiece of the Black Hills. Still operating in the 1920's, his nephews, Leland V. and Earl B. Morford, became associated with him in the management of the newspaper. In 1901 the Evening News was started by Ira Hungerford but it lasted only through the 15th issue, a much briefer career than the earlier Evening News, published in 1879-81.

Remembered well by many old timers at the turn of the century were the Independent, the Equality and The Lantern, all founded by Freeman Knowles, a congressman for several years.

Deadwood, S. D. — "Buster" the best known dog in the Black Hills, is dead. He was the property of W. L. McLaughlin, the manager of the Mogul Mining company. "Buster's pet trick was to watch the eastern mail sacks as they were thrown from incoming trains and permit no one but the mail clerk to touch them. He was the only passholder on the Burlington railroad who was not an employee and used to ride to and from the Mogul mill at Pluma at will, occupying one of the seats as a regular passenger.

Minneapolis Journal
Nov. 28, 1907

# Lead Daily Call

# EXTRA

**Lead, South Dakota, February 15, 1903.**

## BIG BLAZE AT DEADWOOD

### Fire Broke Out at Eight O'clock in the Postoffice Building.

Fire broke out in the furnace-room of the postoffice building at Deadwood this morning at 8 o'clock. The flames in a remarkably short time spread through the postoffice building. The mail and most of the postoffice fixtures were saved, being transferred to the Syndicate block.

Low water pressure retarded the work of the fire department and enabled the blaze to gain great head way in a very few minutes time.

Postmaster Bonham at 9:30 telephoned the Call that the fire was under control, having been confined to the building in which the postoffice was located. He says the department practically suffered no loss, except from smoke and water, the mail having all been removed.

### Washington School House Fire.

Last evening about 7:30 o'clock fire was discovered in the south wing of the second story of the Washington school building. The alarm was turned in and in a very short time the Highland Park hose team boys were on the ground and had a stream of water turned on the blaze, which was fortunately subdued in a short time.

The up stairs rooms, particularly the one in which the fire started, sustained considerable damage, and it will probably be some days before school can be resumed in these rooms.

In 1906 there appeared the newspaper called the Deadwood Telegram, which was purchased two years later by E. L. Senn, a crusader, who hoped, through the columns of the paper, to clean up the vice and corruption in Deadwood. After his son Albert purchased the plant it continued as the Deadwood Telegram and the Black Hills Weekly. It eventually became the Black Hills Weekly, and later was consolidated with the Whitewood Plaindealer. The Black Hills Weekly is still printed each Wednesday by Seaton Publishing Company, which, in 1946, purchased both the Deadwood Pioneer-Times and the Lead Daily Call, and is now published as one paper under a combined masthead on presses located at Lead.

Robert Sloss, 18, while working for the contractor tearing down the old Burlington depot, discovered a cache of $20 bills which totaled $1,160. The discovery of two other bills brought the total to $1,200. No trace of the owner or owners of the money could be found and it was retained by the finder.

Deadwood Pioneer-Times
July 14, 1950

Other newspapers which belonged to the area briefly but played their part in the history of the region were the Black Hills Mining Review, a weekly devoted to the mining interests of the Black Hills, which ceased publication in 1907; the Black Hills World, 1901; Black Hills Blade, Lead, 1904; The Register, Lead, 1906; the Terry Record, which ceased operations in 1909 after 15 years of publication; the Bald Mountain News which went out of existence in 1901, also after 15 years of printing; and the Spearfish Enterprise which went out of business in 1916 after 20 years of publishing.

In addition to the Lead and Deadwood daily and the Black Hills Weekly, the only other papers still being published in Lawrence at the end of its first 100 years, are the Queen City Mail, Spearfish, and the Whitewood Centennial that was established in 1974.

Another form of communication, the radio, came to Deadwood on July 2, 1947, when the Daniels brothers, Eli and Harry, started broadcasting from a somewhat makeshift studio in the Franklin Hotel. The transmitter site was located four miles from Deadwood on the Boulder Canyon road on land purchased by the Daniels. The station, with call letters KDSJ, started with only 250 watts on 1450 kilocycles in 1947 but six years later it began broadcasting with 1,000 watts, day and night on 980 kilocycles. When the studio in the hotel proved inadequate the office was moved to the City Hall building, where the station broadcast until it was destroyed by a fire in 1952. This brought about the purchase of the Buehler Building at 745 Main Street, where it is still located.

"By ironic fate, Harvey Fellows in his feeble old age was mortally injured at Deadwood's Days of '76 celebration while alighting from his coach which he had piloted 300,000 miles carrying some 90,000 passengers without an accident."

Lee Case, Lee's Official Guidebook to the Black Hills and Badlands, Sturgis, 1953

The Deadwood-Lead area joined the new world opened by television as early as 1955 when WTVS pioneered in the field. Although reception and facilities were inadequate, it gave the viewing public a taste of what was to come and Deadwood, Lead and Spearfish welcomed the South Dakota Cable TV which took over the operations in 1969. The cable system also serves Belle Fourche and Hot Springs. Non-subscribers receive viewing limited to two Rapid City stations from translator towers located on White Rocks in Deadwood and others in Lead and on Terry Peak.

# chapter XXIV

# The Mighty Homestake

**Ten levels below the surface and three above are shown in the cutaway picture of the railroad operations in the Homestake Gold Mine.**

Tremendous technological achievements and expansion into other mining areas around the nation and world have highlighted Homestake progress in the Twentieth Century. The transformation of Homestake from a boomtown mine into one of the country's major mining corporations was accomplished by a great deal of planning, patience, and foresight on the part of the mine superintendents. Around 1900 T. J. Grier, superintendent from 1884-1914, continued to reorganize and expand the gold mining operation. Mine improvements were implemented rapidly after Homestake purchased all the mines and their mills in the Lead-Terraville-Central City district.

Homestake officials were constantly searching for better ways to improve mining activities. After 1900 square set timber stoping was used in conjunction with shrinkage stoping because large amounts of timber were required for the square set method. Rock pillars 60 feet high were left while the rest of the ore was removed by the square set method. Cut and fill horizontal stopes are used at the present time in the mine. The stope is cleared of all accessible ore, filled with a ten foot layer of sand from the mills, and capped with a six inch layer of cement. Filling equalizes ground pressure and prevents ground movement. Cut and filling is repeated until all the ore is taken from a mining area.

Carbide lamps replaced the kerosene or "sunshine lamps" used by the underground workers about 1913 and candles used since 1876. In 1934 electric cap lamps were introduced. Safety in the mine has progressed a long way since the days before electric lamps, hard hats and safety glasses. Safety equipment and procedures quickly became very important aspects of Homestake's operation.

Prior to the turn of the century, post-mounted compressed air (pneumatic) drills were employed in the mine. The pneumatic drills were heavy, awkward machines and they produced great amounts of

Our Black Hills banks felt the first shock of the Panic of 1907 . . . . It was a money panic and we were a gold mining country. The largest gold mine in the Black Hills, the Homestake, refused to deliver its bullion to the U. S. Mint, uness it received gold coins in return . .. . Homestake got its gold coins, because the U. S. Treasury could do nothing but accede. The result was that the Black Hills banks remained on a specie basis — perhaps the only banks in the country where such a situation existed.

Robert E. Driscoll
Black Hills of S. D.
Its Pioneer Banking History

Lead, S. D. — While mines and mills closed down for the day, every employe of the Homestake Mining Co. and many citizens of both Lead and Deadwood and the surrounding country, celebrated at City Park with a mammoth picnic, the successful termination of the fire that threatened last spring to cost the company much more than the one million dollars figured as the loss. The day commenced with a big parade in which William Bartelero was marshal and every band from this section of the Black Hills participated . . . . Speeches were made . . . . followed by the feeding in the open air at long rows of tables, between two and three thousand people, a small army of chefs and waiters being employed therefor by the association. It was a big day in Lead never to be forgotten.

Argus-Leader, Sioux Falls
Oct. 8, 1907

**Unknowingly sitting on top of the fabulous Homestake was the Oro Hondo Mining Co. When directors refused to authorize funds to go deeper, the Oro Hondo was sold to HMC in about 1920. It was another bonanza for Homestake as the previous owners had missed the main vein of gold by a few feet. It was a lifesaving streak of good fortune, giving many more years of life to the company.**
**(Centennial Collection)**

dust. The dust and insufficient lighting made working conditions very difficult. The drills of the 1920's and 1930's were post-mounted water leyners (pronounced liners). The leyners operated with water to control the dust problem. However, these drills consumed large quantities of drill steel since the cutting edges dulled quickly. Drill bits originally forged by hand gave way to machined and detachable bits.

Due to the hardness of Homestake ore, diamond drilling has been used extensively in the mine. Diamond drilling dates back to 1916 and has been used ever since for exploratory and geological activities in the gold mine. Gradually, the diamond drills over the years have been considerably improved. The Homestake now uses tungsten carbide and diamond drill bits. Blasting techniques have greatly changed. Blasting in the 1876 era was done by a gelatin explosive, a recent invention of that time, and later dynamite. A variety of explosives are used today as dynamite is being phased out of mining operations.

Advances in the Twentieth Century have also been made in the transporting of men, supplies and ore underground and on the surface. Although compressed air locomotives were introduced in 1901, mules and horses continued to be employed for another decade. Compressed air locomotives were eventually supplemented by electric locomotives. Only a few compressed air locomotives are in use today. Homestake incorporated other forms of transportation in its mining enterprise. The company purchased its first truck in 1918 and at the present time Homestake has a fleet of modern cars and trucks.

At the beginning of the Twentieth Century, Homestake's main shaft was the B&M. This shaft was built in 1878 and was continually modified until dismantled in 1935. Developmental work at the Ellison shaft was accelerated in the early 1900's and the Ellison soon became Homestake's deepest shaft. In 1921 a new electric hoist was installed in the Ellison hoist building, replacing an old and delicate steam-driven hoist. During the same year, it became apparent that the Homestake surface works near the Open Cut had to be moved due to gradual ground slippage.

The B&M shaft, the Star Mill, Homestake's largest stamp mill, and many other surface plants were either dismantled or torn down. The B&M No. 2 shaft, built in 1924 to supplement the threatened B&M No. 1, was erected too far from the main ore body and later became part of the ventilation system of the mine. The ruins of the headframe of the B&M No. 2 can still be seen on the hill next to the Open Cut. On the opposite side of the gulch, the South Mill was constructed to replace the doomed Star Mill. Developmental work continued at a rapid pace at the Ellison to offset the probable loss of B&M No. 1. The 900-foot tramway from the Ellison to the Star

Mill was modified to serve other mills and in the 1930's the tramway was torn down.

Lead was a city on the move during the period from 1919 to the 1930's when the center of the business district began to sink as the old stopes beneath the town gave way. The Open Cut sinkage eventually subsided, but not until Homestake was forced to move its surface works and the City of Lead was forced to move its entire business district. Today the huge, gaping hole known as "the Open Cut" is a famous landmark in Lead.

During the depression, Homestake continued to expand its operations by enlarging underground workings and constructing new surface plants. The Kirk Power Plant, which was later sold to Black Hills Power and Light Co., the South Mill addition, and the Ross shaft and hoist building were built in the 1930's. The mine was making a profit even though it was hiring new workers and expanding underground and surface facilities. The Ellison shaft in the late 1930's began to show the effects of underground slippage. Plans were made for the erection of a new shaft and hoist. In 1941 the new Yates shaft and hoist building were completed. The hoisting equipment was the most modern available at the time and continues to efficiently serve the mine. Conehead crushers and advanced crushing equipment were installed in the Yates crusher building.

Then the mine was ordered closed by the War Production Board during the Second World War. Gold mining activities at the mine were suspended and the surface shops were converted into war materials factories. Miners either looked elsewhere for work or joined the armed forces. Only a skeleton crew remained to keep the mine ready for reopening after the war. The once thriving city of Lead became a virtual ghost town with half of its population gone. Many businesses closed and homes were boarded up. When the war ended, new activity at the mine insured Lead's return to prosperity.

From 1950-1970, Homestake began a huge program to completely modernize surface and underground mining operations. On the surface, ore crushing, grinding and recovery processes were updated. One of the innovations pioneered by Homestake was the development of a more effective cyanide treatment. This process, perfected in 1899-1901, is still used today with a few modifications to replace the amalgamation process which was discontinued for the most part in December of 1970 due to environmental considerations. In the mine, improved mining methods were introduced. Mining activity reached the 6,800 foot level and plans for even deeper exploration were made.

In the 1950's, the Homestake began to diversify its mining activities. Homestake has or has had interests in uranium, zinc, silver and lead mines in the United States; potash mines in Canada; and iron ore mines in Australia. Recently, work has begun on sinking a shaft to deeper levels of the mine.

**Gold was still plentiful in the sluice box of Harry and Jessie Pouriea in 1908 — over 32 years after the first big strike near this site in Blacktail Gulch above Deadwood. (Courtesy Mrs. Clarabelle Pouriea)**

It was found necessary this morning to use dynamite in blasting for the trench which is being dug on South Gold Street, Lead, to be used for the rock conveyor which will be used in filling the cavein, several squibs being used, and while considerable rock and debris was jarred loose in the trench the force of the explosion was not sufficient to jar loose any earth in the cavein. Quite a number from the surrounding towns and cities were in Lead this morning to gain a view of the Gold street cavein.

Two empty cars, one a refrigerator and one a steel coal car, got away in the local Burlington morning and kept going until they brought up against the corner of the Rewman stable on the east side of Sherman street. Neither the stable nor the cars were injured, but the sidewalk was damaged to some extent.

Lead Daily Call
March 8, 1911

The city of Deadwood and the Homestake Mining Company narrowly escaped a dire disaster yesterday afternoon when the Slime Plant of the big company was saved from destruction by fire through the united efforts of the local fire department and the employees of the company.

Deadwood Pioneer-Times
Oct. 3, 1907

Lead — As an evidence of their generosity and the liberality for which they are noted, the Homestake Mining company through T. J. Grier, the superintendent, has presented the Lead City fire department with a check for $1,000 as a reward for their success in saving one of the big Homestake mills from destruction during a recent fire . . . . The money will be distributed pro rata among the various fire companies in the city and will be used toward defraying the expense of necessary repairs to the fire houses.

Sioux Falls Argus-Leader
Jan. 10, 1908

Lead — An event of importance among the two thousand miners in the employ of the Homestake company was the annual meeting of the Homestake Veterans Assn., just held. The organization, now two years old, is composed of many men who have grown gray in the service of the big company, and whose loyalty has never faltered. Most of them own their homes in this city, and all are old timers. The annual report of the secretary, Robert Fraser, showed that during the year the membership had trebled, until it now reaches 145 men . . . .

Argus-Leader, Sioux Falls
Dec. 24, 1907

"Our summertime Homestake Band is a luxury that unfortunately we can no longer afford," stated James O. Harder, vice president and manager of Homestake's Black Hills operations in announcing the discontinuance of this well-known musical organization. "We were pleased to have been a part of many fine Black Hills celebrations . . . . We sincerely regret that we can no longer participate in these celebrations," he stated.

Lead Daily Call
March 16, 1972

**Historic Ellison Hoist was destroyed by fire in 1931. Fiery cables melted and three men died as the cage they were riding plummeted to the bottom of the shaft.**

**(Art Jobe Photo)**

In 100 years, the Homestake Mine has produced over one billion dollars worth of gold based on the government-set price of $35 an ounce. If the production of the consolidated Homestake Mines, the Highland, Deadwood-Terra, the Caledonia, and the Father DeSmet was included, the amount would be even greater. At today's price of gold, averaging about $145 an ounce, the total amount of gold produced by the Homestake and its consolidated mines is astronomical. During those first 100 years the company has paid over $100,000,000 in federal, state and local taxes, over 100,000 employees have been paid $300,000,000 to support themselves and perhaps 400,000 dependents. Operating expenses, mining supplies and expansion programs throughout the years have totaled in excess of $275,000,000 and dividends of over $220,000,000 have been paid to thousands of stockholders.

Despite the impressive figures, the mine was experiencing some of its leanest years in the late 1960's. Inflation, high taxes, and high labor costs reduced profits to a minimum. The 1968 rise in the price of gold and the subsequent increase in the world gold price have placed the mine on a financially sound basis. And what of the future of the mine? Gold ore reserves are expected to last many years, but who knows how long? When the price of gold approached $200 an ounce in late 1974, interest was expressed by mining concerns in reopening and redeveloping the numerous old gold mines in the county. High costs of labor, materials, and ore processing have made reopening these mines very difficult. Only a large operator like Homestake would be able to make any new mining venture pay off. Recently, the Homestake has done exploratory work at the Deadbroke Mine near Maitland and at the Mogul Mine near Trojan in a renewed search for gold-bearing ore in long dormant shafts.

Homestake progress hasn't been easy. The mine, like any other large industrial complex, has had its share of problems. Mining disasters, fortunately, have been rare. In 1907 and again in 1919-1920, mine fires forced Homestake officials to flood the underground workings. Another mine fire, discovered in 1945, was controlled by sealing off the burning areas with airtight bulkheads. Minor problems have plagued the mine occasionally. The Ellison shaft building in 1931 was destroyed by fire and in 1965 an ore train jumped the tracks on the South Mill Tramway. An underground fire in May 1975 forced the mine to close for a week and a half.

The Homestake Mine has also been temporarily closed because of labor troubles. Between November, 1909 and January, 1910, and during the late summer of 1972, the mine was shut down by strikes. The unionization of Homestake employees is not a recent event. In 1877, the Lead City Miners' Union was organized. The union was formed for the purpose of promoting the members' common interests. During the early years, the union, more of a club than a labor organization, sponsored dances, picnics and Labor Day parades.

In the 1890's changes began to take place. The local union became affiliated with the Western Federation of Miners, a radical group. In 1894, the union built one of the finest buildings in the Black Hills to serve as Union Hall. The union had its own paper, loaned money to other labor unions, and rented out the hall for various social events. Many of Homestake's employees were not dues-paying members of the City Union. Nevertheless, the labor organization was concerned for the members it did have. Eight dollars a week compensation was paid to sick workers and accident victims were paid up to sixteen weeks. When a union member died, he was given a $75 funeral by the union.

Homestake officials before the turn of the century tried to improve working conditions and hospitilization, anticipating the demands of labor. But other issues were at stake. The union wanted a closed shop. The City Miners' Union as early as 1891 requested a closed shop, but it was refused by Homestake management. Around 1900 Homestake officials and labor had no open conflicts. It was a time of caution. The miners did have complaints. Working conditions were not good in the mine. The miners of the early 1900's worked by candlelight and used pneumatic drills that produced great amounts of dust. Furthermore, the miners had worked ten-hour shifts every day of the week since 1876. The work was hard and the hours long, but the pay was the best in the mining industry.

The Black Hills Register, started in 1906, became the voice of the local miners' union. The Register frequently lampooned Homestake and its officials. The Lead City Miners' Union asked Grier for an eight hour day in 1906 and it was granted the following year. However, Grier's decision was made independent of the union. Later the union asked for a closed shop and again it was refused.

The Western Federation of Miners, noted for violent tactics, sent a representative to Lead in 1909. The local union began to use pressure to force the non-union Homestake workers to join. Conflicts appeared in the labor ranks. Soon after the union demanded a closed shop and Grier refused. Finally, a strike was called in late November. Homestake in defiance of the union, began hiring non-union workers. This practice infuriated some of the more outspoken union members and acts of violence and attempts of sabotage on company property occurred. Homestake hired guards and detectives to watch mine buildings and to protect Homestake officials and their families.

The strike, controversial from the beginning, financially ruined many miners and their families. Miners wanted to go back to work. Grier, who would not hire a man unless he declared he was non-union, resumed mining operations with a number of non-union and former City Union men in January 1910. Grier had broken the union and it was finished. Grier realized that conflicts between labor and management would probably occur again sometime in the future. He

**The Gold Nugget most miners sought when thirst took priority over quest, was this brand of beer brewed and bottled in Central City up until the time of prohibition.**
**(Centennial Collection)**

Union and Homestake friction created hot tempers and words. A union representative warned Supt. T. J. Grier of the company: "All I have to do is snap my fingers and I can stop every wheel at Homestake." Grier agreed but fired back: "That may be very true, but you can't snap your fingers and start them up again!"
Circa 1909

**Thomas J. Grier was born in Canada in 1850. He worked as a telegrapher in Montreal and Utah before coming to the Black Hills in 1878. In 1884 he was chosen superintendent of the Homestake. During the period he was superintendent, he enlarged and consolidated the holdings of HMC. He initiated free hospitalization and built the recreation building which provided free recreational facilities to the miners. He weathered the lockout of the union members in 1909-10. Grier demanded and received gold coins from the Treasury Department for Homestake bullion during the money panic of 1907. He continued as superintendent until his death in 1914.**

Gold bullion was well guarded until it could be delivered to the U. S. Mint. Riding shotgun on this display is the man seated at right. He is backed up by Homestake employees and officials.

(Centennial Collection)

made some changes to benefit the workers. Hospitalization became free for the miners and their immediate families. An aid fund was also established for the families of workers who died.

Numerous attempts by national labor organizations to represent the Homestake workers were voted down by large majorities of the employees. United Mine workers tried in 1947 after a 40-year absence of a union in Lead, but the Mine Workers were soundly defeated. The United Steel Workers were more persistent and tried on a number of occasions to bring unionization back to Lead. The miners had consistently voted down union representation because with free hospitalization, surface rights for homes, a free recreation center including a library, good hours and fair wages they really didn't need a union. Times were changing. In the 1960's, the same inflation that affected the Homestake Mine was eating into the pocketbooks of many miners and something had to be done. Finally in 1966, the United Steel Workers of America won the right in an employee election to represent the Homestake workers. A strike later followed. The strike of the summer of 1972 was very different from the "Trouble" of 1909. The strike of 1972 was basically a conflict over wages, a five-day week, and a pension plan. Violent tactics were not used in the strike and management respected the closed shop. Fortunately for all parties involved, a settlement was reached quickly.

The mines located at the edges of the Homestake Lode, the center of mining activity in Lawrence County, were for a variety of reasons not as fortunate as Homestake. These mines were profitable at times. However, they were for the most part characterized by sporadic mining activity, numerous consolidations, faulty financing, and in the end complete shutdowns. Mining activity was at a peak during

Over 15,000 people greeted President Howard Taft in Lead. The president visited the Homestake underground workings and he later said that the tour was the chance of a lifetime.

Lead Daily Call
October 23, 1911

The Homestake properties at Terraville in the early 1900's showed the Caledonia (left foreground) which HMC purchased and renamed the Monroe. The Deadwood-Terra (center right) was renamed the Pocahantas. The wood chutes (upper left) supplied cordwood to fire the boilers. Back of the chutes, the Terraville side of the "Open Cut" is visible.

(Centennial Collection)

the turn of the century. In the Bald Mountain area and the Ruby Basin district west of Lead, three mining companies almost as large as Homestake at that time — the Portland (Bald Mountain), the Mogul, and the Golden Reward — were active gold producers in 1900.

The Portland Mining Co. reorganized in 1911 and became the Trojan Mining Co. The Trojan operated with some success until 1923 when inflation forced the company to close. Five years later the Bald Mountain Mining Co. reorganized the properties of the Trojan and began a temporary developmental program employing 30 men for two years. The mining property remained inactive until an increase in the gold price made its reopening financially feasible.

The mine was closed during World War II by the War Production Board. The Bald Mountain reopened after the war and a modernization program was started in the mine and mill. Inflation dealt the final blow in 1959, closing the mine for good. Neverthless, the Bald Mountain was the second largest gold producer after Homestake in Lawrence County. Although mining activity ceased, a group of promoters organized the "Top of the Mountain" project with the intention of turning the surface buildings into a tourist attraction. Financial difficulties plagued this idea from its conception and ultimately it was abandoned.

The Mogul Mining Co. of Trojan was reformed by a merger of the Horseshoe and Mogul Mining companies in 1905. The Mogul continued to operate until 1917 when the lack of materials and high prices forced it to close during World War I. Prior to the actual shutdown, two disastrous fires destroyed two major mills. In 1939 the Mogul became the property of the Bald Mountain Mining Co. Today all that remains of the Mogul are a few tunnels and dark, dangerous shafts, and a pile of rotting timbers where a mill once stood. In its time the Mogul was a very productive mine. The Mogul hasn't been forgotten. The Homestake, in partnership with another mining firm, was conducting exploratory work in the mid-1970's below the old Mogul workings near the Terry Peak Chairlift.

The Golden Reward closed in 1918 when either inflation or lack of materials during the First World War made it impossible to continue. The idled mine soon filled with water. Although the mine did not last long, the Golden Reward was one of the largest gold producers in the county. The last chapter of the Golden Reward story ended when the Homestake in the 1940's did exploratory work in it and found little profitable ore.

Another less important property in the Ruby Basin district was the Lundberg, Dorr and Wilson Mining Co. which operated until 1913 and produced large amounts of gold and silver.



The Black Hills Grub Staking Concern is a South Dakota corporation organized with stock of $50,000 which is composed of $26,000 common stock and $24,000 preferred stock. Its purpose is to promote the development of the resources of the Black Hills by aiding prospectors by providing them with food and clothing for one year or more. The prospector, on the other hand, must enter into a written agreement, which states that one-half of the profits of his finds belong to the Black Hills Grub Staking Concern. I. A. Herrick of Deadwood is president and manager.

Illustrated Booster Nugget
Lead High School, 1912

For the third consecutive year, employees of the Homestake who during the year, worked 300 or more shifts underground without having suffered a single lost time accident, are being given the usual token of appreciation (a new $10 gold piece) by the Company for the careful manner in which they have performed their work.

Lead Daily Call
Jan. 15, 1926

**Stairway to the Stars? Not exactly. But there were many residents of Terraville who thought so, making the climb from the Central City vicinity. Workers living in the gulch made the arduous climb to work daily.**
**(Centennial Collection)**

The Wasp No. 2 Mine in the Yellow Creek area south of Lead, the Hidden Fortune and Cutting Mine near Lead, the Maitland group, the Belle Eldridge in Spruce Gulch, and the Monarch Mine in the Two Bit area were all substantial gold producers. The Galena area mines, the Branch Mint, the Gilt Edge, and the Golden Crest, produced silver or gold on and off until they were closed after the turn of the century. Mining activity northwest of Lead in the Ragged Top district at the Deadwood Standard, Spearfish Gold, Dacy, Ulster, and Victoria mines didn't last 20 years. New development at the Cleopatra Mine on Squaw Creek in the Carbonate district brought new life to the area for a few years around 1900. But the Black Hills Tin at Tinton and the Clover Leaf at Roubaix were worked well into the 1930's. Most of these mines closed not long after 1900 due to financial pressures and the lack of high grade mineable ore.

And, what has happened to all those old mining camps with those colorful names? The Trojan, Terry, Balmoral, Preston, Carbonate Camp, Flatiron, Two Bit, Maitland, Galena, Roubaix, and Tinton. Homes or cabins can still be seen in and near most of these ghost towns, but now the old camps are only relics of a golden past. Looming over them all, and symbolic of that exciting era, is the only survivor of that turbulent past — the mighty Homestake!

The Tinton Mining Mill at Tinton was completely destroyed by fire early this morning. The loss was estimated at $200,000. The mill, owned by the Black Hills Tin Co., R. J. Beatty, Chicago, president, had been under lease to the Bald Mountain Mining Co., Trojan, since Sept. 1.

Deadwood Pioneer-Times
Nov. 27, 1953

**The mining town of Terry, near Lead, had its troubles in the flood of 1909. The photo was taken after water had poured through Main Street on the left and over the Chicago, North Western Railroad tracks on the right.**
**(Centennial Collection)**

# chapter XXV

# Culture, Crisis And Consolidation

**Through the Andrew Carnegie Foundation and local women's club fund raising socials, Deadwood has had one of the top libraries in South Dakota for many years. A complete file of early-day Deadwood newspapers dating back to 1876 are available to researchers and historians.**

After a full century, the residents of Lawrence County continue to show concern for education by improving their school systems and increasing their patronage of two of the oldest libraries in the state along with two which were more recently established. The Deadwood Daily Pioneer, November 8, 1905, stated: "Had Andrew Carnegie been present himself last evening at the official opening of the Carnegie Free Library on Williams Street, he would have swelled with pride . . . doors, windows, nooks, aisles and every conceivable spot where one could stand was taken by someone anxious to see and hear the program." And through the years, Deadwood's library has held the "cultural" spotlight, filling the need for education and entertainment. Most of the books were purchased from money raised through entertainments staged under the auspices of the ladies clubs and the women were credited by a dedication speaker with "building for themselves a monument that will last until the end of time."

A highlight of the opening was the presence of Mrs. Phoebe Hearst, mother of William Randolph Hearst, who as a guest of the Homestake mine superintendent and his wife, Mrs. T. J. Grier, Lead, drove down to be present at the big occasion. A year later, to purchase new books, a May Day Library Ball was held with tickets selling for $2 each and a total of $206 sold. Money problems continued to haunt the library and expenditures were carefully scanned. Detailed records were kept and by the end of ten months, it was noted that 21 light bulbs had burned out during the year! A clock, costing $45 and badly needed by the library, was purchased with a $20 down payment and the promise to pay the balance in monthly installments. Financial problems were somewhat alleviated by a city mill levy which was replaced by a county-wide levy initiated in 1975.

Deadwood's Library has gained recognition for its outstanding collection of books on the history of the Black Hills as well as its complete files of daily and weekly newspapers dating back to 1876,

Mrs. Phoebe Hearst, a philanthropist, visited the library and kindergarten in Lead supported by her contributions. Many people from the Lead and Deadwood area came to greet the famous lady. A reception was conducted in her honor at the home of T. J. Grier, mine superintendent. Homestake workers were given the day off to see Mrs. Hearst.

Lead Daily Call
Nov. 6-9, 1905

The Deadwood Public Library yesterday received a very valuable gift in the form of two volumes written by the wife of Rev. Henry Weston (Preacher Smith) early day Black Hills missionary, who was killed by the Indians in 1876 while en route from Deadwood to Crook City to conduct religious services. The books were donated by the daughter and grand daughter of Rev. Smith who are in Deadwood on a visit of this time, Mrs. Franklin Smith, librarian, stated.

Deadwood Pioneer-Times
Aug. 4, 1933

all of which are being placed on microfilm for further preservation. The extensive archives, compiled for the 100th birthday of Deadwood, will also be housed in a Centennial Center in the library at the end of 1976 for the enjoyment of the public for generations to come.

When the Homestake Recreation Building was opened to the public in 1914, it was a gift from the mining company, "a place where anyone could find fun and entertainment," stated Grier. But one of its main objectives was to provide a permanent and spacious home for the Hearst Free Library, which was established for the city in 1894. The library, in 1912, had grown to over 10,000 volumes and had served over 56,557 visitors that same year. It needed room to grow. And that it did — from 4,000 books in 1900 to 28,061 in 1975. The Homestake acquired the contents of the entire library in 1925 from the Phoebe Hearst estate and operated the facility until 1972 when the mining company donated it, along with the entire Homestake Recreation complex, to the City of Lead. One of the unique sections of the library is its foreign language books which contains 1,000 volumes in 11 languages, representing the ethnic groups which populated the community during the early years of the Homestake. Also of prime value are the music, literature and technical sections. as well as a complete file of the early city newspapers on microfilm and many rare and out-of-print books.

The 1914 Homestake Recreation building was a grand complex. It included a pool room, swimming pool, bowling alleys, and social rooms, in addition to the second floor library and an opera house. All of which was enthusiastically enjoyed free of charge by the entertainment-loving population of the hard-working city.

Lead — The annual meeting of the Golden Star Athletic club, the leading social and athletic organization of the city, showed the largest membership the club has enjoyed in years with a greatly decreased indebtedness. The club chose a new directorate composed of J. G. Stanley, Charles Mendelsohn, William Peters, Edward Rochold, Dr. Bickford, A. L. Coolidge, G. L. Scott. The club has a band of its own that is considered one of the best in the Hills.

Sioux Fall Argus-Leader
Feb. 15, 1909

Young men of this city have organized a gymnasium association which was named Olympic Athletic Association, and start out with 40 members. The second story of the L. R. Graves building which is occupied by Haines and Heyn has been secured and steps are being taken to fit it up at once with all the equipment found in the first-class modern gymnasium.

B H Daily Times
Feb. 4, 1894

Matt Bender plans to add a merry-go-round at his amusement park.

Evening Call
April 25, 1896

Yesterday for the first time in her history, Deadwood saw a real live female bicycle rider. Not one of your three-wheel affairs, but the regulation safety kind and "Oh Horrors," the lady rode without a side saddle, and she seemed to get along very well, in fact as well as many of the male riders who show themselves occasionally.

B H Daily Times
Aug. 10, 1892

**Fun-loving Germans erected the first bowling alley where the Claim Jumpers Motel is now located in south Deadwood. John Treber, one of the gold rush pioneers is second from the right (No. 16). His son Albert, sitting on the roof, will be 94 in the Centennial Year. For many years he was one of the top local bowlers. (Centennial Collection)**

Of the four public libraries in Lawrence County, Deadwood's and Lead's are among the oldest in the state. Spearfish has two libraries — one at the Black Hills State College and the other, the Grace Balloch Memorial Library, a City institution since 1945. Originally located in the Spearfish Hotel, the Queen City's library now has permanent headquarters in its own building where it opened in 1971 and which has permitted it to expand its 5,000 book collection close to 10,000. The college library traces its beginnings to the fire in 1925 when its collection was reduced to only 46 books. But donations enlarged it to about 600. By 1975, the library, known as the E. Y. Berry Library Learning Center, boasted 83,000 volumes, 25,000 microfiche and microcards plus 853 reels of microfilm or a total of 109,000 volumes. In a new building, dedicated in 1972, the library contains a wide collection of important documents from Berry's 20 years of service in Washington as a congressman. In addition, it is adding the Leland Case Western Americana History collection as well as the extensive book and map collection of the late Spearfish historian, Rev. Eugene Szalay. The Whitewood library, formerly a club project, first received public funds in 1959 and is now located in a city-owned building. It offers that small community the use of over 4,000 volumes.

A very interesting cockfight took place last evening at Sutton and Carr's saloon. The first fight was between a Lead and a Deadwood bird, Lead winning. The second was between two Lead birds owned by Cotton and Andrews and Frank Heitler, the latter winning. It was witnessed by a good sized audience.

B H Daily Times
Jan. 14, 1894

A souvenir book descriptive of Deadwood and its resources issued by the Deadwood board of trade, was received yesterday. It is well filled with reading matter of an excellent description, and various cuts of buildings and points of interest around the city. Among the buildings represented are the city hall, syndicate block, schoolhouse, and the residences of Messers. Bullock, Selbie, Treber, McLaughlin and others. The books will be distributed throughout the east and will undoubtedly do good.

B H Daily Times
June 13, 1892

Great progress has also been evident in the county's school system.

At the turn of the century, Lead's pupil enrollment totaled 2,100 with seven schools and a staff of 41. Deadwood had six brick buildings for its 1,200 students and 24 teachers and Spearfish recorded 230 pupils with five teachers. The school system in Spearfish, grew like its town, gradually. Its present high school was constructed in 1923 to replace the building which housed the kindergarten-through-high school system. In 1938 a new elementary school was built on Jackson Boulevard to replace the one which had been used since 1889. By 1960, an addition was constructed to the high school for junior high classes and in 1962 the West Elementary school joined the system. By 1975, Spearfish enrollment was at 1,515 and 72 full-time teachers comprised the staff.

Spearfish, S. D. — Hereafter all grade school teachers will receive $70 per month for work in the local schools, this being a raise of $5. The board of education while raising the salaries of teachers declined to raise the principal on the ground that he now had sufficient and the disparity between the salaries of the principal and teachers was too large.

Argus-Leader, Sioux Falls
Oct. 5, 1907

Lead, which enters the Centennial Year with its last payment made on its school buildings, has had a steady construction program since the turn of the century. In addition to the Central Campus building, constructed in 1895, a grade school at South Lead opened its doors in 1900. Outliving its usefulness, it was razed in 1968. Another grade school was needed for the West Lead area and this was built in 1901. The older structure, replaced in 1955, was destroyed by a fire in 1975. A grade school building was added to the Central Campus in 1914 and this is still in use as well as the annex which was constructed there in 1926. Remodeled at that time was a portion of the 1895 high school, which is also being used today. However, the

Assembly Hall, which was constructed on the campus in 1903 and housed the first school gymnasium in the Black Hills, was razed in 1974. Replacements were constructed in 1955 in the Washington area for the school which had served since 1900 and at West Lead for the 1901 building. The most extensive building program was in 1940 when the new high school was constructed on its present location to replace the Central campus, which showed signs of surface slippage. The last major construction occurred in 1965 when an addition was made to the high school and the Hunkins building was added to the Central Campus. At the end of 1975, total registration for the Lead-Deadwood system was at 2183 and 130 full-time teachers were on the staff.

Deadwood, S. D. — No more punch or lemonade with "sticks" in it for the students of the Deadwood High school who attend dances in the Masonic temple at regular intervals. The high school board of education has set its foot down on such practice good and hard, and hereafter the students are expected to pay less frequent visits to the anteroom, where refreshments are served. The trouble came about through the talk of one youngster whose liking for the punch caused his mother to start an investigation . . . .

Argus-Leader, Sioux Falls
Oct. 19, 1907

By the early 1900's Deadwood had one of the finest school systems in the area. In addition to the high school which had been built in the late 1880's, voters had approved a bond issue of $35,000 for an annex to the structure; had built a new school house in First Ward, and made improvements to one in Fourth Ward as well as to those in the outlying districts, all a part of the system. By 1925, a new high school building had been built in front of the old structure and the two combined. The old manual training building was razed. A new grade school annex was built in 1951 and a second story added in 1956 when the Gym-Armory was constructed, providing the district with additional classroom space and gym facilities.

Pay hikes for teachers were of concern even back as early as 1905 when a committee recommended that individual requests be denied. That year, with R. N. Ogden as chairman of the board, the principal was hired for $85 a month on a 10-month contract, high school teachers for $1,000 a year, grade school instructors for $70 or $75 a month and teachers in the Gayville, Maitland, Two Bit and Mountain Ranch schools at $50 or $60 per month.

Pioneer-Times
June 28, 1971

Of the church-supported schools, those in the Twin Cities were the only ones that survived for any period of time. St. Ambrose Catholic grade school, started in 1918 in Deadwood with 91 students, was operated by the Benedictine Sisters and closed in 1966. The Sisters of Charity took over the spasmodic operation of St. Patrick's grade school in Lead and operated it continuously from 1916 until 1965. St. Patrick's High School, operated by the same order, opened in September, 1949, but closed in May, 1958.

The independent school districts all felt a pre-World War II "baby-boom" in 1940 when Deadwood had a record enrollment of 705 pupils. Lead had 1537 and Spearfish, 655. While the independent districts were growing in Lawrence County, the country schools were on their way out. In 1960, of the 37 school districts, only 15 operated schools. Twenty-two had closed their elementary schools and were transporting students to Spearfish, Lead and Deadwood on a tuition basis. All 34 common school districts also sent their high school students to the three independent districts for education.

Maintenance and improvements were worries clear back in 1907 — when among those recommended were "calcimining the ceiling of the assembly room, remodeling of the bin crosswise so that a car of coal can be stored, wire netting for cupola windows to keep pigeons out, electric motor to replace gas engine for manual training, new fire pot for the heater in the fourth ward school and move the stove to the center of the room or to a better location."

Pioneer-Times
June 28, 1971

During the fairly calm years until the 1960's, all schools experienced the problems of maintenance and improvement plus ever-increasing salaries, with Lead perhaps the exception. Located in the rich mining district, its tax receipts helped keep the school out of the red longer than others in the county. But for Deadwood, 1964 was the beginning of one of the most stormy seven years in the history of the district. County reorganization was underway with several small common districts going to Deadwood, requiring additional teachers and increasing transportation costs for the rural students. Increased budget totals, mill levy hikes, spiraling costs and less tax money resulted in the "handwriting on the wall" with every avenue of relief investigated. Finally the district went deeper in debt each year and the mill levy limit was reached.

In spite of cutting all possible corners, the board found itself up against the proverbial wall and by October, 1967, had voted to dissolve the district at the end of the 1968 school year. Adding to the problem, Lead and Spearfish both rejected the idea of reorganization into a county-wide district. Deadwood had no other avenue of escape and tossed its problems into the lap of the State Commission of Elementary and Secondary Education, which ordered the attachment of Deadwood to the Lead district. Petitions for a "new look" at the dissolution of the Deadwood district failed to change the commission's ruling and Lead was faced with a storm-clouded year for merging the two schools on July 1, 1971.

Conversion was carried out much faster and easier than had been anticipated by the highly competitive sister cities. Deadwood's former high school became a junior high with Lead pupils bussed to the Historic City and Deadwood High School students attending in Lead. Although not all financial problems were eliminated with the merger, what has evolved is a well-balanced school system with many educational opportunities for the youth of the Twin Cities which might never have otherwise been available as separate districts.

When the feverish gold rush era simmered down in Lawrence County after the turn of the century, residents, especially of the Lead, Deadwood and Spearfish areas, hungrily sought the excitement and competitiveness of sports. Limited for space and athletic facilities, foot and hose cart racing by the various fire-fighting organizations held the early limelight. Well-known foot racers were imported into the Northern Hills under assumed names to represent Lead, Deadwood, Central City, Spearfish and Whitewood. Pre-race excitement ran high and wagers were big on the outcome of these events, usually held on special days such as July 4 and Labor Day. The many hose cart teams from the fire departments in the county also were spiked with professional athletes to assure victory. Of the various races, the Hub'n Hub was the most exciting and exacting with the winner determined by a time watch. In this race two teams at a time would run 600 feet, lay out 250 feet of hose, spin on the nozzle and start a stream of water. The fastest time was usually around 39 seconds. A lot depended on the expertise of the nozzle man who joined it expertly to the hose with a quick twist of the wrist.

Lead High School has been named the National Bellamy Award School for 1970. Glen Hogen, superintendent, made the announcement at a special student assembly. The National Bellamy Award is presented annually to a high school in one state. The school chosen is judged the most representative of all fine schools in that state and will be the standard-bearer for all schools in that state for a period of 50 years, until the honor again rotates. Lead High earned the Bellamy Award as the result of 7 years of uninterrupted education, kindergarten through grade twelve, with the fundamental values of America's heritage stressed and implemented.

Lead Daily Call
September 8, 1969

Upwards of 100 persons enjoyed a walk over the new road on Park Avenue, the approach to the new city park, last evening . . . Deadwood plans the park on the east side of McGovern Hill as one of the permanent improvements the city could and should afford . . . The path to the new park would be illuminated with incandescent lights . . . Deadwood is the metropolis of the Hills and there is every reason why we should have a beautiful city park for holding picnics and conventions.

B H Weekly Times
July 18, 1896

The automatic weigher, lifter and blower which for sport calls for a nickel in the slot machine, is one of the attractions at Fassold's club rooms, and to judge from the patronage it is a very popular affair. Some of our heavy blowers are talking of getting up a contest to be followed by the lifters and heavyweights. The machine gives your correct weight and height as well as lung power and lifting capacity, to ascertain which, drop a nickel in the slot and the whole story is told.

B H Daily Times
Dec. 14, 1891

**Lead has one of the most unique athletic fields in the nation. The top of a mountain was cut off at a cost of $15,000 to give the Mile-Hi City a baseball diamond and football field.**

Babe Ruth and Bob Meusel arrived in Deadwood yesterday afternoon as scheduled and took part in an exhibition baseball game at the Amusement park, Ruth playing on the Deadwood team and Meusel on the All-Star team, consisting of selected players from the five Black Hills League teams outside of Deadwood. Both stars started the game on the initial sack and shortly after 2 o'clock, the stage was all set and the large crowd was ready to go wild with applause at the first possible provocation.

| All-Stars | AB | R | H | PO | A | E |
|---|---|---|---|---|---|---|
| Gordon, ss | 3 | 0 | 1 | 2 | 2 | 2 |
| Remschell, rf | 2 | 1 | 1 | 0 | 0 | 0 |
| Gronert, lf | 2 | 0 | 1 | 0 | 0 | 0 |
| Meusel, 1b | 4 | 0 | 1 | 3 | 2 | 0 |
| Cole, cf | 4 | 0 | 1 | 0 | 0 | 1 |
| Yonzick, 3b | 4 | 0 | 0 | 0 | 0 | 1 |
| Townsend, 2b | 4 | 0 | 0 | 5 | 0 | 0 |
| Hale, c | 4 | 1 | 1 | 12 | 0 | 1 |
| Hejde, p | 0 | 0 | 0 | 0 | 1 | 0 |
| Mead, p | 2 | 0 | 0 | 2 | 1 | 0 |
| | 35 | 2 | 6 | 24 | 6 | 5 |

| Deadwood— | AB | R | H | PO | A | E |
|---|---|---|---|---|---|---|
| Arsers, rf | 2 | 0 | 0 | 0 | 0 | 0 |
| Eilers, J., rf | 2 | 0 | 0 | 1 | 0 | 0 |
| Eilers, C., c | 3 | 0 | 0 | 17 | 1 | 1 |
| Morford, F., | 4 | 2 | 1 | 0 | 1 | 0 |
| Ruth, 1b | 3 | 1 | 2 | 8 | 1 | 0 |
| Gorum, p, lf, | 4 | 0 | 0 | 0 | 3 | 0 |
| Rakestraw, ss | 4 | 1 | 2 | 0 | 2 | 1 |
| Ewing, cf | 4 | 0 | 0 | 0 | 0 | 0 |
| Nussrallah, lf | 1 | 0 | 0 | 0 | 0 | 0 |
| Gill, p, 1b | 3 | 0 | 0 | 0 | 0 | 0 |
| Morford, L., 2b | 2 | 0 | 0 | 0 | 0 | 0 |
| Elward, 2b | 2 | 0 | 1 | 1 | 0 | 0 |
| | 34 | 4 | 6 | 27 | 8 | 2 |

Summary: Three base hits, Gronert. Two base hits, Hale, Ruth, Gordon, Meusel. Base on balls, off Gorum 1, off Hejde 3. Struck out, by Gorum 7, Gill 6, Ruth 4, Hejde 3, Mead 4, Meusel 3. Hit by pitcher, Hejde. Time of game, two hours. Umpires, McCumsey and Gorman.

Score by innings—

| | 1 | 2 | 3 | 4 | 5 | 6 | 7 | 8 | 9 | T |
|---|---|---|---|---|---|---|---|---|---|---|
| All-Stars | 0 | 0 | 0 | 0 | 0 | 0 | 0 | 2 | 0 | 2 |
| Dwd. | 0 | 1 | 2 | 0 | 0 | 0 | 1 | 0 | x | 4 |

Runs were made by—Deadwood. Morford E. 2; Ruth 1; Rakestraw, 1—All stars Remschel, 1; Hale, 1.

Baseball caught on fast in the Lead and Deadwood areas after locations suitable for a diamond were found in the mountainous terrain of the two communities. Lead eventually cut the top off one of its mountains to gain a park spacious enough for baseball or football. Many a home run resulted in the loss of the ball as it sailed into space beyond the edge of the Mile High park.

By 1903 regular games were played by the Golden Stars of Lead and Deadwood's Olympic Club nine. From 1908 through 1922 the competition was so intense, Lead, Deadwood and Spearfish brought in professional ball players from distant leagues to assure victory. In 1922 Deadwood won the Black Hills league pennant and as a season-closer treated the baseball fans to a special event. Famed Babe Ruth and Bob Meusel of the New York Yankees were invited to play in an All-Star game against the champs. A huge crowd attended the game at the Deadwood Amusement Park. On every pitch, the fans waited for the mighty Babe, better known as the "Sultan of Swat," to blast the ball out of the park. Babe really connected with many of the pitches but the long balls landed foul over the fence at the north end of the park. Intercity games faltered in the late 1920's and were kept alive only by the Homestake League. When the league died in 1956, organized baseball became a thing of the past in Lawrence County.

Deadwood and Lead had their differences down through the years as they vied for political and business advantages, but when it came to high school sports there was no compromise — it was win or else! Both schools had state and conference championship teams, but whether it be football, basketball, track, wrestling or even a minor sport, the entire season was climaxed in the Lead-Deadwood game. Even when both teams had a losing season it was the "super battle" of the year whenever the two clubs were matched. In the early part of the 1900's, feelings were so intense that when the Deadwood team went "up the gulch" to play Lead, it made sure it had a quick exit from the town with a massive bodyguard — especially if it was victorious. Lead teams would do likewise when they went "down the gulch" to play.

In the early 1920's, one game became so rough the Deadwood coach took his team off the field and went home. Lead fans started a massive invasion on the downgulch city. Police finally restored order and the up-gulchers went home, leaving their arch enemies thankful that the town hadn't been torn down brick by brick. The intense rivalry continued until financial difficulties of the Deadwood school system necessitated consolidating with Lead in 1971. This blow fell like a sword to end the fiercest, yet finest, rivalry local sports had ever known.

Deadwood Bears showed state basketball fans everything in the books Saturday night in their exciting victory over Gregory, 38 to 33. The Bears made history on the Brookings Armory floor, taking state-wide Class "B" honors twice in succession.

Deadwood Pioneer-Times
March 10, 1940

**This fine looking group of young Lead baseball players from back about the turn of the century would be in style again now with most sporting fancy mustaches. Pipe the guy with the stovepipe hat!**

**(Centennial Collection)**

It was a festive celebration — either the Fourth of July or an Elks convention. The building with the light-encrusted Elks head is the present Bodega building on Deadwood's Historic Main Street.

(Adams Museum)

# chapter XXVI

# Making The Headlines

Floods were frequent in the Northern Black Hills due to the fast runoff from the hills and gulches. In 1908, Pluma, halfway between Deadwood and Lead, caught the brunt of this deluge. The depot in the background was washed from its foundation.

(Centennial Collection)

Within a period of 20 years, the Northern Black Hills survived three major disasters, ranking closely in scope to those experienced in the early days of settlement.

The blizzard of 1949, which started just as a snow storm in the Black Hills on January 1, was only a taste of what was to come for an entire month. Blizzard conditions continued in the Hills with only a few days of respite between storms until by the end of the month a record total of 77.4 inches of snow had been received in Deadwood. While the blizzard of 1888 had been short-lived, lasting around 12 hours, the first blizzard of the 1949 series lasted four days and left Lead and Deadwood virtually isolated from the outside world. It started on January 4 and blanketed Deadwood with 31 inches of snow. Telephone communications were the only means of reaching distant points. All roads into Lead and Deadwood, county, state and federal, were piled high with snow drifts. Snow was about three feet on the level and drifts were piled up four and five feet deep. On the second day, the thermometers in Lead and Deadwood dipped to 13 below to add to the discomfort. Old-timers in the Lead and Deadwood areas scratched their heads and started recalling the "big blows" of past years. Many were of the opinion that if this wasn't the worst in the area's history, it wasn't far behind.

Lawrence county's judiciary took time out this morning to shovel the snow out from the rear of the county building on Sherman street. Along with the rest of the male personnel of the court house, Judge Alex Rentto of the eighth circuit; Judge Matthew Furze, of county court, and Justice of the Peace Richard Murray, wielded shovels.

Lead Call
Jan. 7, 1949

By Wednesday, January 5, Deadwood had recorded 43 inches of snow in 48 hours and Lead, with its narrow and hilly streets, was paralyzed beneath 42 inches. Deadwood and Lead still had no train or mail service; there was no milk in either city except for a few bottles saved for babies; winds continued to blow the newly-plowed paths shut as fast as they were opened and state highway crews were trying to get roads open to Spearfish and Sturgis. According to the U.S. Forest Service records, there were 12-foot drifts in Spearfish Canyon, and the County Highway Department reported encountering drifts from 15 to 20-feet high. Over 200 men and boys in the two cities volunteered their services to help clear out the four feet of snow; business was at a standstill and schools remained closed.

By January 6, the drifted snow was beginning to diminish with a rise in temperature. However, neither the Burlington nor North-Western Railroad was able to get through. Dynamite was used to loosen the ice jam in Whitewood Creek back of Ayres Hardware Store in Deadwood. It was not until January 12 that most of the highways were opened and passenger and freight trains chugged into the area. However, within another five days there were high winds to cause more drifting and 11 more days of sub-zero weather with intermittent high winds, complicating the month-long problem.

Eighty years to the month after Deadwood suffered its first major fire, flames were licking at its outskirts, but this time the danger originated in the forest land which surrounds the city instead of in the business district as in 1879. The fire was caused by an ignited piece of paper which blew out of a trash burner onto dry grass before the burner lid could be replaced. The incident occurred at 1:10 p.m. September 8, 1959, at the Hillcrest Manor, one mile west of Deadwood along the Central City road between Deadwood and Lead. Although the fire was discovered within one minute and was attacked within three minutes by three men using shovels, it burned into the timber, crowned and was out of control five minutes later. It had been 42 days since the area had received its last rain of only one-tenth of an inch, the fire danger was rated 95 and the temperature was 96 with a 13-mile-an-hour wind.

While pumpers, handtools and many men were used on the fire, the flames, upon reaching the ridge, received the full effect of a wind blowing 44 miles per hour. One hour after starting, the fire had burned a swath one mile wide and two and one-half miles long, crossing U.S. 14 at Pine Crest north of Deadwood over the heads of the firefighters. The fire continued toward the northeast until a weather front moved through the area, after which the wind shifted and blew the fire toward the southeast, thus endangering Deadwood again.

A total of over 3,600 men supplied by the Forest Service, Homestake Mining Co., Ellsworth Air Force Base, area fire departments, City and County workers and volunteers worked on the ground while slurry bombers dispensed a flame retardant mixture of bentonite and water from the air to control the flames. By 4 p.m., the city was ordered evacuated and residents fled their homes to nearby Lead and some even traveled as far as Spearfish, Sturgis, Rapid City and the Southern Hills in the belief that there would be no stopping the flames in the tinder-dry forest. By early that first evening Deadwood resembled a war front as heavy equipment, bulldozers, tankers and trucks rumbled through the dark smoke-laden streets. Street lights

It took Dr. G. C. Fehliman of Lead and his brother-in-law, P. L. Harms of Minneapolis four days to negotiate a trip of 210 miles during the blizzard which swept the midwestern area this week . . . . Each day they came as far as the snowplow had opened the highway, and finally reached here Thursday afternoon.

Lead Call
Jan. 7, 1949

Morris Bryan and Charles Borup, Spearfish highway workers, plowed a coyote under with their snow plow out in the canyon country. Bryan covered the coyote with snow and then Borup attempted to hit it with a shovel, but the coyote got away from them. The snow in the canyon is very deep.

Lead Call
Jan. 7, 1949

Philip Furze, Lead mail carrier, on his usual route Wednesday morning, stumbled on an object as he ploughed through deep snow. Reaching down to investigate he got hold of a man's coat and finally uncovered a man asleep in the snow.

Furze called the police department and an officer assisted the fellow to his home where he continued his snooze. He had fallen down a short time before and had gone to sleep. Officers said the man was none the worse for his short rest except possibly a hangover.

Lead Call
Jan. 7, 1949

were out and only a few homes, housing the handful of residents who remained behind, were illuminated. Adding to the confusion and danger, about 3 p.m. that same afternoon, was another fire which burned 273 acres of federal and private land, 13 miles southeast of Deadwood near Nemo, before it was controlled 11 hours later. High winds had blown a tree across a power line to start that fire.

Forest Service officials considered the fire controlled by 10 a.m., September 9 but mop-up operations continued until September 19 and the fire was considered completely dead on September 23 — 15 days after it had started. A real aid to night fire suppression activities that near-fatal first day was a drop in temperature to a low of 26 degrees.

Burned over were a total of 4,501 acres of intermingled private and public land. There were serious injuries but no casualties on the fire, although several minor accidents did occur. Two dozer operators were burned when fire overran them while they were working. A crew of men was temporarily trapped, but was led to safety by a helicopter. Power lines were down, and threatened the safety of firefighters until the power was cut off. Total direct costs of the fire were approximately $1,678,000 and indirect losses and resource damages were also extensive. Several homes on the Mount Roosevelt road were destroyed by the fire as well as a tourist camp on the Spearfish highway and a post and pole treatment plant between Deadwood and Pluma.

And after it was all over and the hillsides were blackened reminders of the vicious flames, there was the potential danger of flooding. Started immediately as a preventive measure was the contouring of the steep mountainsides to the north of Deadwood with bulldozers cutting trenches parallel to the hillsides. After the bulldozers had done their work, the deep trenches horizontally ringed the burned-over mountainsides with 31 miles of terraces to slow down moisture runoff. Aerial seeding was launched and even before the snows had come, a few areas had been replanted with pine seedlings, a project which was accelerated the following year.

On Friday, May 14, 1965, a flood, one of the worst on record, ravaged the communities of Deadwood and Spearfish. Whitewood Creek, already swollen by the runoff of a one-day spring blizzard that dumped 32 to 34 inches of snow on the Northern Hills, reached flood stage after a heavy rainstorm poured six to seven inches on the Lead-Deadwood area. The flood was the worst natural disaster to threaten Deadwood since the fire of 1959. Electric power went out in Deadwood but was quickly restored. The high water damaged many business buildings and homes, flooded numerous basements, and wiped out bulkheads along the creek through the business district. Spearfish experienced its worst flood since 1933. About 125 homes in Spearfish had water or mud in their basements and at least 25

The Whitewood Volunteer fire department postponed a regularly scheduled meeting Wednesday night because the fire hall was nearly covered by a 12-foot drift. The building is now dug out and a special meeting was called for tonight.

Lead Call
Jan. 7, 1949

Mr. and Mrs. Konfrst of Aurora, Ia., had their honeymoon interrupted Tuesday when they attempted to leave Deadwood via U. S. 14-85. Told the road was closed, they went back to Deadwood. An officer stopped them and asked Konfrst to volunteer for fire fighting. He did so while his wife drove back to Brownsville Store on U. S. 385, the route they had used coming to Deadwood. He joined her there later after some hours on the fire line.

Pioneer-Times
Sept. 10, 1959

Although it was the largest forest fire in the Deadwood area since 1879, it was not the worst fire in the Hills by any sense. The Tilford fire in 1939 burned more than 7,000 acres and the McVey fire north of Hill City in the 1930's burned 23,000 acres.

Pioneer-Times
Sept. 10, 1959

One small Spruce Gulch boy, who had started to school this week before the fire, watched his mother hastily packing various items in preparation for evacuation. "Mommy," he said, "What can I do to help?" She told him not very much, she guessed he would just have to pray. He looked at the huge clouds of smoke rolling over the hill and said, "I don't think I can. My guardian angel just burned up."

Backlog — Camille Yuill
Sept. 15, 1959

The old Gem Theatre piano which for many years had a prominent place in the night life at that popular early day Deadwood rendezvous has returned to the city after a long absence and has found a safe harbor at the Adams Memorial Hall here, where it was recently placed among the exhibits.

Deadwood Pioneer-Times
May 29, 1933

"Monseieur Beaucaire" was featured at the opening of the Deadwood Opera House in 1906 with great fanfare. The ladies wore their most beautiful evening gowns and jewels; the men were resplendent in ruffled white shirts, black ties and longtailed coats. Admission was $5, and box seats sold for $25. It was the social event of the season. Afterwards, the people crossed the street to the luxurious Franklin Hotel for champagne parties.

families were forced to evacuate their homes. Rampaging Spearfish Creek washed out portions of the Spearfish Canyon highway and a number of bridges. Lead, on the high ground, received the most rain and the least damage. Many homes and businesses reported only flooded basements, stained ceilings, or collapsed retaining walls.

By Wednesday, May 19, the waters had subsided. No lives were lost and only minor injuries reported. The flood caused an estimated $5 million damage to buildings, bridges, and roads in the county. The cities of Deadwood and Spearfish were the hardest hit with each sustaining over $330,000 in damages. Immediately after the flood, repairs on bridges and roads began and the communities of Deadwood and Spearfish undertook extensive clean-up operations.

Twentieth Century disasters also had a profound effect on the county's cultural facilities.

In 1902 the Gem Theater had burned to the ground. The mining camp theatre, after a long life of prosperity and gaiety, died in Deadwood in the second year of a century to which it did not belong. Al Swearengen, one of its former owners, who reportedly took in $5,000 on many nights and as high as $10,000 on other nights, left Deadwood penniless. Swearengen reportedly enticed a number of young women to Deadwood and the Gem with promises of honorable, high-paying jobs which never developed. Instead, they were forced to travel down the one-way street of sin.

The theaters improved as the years glided into the 1900's. One of the greatest social events of 1906 was the opening of the Deadwood Theater, where for the first quarter of a century of its existence, musicals were produced by summer stock groups with 40 to 60 in the cast. The theater was also the site for stock companies which played for long engagements, a performance by the San Carlos Opera Company of San Francisco, California, and a Minneapolis, Minnesota symphony orchestra. George N. Butler, an early-day resident who worked back stage at the theater from the time he was about ten years old, recalls that another highlight of the entertainment center was the appearance of the Christy Minstrels, a large company complete with a band that paraded down Deadwood streets. The theater's engagements, however, were not limited to musicals but also attracted outstanding wrestlers, which according to Butler, "were the world's best." With the coming of the "moving picture," the Deadwood theater was converted into a movie palace, where the latest productions were shown, complete with "Bank Night" and "Ten-O-Win" during the depression years of the 1930's.

When the fire of 1952 destroyed the City Hall and the theater, the entertainment center was not rebuilt. Instead movie lovers drove to nearby Lead to attend shows at the Homestake Theatre.

The Opera House in Lead, built in connection with the Recreation Building, was second to none in the area. It hosted Grand Opera from New York City during the first few years of operation. It also featured a three-piece orchestra and stock companies performed a week at a time with a different show featured each evening. Vaudeville performers were also a major attraction and silent movies were shown at five and ten cents admission when the live performances were not scheduled. However, the coming of the "talkies" spelled the eventual downfall of the stock companies.

Although motion pictures sounded the death knell for live theatre in Deadwood Gulch, attempts were made to keep it alive by faculty groups, home talent efforts, oratorios, minstrels and pageants. A documentary of Deadwood was presented during the Days of '76 in 1927 when President Calvin Coolidge attended the celebration. One of the more serious attempts to revive an interest in stage productions was the Northern Black Hills Little Theatre, which served the community from 1948 to 1957 with a membership at one time of 240. Television viewing at home was blamed for the decline in the audience through the years and the eventual demise of the group.

Through the years the drama department of Black Hills State College, Spearfish, has also presented an annual series of student-produced dramas and musicals. But before the century of theater entertainment in the Northern Hills could end, live stage productions have been reborn through the efforts of the Lead Fine Arts Association, the Homestake Mining Co., the Deadwood-Lead '76 Centennial Inc. and patrons, who have financially sponsored the establishment of summer theatre at the Homestake Opera House, which through a federal grant, is being restored to its 1914 baroque elegance.

Spearfish also had its Matthews Opera House, which was built in 1906 and housed touring shows, minstrels, vaudeville and Shakespear plays. Through the years the "grandest show place in the state" has been a motion picture theatre, shooting gallery, dance hall, and eventually a pigeon roost. Renovated in 1966, the old Opera House is presently known as Stagecoach Theatre, a Black Hills State College-sponsored summer theatre.

With the decline of the theatres and traveling artists, a need for professional talent was seen and the music lovers of the Lead and Deadwood communities, with the help of local clubs, organized the Northern Black Hills Community Concert Association in 1940 to bring concerts to Lead. With the exception of the World War II years, the organization has provided the Twin Cities with nationally and internationally famous artists, scheduling three or four concerts each season. So popular did the concerts become that Spearfish realized the need in that community also and, with the financial assistance of the college students, organized the Black Hills State Community Concert in 1968, operating under a similar schedule of concerts and artists.

**Lead's ornate opera house, built by Homestake Gold Mining Company in 1914, has been a showplace for half a century. It has been designated as a National Historic Site.**

**Historic Matthews Opera House, Spearfish, is shown at the height of its beauty after the turn of the century.**

**Charlotte Cushman Clark of Lead, wife of the late Horace Clark, is the oldest living member of the Black Hills Society of Pioneers. She came to Deadwood with her father, Samuel Cushman, by stagecoach in 1876. She celebrated her 100th birthday in the Historic City in 1975. Her husband was known as "Mr. Realtor" of Deadwood and Lead, at one time owning most of the property in the two towns, starting his business venture back in 1882. Their sons, Cushman and Rodgers Clark, continued to operate his business after his death — another three-generation Deadwood family.**

Deadwood, S. D. — Secretary Deetken of the Black Hills Pioneers is busy raising funds to carry on the work of the society among its sick and enfeebled members. A special amount for a life membership card was named by the board of directors and quite a number of the old timers have been secured in this way. Among the number are United States Marshal Seth Bullock, Jack Gray, Sol Star and others. At the present time the membership roll shows but 110 members and it is probable that at the next annual meeting in January, the year limit will be raised and those who came to the Hills in 1877 will be permitted to join this filling out the ranks again.

Argus-Leader, Sioux Falls
Oct. 11, 1907

Art has not been neglected in the cultural development of the area since 1962. It was in that year that the Black Hills Art Association Inc. was established in Lead and Deadwood. Now enlarged to include eight towns of the Black Hills, with the exception of Rapid City, the non-profit organization has sponsored annual national exhibits, each judged by an outstanding professional artist from another part of the nation. In addition to encouraging the individual development of the artist, the association works closely with other smaller art groups in the area.

One of the most active groups in preservation of the area's history is the Society of Black Hills Pioneers which established the monument to Rev. Henry Weston Smith on the Deadwood-Spearfish highway in 1914; sponsored the erection of the monument to Theodore Roosevelt on Mount Roosevelt near Deadwood in 1919; and was instrumental in establishing the gold discovery monument in Custer in 1921, the monument to Annie D. Tallent near Custer in 1924, the rebuilding of the Gordon Stockade near Custer in 1925 and the erection of a State historical marker at the monument to Rev. Smith in 1975.

Today, annual dinner meetings are held on the Sunday afternoon a week ahead of the "Days of '76", which is held yearly as close as possible to August 1. Except for one 1878 pioneer, all members today are direct descendants of those coming to the Black Hills prior to the date of the big Deadwood fire of September 26, 1879. This change in the membership eligibility date was made in 1932. Another group interested in the preservation of the area's heritage is the Lawrence County Historical Society which was formed in 1969. It is sponsoring oral tapes of interviews with early-day residents and their recollections of life in those pioneer days. It is also marking some of the vital historical sites throughout the county.

By the turn of the century, the Northern Black Hills faced the necessity of bringing to the outside world the potential of its mineral resources and to enlist outside capital in the development of its hidden wealth. With this as a goal, the Black Hills Mining Men's Association was formed on September 3, 1901, with a board of directors which included local businessmen as well as prominent mining company officials. It was successful in its first project — to take a mineral exhibit to the Festival of Mountain and Plain in Denver that fall. So successful was the endeavor that by the next monthly meeting the membership had increased from 50 to over 400. Encouraged by such support, the organization pledged its efforts to securing the American Mining Congress for the cities of Lead and Deadwood and sent a delegation of its most prominent members to the next meeting of the Congress at Butte, Montana, the next year. Again, its efforts were rewarded and the Congress convened in the Twin Cities in 1903, convincing the rest of the mining world of the important mineral deposits located here. While the Mining Men's Association may not have

**Deadwood and Lead businessmen built a palace to display the abundant materials found in the northern Black Hills. The building was located on the corner of Main and Shine streets where the Franklin Hotel now stands. The time was 1901.**

**(Centennial Collection)**

solved all the problems of securing capital investment for the area, the organization can be credited with "planting the seed" for the Northern Hills' second century gold rush — Tourism.

For it was about this time that the commercial clubs of Lead and Deadwood, and a group in Spearfish, realized that not only was the mineral wealth of the Hills of value but also its scenic beauty. And with that realization — the state's second most important industry was born.

Revived in December of 1901 as a successor to the Deadwood Club, which proved mostly a social organization, was the Business Men's Club. Realizing the faults of its parent organization, the new club's goal included "the general interests of the city, development of its resources and the uniting of citizens in an effort to accomplish these ends." Its 150 members were enthusiastic about the civic activities and, incidentally, also about the club's sideboard which offered refreshments and cold lunches to the tired businessmen. Not enough praise and credit can be given to those early Twentieth Century businessmen. They were responsible for the erecting of the present Franklin Hotel and they led the drive for a correct city census which confirmed the city's population growth. Even in 1902 these businessmen were seeking quicker and better mail service and extended their efforts toward securing a franchise for an electric motor line from Spearfish to Deadwood. Highlighting the attainments of the group was the passage of the Omnibus Bill in Washington with the rider granting $200,000 for a local federal building. Other objectives were obtaining an appropriation for the present Deadwood Carnegie Library, the attraction of mining interests to the city, the postal telegraph, a flour mill and enticing the Chicago and North Western Railway tracks into the city.

An unpredicted tornado, cloaked by a thunderstorm and heavy rain, swooped down on the Black Hills National Forest southwest of Lead . . . cutting a 20-mile path through a heavily timbered area.

Although timber loss was heavy in the ten square mile area, there was no damage to property or any loss of life or injuries as far as U. S. Forest Service officials were able to learn . . .

. . . . A rough estimate of the timber loss was set at $250,000 by forestry officials who reported that about one fifth of the destroyed timber was on land owned by the Homestake Mining Company. A total of 6,400 acres was leveled.

Lead Daily Call
July 13, 1965

Lead, S. D. — On his first trip to the Black Hills Dr. William Mayo, the celebrated surgeon of Rochester, Minn., was tendered a reception and banquet by the local and Deadwood physicians at the Franklin hotel in Deadwood. Dr. Mayo declared that it was his intention to recommend the Hills to many of his patients in the future.

St. Paul Dispatch
Oct. 17, 1907

In her regal finery, Carrie Tippie was crowned queen of the Deadwood Elks Lodge Carnival in 1908. Carrie was the daughter of Anson Tippie, the bartender in Saloon No. 10 when Jack McCall shot and killed Wild Bill Hickok. (Adams Museum)

Reorganized in 1929 as the Deadwood Chamber of Commerce, the group continued its community endeavors but with emphasis on the value of preserving the city's early-day history as a means of attracting the tourists, an industry which has multiplied through the years. Guiding the Chamber since its earliest years and instrumental in building up Deadwood's legendary past was Nell Perrigoue, executive secretary.

Miss Perrigoue is credited with perpetuation of the "Trial of Jack McCall," also geared to the preservation of some of Deadwood's early history. The production is based on the actual farce of 1876. It annually attracts thousands of visitors to Deadwood. The play was first introduced in about 1928 as part of the Days of '76 celebration and was presented at the "Bucket of Blood." After a few years as a specialty of the annual celebration, it was taken over by Miss Perrigoue and Mrs. Pat Woods as a private venture. It has been produced on a regular basis during the summer season since the late 1930's by a cast of local residents, college students and teachers.

Before their deaths, Mrs. Woods and Miss Perrigoue also formed the corporation which owns and operates the Ghosts of Deadwood Gulch, an authentic wax museum featuring a rare collection of more than 70 life-size figures in authentic settings, tracing the history of the area through its gold-rush days. Also promoted as an attraction is Mount Moriah cemetery which over a hundred thousand tourists visit each year to view the graves of the many early-day residents who added much color to the history of the area. Buried there, with appropriate grave stones, are Wild Bill Hickok, Calamity Jane, Potato Creek Johnny, Seth Bullock and Preacher Smith. Various sections of the cemetery, established in 1877, tell a true story of life — and death — in the early-day mining camp. A children's section resulted from an epidemic that swept the gulch from 1878 to 1880; the Masonic Section, established by the oldest lodge in South Dakota, laid out in a perfect circle with the Holy Bible as a centerpiece; the Hebrew section which contains the graves of many of the prominent Jewish families who contributed to the growth and welfare of the surrounding community; and the rustic Chinese area which tells a vivid story of the part this group played during the gold rush and the mellower days that followed.

Also recalling early-day history is the Broken Boot Gold Mine, a subsidiary of the Deadwood Chamber of Commerce which gives visitors the only opportunity in the Northern Hills to inspect underground gold mining operations. Originally the Seim mine, it was discovered in 1885 and abandoned in 1904 when the Deadwood smelter ceased operations. Lying dormant for more than half a century, the old mine was reopened in 1954 for tourists. The main drift runs approximately 840 feet back into the hill along which visitors are guided to the large open stopes where the rich gold ore was removed before the turn of the century.

The pages of history are also turned back for three days of each year on the first weekend in August when Deadwood relives the "Days of '76." The giant morning parade depicts the history of transportation in the discovery, settlement and development of Deadwood Gulch and pageantry is the theme for the three-day rodeo which rounds out the celebration. All of the horse-drawn vehicles, which are restored and maintained by the Chamber of Commerce are on display at the '76 Museum located near the rodeo grounds.

One of the most popular attractions for visitors to Deadwood is the Adams Memorial Museum, erected in 1930 at the corner of Sherman and Deadwood streets. Yearly about 100,000 persons visit the museum to enjoy the numerous historical exhibits and Indian artifacts. The building, constructed at a total cost of about $75,000, was financed by W. E. Adams, pioneer grocery wholesaler, who intended the museum to also be a home for the Society of Black Hills Pioneers in Deadwood. The museum, which is operated by a trust fund established by Adams, is also supported by a City levy and through the donations left by those who visit it daily and appreciate the heritage which it is entrusted to preserve.

Scheduled to start operations in the Centennial Year is a narrow-gauge railroad, that will travel from the large parking area below the '76 Arena to the historic business district. The line, named after the pioneer Deadwood Central Railway, was planned to solve an ever-increasing traffic and parking problem in the congested area.

Pledging to advertise the scenic and mining resources of Lead and the Black Hills, the Lead Commercial Club was organized in 1902. One of the most unique projects ever handled by the club was the creation of the Lead Coliseum Company to erect a large building to be used as a skating rink during the winter, and for meetings. Ten thousand dollars was raised and the building erected on Main Street at a total cost of $10,400. It was opened in December, 1904, complete with band music for the skating rink on Wednesday and Saturday evenings. The revenue for the first two months was $2,400 which qualified it as a great success. The club also spearheaded a permanent mineral exhibit which was located in the Hearst Library. It also sponsored the presentation of a $1,500 loving cup for Mrs. Phoebe Hearst as a reminder of Lead's esteem for her benevolent contributions to the city. All of the funds to purchase the cup were donated by the men, women and children of the city with the exception of a $63.10 balance which was contributed by the Commercial Club.

The club also led the way towards the establishment of a commercial college for the city, which opened in the fall of 1903. By the next February there were 200 day and night students with a staff of four teachers. In its later years, the club went all out for publication of folders, printing of auto stickers, pamphlets and maps and spon-

**Deadwood's new courthouse, looking as regal as most capitol buildings, proved a perfect backdrop for President Taft when he visited Deadwood in 1911. Note the "bunting in bloom" on the side of the courthouse — back when patriotism was a way of life.**
**(Centennial Collection)**

Three more conventions have been secured for Deadwood. Next July the state medical board will hold its sessions here, while the state dental society has also chosen the same month to meet here. The South Dakota's Bankers' Association is planning the biggest annual meeting it has yet held in this city the middle of July, and hotel reservations have already been made for the event.
**B H Daily Times**
**Jan. 31, 1909**

W. E. Adams reportedly paid $9,000 for the museum site, which back in 1876 was the location for the Minnesota store, owned by Thomas Whittaker. Conducting his business in a rude unfinished shack, Whittaker exchanged gold dust for commodities such as beans, bacon etc. Although destroyed in the 1879 fire, Whittaker rebuilt at once, increasing its size. Part of the buildings were still standing when it was razed for the museum.
Circa 1930

**When the carnival came to town it was the biggest thing ever — especially for the young people who appear entranced by the sideshow. (Centennial Collection)**

soring the erection of roadside mileage signs. Realizing that accommodations must be provided for the visitors they were trying to attract, the organization also undertook improvements of the Mile High Free Tourist Camp at the City Park and the establishment of a Mile High Pay Camp near the Washington School area.

Lead, also proud of its heritage, plans to restore the Homestake Opera House to its early-century interior. Serving as headquarters for summer theatre productions, the Opera House attracts visitors for afternoon variety shows, a tour of the elegant facilities, and a concert on the 1880 pipe organ.

The Mile-High City also has its own special restoration project, thanks to the Woman's Club of that city. At one end of the Sinking Gardens, with the spectacular Open Cut as a backdrop, stands the former Finnish Lutheran Church which serves as a club meeting place and gallery for the display of local, state and national art. Built in 1891, the edifice was moved to its present location from East Main Street in 1963. The Woman's Club dedicated the structure to the memory of Mrs. Ira Sweatman, who bequeathed a sum of money to the organization, and opens the gallery to the public during the summer.

Perpetuating the history of its gold-mining origin, is another Lead attraction, which is conducted by the Lead Civic Association, a nonprofit corporation. The organized tours of the Homestake Mining Company's surface plants and gold ore processing have been conducted since 1920, with proceeds used for civic endeavors. Records show that in 1945 there were only 812 visitors. The peak day has been August 4, 1970, when 1,671 persons took the tour. The largest attendance in 1975 was reached on August 5 with 1,381.

Although the Lead Commercial Club joined the U.S. Chamber of Commerce in 1935, it did not technically change its name to the Lead Chamber of Commerce until 1965. In addition to all its efforts in support of the business district, the Chamber, along with Deadwood's, has been active in promoting the Twin Cities as a winter sports area for snowmobilers and skiers, to make the area a year-round vacation land.

Three small specks of gold, the magic mineral which spurred the settlement of Deadwood in 1876 and led to the death of James Butler (Wild Bill) Hickok, figure prominently in the statue of the two-gun marshal to be dedicated in Deadwood, June 21. It is ironic that 75 years after Hickok's death at the hand of cowardly Jack McCall, gold should unexpectedly be found in the block of granite from which sculptor Korczak Ziolkowski is carving the bust of the frontier lawman.

Pioneer-Times
May 24, 1951

Colonel Charles A. Lindbergh and the other half of his famous "we" — the "Spirit of St. Louis" — flew over Deadwood yesterday morning and dropped a message of greeting to the citizens. "We" flew over the comparatively low buildings at a height variously estimated at from 100 to 200 feet from the streets and circled and returned repeatedly without rising above the walls of the narrow gulch. In several instances he grazed the tops of buildings with a few feet to spare. After flying over Deadwood, "Lindy" headed off in the direction of Lead and later flew over the city and also over Spearfish.

Pioneer-Times
Sept. 3, 1927

Famous opera singer Mary Garden and Gutzon Borglum, creator of Rushmore Memorial were treated to a luncheon on the 2,000 foot level of the Homestake Gold Mine at Lead on October 20, 1931.

Mildred Fielder
Treasure of Homestake Gold

Now playing at the Homestake Opera House William Fox's production of "Cleopatra" starring Theda Bara.

Lead Daily Call
September 24, 1919

Tootsie, the South Dakota coyote, was designated the state animal by Gov. George Mickelson in 1949. Tootsie and her owner, Fred Borsch of Galena, were popular with the tourists in Deadwood, on television and on a 10-state tour. Tootsie, found as a pup at the foot of Custer Peak, 20 miles from Deadwood, was domesticated by Borsch. She died in 1959.
(Fred Borsch Photo)

A group of Deadwood and Lead businessmen in 1936 met over coffee in Lead and organized what was called the Bald Mountain Ski Club. Pioneering in the field, these men spent much of their time in cutting trails and putting up two rope tows on land which had been donated to the club and is now known as Stewart Slope. At first it was mainly a family and friends type of operation that never numbered over about 100 ski enthusiasts. When World War II came, all activity ceased. However, after the war, more runs and facilities were developed. By 1952, the same group adopted the name of Black Hills Chair Lift, Inc., and organized to build and operate a chair lift. From then on developments were extensive with the club concentrating its resources on junior racing. It paid off with some of the youngsters going on to college teams and one even becoming a member of the U.S. Olympic team. In 1971, the ski jump was built for the North Central Ski Association which met at Terry Peak. Presently, Terry Peak is concentrating on expansion to include another chair lift to provide more family type facilities to conform with the popular trend of the sport nationwide.

Deer Mountain Ski Area, two-and-one-half miles from Lead, was started in the fall of 1970. It features two Poma lifts and two smaller lifts. Both Terry Peak and Deer Mountain attract ski enthusiasts not only from the local area but also from surrounding states.

Spearfish, above all, was cognizant of what the beauty of Spearfish Canyon and the surrounding Hills could mean to it as a community and so a group of businessmen formed the city's Commercial Club in 1910. One of its first and most important projects was to spearhead a drive to open a Spearfish Canyon road. About 100 men, by the sweat of their brow, constructed a road from Spearfish to the Homestake power plant, aided partly by an access road which was built by E. C. Dickey, father of Walter Dickey, Spearfish, for delivery of lumber and boilers to the sawmill.

Lead, S. D. — To arrange if possible a circuit for the leading towns of the Black Hills for either high class legitimate or vaudeville shows, Frank Phelps, treasurer of the Krug theatre in Omaha, is here. It is said that he is backed by eastern capital that is desirous of placing their syndicate attractions in the Hills and establishing new theatres here. As Lead, Deadwood, Spearfish and Belle Fourche have within the past year erected new theatres for the better class attractions, Mr. Krug is meeting with some opposition in his efforts.
Argus-Leader, Sioux Falls
Sept. 30, 1907

It wasn't enough that Deadwood had been "wild and woolly" since its birth in 1876. No date is available for this cowboy and Indian wild west show. The grandstand in the background had its back to Main Street about where Schwarzwald Furniture Store is now located. The arena had to be between the grandstand and the bulkhead for Whitewood Creek to the right of the picture.

(Adams Museum)

The granddaughter of Henry Weston Smith Sunday stood on virtually the same spot where he was killed 85 years ago and placed a wreath on the monument which honors the first missionary in the Black Hills. The observance of the death of Preacher Smith was held at the Preacher Smith Monument on U. S. highway 85 north of Deadwood and was highlighted by the presence of Mrs. Geraldine Holden, Shrewsbury, Mass, granddaughter of the Methodist minister.

Deadwood Pioneer-Times
Aug. 20, 1961

The Spearfish Chamber, since 1938, has worked closely with Josef Meier who chose the community's peaceful setting as the permanent location for the Luenen Passion Play. By the following year a site was selected and stage buildings constructed. So well was it accepted by the community and the travelling public that attendance at the giant outdoor amphitheatre has increased annually. Established as the Black Hills Passion Play, the cast of 35 professionals, which is supplemented with about 150 local people, headquarters in the winter months at Lake Wales, Florida, where the seven last days of the life of Jesus of Nazareth are reenacted during February, March and April. The only interruption of its 37-year summer run in Spearfish was during World War II when travel was limited and the production was discontinued from 1943 through 1947. The world-famous production has since attracted visitors to Spearfish in numbers comparable to the throngs of gold-seekers who first swarmed into the region a century ago. The Passion Play, plus the spectacular beauty of Spearfish Canyon, is chiefly responsible for bringing Spearfish into the galaxy of Black Hills tourist communities.

**One block of Deadwood's Main Street was missing when this photo was taken in the early 1900's — probably another bad fire. It must have been a gala, holiday celebration with a balloon ascension as the main attraction. Schwarzwald's Furniture Store (same location as today) can be seen to the left of the balloon. (Adams Museum)**

# chapter XXVII

# Violence And The Vanishing Angel

Violent deaths, so numerous in Lawrence County's early history, also brought unwanted notoriety to the Twin Cities of the Northern Hills in the Twentieth Century. A number of assumed murders, as in earlier years, defied solution in the second and third decades of the new century. The first of these unsolved deaths was the case of Mrs. John Niemi whose charred body was found in the furnace of her daughter's home in Lead on December 7, 1919. The daughter and her husband were charged with murder, but they were acquitted and the grotesque case was never solved.

Father Arthur Belknap, rector of St. Patrick's Church in Lead, was the victim of the second unsolved death in that community in the Twentieth Century. The young priest had been summoned by an unknown caller at about three in the morning on October 26, 1921, to attend a sick person in the region of Bender's Park, a Homestake storage area. His mercy mission was never completed as he was struck on the head and shot in the heart while walking near the park. Three cartridges from a Colt 45 were found near the body. A few days after the murder a colt 45, a hammer, and a blood-stained glove were found in the boarding house room of a young man who had hurriedly left town shortly after the crime. The fugitive became the prime suspect, but he was never apprehended. The motive for the murder of Father Belknap, a popular priest with no known enemies, baffled the community as well as the investigating authorities.

Another unsolved murder shocked the people of Deadwood on September 6, 1926. Frank S. Peck, engineer in charge of state highways, was fatally injured when a tire pump, loaded with nitroglycerine, exploded as he handled it in his garage on his way to work that morning. A hand pump was standard equipment for every car in those days as tires were prone to blowouts. Peck, seeing the pump in the garage, picked it up and pushed the handle down, discharging the explosive and blasting his legs. Amputation of the

LEAD DAILY TRIBUNE

EDWARDS & GRACE, Owners.

G. H. GRACE, PUBLISHER

Published every day in the year except Sunday at 103 Main Street, Lead, S. D.

TERMS:
$3.00 per year; 25 cents per month delivered by carrier or by mail. Advertising rates made known on application.

(Entered at the postoffice in Lead as mail matter of the second class)

**Colonel Parker Stand Up**

(By McCormick Clawater)

Colonel Parker the Tribune has it's hat off to you—It wants to compliment you on your bold, manly, vigorous stand in defense of Civic morality, purity and decency.

Colonel Parker, the Tribune is glad that that there is a MAN in the chair of the states attorney and extends the hope that you will continue to be the William Travers Jerome, the Joseph W. Falk of Lawrence county.

Colonel Parker, if you follow along these lines there are higher honors in store for you. South Dakota, like every other state needs men of integrity and honor, intensity and backbone, and will be glad to honor them.

Colonel Parker, the Tribune is glad that you realize that Lead and Deadwood are no longer mere mining camps, filled with the riff-raff of civilization, but communities occupied by decent, law-abiding and, for the most part, God fearing citizens, who applaud your action, and for every enemy your manly effort has cost you, you may count ten new friends.

Colonel Parker, the Tribune asks you to continue your work. The saloons should close at eleven o'clock at night. Those who can't get enough to drink by that hour can buy more and take it home, thus avoiding the nightly bands of midnight destroyers of the peace.

Colonel Parker, for what you have done and for what the Tribune thinks you will continue to do. we thank you.

Colonel Parker, again we thank you. You may sit down.

Prentice Bernard, alias George Perry, alias "Vinegar" Rowan is dead in the undertaking establishment and Dick Moran is lying in St. Joseph's Hospital with a bullet in his body and his life in the balance, as the result of a shooting scrape which occurred at 5:30 o'clock yesterday evening on the third floor of the Mansion building at the corner of Main and Wall streets.

Deadwood Pioneer-Times
Dec. 10, 1907

An unsolved murder in Lead. On Oct. 26, 1921 Father Belknap, answering an early morning mercy call, was struck from behind and shot through the heart as he walked near the summit of what is now Glendale Drive.

Lead, S. D. — Through the arrest of Anna Miljas, her husband Chris, and her uncle Matt Seimbela, a bold attempt at extortion with T. J. Grier, the wealthy superintendent of the Homestake mine, as intended victim came to light. The two wrote an anonymous letter to Grier demanding that he place $20,000 in an envelope at a stated time or place or be blown up in his home. Grier turned the matter over to Sheriff Trathen, and was instructed to leave a dummy letter. This was done, and the woman took the bait and was promptly arrested by a concealed officer. Grier left here Sunday for a trip to Scotland, but has been notified of the arrest. The Miljas woman has been out on bail for a daring attempt to pass a bunch of lost checks last summer. Mrs. Miljas is 26 and pretty. Grier received two letters, one two weeks ago, another Saturday. The letters were signed "President" and said an organized band of 300 wanted money or the Homestake mines and mills and the Grier home and children would not be safe. It named Sunday at 10 a.m. as the hour for placing the envelopes with greenbacks under a corner of the Ellison hoist building. The woman made two trips there Monday under pretense of tying a shoe. She secured the dummy envelope and hurried home, followed by the detectives. Fifteen minutes later she was arrested in her bed, where she said, she had a sick headache. The arrest of her husband who recently returned from Goldfield, and of her uncle, who was supposed to be well-to-do, followed. Shortly after Grier received the first letter, Mrs. Grier and the children departed for Europe, and Grier followed himself on Sunday after the receipt of the second letter.

Omaha World Herald
Oct. 16, 1907

severely-damaged limbs failed to save his life. Police officers investigated, but could find no clues to the murder.

Added to the list of unsolved murders was the death of Bernard L'Esperance who body was found in the late afternoon of May 8, 1958, at his home by his sister, Lea L'Esperance, when she called to see him. His body was lying just inside the front door of his Main Street home in Deadwood and it was believed that he had died several hours earlier. An autopsy revealed death was attributed to several blows on the head with a blunt instrument. Robbery as a motive was discounted after an investigation revealed that about $1,000 was found untouched in his home.

The murders of three law enforcement officers brought more headlines for the Northern Hills area as details of the killings were carried in newspapers throughout the region. On November 22, 1938, Milan Miller, a State Highway Patrolman, was shot and killed by a Charles Fowler, who alleged that Miller had treated him in a brutal manner while he was a prisoner in the Lead jail. Charged with murder, Fowler had a speedy trial on December 13, less than a month after the murder. He was found guilty of manslaughter in the third degree by a jury which recommended clemency. Fowler was sentenced to 15 years in the state prison.

Long remembered was the apprehension and conviction of George S. Sitts, 32, for the murder of Tom Matthews, Spearfish, State Agent, and Sheriff Dave Malcolm, Belle Fourche, on January 24, 1946. Once again justice was speedy and it was just a matter of eight weeks after Sitts shot the two officers as they attempted to stop him for questioning, that the jury brought in a verdict of guilty and recommended the death penalty. The late Judge Charles R. Hayes presided over the trial in Circuit Court and sentenced Sitts to death by electrocution in the state prison.

Sitts, who had escaped from the Minneapolis jail, was being held there for transfer to the state prison at Stillwater to start serving a life term for the slaying of a Minneapolis liquor dealer. After his escape he stole a car and fled across South Dakota. His abandoned car was found the day following the murder, on the old Crook City road near Deadwood. For four days after the murder, Sitts hid in an abandoned schoolhouse, six miles from Deadwood. Driven out by cold and thirst, he made his way to Deadwood, where he hid in the basement of the home of Police Chief Ross Dunn for about a week. On leaving his hideout, he kidnapped a local man, Leonard Ronneberg, and forced him to drive him beyond Beulah, Wyoming, where he let the driver out and drove on across Wyoming. He was captured the next day at Lysite, Wyoming, and returned to Deadwood, where he was held for trial, with Clinton G. Richards as the prosecuting attorney and John T. Heffron, one of the ablest criminal lawers in the area, appointed by the court to defend him. Sitts was electrocuted at Sioux Falls, April 8, 1947.

The sanctity of the home and the violent deaths of two of the main witnesses to a shooting death were believed responsible for the unexpected acquittal in a trial held in Deadwood in 1905 before Judge William Rice. Charged with the death of Richard Galvin, March 13, 1905, at the Silver Queen Mine in Galena was Eli Farnham. Galvin, who lived for five days following the shooting, was questioned at the hospital in regard to his relations with Farnham's wife and made a dying statement. One of the two witnesses who were present at the time of the shooting was sitting in a room by the stove and was killed when lightning struck the chimney. The other witness drowned while crossing a stream of high water.

In the 100-year history of U.S. District Court at Deadwood there have been only nine federal judges. Appointed for life, it was not until 1957 that Congress provided for two judges for South Dakota. The U. S. Attorneys, who serve by appointment of the President and are confirmed by the Senate, usually change with every national change of administration. As a result 25 different attorneys have been appointed to this office to date. It should be remembered that prior to statehood the territory had a U.S. District Court with jurisdiction over federal matters, although the same personnel operated as a state court and state officers until 1889. Many historical trials, involving civil matters as well as criminal, have marked the calendar of the U.S. District Court through the years. However, the longest case for trial and the biggest verdict ever awarded in this court in South Dakota took place in 1965 at Deadwood.

The case of Summit Construction Co., plaintiff, against Peter Kiewit Construction Co., defendant, and General Insurance Co. of America, third-party defendant, started July 12, 1965, before Judge Fred J. Nichol on the question of liability. A verdict for the plaintiff was rendered in October of the same year. A few days later the trial was resumed on the question of the amount of damages, and continued to February 11, 1966. The verdict was rendered for damages of approximately one million dollars. Later the court added pre-judgment interest in the amount of $190,000. After the allowance of some set-offs, the defendants paid the final judgment with a check for $1,025,000. The trial required 32 days before the Court, without a jury, and another 84 days before the Court with a jury.

**William Green Rice was judge of the Eighth Judicial Circuit Court in South Dakota for Lawrence, Butte and Meade Counties. He was born in Memphis, Missouri, February 1, 1858 and died in Deadwood July 7, 1948.**

Deadwood — In a quarrel over a mongrel yellow dog, William Frazer, a well-known local politician, last night shot and badly injured Ike Trotter, a bartender. Frazer accused Trotter of trying to humiliate the dog by putting turpentine on it. Frazer was released on six prominent men signing a bond for $5,000, the exact figure at which he has often said he valued the dog.

Minneapolis Tribune
Feb. 7, 1909

Pioneer sheriff of Lawrence County, Seth Bullock, died of cancer and was buried near the base of White Rocks above Deadwood.

Lead Daily Call
September 23, 1919

Pierre — Former Gov. George T. Mickelson and Deadwood attorney Clinton G. Richards are slated for appointments to the U. S. District Court.

Deadwood Pioneer-Times
May 11, 1953

The name of Kellar is synonymous with a century of law and order in Deadwood Gulch since the gold rush of 1876. Chambers Kellar started practicing law in Deadwood in 1897. In 1904 he was appointed general counsel for the Homestake Mining Company and moved his office to Lead. His son, Kenneth Kellar, joined the firm, and, following his father's death, became chief counsel for the mining company, which post he held as well as serving as a director, until his retirement in 1976. Seth Bullock, one of the original pioneers who came to Deadwood in the 1876 gold rush and served as the first sheriff, was Kenneth Kellar's grandfather, rounding out 100 years for the family in the area's history.

Even his political enemies agreed that U. S. Senator G. C. Moody from Lawrence County, elected in 1902 was an able legislator.
Black Hills Blade
August, 1904

In the early 1900's the bar at Deadwood numbered about 80 lawyers and was composed of some of the ablest and shrewdest attorneys in the West, including Judge Granville E. Bennett and Judge Gideon C. Moody, two of Deadwood's most famed men of justice who had been identified with Black Hills legal history since 1877. Among other members of the Deadwood bar at that time, who had practiced in the Black Hills courts since their establishment in 1877, were Frank J. Washabaugh and Edwin Van Cise. Washabaugh, who was identified with every public movement for advancement of the Black Hills and the State, was elected a member of the Territorial Council and State Senate for seven consecutive terms. Van Cise, who before the turn of the century was in partnership with John R. Wilson, was "a conspicuous figure in the bright galaxy composing the Deadwood bar." While some of the attorneys figured prominently in the big business concerns of the area, other emminent attorneys were associated with the Homestake Mining Co.

Perhaps one of the most prominent attorneys to practice in Lawrence County was Chambers Kellar. Associating himself, in about 1890, with Judge Moody, who was serving as legal counsel for Homestake, Kellar rose to a positon of power and prominence by the time that T. J. Grier died in 1914. As Mildred Fielder describes the man in her book, The Treasure of Homestake Gold:

> "Kellar's position as chief counsel for the Homestake Mining Company put him in a spot which could touch not only on the mining industry but could bring influence to bear on the entire town, the county, and the state. He was a gentleman of the old school, wearing his rimless pince-nez glasses and his well-tailored clothes with an air of authority. If he had one weakness it was for flamboyant neckties, and the town saw him with one flash of color more often than not."

But, not unlike most contemporary leaders of the community of the time, his temper was such that on occasion he could let it fly (along with his fists) as he did once with Freeman Knowles who was an editor of a pro-union newspaper in Deadwood during the Homestake Lockout.

Moody, as described in Joe Cash's book, Working the Homestake, was a "master politico in territorial days who later became United States Senator from the springboard of his position as chief counsel. Moody's leadership in the Republican party not only marked the open emergence of the Homestake Mining Co. in politics, but also tied the majority of the citizens of Lead to the GOP (this even though the Hearst family were Democrats in an active way)."

Judge Moody's clerk and aide while in the Senate, Robert Hayes, also settled in Deadwood, where he engaged in a successful, scholarly practice of law. His son, Charles R. Hayes, also a Deadwood attorney, achieved the position of State Supreme Court Justice before retiring to Deadwood to resume his career.

One of Hayes' first associates, Clinton G. Richards, has practiced law in the Black Hills for nearly 50 years, including an appointment as U.S. District Attorney. In 1975 he was joined in his law firm by his son Reed.

Of more recent legal fame is Alex Rentto, a native son of Lead, who rose from the depths of the famous gold mine to the highest judicial post in South Dakota, the Supreme Court. Judge Rentto, proud of the fact that Homestake permitted him to work as a gold miner to finance his way through law school, graduated from the University of South Dakota. Named Circuit Court judge in 1947, eight years later he was elevated to the Supreme Court bench where he served until retirement in 1974.

Lead Municipal Court, which originated in 1911, was terminated in 1969 when it was absorbed into the Magistrate Division of the newly-formed District County Court system. Only five judges served on the bench during its 58-year history. John H. Rogers held a term from May 1911 to May 1915; John Walsh, May 1915 to February 1930; Walter R. Curnow, February 1930 to October 1943; E. A. Steinback, October 1943 to October 1954 and Richard A. Furze from November 1954 until it ceased in 1969. In a wide-sweeping change in 1975, which involved Lawrence County courts as well as all other counties in South Dakota, all courts were incorporated into a judicial system controlled and financed by the State government.

One of the longest legal practices is held by Francis J. Parker, who is still an active attorney at the age of 90. Starting his practice in Deadwood in 1910, Parker has witnessed the long transition from a bustling frontier to the more staid times of today. His personal recollections date back to the times when in court and in his office, the protection of the rule of law was subordinated by individuals emboldened by loaded six-shooters. Utilizing his philosophy of standing and fighting rather than turning to run, Parker either disarmed them and sent them running out of his office in flight for their lives or left them to the processes of the law, making them more considerate of the proper rules of debate and persuasion.

He recalls details of a case that he was prosecuting for the State during prohibition days. The defendant, the alleged moonshiner, took the stand and admitted all of the pertinent points in the case: he had made the alcoholic stuff and was selling it. The jury went out and shortly returned with a verdict of "not guilty." Later in chambers, the judge inquired of Parker the reason for the jury's verdict acquitting the defendant when he had admitted all charges on the witness stand. "Obviously," replied Parker, "the jury didn't believe him."

Another chapter in the practice of law was John T. Heffron, a criminal trial attorney whose skills commanded great respect. The story is told, however, that his eloquent summaries to the jury were

A truly Centennial family, covering almost 100 years in the city of Deadwood, is the Parker family. William H. Parker rose from a 15-year-old drummer boy to a colonel during the Civil War. He started practicing law in Deadwood in July, 1877, and was a member of the Constitutional Convention in 1885. Elected a member of the National Congress in 1906, he served until his death in 1908. His son Francis J. Parker has carried on in his father's footsteps in the legal profession, still active in law in Deadwood at the age of 90 in 1976. Francis has held every office from state's attorney on up to being a member of the State Legislature. His son, Thomas H. Parker, entered the family law firm and is now a Circuit Court judge in Rapid City, S. D. A nephew of Francis Parker, William Parker, also a native of Deadwood, worked his way through law school serving as a police officer and rose to chief of the Los Angeles Police Department where he served until the time of his dath.

**John T. Heffron was one of Deadwood's leading criminal lawyers. He served four years as state's attorney, sixteen as city attorney and ten as U. S. District Attorney.**

somewhat repetitious and based on the same quotations and examples. On one occasion, as Heffron was wrapping up his summation in the newly redecorated courthouse in Deadwood, he made reference to the angel of justice and pointed to the spot where the august figure was painted on the ceiling. Upon turning his gaze to the place where he was pointing, Heffron was shocked to find that the angel of justice had been painted out in the remodeling. It was said that his closing arguments were never again the same.

One of the stories told about Attorney Henry Frawley involved a case where Frawley was engaged to defend a man accused of a crime. The defendant had a large family and all members of it were in the front row of the courtroom for the trial. Obviously informed that if their emotions showed, it would not hurt and, possibly might help the defendant's case, the wife and the children were more and more audible as the case wore on. Finally the defendant himself took the stand and told his tale of woe. The sad chorus of the family grew and was joined by the family dog who had crept in unnoticed in the commotion. Soon his howls joined the family. At this point the judge promptly stopped the proceedings and peering down on Attorney Frawley, he instructed, "One at a time, please counselor, one at a time!"

Though the angel of justice has been painted over and the dog's howls are gone, the legal halls of Lawrence County still echo with the cases of those early settlers with their problems and complaints. More than other professions, perhaps, the taste and touch of tradition is felt by those who follow the same paths of early miner-lawyers.

Henry Frawley was born in Washington County, New York, in 1850. He graduated from the state university at Madison, Wis. in 1874 and came to the Hills in 1877 as a practicing attorney. For many years he was a prominent member of the Deadwood bar. He purchased a number of ranches in Centennial Valley, consolidated them and improved them into one of the largest ranches in the Black Hills. He died in 1927. His son, Henry II, and grandson Henry III, continued to operate the historic ranch site in Centennial Valley between Deadwood and Spearfish.

**A little country town was Spearfish back in 1918. Looking at Main Street, note the patch of grass in the foreground of the dirt road.**

# chapter XXVIII

# Villages With Vision

**A new hotel was the turn of the century highlight for Spearfish which was experiencing a building boom.**

**(Centennial Collection)**

Spearfish, the Queen City, was a quiet and peaceful town during the turn of the century. Although visions of Spearfish as a great mining and industrial center faded in the early 1890's, the town, because of its unique location and tranquil atmosphere, grew and prospered. In the early 1900's, Spearfish vied with Terry for the title of the third largest city in Lawrence County. The population of the city ranged between 1,500 and 2,000 during the first decade of the Twentieth Century. Building activity was bustling throughout the early 1900's. New hotels, businesses, and many homes were built. In 1900 construction began on the Matthews Block and the building was completed a few years later. The Matthews building contained many businesses and shops. As the town grew, critics of the aldermanic form of City government demanded that the City convert to the commission plan to govern Spearfish. Two attempts to change the form of City government were voted down in 1910 and 1911.

The Homestake Mining Co. in the early 1900's looked at Spearfish as a possible site for a hydro-electric plant. The Homestake Hydro No. 1 Plant, after two years of construction, was completed in 1912. A four-and-a-half mile-long cement lined tunnel was built to divert water from Spearfish Creek to a dam near the Spearfish City limits and several thousand feet of steel pipe were laid to carry water to the generators. Approximately 33,000 volts of electricity were sent over power transmission lines to the mine at Lead. Many Spearfish citizens were employed by Homestake to operate the electric generating facility.

The First World War brought a number of changes to Spearfish. It was a time of sadness and celebration. Many young Spearfish men lost their lives in Europe during the war but the citizens of Spearfish, like their counterparts in Lead and Deadwood, celebrated jubilantly when word was received that the war was over.

A Glimpse As We Pass

Where the Spearfish sings through the canyon gash,
By fall and rapid our motors flash,
And we halt to view the magic work,
Of engineers on the Beautiful Fork,
Where a river is sucked from its valley bed,
And the thirst of an alien empire fed.
For substance and home and comfort link
When a desert is given a flood to drink.

Doane Robinson

**January 15, 1925 was the worst night in the history of Spearfish Normal (Now Black Hills State College) when a holocaust left a fiery skeleton of this once-proud hall of learning. (Centennial Collection)**

The new metallic circuit telephone line between this city and Spearfish is practically complete. The wire is all strung and all other details will be finished and the line in shape for use in a few days . . . .

B H Daily Times
Jan. 12, 1894

Spearfish, S. D. — Greater demand than it expected, has placed the Black Hills Traction company in a position where it will have to build another power plant to meet the requests of customers for electricity. The company recently completed a large water plant here which will generate 1,200 horsepower. So many mining companies and firms have contracted for the use of the electricity that the company is now figuring on plans for the erection of a larger plant at Beulah, Wyo., west of Belle Fourche, some time this winter. This plant will insure sufficient power for the operation of the proposed trolley line between Deadwood and Spearfish, which it is believed, will give the North Western railroad an opportunity to tap this section of the country.

Rapid City Journal
Oct. 25, 1907

During the early 1900's Spearfish lacked a dependable water supply. The city had tapped Hungry Hollow Springs for water but the springs were beginning to dry up. In 1919 the voters approved a bond issue for $50,000 to update and improve the water system. Wooden water mains were laid from Spearfish to the new water source in Spearfish Canyon. After the flood of 1933, the wooden mains were replaced with cast iron pipe.

The decade of the "Roaring Twenties" was a time of growth and change for Spearfish. In 1924 the building that housed the agricultural exhibits for the Lawrence County Fairs of the 1890's was moved to the east side of Spearfish Creek in the north-central part of town. The County Commissioners felt that the building could be better utilized in a different location.

During one of the most critical periods in the history of the Black Hills Normal School at Spearfish, a disastrous fire and a political struggle nearly prevented the school from becoming a state college. The Main Hall of Black Hills Normal was destroyed by fire on January 13, 1925. Main Hall contained the school's administrative office, a number of classrooms, and a library of about 15,000 volumes — believed to be one of the best in the state. In 1925 Black Hills Normal had 500 students and a varied curriculum. The following week classes resumed in an old vacated Spearfish public school building. A few days after the fire, aid in the form of money, books, and even chairs began to pour in from the nearby communities of Lead, Deadwood, and Belle Fourche. The Spearfish community donated hundreds of books and large amounts of money. The cause of the fire was never determined.

The rebuilding of Main Hall was not the only problem. The Governor and many members of the State Legislature doubted that Western South Dakota could support a teachers college. Lawrence County representatives to the State Legislature were able to convince the reluctant Governor otherwise and an appropriation of $350,000 was granted for the rebuilding of Main Hall, renamed Woodburn Hall. The legal conflicts remained unresolved until 1939 when the Legislature decided to include Black Hills Normal among the state colleges. Two years later the school was officially renamed the Black Hills Teachers College. Since the fire of 1925, the school has gradually grown. The campus of the college now has ten buildings compared to only four at the time of the fire. In 50 years the enrollment at the college has more than tripled. At present the college has about 1,600 students and it is now known as Black Hills State College.

In 1928 three blocks of Main Street were paved at the request of the Spearfish Commercial Club. Civic improvements continued into the next decade, the depression years. New telephone lines and wires for electricity were strung on joint poles throughout the Queen City in November 1933. Federal programs, organized to combat the economic depression were implemented in Spearfish. A Works Progress Administration (WPA) sewer system project was begun in 1938 and completed a few years later at a cost of over $200,000. In September 1937, Spearfish was selected as a site for a new federal post office. The building was finished in November 1940.

The stock market crash of 1929 and the depression of the 1930's had a great effect on the farmers and ranchers in the Spearfish Valley. The difficulty in getting bank loans or mortgages and the drop in agricultural prices forced many farmers and ranchers into debt. The Spearfish business community was hurt by the loss of business from area farmers and ranchers. An encouraging sign for renewed prosperity for Spearfish was the continuing growth of the tourist industry. Spearfish's location on the northern edge of the Black Hills and at the entrance to Spearfish Canyon, has long held special attraction to tourists. With the coming of the automobile and improved roads for the contraptions, visitors frequently came to Spearfish. In the 1920's and 1930's, tourism was becoming an important part of the area's economy. In 1930 the road through Spearfish Canyon, one of the most scenic highways in the Hills, was completed. But the effects of the depression were felt in the Spearfish area and the blossoming tourist industry suffered.

Unfortunately, the automobile that helped Spearfish's economy also harmed it. The Burlington Railroad was forced to cut back service on its route through Spearfish Canyon since the automobile hurt business. The early tourist industry of Spearfish received a severe setback in 1933 when one of the worst floods in the town's history washed out the highway and railroad grade in Spearfish Canyon. The canyon highway was later rebuilt but the railroad line was abandoned in 1934. After WWII and the return of the men who had served in the armed forces, Spearfish began to experience a new growth. The population, which had stabilized at about 2,000 between the two world wars, had grown to 3,680 by 1960. The decade of the 1950's was a period of much building activity in the Queen City. Many motels were built to serve the large numbers of tourists that came to see the Passion Play, Spearfish Canyon, and the Black Hills.

In 1940 the Homestake Mining Co. relocated its large sawmill at Nemo to Spearfish. The sawmill and hydro-electric plant provided employment for many residents of the city and the annual payroll of nearly one quarter million dollars gave a boost to the community. Unlike Lead, Spearfish was not greatly affected by World War II. The closing of the mine in Lead did not force the Homestake sawmill to curtail operations. The Harmony Heights housing development was begun in 1955 on a location south of the Homestake sawmill and near the teachers college. In the late 1950's a new fish hatchery was built eight miles west of the city to supplement the hatchery in Spearfish.

Spearfish, S. D. — When L. N. Snow, a small rancher near here, took a chance shot at a wild duck flying overhead, he did not expect to get a Christmas present. His aim proved true and the bird fell. When dressed a large gold nugget fell from its craw. Snow is having the nugget made into a ring for his wife and some prospectors have started out to find the placer bed from which the duck picked up the yellow metal.

Minneapolis Tribune
Dec. 2, 1907

At an early hour yesterday morning the Burlington agent at Spearfish, found the dead body of "Bishop" Mann, lying in the creek a short distance from building occupied by the deceased. The old gentleman had spent the previous evening in one of the saloons of Spearfish. He was under the influence of liquor and it is believed he died from cold and exposure rather than that he was drowned. George Mann was one of the first settlers of the Spearfish country coming from Montana in July, 1876.

Pioneer-Times
Dec. 28, 1907

**The devastation following one of the worst floods in the history of Spearfish is evident in this picture of damaged railroad tracks, taken May 24, 1933. This led to the abandonment of the Burlington's Spearfish branch. (Black Hills State College)**

SPEARFISH: A peerless residence town.
No boom — no slump.
Valuable educational facilities.
Safe, religious environment.
Two banks — firm as Gibraltar.
U. S. Fish Hatchery—stocks Black Hills streams yearly.
Homestake Hydro-Electric Plant—generates power for mine at Lead.
Pure Water—moderate altitude climate with zip, air with snap.
Summer insect pests all but unknown.
Fine camping sites
Good graveled roads among scenic grandeur to all parts of the Black Hills.
Wonderful crops of wheat, corn and alfalfa; potatoes, onions and beans.
Home of widely known Spearfish Apples and Vegetables.

Sunshine State Magazine
May, 1926

**Spearfish Valley was a prime agricultural area and proved to be the "breadbasket" for the Deadwood-Lead mining areas after the gold rush.**

**(Black Hills Illustrated)**

In 1954 Dr. Arthur A. Schade, a retired minister, considered quiet Spearfish to be the perfect location for a retirement home for the aged. The David M. Dorsett Home was completed in 1956 under the supervision of Dr. Schade in the northeast corner of Spearfish near Lookout Mountain. The estate of Mr. and Mrs. Dorsett of Spearfish and other large donations from the Clarkson family of Belle Fourche and Buffalo, South Dakota, were instrumental in starting the home. The home, a place where the elderly could be cared for professionally, has always been filled with residents. Plans for future expansion of the home have resulted in a number of additions built throughout the years. The Lookout Memorial Hospital, located on the northern edge of Spearfish, was opened in 1963. The 20-bed hospital has a staff of four doctors and a number of nurses. A clinic has been opened during the past few years. The present medical facilities are considered to be adequate for the community of Spearfish and no definite plans for expansion have been made.

In the early 1970's, Spearfish had a population of about 4,700. The town is still known as an agricultural, cultural, and tourist center. Farmers in the fertile Spearfish Valley produce large amounts of apples and vegetables yearly. Continual expansion of Black Hills State College has made it an important institution for higher learning in the state. Tourism has continued to grow in Spearfish. The town has become an important tourist stop for campers and visitors to the Hills. A new luxury motel was built in the 1970's near I-90, not far from the Spearfish Canyon entrance, to serve the increasing number of tourists. The town has also become a retirement center. The Dorsett Home retirement complex for the elderly ranks among the finest in the state. When one visits Spearfish today it is difficult to believe that the town had its beginning as a small wooden stockade besieged by Indians in 1876.

Since pioneer days the agricultural wealth of Lawrence County has been centered in Spearfish and Centennial valleys, picturesque, park-like regions ringed by pine-studded hills. By 1905 Spearfish Valley, about ten miles long and from one to two miles in width, was all under irrigation and cut up into small farms of from five to 50 acres. Stately residences with orchards bending under loads of fruit, gardens and vineyards, golden wheatfields and lush corn and other grains of every description were interspersed with meadows of tall waving grass. The crops virtually never failed and there was always a ready market for all produce in Deadwood and adjacent mining camps.

It was boasted that the finest oats in the world came from spacious Centennial Valley and other foothill areas of the Black Hills, averaging around 60 to 100 bushels per acre. The agricultural land near Whitewood was considered at the turn of the century to be the best wheat-producing area west of the Missouri River. Most of the wheat harvested in the Hills region in the early 1900's was within 15 miles of Whitewood. The first farms in the St. Onge area were 160 acres in size. But by 1907, while the size of the farms had increased, the number of them had decreased.

In the early 1900's horse breeders in the St. Onge locality could no longer make a profit due to the higher costs and the decreasing demand for horses after the coming of the railroad and the building of roads. The owners of the JB horse ranch near St. Onge sold most of their animals in 1903. At the turn of the century, some of the best cattle ranches in the state were located near Whitewood. Only 2,000 cattle were shipped from Whitewood in 1903 because most of the cattle business was transferred north to Belle Fourche.

Area farmers continually experimented with farm machinery to improve crop yields. A rancher near St. Onge around 1900 tried a horse-operated threshing machine. The cumbersome thresher required a level field to operate since any tilt would throw the machine out of order. The machine was too difficult to keep running and it was quickly replaced by a steam-driven threshing machine. Today the county farmer uses modern combines and powerful tractors, the result of great technological achievements.

The years after the First World War were perhaps the most profitable ever for the county farmers. Grasslands thrived and wheat fields yielded huge harvests. For the first time, the farmers could buy their own steam-operated threshing machines and tractors. The farmer could purchase more land to plant more crops to pay off his loans or debt.

But the 1930's were a time of disaster for the county farmers and ranchers. During the spring of 1934, huge dust storms blew the topsoil from the fields near St. Onge so crops could not grow. An extended drought devastated many cattle herds. Grasshoppers destroyed trees and bushes and dense clouds of locusts filled the air. It was a difficult time for farmers and ranchers. The economic depression of the 1930's forced banks to close in the area and many farmers and ranchers went into debt. Federal assistance programs and World War II helped the area agricultural industry to recover quickly. One of the most important innovations in the county agricultural industry was the advancements made in the dairy business. In the early 1930's, pasteurization was introduced in the county. Grade A milk was bottled by local dairies in 1949.

The number of farms in Lawrence County has greatly changed. Farms have decreased in number from a high of 490 in 1935 to about 350 in 1975. But the average size of the Lawrence County farm is increasing. The farms in 1900 averaged 256 acres and by 1974 they averaged 1,130 acres. The number of farms over 1,000 acres has steadily increased from 42 in 1935 to over 50 in 1964. However, the

**The Latchstring Inn at Savoy in Spearfish Canyon has attracted many notables during the past century, including Teddy Roosevelt before he became President.**
**(Black Hills State College)**

. . . Beginning in 1883 the Dakota Normal School provided courses for those who had 'finished or nearly finished the common branches' in the public schools. From 1883 to 1900 the course of instruction embraced four years of work. In 1900-1901 a fifth year was added, and in 1905 a Sixth Year Course was established. In 1926 the first four-year college class with the degree Bachelor of Science in education was graduated. Between 1932 and 1939 the institution offered only a two-year program. Now four-year curricula are again offered and another degree, Bachelor of Science, has been granted since 1946.

Quarterly Bulletin
B H Teachers College
April, 1948

Spearfish, S. D. — That this is surely a land "flowing with milk and honey" was emphasized by the find of "Bi" Bolster, a rancher living near here. Workmen on the place cut down an old pine tree that stood over 100 feet in height and were surprised by a colony of bees that savagely attacked them and drove them off. Bolster at once swarmed the bees into home-made hives and then proceeded to take out the honey from the hollow of the tree. Before he had finished he had secured 300 pounds of the bees' product that filled the trunk 18 inches in diameter at the bottom, 35 feet up.

Argus-Leader, Sioux Falls
Nov. 29, 1907

Mr. and Mrs. Alfred Hofeldt of St. Joe, Mo., were arrivals on the Burlington yesterday coming to attend the funeral of Mr. Hofeldt's stepfather, Charles Zumach, pioneer resident of the Black Hills which was held yesterday afternoon in Spearfish. Zumach who was born in 1844 in Germany came to the Black Hills in 1877 and after working in the mining camps, constructed and operated the old Cliff House or what is now known as the Half Way House on the Deadwood-Spearfish road until 1884 when he sold out and went to live in Crook County, Wyo.

Pioneer-Times
Aug. 31, 1932

St. Onge, S. D. — While out hunting near here, Felix Cardinal shot a large pelican, believed to the the first of its kind ever seen in this part of the country. The bird had the appearance of having traveled far and was easily bagged. It measured nearly nine feet from tip to tip of wings and had a bill thirteen inches long . . . The bird was sent to Deadwood where it will be mounted and later will be presented to the state curator. So few persons had seen a pelican that it required an expert to determine what Cardinal had shot.

Argus-Leader, Sioux Falls
Oct. 15, 1907

trend since 1964 has been more people farming smaller acreages of land. Most of the 230,000 acres of farmland in the county are used for pasture land. The rural population of Lawrence County at the time of the 1970 census was 4,963.

Recently, farm income in the county, despite a few bad years, has gradually increased — mainly because of inflation. In 1973 a large percent of the farm income of $5,574,000 came from the sale of livestock and livestock products, including cattle, calves, dairy products, hogs, sheep, and chickens. In 1974 the total value of livestock in the county was nearly $9 million. A smaller percentage of farm income in 1973 came from alfalfa, oats, winter and spring wheat, corn, and wild hay. The total value of crops sold or used on the farms amounted to over $2 million in 1974. The building of Interstate 90 through Spearfish Valley has had little effect on agriculture in the area.

Inflation, higher feed and machinery costs, and unstable livestock prices have had a great effect on the area farmers and ranchers. It is a time of uncertainty for the county agricultural industry. Nevertheless, the income from the sale of agricultural products is still an important part of the economies of Spearfish, Whitewood and St. Onge.

Whitewood in the early 1900's had a population of about 500. The town had three hotels, a bank, a doctor's office, numerous retail businesses, and a sawmill. The Lane Hotel, a popular place, was built by Enos Lane in 1904 with sandstone from a quarry near Whitewood. The hotel had a special parlor for women and well kept rooms. Another stone structure, erected about the same time, was the Bonniwell Hall, later called the Golden Wheel Dance Hall. The sawmill, the main timber supplier for the surrounding area, and the Elkhorn Railroad, later called the Chicago and North Western, were the most important employers in the town around the turn of the century. In the early 1900's, the City of Whitewood sponsored Labor Day celebrations and special trains brought many visitors from Deadwood, Belle Fourche, and Rapid City. The celebration faded when Labor Day began to be observed by the Homestake in Lead. In 1910 a rodeo was organized in Whitewood but it did not become a yearly event.

During the Jazz Age of the 1920's, Whitewood had a theater and a thriving newspaper. In 1925 the Legion Theater in Whitewood showed movies every Wednesday and Saturday evenings. The office of the Whitewood Plaindealer, a weekly newspaper, was located next to the theater. The Plaindealer, once the official county newspaper, started in 1888 and was sold in 1946 to an area publishing company. It was later replaced by the Whitewood Centennial published in Sturgis. The Works Progress Administration during the depression of the 1930's built a gymnasium in Whitewood. After the high school closed in 1943 and the students attended school in other towns, the gymnasium was used for community events.

In 1932 one of the last bank holdups in the Northern Hills occurred when the Whitewood Banking Co. was robbed of $25,000. The bandits were later apprehended. The bank closed permanently six years later. Today Whitewood is served by a branch of the Miners and Merchants Bank, Lead.

Whitewood in 1940 had a stockyard, but the yard was moved to Sturgis when a larger one was built in Belle Fourche, the cattle shipping center for the region. Soon after the Chicago and North Western, employer of many Whitewood residents, began cutting back service to the town. In 1958 the passenger depot was closed.

Today Whitewood, with a population of about 700, is known as a residential community. Many people who live in the town commute to jobs in nearby cities. Wood products is probably the most important industry in the small town at the present time. The grade school is operated by Meade District 101 and junior and senior high school students are bussed to Sturgis.

In 1900 neighboring St. Onge had a population of fewer than 100 inhabitants. The small building boom of the 1890's continued into the Twentieth Century. A new hotel, bank, a creamery, and a church were built. The little town was becoming a community of some importance along the Chicago and North Western Railroad route and the town leaders decided to incorporate St. Onge as a township in 1906. St. Onge continued to grow. Before the First World War, the town had a cafe, a boarding house, a tavern, grain elevator, numerous retail businesses, a barber shop, and a newspaper. The first issue of the St. Onge newspaper, the St. Onge Quiet Tip, was printed in Whitewood on March 16, 1910.

The years between the end of the First World War and the stock market crash of 1929 were good years for the citizens of St. Onge. Land and farm prices were high and farmers were getting good prices for their crops. For the first time, many farmers could afford to buy a car. But, there were tragedies. St. Onge had an unsolved murder case in the 1920's. On August 8, 1929, a grocery store owner was brutally attacked by an unknown assailant. The store owner later died. The murderer was never found and the incident still remains a mystery.

The years between 1930 and 1960 were years of many changes in St. Onge. The economic depression of the 1930's forced the St. Onge Bank to close it doors. The local farmers and ranchers recovered only a small portion of their savings. Despite economic difficulties, highway construction and railroad improvements brought income into the community. The town slowly recovered from the effects of the depression in the 1940's. In 1948 a rodeo was organized in St. Onge and rodeo grounds were built with local funds. The popular Rough Riders Rodeo has been sponsored by the St. Onge Saddle

**The name of Dickey has also been synonymous with Black Hills history for over 85 years, especially in the Deadwood and Spearfish areas. Eleazer C. Dickey, an excellent lumberman, became affiliated with John Hunter and James M. Fish in 1891 and worked for Fish & Hunter in the Black Hills before coming to Deadwood in 1912. He took care of the company's retail lumber yard until his death in 1928. Walter Dickey, his son, born in Deadwood in 1896, started his banking career with the American National Bank of Spearfish. After consolidation with the First National Bank of the Black Hills, he was named vice president and manager of the Spearfish branch, a position held until retirement in 1961. Dickey, still living in Spearfish, is active as a director of the Fish & Hunter Co. He was instrumental in bringing Josef Meier's Passion Play to Spearfish and establishment of the Dorsett Home and Lookout Memorial Hospital.**

Club for many years. Not all the changes were beneficial to the town. The North Western Railroad in the early 1900's began to bypass St. Onge as a cattle shipping center and in 1956 the railroad stockyards were torn down. These losses, however, were partially offset by the building of Madden's Livestock Market just east of town. It serves the Tri-State area and remains popular with cattle buyers and sellers to this day.

Today St. Onge is a quiet agricultural community of about 90 residents. Both the small communities of Whitewood and St. Onge have contributed a great deal to the development and growth of Lawrence County. They have retained their essentially rural characteristics since their beginnings. They prefer it that way.

This picture shows the Mill and Bleeker street areas following the Lead fire of March 8, 1900. The Star Mill, tramway, home of the Homestake superintendent and the Ellison are behind the Hearst Mecantile building (upper left center). (Centennial Collection)

# chapter XXIX

# Where The Past Still Lives

A remnant of the past is this wooden Indian which stood outside the Butler Jewelry store. George Butler, son of the pioneer Deadwood merchant, still lives in Deadwood.
(Centennial Collection)

By 1900 the colorful pioneer days were over and the mining community of Lead was prepared to accept the challenges of the Twentieth Century. Some of the challenges were to be difficult. A brief, but disastrous, fire occurred in 1900 that momentarily stunned the citizens of the mining town. Lead had been fortunate to escape a destructive fire like the Deadwood blaze of 1879. Mining towns were not meant to be permanent communities and were built mostly with wood. Fires were a constant fear to the citizenry. The fire started early in the morning in a butcher shop and quickly spread throughout the business district. The Evening Call of March 8, 1900, reports that numerous buildings were leveled by explosives to prevent the blaze from spreading to the Brick Store, other businesses, and the Homestake stamp mills. The fire was under control by 9 a.m. but the cause was never found. The Call praised the firefighters whose heroic efforts helped extinguish the blaze. The fire destroyed a large portion of the commercial area and the business district was rebuilt with attention given to making the new buildings as fire resistant as possible. Buildings of brick replaced many wood frame buildings. One of the new buildings constructed was a hotel. The Smead Hotel, "The Pride of the Northern Hills," was an imposing four-story structure built on the corner of Pine and Mill Streets where Mooney Park was later located.

After the fire of 1900 many civic improvements were made. The City Fathers were concerned that a town of over 6,000 did not have sewage and water facilities and paved streets. A sewer system was built in 1900-1901. The sewer was inadequate since it only served an area near Main Street and drained into Gold Run Creek. A water main was laid under Lead's Main Street the next year. The water was pumped by Homestake from Hanna Creek west of Lead to reservoirs in the mining town. The January 1, 1905, issue of the Lead Daily Call mentions that Lead's Main and North Mill Streets were paved

Grist of Gold

Our way passed through the heart of the Hills,
Leading us on to Homestake mills,
Where mountains are into the hopper rolled,
And ground and bolted to grist of gold.

Doane Robinson

At the turn of the century, Lead had two famous "houses." They were known as the "North Bleeker Street House" or "Annie's Place" and the old "Green Front." Orchestras were hired for the customers' entertainment in the houses and Lead holds the dubious honor of having one of the popular songs of World War I days written as a love note to an inmate of "Annie's Place."

Lead residents still remember George Norton, a house piano player who fell in love with Maybelle, who some claim was not one of the prostitutes. The song, which came to be known as "My Melancholy Baby", was written on the back of an old envelope while Norton was waiting for the lady of his choice in a railway depot. It was set to music especially for one of the little orchestras which often played for the famed Annie Woods. Later Norton contracted tuberculosis and Maybelle found other fields. The words were set to music by Ernie Burnett, but Norton, it is claimed never collected either a cent of money or the love of his beautiful "lady" and he died shortly after the song was published.

Helen Morganti
Lead, S. D.

Lead — When and where some mail train in the west was robbed of letters on their way to the Black Hills is a question that local merchants would like to have answered. For the past few days the merchants and banks have been receiving badly mutilated mail, in some cases the contents being partly missing. On each letter there was plainly stamped the words, "Mutilated by pouch robbers," but as the letters came from the office of the chief clerk of the postal service at Omaha and no other information was vouchsafed, the robbery is something of a mystery. The local banks' mail included some of these letters, but the checks were not negotiable and were still in the envelopes, only money apparently being taken by the robbers.

Omaha World-Herald
Dec. 22, 1908

with brick at a cost of nearly $80,000. The paper editorialized that the emergence of the mining community from the mud was something to behold.

In 1902 an electric trolley line was built between Lead and Deadwood. Later the trolley line was extended up Lead's Main street to the City Park on the western edge of town. The Burlington Railroad purchased the trolley line and changed it to a bus line in 1924. The same year the trolley was built to Lead, the Elkhorn Railroad, later purchased by the Chicago and North Western, started passenger service to the mining town.

A new banking institution made its appearance on the Lead scene in April, 1903, and opened its doors under the name of the Miners and Merchants Bank. While it was authorized to perform all types of banking, "savings" was emphasized to encourage the miners to transfer their money from its hiding places and put it in an independent bank. In addition to its branch office in Whitewood, established in 1972, the Miners and Merchants opened a drive-in branch at the top of Glendale Drive in Lead in late December 1975. In 1935, the First National Banks of Deadwood and Lead were consolidated with the Deadwood bank as a branch. Three years later, the First National Bank of Lead changed its name to the First National Bank of the Black Hills, Rapid City, and the main office was moved to the Gate City.

The entire mining district was experiencing a boom in the early 1900's. The nearby towns of Terraville, Central City, Terry, and Portland (Trojan) were thriving little communities. Lead had experienced a tremendous population surge in the 1890's and was growing just as fast in the early 1900's. Lead was easily the largest city in the Black Hills and around 1905 the second largest in South Dakota. The mining city averaged approximately 10,000 population until World War I.

Lead was a peaceful and stable town during the early 1900's until the "Trouble of 1909," when the struggle between the Lead City Miners'

**Boarding houses were a way of life in early-day Lead as young, hungry miners came from all over the nation to work for Homestake. This was Mrs. Abe Niva's Miner's Boarding House in 1912. Mrs. Niva served miners for over 20 years.**

**(Centennial Collection)**

Union and the Homestake Mining Co. erupted. Although violence was minimal, fear gripped the town. The threat of violence was always present. The strike of the miners during 1909-1910 was ignored by Homestake management and the town went back to normal. The Lead City government was changed after the strike of 1909. The aldermanic form of City government was replaced by a three-member commission in May 1912. Two City Commissioners and a Mayor are still elected in Lead.

"The stranger is first impressed with the municipal, street lighting and the many electrical signs in the District. The City of Lead is installing an ornamental lighting system which will be placed in service on June first. The system will consist of thirty-four ornamental iron brackets mounted on the steel trolley poles along Main Street. Each bracket will support four fifty candle-power tungsten lamps. All lamps will burn until midnight and one on each pole will remain burning all night as a night lamp . . . . The complete installation will make a brilliant display along Main and will be an improvement of which every citizen will be proud.

Nugget Booster
1911

Bicycles, motorcycles, and horseless carriages had appeared on the Lead streets by 1913 and occasionally a flying machine would pass overhead. The Burlington trolleys and the Chicago and North Western passenger train service were used extensively by the residents of Lead and Deadwood. The Homestake opened its large recreation building to the public in 1914. Reminders of the pioneer days were always present in Lead during this time. Many gambling halls and bawdy houses were still accepted by the citizens of Lead although the citizens believed Lead was as respectable as any eastern city.

The First World War brought a number of changes to Lead and the surrounding area. Prices were high, materials scarce, and labor was in short supply. The Golden Reward and Mogul mines near Portland were closed. With the exception of the Homestake, mining activity declined. The mine experienced labor shortages as miners left the area for service in the armed forces. The population of Lead dropped to about 7,000 and averaged that number until the Second World War. The World War I years were a time of much grief to Lead citizens and their families. Not only had the war taken the lives of many of Lead's young men but also the influenza epidemic of 1918 had taken its toll. Ninety-four persons died during the last three months of 1918 and it was believed that 2,000 had been affected by the illness. Despite the gloom in the town, the people celebrated frantically when the announcement came that the war had ended.

**Thousands thronged to Lead on July 4, 1916 to see Ivy Baldwin cross the Open Cut on a tight wire, a distance of 450 feet and a drop of 500 feet. Later in the day Baldwin gave his audience another thrill by jumping from a balloon and parachuting down over Lead's ball park.**

**(Art Jobe Photo)**

The end of the First World War was followed by a decade of celebration — "The Roaring Twenties." The new decade of women's rights, prohibition, speakeasys, and the "Charleston" brought further challenges to the city of Lead. The greatest challenge to the mining community was the ever enlarging Open Cut. The chasm was made as gold ore and waste rock was mined from below. Inadequate backfilling methods and the collapse of rotting timbers supporting the underground workings caused the area near the Open Cut to settle.

Buildings in the early 1920's began to show the effects of the subsidence and water mains and sewage lines frequently broke. During the next 20 years many business buildings in Lead and a number of Homestake surface works were razed. Even the tracks of the Burlington trolley that had served Lead for 20 years were taken up. The May 17, 1953, issue of the Lead Daily Call describes

Work had already commenced on the United States Post Office, which will be built on the corner of Main and Stone Streets. Several years ago a sum of money was appropriated by congress to build a post office in Lead. After many delays the contract was let to Mullen & Rourke at a figure a little less than eighty thousand dollars.

Illustrated Booster Nugget
Lead High School, 1912

**No, this isn't Lead in 1876. The scene shows part of Jubilee Camp, erected between Lead and Central City by Homestake in 1926 to commemorate the company's 50th birthday. (Art Jobe Photo)**

the change in the business district: "Gone are such landmarks as the Northwestern depot, the Smead Hotel, the First National Bank Building, the Smith Block, the Campbell House, Cotton and Andrews building, the Ford Theater, the home of the Homestake superintendent, and all the other buildings that formed the hub of activity."

The business district was moved three or four blocks west. The First National Bank was built on the foundation of the old Lead City Miners' Union building on the corner of Main and Wall Streets. The Hearst Mercantile, or the Brick Store, was reconstructed on a site next to the recreation building vacated by the Episcopal Church which was dismantled brick by brick and rebuilt farther west on the corner of Main and Paul Streets. The new Brick Store was the largest department store in South Dakota. The Highland Hotel, later the Gold Run Inn, was built to offset the loss of the Smead.

Many businesses were rebuilt in Lead; however, many were moved to Deadwood. Today Deadwood is the commercial center for the Lead-Deadwood community. Home owners, who had to move their homes, rebuilt in other areas of the mining town. The Homestake Mining Co., after examining each claim against the company, reimbursed property owners for losses suffered during the subsidence. The salvaged materials from the buildings were used in the reconstruction of the Homestake mills.

By 1940 Lead's appearance had completely changed. Homestake relocated all its major surface plants on the south side of the gulch. The Ellison tramway and the Chicago and North Western bridge, once near the business district, were gone. After the subsidence ended, Homestake engineers estimated that the intersection of Mill and Main Streets had settled about 28 feet. Lead's unusual sound, the booming of the stamps, began to disappear as Homestake converted its stamp mills to modern crushers. The old business district is the present site of the Sinking Gardens, Mooney Park, the Blackstone housing development, parking lots, a band shell, and the Homestake Tours office.

On August 6 and 7, 1926, the Homestake sponsored the largest celebration in Lead's history, the Golden Jubilee. The festival, honoring Homestake's first 50 years, was highlighted by a pioneer mining camp exhibit located in Poorman Gulch, known today as Glendale Drive. A gold rush parade and a historical pageant were also viewed by several thousand citizens. Then came the stock market crash of 1929 and the subsequent depression of the 1930's. It was a time of drought, locusts, and financial troubles. The worldwide depression forced many countries to devaluate their currencies and gold became very much in demand. After Congress passed the Federal Gold Reserve Act of 1934, which set the price of gold at $35 an ounce, gold mining towns like Lead boomed. The unemployed came from all over the county to work for Homestake. The mining company was the only area firm doing any large scale hiring.

Building activity at the mine and in the town, reminiscent of the 1890's, was at an all-time high. Many buildings threatened by the subsidence still had to be torn down and new business and apartment buildings were constructed. The Wayland Building, famous for the large house perched on its roof, was completed and plans for a new high school were begun. The boom didn't last long and another challenge to the City of Lead materialized.

'Due to the influenza epidemic in Lead the following places will be closed: all churches, theaters, pool halls, bowling alleys, lodges and fraternal organizations, clubs, the plunge, public meetings, dances, the public library, and rest rooms. Spitting in the streets is forbidden. Parents are requested to keep their children off the streets."

J. G. Freeman, health officer
Dwight Casner, Mayor
Lead Daily Call
November 11, 1918

In the 1930's, while the rest of the country was languishing in a severe depression, Lead was booming. In the early 1940's, after the mines were closed by the federal government, the rest of the country was gearing up for war production and the mining town of Lead experienced its own depression. Many of Lead's young men left the town and entered the armed forces. Lead's population dropped to about 3,000, mostly women and children waiting for the war to end and the return of fathers, husbands, and sons. On August 31, 1942, the largest department store in the state, the Hearst Mercantile Company, was destroyed by fire. A large supermarket was built on the former site of the Brick Store in 1957.

Occupants of 17 apartments fled early morning flames which brought a loss of between one-quarter and one-half million dollars to Lead's Main Street and injuries to three Lead firemen. Escaping with only night clothes they were wearing, all occupants of the Wayland Apartment building had been located at noon today and were safe. Deadwood Fire Chief Elmer Pontius suffered a fatal heart attack while fighting the fire.

Lead Daily Call
July 1, 1969

By 1950 the Homestake resumed normal mining activities and the mining community of Lead returned to prosperity. Even though Lead's population did not reach the pre-World War II levels, the city experienced a housing shortage since many retired residents remained in their homes instead of leaving the area. In 1950 Lead had a population of 6,400; the population decreased by 200 in 1960, and ten years later Lead had 5,500 inhabitants. Reasons for this continuing drop in population were numerous. The Homestake expansion program of the depression era was completed by 1953 and fewer men were needed for mining operations. Newer mining techniques eliminated many jobs. Many people lived outside of Lead in the rural area or in the nearby towns of Deadwood, Spearfish, and Sturgis and commuted to work. In 1959, the Bald Mountain Mining Co. closed and the workers and their families who had lived in Lead left. Despite the drop in population, a housing shortage existed. The Homestake, in order to house its workers properly, built a six-building apartment complex.

Deadwood, S. D. — Word from Goldfield, Nev., conveys the news of the death of John Steinmetz, known here since the early days as "Colorado Johnnie" who was 62 years old, came here in February, 1876, being one of the first pioneers. He went to Goldfield with the rush two years ago.

Minneapolis Tribune
Oct. 4, 1907

Nevertheless, building activities continued in the mining community at a rapid pace. In 1950 Homestake remodeled its recreation building and in the 1970's the Center, with the exception of the theater, was turned over to the City. During the 1960's work began on Mooney Park, a softball field, and the Blackstone housing development. A two-story cement parking lot was erected in 1975 on the site of the former Wayland Building that was destroyed by fire during the summer of 1969. Today Lead can be characterized as a stable community.

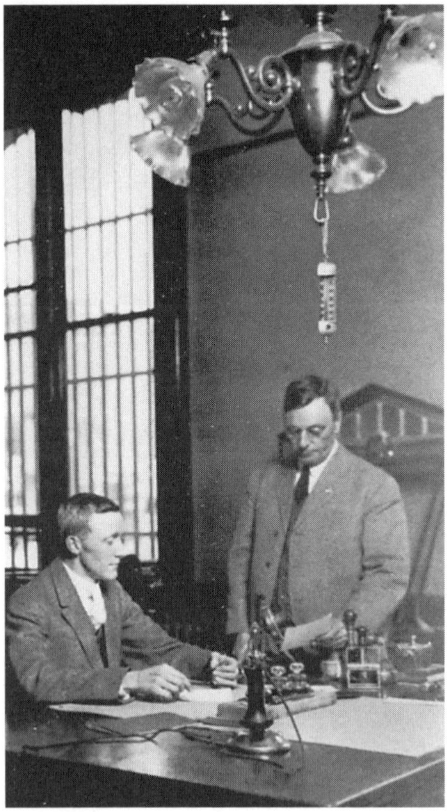

Colonel William J. Thornby came to Deadwood in April of 1877 and worked as a writer for the Deadwood Pioneer. He was the first city judge at Custer and the first justice of the peace in Custer County. Together with Professor W. P. Jenney, he located the thermal springs at Hot Springs. In 1898 he was named assayer in charge of the U. S. Assay Office, which was located in the Apex building on Deadwood's Main Street. He is shown with Jesse Simons (left) when the office was moved to the new post office building. His daughter, Kathryn Thornby, is the curator of the Adams Memorial Museum, Deadwood.
(Centennial Collection)

Russ Appleman, Colorado Springs, Colo., former resident of Deadwood, remembers that during the 1907 money panic, businessmen refused to give change for a nickel. If two cents were due, that amount was dropped. However, if the balance due was over three cents, a nickel was tendered in exchange. No change was given at the Post Office, instead stamps were given in exchange.

The Twentieth Century will continue to challenge the community of Lead. Lead's future is the future of the Homestake Mine. The future of Homestake's operation at Lead depends on gold ore reserves and the fluctuating price of gold, the metal that started it all back in 1876.

Deadwood's future is based on its past. It is one city that has made the most of its reputation — good and bad. It's just that simple. During the first 25 years of its existence, Deadwood didn't need to go out of its way to attract publicity for everything that happened in the roaring mining camp made headlines in the eastern newspapers. After the turn of the century, when Deadwood lost its standing as the largest city of the Black Hills, it still had not lost its importance. And if the active Deadwood Business Club had anything to say about it, it wouldn't. The club sought investors with capital to develop the wealth that lay hidden in the ground and promoters flocked to the Black Hills — and headquartered in Deadwood.

Deadwood was the county seat, an assay office was located there, a new courthouse and a federal building were in the mill, the new Franklin Hotel had opened its doors in 1903, Homestake had constructed the Slime Plant in 1906 to recover the 12 percent gold that was going down the creek, and in 1907 work was even underway to pave the streets with bricks! Although narrow gauge railroads ran in every direction to mines and smelters, changes were developing fast. As the smaller mines petered out and others came under the protective and guiding arm of the burgeoning Homestake, the mills, railroad tracks, smoke stacks and other mining equipment started disappearing from the steep sides of the surrounding gulches. The scene was changing and while Lead was well on its way to becoming the hub of the mining industry, Deadwood was fast developing into a banking, wholesale and commercial center for the four-state area of Montana, Wyoming, North and South Dakota.

Deadwood was also the medical center for the same area and St. Joseph's Hospital, which had been taken over by the Benedictine Sisters of Sturgis just before the turn of the century, was providing nursing care for the region. While no records were kept when the hospital first opened, costs for care right before the turn of the century were $1 per day, including board, room, and special services. However, by 1900, the costs had risen to $10 per day plus an additional $5 if the patient needed surgery. Additional charges were made for medicine, dressings and the "use of night shirts." A new addition to the hospital was erected in 1904 and two years later St. Joseph's began to train student nurses and gained the honor of being the first hospital in the state to establish a School of Nursing. A total of 167 nurses were graduated before the school was discontinued in 1943 because of space limitations.

In 1917 a fourth story was added to the main building and with this new section, a solarium, or sun parlor, was built for the patients who were able to be out of bed. Other new wings were added in 1952 and 1962. However, it was in 1961 that the original building and the first addition were demolished to make room for the other new wings, resulting in the present structure, the oldest portion of which dates back to 1952. In November, 1969, St. Joseph's Nursing Home was opened and in 1972 the former Twin Cities Hospital, constructed in 1968, was purchased and converted to a 44-bed nursing home the following year. The Homestake Hospital and St. Joseph's merged in 1974 and the Lead hospital is now used strictly for emergency care and doctors' offices for treatment of out-patients.

Early-day newspapers reveal that the need for a new courthouse in Deadwood was apparent for several years before action was started on it in about 1905. Some feared that to suggest construction would bring about a movement to take the county seat to another city. The urgent need for the new home for county business was brought home to the people when the District Court was forced to adjourn an important case one day because of rain dripping through the roof on the stenographer's notes and forming in pools on the floor in front of the judge's bench. Deadwood voted $10,000 toward the structure and at election time the County vote was 2,347 for and 543 against. It took most of the years of 1906 and 1907 to construct the brick and stone structure at the same location as the one purchased in 1879, the corner of Sherman and Pine. Three stories high, with a rotunda reaching from basement to tower, it was "more impressive than some state capitols."

The commissioners held the first meeting in the new building in December, 1907. Some of the offices had already moved in; others were transferred early in January, 1908. The rotunda was painted with scenes typical of the county, and so were the courtroom and commissioners' room. The building was lighted with electricity but the cautious commissioners, because the electricity was new, also installed gas fixtures to be used in case of emergency. Judge W. G. Rice presided at the first session of court. Present were such attorneys as A. J. Plowman, Judge G. G. Bennett, Thomas Harvey, Eben W. Martin, Henry Frawley, James Stanley, James Fowler, H. P. Stewart, James Hodgson, Freeman Knowles and Thomas Redlon, nearly all of whom were powerful figures in legal circles. A public dedication was held later, at which time it was announced that the cost of the courthouse and jail was approximately $129,824.

Dedicated at the opening of the Centennial Year was a new County Jail which has been designated as the Lawrence County Regional Public Safety Center. The structure, located at the rear of the old County Jail which served the community for 75 years, was constructed at a cost of about $1,208,772.

Deadwood — Women in the laundries, factories and stores, have organized a union, known as the Black Hills Working Girls' union as the first step toward the protection of the many women employed in the northern Black Hills towns. The union includes in its membership girls and women from each of the towns and is affiliated with the Trades Assembly.

Sioux Falls Argus-Leader
Feb. 6, 1909

In Deadwood an ornamental lighting system was installed in December consisting of fifty-nine cast iron posts with five fifty candle-power lamps on each post. This system makes a beautiful display and lights the City effectively. The citizens of Deadwood are very proud of it and the lighting is commented on by every stranger. The Cities of Spearfish, Belle Fourche and Whitewood are also installing up-to-date lighting systems. The stranger is also impressed with the many illuminated electric signs. This is the modern way of advertising and the merchants of the Black Hills have been quick to realize the advantages of this advertising and have adopted it extensively.

Nugget Booster
1911

Favored with a splendid, open fall the street pavers have now completed their work, and the city has nearly three-quarters of a mile of brick paving. A 6-inch foundation of concrete was laid under the bricks, but the hardest work was that of excavation, one street requiring prying with a board on which six men stood acting as a lever. The total cost of the work was approximately $165,000, which will be paid by the property owners, the assessment standing as a first lien on the property.

Tribune
Dec. 7, 1907

**W. E. Adams came to Deadwood in 1877 from Bismarck, D. T. in a party of 300 people and 65 teams. Four of the party died in a raging blizzard north of Deadwood. He became Deadwood's leading wholesale grocer, served as the city's mayor, was instrumental in the erection of Mount Roosevelt Monument honoring President Teddy Roosevelt. He gave the Adams Memorial Museum to the city of Deadwood to perpetuate the memory of its pioneers and as a memorial to his family.**

Another highlight of the early 1900's was the construction of the present U.S. Post Office and Courthouse, a new home for the post office which had been located in the Wagner Hotel Building. A report from the Senate Committee on Public Buildings and Grounds, printed on February 10, 1902, stressed the necessity for a public building by including the following extract from a report of a United States grand jury at Deadwood:

> "We further report that we have found the sanitary condition of the building and rooms leased and rented for the purpose of holding the Federal court herein, and occupying same for the United States court purposes, in a very unhealthy and nauseating and dangerous state. No water-closet has been in said building during our session and we have been impeded in our business; and the health of the grand jury and others in attendance upon this term of court has been endangered; and we believe a continuance of the foregoing conditions would be a public disgrace and an utter outrage on public decency, public health, and proper administration of United States court in said building."

The Olympia Club spearheaded a drive for a Federal building and with the help of Congressman E. W. Martin, approval for the building was obtained and $200,000 was allocated to build it. Ground was broken and construction started in October, 1903. The building was completed in July, 1907. In 1965, between $200,000 and $300,000 — more than the original cost of the building — was spent to remodel the post office, centered mostly in the U. S. Court areas on the second and third floor, including an elevator and air conditioning. The chandelier from the courtroom can now be viewed in the Adams Museum; the original brass light fixtures were purchased by the Bodega Cafe where they are presently in use; the marble from the stairway, removed to accomodate the elevator, was nearly all purchased by local residents and is preserved in their homes or businesses.

Deadwood, S. D. When the 1906 taxes become delinquent next week the list of those who have not paid will be unusually low. The annual taxes for Lawrence county amount to $400,000 and Treasurer Corum reports that of this sum that practically all is now paid in. The county is in a flourishing condition notwithstanding the payment of $100,000 on the new court house which is nearly completed.

Argus-Leader, Sioux Falls
Sept. 30, 1907

Loss of train service meant many service adjustments for the post office, with the changeover to highway transportation of the mail. Another major change was necessitated in late 1975 when air transportation was initiated for all first class mail and the mail carriers of the Lead Post Office were ordered transferred to Deadwood, which became the mail sorting center for the two cities.

Deadwood, S. D. — After a year's effort to secure a suitable site for a new home of their own, Deadwood Lodge No. 508, B.P.O.E. have purchased for $7,000 the Rosenthal building on Main Street. The building will be renovated and made over into luxurious clubrooms.

Tribune
Sept. 30, 1907

The second decade of the century was marred by the loss of lives in World War I and from the flu epidemic, both of which touched nearly every family in the community. A cause for rejoicing during that period was the construction of the Deadwood Municipal Auditorium in 1913, spearheaded by the Deadwood Business Club which in 1915 turned it over to the City with an indebtedness of only $6,500. Used through the years for Chatauquas, dances, auto shows and for a long period as the high school gym, the building, in the early

1960's, was converted into a City Recreation Center and now features a popular indoor plunge.

It was also during that decade that Deadwood gained recognition as the first city in the world to pay formal tribute to Theodore Roosevelt, the "Great American." On July 4, 1919, the Mount Roosevelt Tower, built by the Society of Black Hills Pioneers, was dedicated. By the Roaring Twenties, Deadwood gave every indication that it was being transformed into a "summer resort," and was finally realizing its potential as a tourist attraction. Firemen added an outdoor swimming pool to the dance pavilion in the First Ward Amusement Park. The City constructed Pine Crest Park in 1925 with a community house and three cabins which were rented at 50 cents a night per car. It raised enough money to pay for operating expenses that summer, with 200 cars in a single night the season's record.

It was in 1924 that the Days of '76 was launched as a two-day celebration, and it became an annual event. Its reputation of "something doing every minute" has carried down through the years. In 1925, a pageant, "The Spirit of Deadwood," was lengthened and presented for three nights. In 1927, the annual celebration attracted President Calvin Coolidge who was in the Black Hills for the summer.

By that time Deadwood residents were priding themselves on the fact that they had five churches, five hotels, a hospital and training school, eight restaurants, four large wholesale houses, a small municipal debt and a low City tax rate! The beloved trolley between Deadwood and Lead, remembered by many a local youth as a special "payday treat" to collect Dad's Homestake check was discontinued in 1924. It was replaced with a bus system, subsidized by the Burlington railroad for the Lead-Deadwood Transit Co. The company merited the second bus certificate issued in South Dakota and was the oldest bus line in the state at the time it was discontinued in 1966.

The burning of Gus Keller's slaughter house below Deadwood on Whitewood Creek Friday night, adds another chapter in the story of the destruction of buildings devoted to the butcher business within the last year . . . . as a matter of fact they are not considered coincidences by the authorities, but are declared to be undoubtedly the work of a fire bug, and one who is actuated by a motive. The slaughter houses have been burned within a year.

Pioneer-Times
Jan. 26, 1908

Deadwood, S. D. — A controversy between Mayor Adams and the L. B. Early Bill Posting company of this city may lead to the enforcement of the Sunday closing hours similar to that in Belle Fourche, where it is now impossible to purchase even a cigar on the Sabbath. Mayor Adams declined to allow billboards to be placed in certain portions of the town, alleging the ordinance prohibiting wooden structures in the fire limits. The Early company came back at the mayor and claims that not only have other wooden structures been permitted to be constructed, but that other laws are not strictly complied with, so the mayor is investigating. So strict are the blue laws in this state that even trains could be stopped from running if they were enforced.

Argus-Leader, Sioux Falls
Oct. 11, 1907

**The Oglala Sioux took President Calvin Coolidge into the tribe during a colorful ceremony witnessed by thousands of people at the annual Days of '76 in Deadwood. It was here in the Black Hills that Coolidge made his famous, "I do not choose to run" statement in 1927.**

**Ching Ong was the last Chinaman to leave Deadwood. The 82-year-old, who had called Deadwood home for 45 years, left on the Burlington train late in December, 1931. Many friends who knew him affectionately as "Teeter," were at the station to bid him goodbye. He was the last vestige of Deadwood's famed Chinatown.**

**(Centennial Collection)**

Deadwood continued to thrive after the stock market crash — partly because Homestake was an economic "gold mine" during those years, and partly because, in addition to being still a trade center for the area, it was also "the fun place to be." There was gambling, liquor could be obtained in spite of prohibition and there were the "upstairs houses." None of this was new to Deadwood — it just had continued there after other places had shut down. The "Bad Lands," common during the first 25 years of the mining camp, had by 1900 extended to include an entire block of two-story brick structures on the west side of Main Street from the Mansion House at the corner of Wall Street down to the end of the block. A druggist said that he used to deliver supplies for his druggist father to the headquarters for the "girls." He said that he could enter at the Mansion House, go through a fire door, enter a hall and deliver the package to the house he was looking for. It was an entire block of girlie houses, each one under different management, a sort of shopping mall of upstairs places!

It was in 1910 that "Gabriel" entered in the person of Edward E. Senn, editor of the newspaper, The Telegram, the last of a long chain of frontier newspapers he owned. It was the time of Carrie Nation and prohibition reform was sweeping the nation. Senn attacked the gambling halls and the brothels. The sporting element fought back. They destroyed his press and attacked him. But Senn persisted. The gambling fraternity left, defeated by a little bald-headed crusading editor with burning eyes.

Again the lid, lifted quietly at infrequent intervals, has been jammed down with a bang and Deadwood once more is closed. Sheriff Trathen slipped into five alleged gambling houses on Main Street during the early hours of the evening and found the games in full swing. Roulette and faro layouts to the value of over $1,000 were seized, along with a number of players and dealers, and moving into the new court house will be celebrated with a large bonfire at the expense of the gamblers. The raid was unexpected in most quarters, and has resulted from the investigations of a detective employed by the State's Attorney Stewart and the sheriff.

Pioneer Press
Dec. 6, 1907

"Were the two towns better off?" a real estate operator was asked.

"Depends on your point of view, I suppose. Economically, no," was his reply. For Senn had closed up two of the most active sporting towns in the country. There were at least 2,500 people engaged or supported by the sporting business in Lead and Deadwood.

With Deadwood officially closed, the era of the bootleggers and the speakeasy began. One of the famous clubs, open only to members known to the management, was located at 555 Main Street and became known as the Three Nickels. Many a railroad man wore a brass buckle with three fives, 555, carved on the face. In the 1920's the message came through loud and clear. When a conductor went down the aisle with his blue coat and brass buttons and a brass buckle with three fives, the modern Bummer Dan knew there was still a place where a shot of bootleg could be obtained, a dance could be had to the tune of a wind-up victrola, and more if he wished. The Three Nickels lasted into the 1930's when prohibition was over and covert operations were unnecessary. The uphill battle of E. E. Senn against sin was over. He had been appointed prohibition officer by the federal government and lived to see the gambling halls, the saloons, and the girls back in business once again.

Many local residents look back with nostalgia on the 1930's. Economically, in comparison with the rest of the nation, those depression years were good years in Deadwood. The town had a marshal named Dick Costello who never wore a gun. His biggest chore was to see that those occasional over-imbibers made it safely home. His job was eased somewhat by each club having its own law enforcement. Just the presence of a big cowboy like one of the McCrorey brothers stopped any trouble before it started. The fact that one of them had cleaned out Jack Dempsey's bar in New York was well known and helped to keep the peace. A world champion bulldogger acted as a bouncer in one club and a champion welterweight performed similar services in another.

**One of the early presentations of the Trial of Jack McCall was held between the Deadwood Post Office and the Adams Museum. It was at Deadwood's Days of '76 in 1930. On the left is the late Judge Charles Hayes, the defense attorney, Clinton Richards for the prosecution and B. K. Bettelheim, the judge, all three lawyers by profession. Richards still practices law in Deadwood.**
**(Centennial Collection)**

The gamblers in the 1930's were members of a respectable occupation. The pioneer gambler dressed the part to show his respectable and substantial station in life. There was the broadcloth suit, string tie or wide cravat with a diamond stickpin that said, "Don't worry, boys, your stake is covered." The gambler of Poker Alice's day would arrive in town with his own layout comprised of a folding faro board, a folding counter and a card bank. The play was in legitimate gambling houses, the games out in the open, with a percentage of one-half to three percent going to the house. The games were fast and large sums wagered and lost. Many of the gamblers became saloon keepers and substantial members of the mining community. The tin horns and the crooked gamblers, according to Poker Alice, were the product of back rooms where gambling was illegal.

Deadwood, S. D. — Remarking to a friend wha sat beside him in a saloon, "this will fix up my headache for a few hours," Robert Armstrong, an old-time blacksmith, drank a large dose of morphine and three hours later was dead. The inquest developed that Armstrong, who had been employed by various mining companies for many years in this section, did not intend suicide, but was trying to find relief from a severe headache which had been bothering him several nights and was unaccustomed to the drug he swallowed.
Journal
Nov. 29, 1907

After World War II, gambling was closed in Deadwood but the houses remained. In the 1950's, a newcomer to Deadwood, a young lawyer, was elected States Attorney. One evening, the daily local newspaper carried the headlines, "Upstairs Houses Raided." There were pictures of the girls and the lawmen raiders. The attendant publicity made national newslines and doomed the political career of the young States Attorney so far as the Deadwood area was concerned. The indignation came mostly from the older native residents. They didn't care as much about the houses being raided as the method in which they were closed. It outraged their sense of fair play. Those older residents knew that to close down the houses all the law enforcement officers would have had to do was pass the word and they would have closed. They had closed before when asked — the madams and the girls just packed up and melted away. The courses of the lives of the residents were little affected. Life went on as usual, but a certain spice, the mysterious aura of a western mining town, was somehow distorted. Those slightly shady stories that had become threads in the warp and woof of the residents' lives had lost some of their unique validity. They had grown up with the houses, all children knew of them — few knew them. The

The Philadelphia Cafe, under the management of Lee Sing Young, Benny Ching and "Philadelphia Kid," three well-known Chinamen of Deadwood, will reopen today in the same building as formerly occupied. "Philadelphia Kid" and his two partners need no introduction to the eating public of Deadwood as they were the former owners of the Philadelphia.
Deadwood Pioneer-Times
July 15, 1920

Once more the famous Spearfish stage coach, ancient conveyor of travelers between Deadwood and Spearfish, leaves its cage in Spearfish park on a journey. But it will not again risk the hazards of Indian hold ups, rocky slopes, or run away horses that formed an integral part of its romantic past. Tucked away safely in a Burlington car it will roll over the prairies to Chicago where World's Fair visitors will smilingly gaze upon its ancient but yet rugged structure.

Pioneer-Times
May 26, 1933

City and county officers joined forces last night in ordering all gambling in Deadwood to cease immediately, and served notice on all the places engaged in the sale of intoxicating liquor to strictly observe all of the provisions of the state liquor control laws in the future.

Deadwood Pioneer-Times
Feb. 27, 1940

In 1974 the Henry Frawley ranch was accepted on the National Register of Historic Places. Features a courtyard style barn. Ranch includes 17 homesteads representing the real beginning of homesteading areas. Reached its present size in 1913. Divided into the upper, middle, lower and east ranches. Upper ranch was once the site of the Centennial Park Hotel, burned in 1883. In 1888 a 17-room hotel and eating establishment was built on what is called the middle ranch. One of the earliest buildings still in excellent condition is a one-story log house found on the lower ranch, believed to have been built in 1870's. The lower ranch also has an early granary with a cutstone first story and horizontal siding on the second. According to the National Register of Historic Places, the 4,750 acre ranch, "encompasses visually and historically the procession of western rural life from the American Indian through homesteaders to the large ranch. The site is also a testimony to the success of one family where many others had failed."

The barn courtyards were used to bed down cattle. At one time the charge was 25 cents less if the horses were kept in the courtyard instead of the stalls.

houses had been tapped for every fund-raising charity known to man and always they had given generously — in cash.

A new minister didn't fare much better. He would park all night on lower Main Street and observe the traffic going upstairs. He would then retire to Brown Rocks above the town and exhort the populace with his loud speakers. Late at night or early in the morning his ghostly voice would float down over the city, exhorting the revelers, the girls and the madames to change their ways. He was not long for Deadwood. It seems evident that a unique people mystique existed in Deadwood — one that formed a protective attitude for the girls and the houses. The girls were never alluded to as whores, harlots or prostitutes. They were called "upstairs girls" and the houses, "upstairs houses." What then has been the moral influence of 100 years of active houses of prostitution on the lives of a small community? A ladies club was polled recently. The members had raised children to adulthood while the houses were running. No dissenting voice was raised against them. However, they did come up with a few stories!

For the next 20 years (1940 to 1960) Deadwood had its ups and downs. World War II and the Homestake Mine shutdown had dire effects on the community; but, on the other hand, the night spots were kept busy by the military until things got out of control and Deadwood was designated as "off limits." After the war, just as the city was looking forward to better times, a rash of fires hit the business district. The series of fires started on May 25, 1948, when a pioneer furniture store and two adjoining bars were destroyed. This was followed by a pre-Christmas conflagration on December 22, 1951, which razed a half block on Main Street occupied by a grocery store, shoe store, children's shop and office supply firm. Within slightly over a month, the third in the series wiped out the City Hall, a jewelry manufacturing firm, the theater, local radio station, an insurance agency, dress shop, shoe store and a group of apartments. The fourth fire occurred in February, 1954, and gutted Deadwood's remaining theater and partially destroyed two more business buildings. Then, in November, 1955, a gas explosion ripped out a western ready-to-wear store, its second floor apartment and damaged a Main Street cafe. In two months another fire wiped out two City warehouses and all of the City's heavy street and water department equipment.

Any other City would have folded up under such gigantic losses but within months after each fire, plans were underway for replacement of the destroyed buildings. Lost, however, was the historic significance of the structures, most of which dated back to the 1880's when Deadwood rebuilt after the fire of 1879. Lost forever, of course, was the City Hall with all of its records. However, the goal to preserve and restore was then launched and the early-day railroad depot was transformed into a new City Hall with all of its offices and departments concentrated in one location.

Since the "Fiery Fifties" Deadwood's efforts have been concentrated on improvement of its business district. The City Council adopted a zoning ordinance in 1971 to control new construction in appropriate locations. Moreover, local businessmen, on their own, undertook the preservation and restoration of the early-day buildings which remained to spotlight the heritage of the community. One of the major projects of the 1960's was the construction of a new highway through the city. Constructed mainly with federal and state funds, the highway covers Whitewood Creek through the city and provides an alternate route to the narrow and colorful Main Street, which proved a bottleneck with heavy traffic. The first phase, from Pine Street to Lee Street, was completed in 1965 and the second phase, from Lee to Lower Main Street, was finished in 1968, at a total cost of over $2 million. The third phase, which has been on the drawing board for over eight years, is meeting with some objections. Local businessmen are seeking an all-weather route which will tie in with the Interstate 90 between Whitewood and Spearfish. Environmentalists, who have delayed completion of the highway, want improvements made to the present routes and a guarantee that no more scenic Black Hills beauty will be damaged by additional roads.

Deadwood is optimistic about its future — it wants to be sure that all the highways into the Historic City are adequate for its "Second Century Gold Rush" — Tourism!

**Deadwood**

A city born without the law:
You had the vital strength to draw,
Out of a rabble run amuck,
Minions of hell and roaring luck,
The mirk of bawdy politics,
The harlot spawn, the Deadwood Dicks,
A company of manly men
Who carried up law's banner when
To stand for common, decent right,
Required the courage of a knight.
Bill Lardner and Seth Bullock sleep,
Below the guard old White Rocks keep.

Doane Robinson

In their Centennial year, both Deadwood and Lead were well prepared to capitalize on the national nostalgia for the past that characterized the nation's Bicentennial observance. Visitors seeking links with the American heritage will find them in abundance there, and in other Lawrence County communities. For most of the elements that shaped the history of the country as a whole can be found in microcosm in the recreated or well-preserved vestiges of Lawrence County's pioneer past. Exploration, Indian conflicts, military campaigns, the settling of a wilderness, frontier vitality and violence, the struggle for independence and self-government, agricultural and natural resource development, and all the color and romance of the historic westering movement. It all happened here — and more recently than in the older sectors of the nation. Here the past still lives because the people who created the Black Hills saga endured too much to ever let it die.

# Selected Bibliography


Anderson, Grant K. "Deadwood's Chinatown," *South Dakota History* 5 (Summer 1975): 266-85.

Bennett, Estelline. *Old Deadwood Days*. New York: J. H. Sears & Co., 1928.

Brown, Jesse, and A. M. Willard. *The Black Hills Trails: A History of the Struggles of the Pioneers in the Winning of the Black Hills.* Rapid City, S.Dak.: Rapid City Journal Co., 1924.

Buecker, Thomas R., ed. "'Distance Lends Enchantment to the View': The 1874 Black Hills Expedition Diary of Fred W. Power," *South Dakota History* 27 (Winter 1997): 197-260.

Casey, Robert J. *The Black Hills and Their Incredible Characters: A Chronicle and a Guide*. Indianapolis: Bobbs-Merrill Co., 1949.

Cash, Joseph H. *Working the Homestake*. Ames: Iowa State University Press, 1973.

Clow, Richmond L. *Chasing the Glitter: Black Hills Milling, 1874-1959*. Pierre: South Dakota State Historical Society Press, 2002.

________. "Wasp No. 2: 'The Wonder Mine of the Black Hills,'" *South Dakota History* 15 (Winter 1985): 261-89.

Clowser, Don C. *Deadwood, the Historic City*. Deadwood, S.Dak.: Fenwyn Press Books, 1969.

Fielder, Mildred. *The Treasure of Homestake Gold*. Aberdeen, S.Dak.: North Plains Press, 1970.

________. *Railroads of the Black Hills*. Seattle: Superior Publishing Co., 1964.

________. *Guide to Black Hills Ghost Mines*. Aberdeen, S.Dak.: North Plains Press, 1972.

Hughes, Richard B. *Pioneer Years in the Black Hills*. Ed. Agnes Wright Spring. Glendale, Calif.: Arthur H. Clark Co., 1957.

Jackson, Donald. *Custer's Gold: The United States Cavalry Expedition of 1874*. New Haven, Conn.: Yale University Press, 1966.

Klock, Irma H. *Yesterday's Gold Camps and Mines in the Northern Black Hills*. Lead, S.Dak.: Seaton Publishing Co., 1975.

Kovats, Nancy Niethammer. "Black Hills Pioneer: First Newspaper of Deadwood, Dakota Territory, 1876-1877," *South Dakota History* 8 (Summer 1978): 193-220.

Lamar, Howard Roberts. *Dakota Territory, 1861-1889: A Study of Frontier Politics*. New Haven, Conn.: Yale University Press, 1956.

Lee, Bob, and Dick Williams. *Last Grass Frontier: The South Dakota Stock Grower Heritage*. Sturgis, S.Dak.: Black Hills Publishers, 1964.

McClintock, John S. *Pioneer Days in the Black Hills: An Accurate History and Facts Related by One of the Early Day Pioneers*. Ed. Edward L. Senn. New York: J. J. Little & Ives Co., 1939.

McDermott, John D. *Gold Rush: The Black Hills Story*. Pierre: South Dakota State Historical Society Press, 2001.

McLaird, James D. "Calamity Jane: The Life and the Legend," *South Dakota History* 24 (Spring 1994): 1-18.

________. "Calamity Jane and the Black Hills Gold Rush in the Writings of William B. Lull," *South Dakota History* 28 (Spring/Summer 1998): 1-68.

________, and Lesta V. Turchen. "Colonel William Ludlow and the Custer Expedition, 1874," *South Dakota History* 4 (Summer 1974): 281-319.

________, and Lesta V. Turchen. "The Scientists' Search for Gold, 1875: Walter P. Jenney and Henry Newton," *South Dakota History* 4 (Fall 1974): 403-38.

Parker, Watson. *Gold in the Black Hills*. 1966. Reprint. Pierre: South Dakota State Historical Society Press, 2003.

________, and Hugh K. Lambert. *Black Hills Ghost Towns*. Chicago: Swallow Press, 1974.

________. "Some Black Hills Ghost Towns and Their Origins," *South Dakota History* 2 (Spring 1972): 89-114.

Price, Samuel Goodale. *Ghosts of Golconda: A Guide to Historical Characters and Locations in the Black Hills of Western South Dakota*. Deadwood, S.Dak.: Western Publishers, 1952.

Rosa, Joseph G. *They Called Him Wild Bill: The Life and Adventures of James Butler Hickok*. 2d ed., rev. Norman: University of Oklahoma Press, 1974.

Rosen, Peter. *Pa-Ha-Sa-Pah; or, The Black Hills of South Dakota*. St. Louis: Nixon-Jones Printing Co., 1895.

Schell, Herbert S. *History of South Dakota*, 4th ed., rev. Pierre: South Dakota State Historical Society Press, 2004.

Stewart, Kenneth. "The Boom and Bust of Central City," *South Dakota History* 2 (Summer 1972): 230-60.

Sulenic, Joe. *Deadwood Gulch: The Last Chinatown*. Deadwood, S.Dak.: Deadwood Gulch Art Gallery, 1975.

Tallent, Annie D. *The Black Hills; or the Last Hunting Ground of the Dakotahs: A Complete History of the Black Hills of Dakota from Their First Invasion in 1874 to the Present Time*. St. Louis: Nixon-Jones Printing Co., 1899.

Wolff, David A. "Pyritic Smelting at Deadwood: A Temporary Solution to Refractory Ores," *South Dakota History* 15 (Winter 1985): 312-39.

________. "No Matter How You Do It, Fraud is Fraud: Another Look at Black Hills Mining Scandals," *South Dakota History* 33 (Summer 2003): 91-119.

Zhu, Liping, and Rose Estep Fosha. *Ethnic Oasis: The Chinese in the Black Hills*. Pierre: South Dakota State Historical Society Press, 2004.

# Subject Index

# Name Index